The Gulf crisis and its global aftermath

The crisis in the Gulf of 1990–91 has affected more than just the regional powers in the area. Rippling outward, its military, economic and political effects are still being felt throughout the international political system, testing American steadfastness in the face of Saddam Hussein's political survival, the EC's ability to form a united front on foreign policy issues and the effectiveness of the United Nations in confronting international aggression.

The rationale behind this book is to investigate and analyse the various aspects of the crisis, especially in regard to the interactions between internal and international politics and repercussions on the prospects for a new order in the Middle East. It also examines the wider effects of the war outside the immediate theatre of action, and includes analysis of Europe, America and the Soviet Union.

Each one of the essays chosen for this volume has been written by an expert in his or her field. This collaboration between historians, regional specialists and political scientists, integrating a variety of research methods in the framework of one book, will be useful to a wide circle of readers, including graduates and undergraduates, political scientists and area specialists.

Gad Barzilai is Assistant Professor in the Department of Political Science, Tel-Aviv University, **Aharon Klieman** is Professor of International Relations in the Department of Political Science, Tel-Aviv University and **Gil Shidlo** is Assistant Professor in the Department of Political Science, Tel-Aviv University.

The Gulf crisis and its global aftermath

Edited by Gad Barzilai,
Aharon Klieman and Gil Shidlo

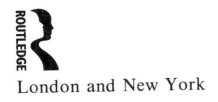

London and New York

First published 1993
by Routledge
11 New Fetter Lane, London EC4P 4EE
Simultaneously published in the USA and Canada
by Routledge
29 West 35th Street, New York, NY 10001

Typeset in 10/12pt Times by Witwell Ltd, Southport
Printed and bound in Great Britain by
T.J. Press (Padstow) Ltd, Padstow, Cornwall.

British Library Cataloguing in Publication Data

A catalogue reference for this book is available from the British Library

ISBN 0-415-08002-9

Library of Congress Cataloging in Publication Data
The Gulf crisis and its global aftermath / edited by Gad Barzilai,
    Aharon Klieman and Gil Shidlo.
        p.   cm.
    Includes bibliographical references and index.
        ISBN 0-415-08002-9
    1. Middle East—Politics and government—1979- 2. World
politics—1989- 3. Persian Gulf War, 1991—Miscellanea.
    I. Barzilai, Gad. II. Klieman, Aaron S. III. Shidlo, Gil, 1956- .
DS63.1.G85   1993
956.05—dc20
                                                            92-42816
                                                            CIP

Contents

List of figures   vii
List of tables   viii
List of contributors   ix
Acknowledgments   xii
Introduction   1

1 Lost in the shuffle: the threatened marginality of the Gulf
   Crisis for international relations enquiry   7
   Aharon Klieman

Part I Middle East tremors

2 Continuity and change in the inter-Arab system   33
   Bruce Maddy-Weitzman

3 Survival at all costs: Saddam Hussein as crisis manager   51
   Efraim Karsh

4 Saudi Arabia's Desert Storm and winter sandstorm   67
   Jacob Goldberg

5 The PLO: from Intifada to war and back   87
   Menachem Klein

6 Migrants and refugees: the human toll   103
   Elizabeth N. Offen

Part II Israel in the post-Gulf era

7 Society and politics in war: the Israeli case   129
   Gad Barzilai

8 Strategic consequences for Israel   146
   Efraim Inbar

Part III Great Power realignment

  9 Origins of the new world order   163
     Robert W. Tucker

10 A changing American-Israeli relationship   176
     Abraham Ben-Zvi

11 Soviet policy during the Gulf Crisis   191
     Yitzhak Klein

12 European reactions to the Gulf challenge   208
     Ilan Greilsammer

Part IV Ripples worldwide

13 Third World arms exports to Iraq before and after the
     Gulf War   231
     Gil Shidlo

14 Petroleum prices, politics and war   250
     Gil Feiler

15 The Gulf War and the media   264
     Dina Goren

Part V Future prospects for calm after the storm

16 Conflict resolution under the veil of uncertainty: the
     Middle East   279
     Gad Barzilai and Gideon Doron

     Name Index   295
     Subject index   299

Figures

6.1 Gulf War migration to Asia, Europe and North America   108
6.2 Gulf War migration within the Middle East   110

16.1 The 'chicken' game   285
16.2 The prisoners' dilemma game between Israel and Egypt   286

Tables

6.1 Stranded foreigners in Kuwait   106
6.2 Remittance of Asian workers in Iraq or Kuwait prior to
    1990   120
6.3 Lost remittance earnings from Arab workers   121

13.1 Third World arms exports to Iraq, 1982–90   233
13.2 Arms exports to Iraq by other countries, 1982–90   234

14.1 Gulf countries' excess oil production in April 1990   252
14.2 World petroleum consumption, by region, 1987   253
14.3 World crude oil prices   254

Contributors

Dr Gad Barzilai is an Assistant Professor in the Political Science Department at Tel-Aviv University. He has written three books and many articles about the social-political sources and repercussions of armed conflicts, interstate and intercommunal encounters, and national security crises, especially in the Middle East.

Professor Abraham Ben-Zvi is an Associate Professor in the Department of Political Science and a Senior Researcher in the Jaffee Centre for Strategic Studies at Tel-Aviv University. He received his PhD degree from the University of Chicago and has published extensively on Middle East issues such as American diplomacy in the Middle East and the cognitive dimension in political behaviour. His most recent books are: *Between Lausanne and Geneva: International Conferences and the Arab–Israeli Conflict* (Westview Press 1989), and *The United States and Israel, 1953–1991: The Limits of the 'Special Relationship'* (Columbia University Press 1993).

Professor Gideon Doron is an Associate Professor and the Chairman of the Department of Political Science at Tel-Aviv University. He has published numerous studies including five books, primarily on game theory and public policy in Western democracies and in the Middle East.

Dr Gil Feiler is a lecturer at Tel-Aviv University and the Hebrew University, and a Research Fellow at the Bar-Ilan Centre for Strategic Studies. He has published articles on labour mobilization in the Middle East and on economic cooperation and development in the Middle East. Currently he is completing a book on the Arab boycott of Israel.

Dr Jacob Goldberg is a former Senior Research Fellow at the Moshe Dayan Centre and Chairman of the Editorial Board of the Moshe Dayan Centre Occasional Papers Series. His fields of specialization are: the modern and contemporary history of the Arab world with particular reference to Saudi Arabia. His publications include: *The Foreign Policy of Saudi Arabia: the Formative Years, 1902–1918*; he is co-editor of *The Soviet-American Competition in the Middle East*.

Dr Dina Goren teaches mass communication at Tel-Aviv and Bar-Ilan Universities. She is author of numerous articles on government and media relations. Among her books are: *The Press and National Security*; *Secrecy and the Right to Know*; and *Communication and Reality*.

Professor Ilan Greilsammer is the former chairman of the Department of Political Studies at Bar-Ilan University and the chairman of the Institute for European Studies at Bar-Ilan University. His main fields of specialization are European studies, especially West Europe and the European Community. He has published extensively on these subjects.

Professor Efraim Inbar is an Associate Professor in the Political Science Department and the Chair of the Bar-Ilan Centre for Strategic Studies at Bar-Ilan University. He has published considerably about strategic issues and international politics of Israel and the Middle East.

Dr Efraim Karsh is a reader in the Department of War Studies at King's College in the University of London. His articles about the superpowers and the Middle East and about Middle East affairs have appeared in numerous journals. He has also published or completed books about these subjects, among them: *Saddam Hussein: A Political Biography* (Free Press 1991), *Soviet Policy towards Syria since 1970* (Macmillan 1991) and (with Lawrence Freedman) *A War of its Time: A History of the Gulf War* (Princeton University Press, forthcoming).

Dr Menachem Klein is a lecturer in the Political Science Department and the Department for Middle East Studies at the Hebrew University of Jerusalem. He has investigated the Arab world and the Palestinians. He has published mainly on the PLO, on the meanings of Islam in the Arab World and on the West Bank and Gaza Strip.

Dr Yitzhak Klein is a lecturer in the departments of Political Science at the universities of Tel-Aviv and Bar-Ilan. His main fields of teaching, research and publication are Soviet-Russia and post-Soviet studies. He has investigated mainly the Soviet armed forces and foreign policy in the Soviet and post-Soviet periods.

Professor Aharon Klieman is a Professor of International Relations and former chairman, Political Science Department, Tel-Aviv University, as well as a member of the Jaffee Centre for Strategic Studies, under whose auspices his book on *Rearming Israel: Defense Procurement Through the 1990s*, co-authored with Reuven Pedatzur, was published in 1991. He is also the author of *Israel and the World After 40 Years* (Pergamon-Brassey's 1991).

Dr Bruce Maddy-Weitzman is a Research Fellow at the Moshe Dayan Centre for Middle Eastern and African Studies, Tel-Aviv University, and was a Visiting Fellow of Middle East Programs at the Carter Center and Visiting Assistant Professor of History at Emory University, 1990–1.

Elizabeth Offen graduated in the Political Science Department at the Massachusetts Institute of Technology. The focus of her studies has been on comparative public policy, with an emphasis on international migration policy. Ms Offen has worked in the field of trauma and victimization. From 1985–91 she was the Deputy Director of the Massachusetts Office for Victim Assistance, where she oversaw policy and services affecting all victims of crime. The themes in this paper are expanded upon in her thesis entitled, 'The Persian Gulf War of 1990–1991: an analysis of migration and the security of states' (1992).

Dr Gil Shidlo earned his PhD from the London School of Economics and Political Science and is an Assistant Professor in the Department of Political Science at Tel-Aviv University and a Visiting Professor at the University of Texas at Austin. He has published extensively books and articles on developing countries in the Third World and on Latin America countries.

Professor Robert W. Tucker is a Professor Emeritus, the Johns Hopkins University's Paul Nitze School of Advanced International Studies, and author, with David C. Hendrickson, of *The Imperial Temptation*, published by the Council on Foreign Relations.

Acknowledgements

We appreciate the co-operation of the various authors who prepared the papers for publication. We also gratefully acknowledge Sarah Shidlo's technical assistance in editing the book. Rose, Pam and Silvia of Tel-Aviv University typed the scripts with great care and patience into an accurate manuscript. Ning Lin of the Institute of Latin American Studies at the University of Texas at Austin assisted in converting the chapters written in numerous word processing languages into one coherent language. Finally, we would like to thank Gordon Smith, Jane Mayger and Catherine Fear at Routledge who helped improve the final manuscript in countless ways.

Gad Barzilai
Aharon Klieman
Gil Shidlo

Introduction

The end of the 1980s seemed to suggest a marked decline in the destabilizing role previously played by the Middle East in international affairs. In contrast to dramatic change in the Soviet Union, Central Europe and Germany, the eastern Mediterranean–Gulf sector appeared refreshingly stable. Termination of the Iran–Iraq war in 1988 was one factor; another, the impression that Ayatollah Khomeini's brand of Islamic fundamentalism was not so rampant as previously feared. Similarly, although the Arab–Israeli peace process had produced no breakthrough, nevertheless, the latent conflict did not threaten to escalate into a new war; even the Intifada and turbulence in Lebanon had become fairly routinized. This false sense of stability came to an abrupt end on 2 August 1990 with the Iraqi aggression against Kuwait.

For seven long months the invasion and subsequent annexation of Kuwait dominated the international agenda, reminding one and all of just how unstable and unpredictable the Middle East region can really be even at the best of times.

The crisis in the Gulf affected many more than the regional players alone. Rippling outward, its military, economic and political effects are still being felt throughout the international political system, testing American steadfastness, the effectiveness of the United Nations to confront international aggression, the EC's ability to pose a united front, and the will of 165 states to pursue common security. So, too, the implications for an increasingly interdependent international economic system.

Following the invasion, an international economic embargo was imposed on Iraq. The loss of Iraqi and Kuwaiti oil, plus the threat to Saudi oil facilities, led to a dramatic increase in oil prices affecting both developed and developing economies. Indeed, worldwide concern for oil pricing and market access reinforced strategic and political anxiety at Iraq's military capabilities and possible pretensions at regional hegemony. So immediate and so grave were these anxieties as to give rise to an unprecedented international coalition which then proceeded to rebuke and even humiliate the Iraqis. But the global alliance fell short of defeating the Saddam regime or denying it any future military option. Thus, towards mid-decade the truly critical economic and political problems of the Middle East region continue unsolved. The crisis aftermath is demonstrating once more the illusiveness of stability in this part of the world.

Yet, at the same time Middle East politics and players have been transformed in a number of important ways by the unsettling Gulf experience. Certainly the three editors of this book have. Prior to August 1990, as colleagues in the political science department at Tel-Aviv University, each of us was preoccupied with our respective areas of teaching and research. Surprised like everyone else at the spreading atmosphere of crisis, in the tense weeks between Saddam's unopposed seizure of Kuwait and the playing out of all the options for avoiding an outright conflict, we were converted into close observers of unfolding events on an expanding chessboard. Once the actual fighting began, but particularly from that unforgettable moment when the first Scud missile without provocation or warning hit Israel, our scholarly pursuits were thrust aside. Finding oneself caught in the middle of a war, with missiles flying overhead, is not exactly conducive to calm reflection, heuristic theory or intellectual breakthroughs. Together with our closest family members, we hunkered down in our improvised, sealed rooms, gas masks at the ready, awaiting each all-clear sound and the next deafening missile alarm siren with equal anxiety.

It was only after the threat had been lifted by Iraq's forced evacuation from Kuwait that we could even begin to seek release from individual suppressed fears and resume our stunted professional activity. In verbalizing these feelings to each other, it became clear that in addition to having experienced first-hand the 'balance of terror' – praxis rather than theoretical abstraction – we were witness to a remarkable international event – quite probably a 'defining moment', and perhaps even system-transforming: one of those rare integrative sequences which bring together personal and impersonal forces; domestic, national, regional and global actors; ideological, social and economic variables as well as technological, political, military and diplomatic ones. From those early post-crisis therapeutic conversations and attempts at putting the whole thing into perspective comes the inspiration for this collaborative effort. That and the twofold conviction that: first, there are abiding insights and lessons to be learned from the Gulf crisis, especially once the dust had settled, rather than instant history or analysis; second, whether for better or worse, the Middle East as a region has every potential for remaining at the epicentre of new world disorder.

Two main issues are at the centre of this collection of original essays. One question is the significance of interactions between domestic politics and the international setting. The second: the wider repercussions of the Gulf crisis. Aharon Klieman's introductory chapter accordingly sets forth a research framework that incorporates the Gulf events into the academic study of world political trends. He stresses that if Gulf-induced renewed interest in strengthening the global community is not to be short-lived, greater effort must go into evaluating how international processes such as realignment and balancing take place over longer periods of time against the backdrop of a changing international order.

Each one of the pieces chosen for this volume was written by an expert in his or her field. We believe this collaboration between historians, regional specialists and political scientists – integrating a variety of research methods in the framework of one book – will be useful to a wide circle of readers. The book itself covers four main areas: the Middle East proper; Israeli domestic and security concerns, Great Power policies and worldwide forces. Opening the first part on 'Middle East Tremors', Bruce Maddy-Weitzman's discussion of the Gulf War centres on enumerating and analysing the elements of both continuity and change in the system of inter-Arab relations in order to provide a more reliable road map for understanding the ever-changing course of Middle East politics. Efraim Karsh explains the latent logic and incentives behind Saddam Hussein's invasion of Kuwait as an aid in understanding his likely future behaviour should he remain in power in Baghdad. Jacob Goldberg, in turn, addresses several lessons about Saudi Arabian domestic and foreign policies; in particular, how and why during the crisis the key word was 'change' while after the war 'restoration' and the 'status quo' became the main theme.

Menachem Klein next analyses the effects of the Gulf War upon the Palestinians. He examines how the PLO entered the war, and with what goals in mind, then contrasts it with the influence the crisis is having upon the organization's internal structure and external policy. In her chapter, Elizabeth Offen deals with the meaning of one of this century's largest and most widespread migrations, whereby more than 5.5 million people from around forty countries were temporarily or permanently displaced by the Persian Gulf.

In the second part of the book, 'Israel in the Post-Gulf Era', Gad

Barzilai's chapter refers to the tendency of democracies to convert to military societies when their national security faces danger. The broad claim is made that such countries become warlike in character with a tendency not merely to react but to initiate military operations. However, his analysis of the Israeli case during the Gulf War produces different conclusions. Efraim Inbar complements this treatment by focusing on the conduct of the Israeli government in responding to Iraqi provocations with almost uncharacteristic restraint. He probes as well into the larger strategic ramifications of the event for Israel and the consequences of the war for national security in this decade.

In the third part of the book devoted to 'Great Power Realignment', Robert Tucker deals with an issue that surfaced during the war in the Gulf – the new world order. In a profound historical analysis he illuminates the fundamentals of the policy engendered by the Bush Administration, identifying elements of both continuity and change in comparison with previous administrations. Abraham Ben-Zvi's chapter then depicts the war in the Gulf as a screen or prism through which the basic components of the dynamic US–Israel relationship are illuminated. He explains why in a variety of situations potential US power and leverage do not always or necessarily translate automatically into actual power, and discusses whether the current state of American–Israeli ties provides the right environment for a more assertive role by Washington in the Arab–Israeli conflict after the US presidential elections.

Yitzhak Klein considers the problem not of ascendancy or hegemony, but of superpower decline in his chapter on Soviet policy in the Gulf crisis. He nicely illustrates the difficulty the former Soviet Union experienced in adjusting Gulf crisis policy to its own internal weaknesses and strained international circumstances. Klein poses the argument that the Soviet Union attempted to play an independent role in the crisis, yet, in the end merely succeeded in dramatizing that its era as a Middle East actor and global superpower was over. The European Community's reaction to the Gulf crisis is the subject of Ilan Greilsammer's essay, in which he seeks to explain the weakness of the EC at a time of major international crisis as deriving from the inability of the twelve member states to act in a collective and uniform manner.

Our final section, devoted to 'Ripples worldwide', deals essentially with three representative systemic-wide issues – Third World arms exports to Iraq; petroleum prices and war; and the media dimension of the Gulf crisis. Gil Shidlo's chapter provides an overview of the defence production capabilities of four developing countries (Argentina, Brazil, China, Egypt) that exported arms to Iraq – before and after the Gulf War. Gil Feiler raises the important question of whether Saddam's power drive to incorporate Kuwait, *de facto*, into Iraq comprised the main reason for his invasion (with financial considerations only secondary) or whether in fact financial objectives and his prospects for dominating the oil market were foremost. In her chapter on the media dimension of the War, Dina Goren punctures the myth of a free, objective mass media in times of crisis and conflict by underscoring various forms of control, including secrecy and censorship.

Concluding the essays, Gad Barzilai and Gideon Doron point us to future prospects, by looking at the possibilities for resolving at least one major source of Middle East turbulence, the Arab–Palestinian–Israeli conflict, in light of the structural changes we are witnessing in the international system in the aftermath of the Gulf War.

1 Lost in the shuffle
The threatened marginality of the Gulf Crisis for international relations enquiry

Aharon Klieman

The great Gulf confrontation of 1990–91 is withdrawing into the recesses of our collective historical consciousness. Not so long ago the most minute details stood out in sharp relief; now only the broader contours remain. And as the overall event recedes still further, what was perceived of at the time as an acute world crisis – indeed, in the eyes of many a defining moment in global affairs – could very well be downgraded, and relegated to marginal status.

An initial discordant note is sounded at the practitioner level, with criticism raised in retrospect at how individual leaders, state actors and systemic agents sought to cope with the stressful Middle East challenge. If taken, for example, as a paradigm for international crisis management, Iraq's aggression against Kuwait and eventual containment yield mixed reviews owing to errors of omission and commission. This disappointment is echoed, in the second instance, because of the secondary impact the Persian Gulf crisis has had thus far in framing the current agenda of international relations. Nor do we find improved prospects for its doing so in the future.

Any subsequent renewed crisis confrontation in southern Iraq only accelerates the act or process of forgetfulness. Because the entire thrust of analysis and commentary is given to the later round of political-military re-engagement at the expense of the earlier phase. If not actually pushed into oblivion, those formative events would merely serve as the background for reminiscence and perspective, but not as a subject in their own right for closer, in-depth study.

CRISIS CONVENTIONS

A good deal of the problem lies in the analysis of data and interpretation of events. When looking at the initial two phases – threat detection and conflict avoidance – it is fair to say that once the crisis erupted the American administration, and President Bush in particular, earn high marks for resolve in painstakingly building up domestic support while simultaneously orchestrating an exceptionally heterogeneous coalition and assembling a credible military option. Yet the fact remains Kuwait was ignored as a potential flash-point prior to 2 August 1990. Arguably, had US intelligence analysis correctly assessed Iraqi intentions early on, and an unambiguous cautionary signal of *casus belli* been transmitted to Baghdad,[1] two cardinal rules of crisis management might have been honoured at the very outset: avoid strategic surprise, and strive to prevent crisis.[2] Moreover, of course, on 17 January 1991 actual fighting did ensue, thereby climaxing a belated, and ineffectual, exercise in crisis diplomacy.

In restructuring the chronology of crisis, the record is similarly inconclusive in the next phase. Here the application of overwhelming military preponderance by the US-led alliance seemed virtually flawless at the time, except that subsequent declassified reports have exposed a number of tactical shortcomings. Major Iraqi military installations that either went undetected or undamaged are merely one illustration; the relatively high casualty rate among allied ground forces from friendly fire another; the mixed performance of sophisticated weapons systems yet another. Still it can be argued that defusing the crisis and bringing it to a satisfactory conclusion – the ultimate bottom line in grading successful crisis performance – were achieved, and achieved brilliantly. What better confirmation than the primary objective in liberating Kuwait and rolling back the aggressor through a limited, controlled war.

Indeed, at first glance this favourable outcome to the crisis suggests outstanding success in the fourth and decisive phase of crisis termination. However, here, too, any inclination to put forward the Gulf as a model for crisis management is dampened by the mounting realization that the denouement on 3 March 1991 in many ways was inconclusive, if not unsatisfactory. Whatever else, surely references to victory (in the strict scientific meaning of the term as unilateral, unconditional and undisputed) were exaggerated and hence inappropriate. The follow-up to the crisis found its precipitator, Saddam Hussein, unrepentant and defiant, his staying power and regional pretensions encouraged by retention of a still formidable conventional arms capability.

Our ambivalence towards how accepted conventions of crisis may or may not have been applied in the case of the Gulf doubtless will further increase the more removed we become from the drama itself. This uncertainty is only exacerbated by the deeper underlying political issues which the conflict failed to resolve, such as the plight of the

Kurds, the lingering insecurities of Iraq's neighbours to the south, oil dependencies, a refuelled regional arms race and, permanently at the background of Middle East politics, the appeal of Islamic fundamentalism and political radicalism.

CONTRASTING PROFESSIONAL RESPONSES

Dissonance over the consequences of the Gulf War, nevertheless, would appear to be having a positive, salutary effect in one sense at least. Picking up where the earlier stream of media commentary left off at the end of the protracted seven-month conflict, a healthy debate has continued among historians. Which is precisely the contrast I wish to make, because it is a source of professional concern that international relations specialists have been slow to rise to the challenge offered by the 1990 crisis, and not solely in terms of possibly refining crisis theory.[3] This does not imply that the agenda for the study of international relations is not undergoing meaningful change in a period of turbulence; only that these changes and new emphases owe less to the Gulf crisis than one might expect.

In fairness, it is perhaps too soon to expect a tremendous output of scholarly work inspired by the Gulf experience. Nevertheless, in this second year of the post-crisis period there is a perception, admittedly more impressionistic than empirically substantiated, of an intellectual opportunity about to be lost.

A MISSED OPPORTUNITY

If our interim assessment is correct, disappointment is that much greater since the Gulf drama had all the makings of a perfect catalyst for professional progress in two directions: 'the breaking of conceptual jails' encouraged by Rosenau,[4] even as we seek 'to isolate those factors that are likely to be the driving forces of history' urged by Mearsheimer.[5]

What recommends Gulf-oriented scientific inquiry are, Halliday's 'three concentric circles' for developing the discipline of international relations: change and debate within the subject itself, the spillover of fresh ideas within other areas of social science and the impact of actual events.[6] This especially holds true when the latter is the genuine article – those rare system-transforming crises with the capacity to alter both (a) the existing structures of a particular international order (the hierarchy of states, the balance of power) and (b) its 'rules of the game' (legal conventions, diplomatic codes).[7]

The Middle East crisis is further distinctive for having posed the first real challenge to the post-Cold War international system. Closely related, it also inspired 'New World Order' enthusiasts to proclaim a new ethic of conduct in world affairs marked 'by acceptance and not by rejection . . . by dialogue and not by violence . . . by cooperation and not by conflict . . . by hope itself, and not despair';[8] in short, the end to what Bull, in his classic study, describes as 'the anarchical society'.[9] The 'new era' – 'new thinking' perspective, by sharing with the school of 'endism' an extreme interpretation of contemporary world history and politics as crossing a great divide, surely calls for the testing and validation of first postulates in light of the Gulf experience.[10]

Lastly, what unfolded in the Middle East also qualifies as an exceptionally integrative event. Few recent global developments quite equal the Gulf power contest for sheer complexity: the multiplicity and diversity of participants, the entanglement of interests at stake, the web of interactions and sequence of moves, the far-reaching ramifications. This interplay of variables in turn highlights, among other things, the strong influence of domestic-external linkages. It recommends the synthesis of all three foci of international relations studies: man (perceptions), the state (interests) and the international system (environmental factors). And it so nicely mirrors the many cross-currents governing prospects for stability at least through this decade. In a word, part of the Gulf's fascination should lie in the presence of nearly every theme we teach, research and argue over within the profession.

To date, however, Gulf-related questions are being addressed by the military sciences more than the political or social sciences, giving an additional boost to security studies broadly defined at the expense of what traditionally fell under the purview of foreign and international affairs,[11] and making it harder to distinguish what Gabriel Garcia Marquez terms the 'ingenuity of politics' from the 'intuition of warfare'.[12]

In so far as international relations studies are concerned the Gulf has failed to register an intellectual shock-wave. What bearing has it had, for instance, on the contention made by Keohane and Nye that sovereign states have all but forfeited their Westphalian saliency to non-state supranational and transnational actors?[13] After 'the mother of all battles', how convincing is Mueller's proposition about warfare sinking into obsolescence, going the way of duelling, slavery and colonialism before it?[14] Have economics, interdependence and functional cooperation really come to supersede geopolitical preoccupations like national identity, territory and security which traditionally have ranked at the top of international concerns?

The point is not the lack of definitive answers, which is understandable. Only that at the time of writing, what might have been a stimulating exchange occasioned by the Gulf over the prevailing wisdom is rather desultory. Before proceeding to volunteer some useful avenues for study and discourse inspired by what we witnessed in the Middle East, I will hazard several possible explanations why international relations specialists might be deterred from wrestling with the theoretical implications of the Gulf conflict.

FIVE MITIGATING FACTORS

One possible deterrent has already been mentioned in passing; namely, the inconclusive outcome. By way of contrast, the positive finish to the 1962 Cuban missile crisis – with everyone a winner – nevertheless must have emboldened Allison to use it as the illustration for his three conceptual models or 'cuts' of state behaviour.[15]

No less treacherous than its mixed signals and subjective, often contradictory 'lessons' is the dazzling complexity of the Gulf affair also alluded to earlier. The weight of detail alone, plus the seemingly limitless number of intervening variables, is intimidating, and could easily scare off many students of international relations. There is, to be sure, the very real fear of not getting the analysis right: by mistaking the key driving forces behind the crisis, by confusing dependent and independent variables, by overlooking the real determinants, or by simply failing to master the flow of crisis events.[16]

No matter how intensely eventful it may have been in its own right, the Gulf chronology of crisis merges like a tributary into the still larger flow of global affairs. Mindful of this, we are led to a set of two additional mitigating factors, the first being that the international environment of the 1990s may discourage our pausing to zero in on the Gulf *per se*. Relentless, accelerated change constantly redirects our attention and professional skills to the latest fast-breaking global development as the world system lurches from one drama and one tension spot to another. Under the ceaseless barrage of headlines, save perhaps for the occasional doctoral candidate who can afford the luxury of dealing in isolation with the ageing tale of Iraqi crime and punishment? The Gulf, in short, threatens to be left behind scholastically, outpaced and overshadowed by ever more current events.

This same tendency to marginalize one of the more formative events of our time, treating it as merely episodic, is also reflected, on the other hand, from a macropolitical perspective. As memory fades, the Gulf crisis even now is being viewed less as a self-contained event than as but another link in the chain of historic events all contributing to, and illustrative of, a larger pattern of worldwide, systemic transformation. Bracketed between the collapse of the Warsaw Pact in 1989 and the collapse of the USSR in 1991, in all probability the 1990 crisis will lose its own distinctive identity together with whatever identifiable boundaries it may have had. The prospect of the Gulf simply being enveloped in the vast reshuffling of international politics is very real.

Going one step further, this line of thinking might argue that the authentic 'sea-changes' in world affairs (a) had little or nothing to do with the Gulf (b) preceded the Gulf and have been in motion since 1985;[17] (c) have come to the fore really only since the Gulf.[18] Whichever, the net effect is to downplay the event's importance. Whereas, conversely, if regarded conceptually as *sui generis*, then the predictive and comparative value of what unfolded on the Iraq–Kuwait border also becomes virtually nil. Both approaches in essence represent disincentives against treating the crisis as potentially valuable for theory-building.

THE MIDDLE EAST DIMENSION

There remains, however, one additional factor that I fear mitigates even more strongly against the Middle East crisis drawing close professional international relations investigation. And this is precisely its regional origin and character.

While the struggle exhibited a strong 'ripple effect', radiating outward and eventually assuming systemic-wide proportions, nonetheless, it can only be comprehended, at least initially, in the narrower context of the Middle Eastern regional subsystem.[19] Except that for years now this part of the world relatively speaking has been an underdeveloped area of regional studies. As a result, when the Kuwait crisis surfaced, catching policymakers off-guard, it also found academia in general, and the discipline of international relations in particular, with few exceptions,[20] ill-equipped to cope analytically or conceptually with its immediate origins in the Middle East.

The Middle East, its languages and cultures, its history and politics are in large measure neglected in the international relations core curriculum. This ignorance we suspect was one of the principal causes for the 'tilt' in American policy towards Iraq throughout the 1980s, when emotionalism – loathing for Khomeini's Iran in the wake of the

US embassy seizure and hostages ordeal – was permitted to become a policy blind spot, and a lucrative one at that.

Without the tools of Middle East specialization and without a sensitivity for the deeper forces at work within the region, fundamental international relations questions will go unanswered; above all, the degree to which the 1990–91 patterns of crisis and political alignment are symptomatic of larger global trends, or possibly indigenous to the region alone.[21] Middle East experts, in turn, professionally have been understandably inclined to limit their analysis to the purely local dimension of the Gulf story.[22] They make little if any reference to the wider professional literature, draw few if any comparative analogies and are reluctant to suggest potential lessons from the Middle East crisis either for extra-regional politics or for the international relations discipline as a whole. Their interest, in short, centres more on the possible impact the Iraq war may be having on a new regional order than for the new world order.

Nevertheless, the above disincentives can, and must, be overcome, and the receding Gulf experience retrieved. The following remarks are meant only to suggest several possible directions and frameworks for incorporating Gulf-related issues into a revised, 'old–new' international relations agenda.[23]

WESTPHALIA REVISITED

The first contribution the Gulf conflict offers is to caution all of us – idealists, realists and neo-realists alike – against the excesses of political Utopianism and wishful thinking. Our generation, like those before it, but also inspired by millenarianism ('towards the year 2,000'), an end to bipolarity and the seeming end of the reign of nuclear terror, is inclined to see itself living in a time zone fundamentally and qualitatively different from past history; or what Roberts traces as 'false dawns in earlier eras'.[24] Yet rhetoric aside, the 'new world order' is guaranteed to have more than its share of not-so-new disorders. The Gulf explosion therefore provided a timely antidote. It may have had its inspiring aspects, but was also sobering in exposing the *problematique* behind attempts at bringing the new world order blueprint to full realization under existing conditions.

Emphasizing elements of continuity becomes the Gulf's second contribution, for it brings us not only back to reality but also back to basics. Centuries-old notions that constitute what I would call 'unquestioned answers' undergirding the modern state system since its inception at Westphalia in 1648 now need to be retested and then redefined, beginning with the basic political unit, the state itself.[25] Thus the sovereign nation-state is the primary but no longer sole actor, forced to share the spotlight – as in the Gulf situation – with a whole range of multistate regional or functional alliances, international regimes and world bodies like the United Nations and its agencies. Today all states have gone from impermeability to permeability,[26] and find themselves subject to a whole host of external influences, indirect as well as direct. Gulf illustrations include: Kuwait's vulnerability to land attack, the Scud missiles fired at Israel, and the outside UN supervision imposed upon Iraq. This mounting sense of pregnability serves as one of the new realities – inspiring (some would say, dictating) a marked shift from the classic posture of self-reliance in defence to creative new common security models, the anti-Iraqi coalition being the latest and best example.

The need for collective frameworks accentuates the fictitious nature of the sovereignty principle to which states cling. Nowadays what government or country, whether superpower or non-superpower, is really allowed to conduct its affairs of state as a free agent? Since none are fully independent, what are we to make of sovereignty? Even more, why are there so many national claimants to this dubious title? Obviously still needing to be worked out from a theoretical, legal and practical standpoint is whether the notion of sovereignty has lost its meaning, or whether in our interconnected world sovereign states can be interdependent and 'semi-sovereign'.

Surely just as mischievous and needy of clarification is that other legacy from Westphalia: the hyphenated nation-state formula. As exemplified by the deep fissures within Iraqi society, between Shi'ites and Sunnis but above all between Iraqis and Kurds, today's present states are anything but homogeneous units; with rare exception (Japan?) they are bifurcated entities – binational or multinational – very much susceptible to centrifugal forces like tribalism, sectarianism or virulent, xenophobic nationalism. Domestic consequences aside, from a purely systemic viewpoint Lebanon and Iraq join with Yugoslavia and the Soviet republics to raise the spectre of civil strife, internal war and appeals for outside intervention.

Yet one more Westphalian postulate was the regularization of interstate relations through endorsement of the principles of equality, reciprocity and nonintervention. After the Gulf conflict, however, Mayall warns of 'a new form of collective imperialism'[27] which may have established a dangerous precedent. In the absence of clear guidelines, interference by the international community in another country's domestic jurisdiction will remain highly arbitrary. What obligation, after all, was there to aid the Kurds? And if the Kurds, why not other oppressed peoples? Likewise, if allied support for the Kurdish rebels is defensible, then the international community has a harder time deploring Turkish assistance to the Kurds against Saddam Hussein which then found Baghdad arming Kurdish separatists in south-eastern Turkey by way of retaliation.

Our purpose is not to argue the rights and wrongs of the case, but rather to emphasize that the principle of 'non-intervention' along with other key international relations concepts like 'sovereignty', the 'nation-state', 'territorial integrity' and 'defensible borders', and 'security' invite theoretical reassessment and updating because of the Gulf in conjunction with other recent global developments.

A REVISED CURRICULUM

If the Middle East crisis succeeds in encouraging greater realism and also forces a revision in our basic terms of reference, then its third contribution should lead to a renewed emphasis upon certain approaches or sub-fields neglected by the discipline.

Taken for granted

The study of power

Outdone only by most world leaders, a good many people in the international relations field still cling to an old-fashioned and simplistic view of 'power' which assumes it to be, among other things, monolithic or uni-dimensional, cumulative and overwhelmingly resting upon material resources. Now, with illustrations from the Gulf power struggle and the aid of works by Nye[28] and others, we ought to be achieving a greater sophistication in understanding the nature of power, what it consists of and how it works. On the one hand, Nye's point is well-taken that in the future 'soft power' will count for much, highlighting a country's qualitative assets: its national will, domestic consensus, morale and sense of purpose; its belief system and commitment to human rights; its image and international standing. But on the other hand, it is equally true that what helped the USA in its leadership role in the Gulf was the enduring relevance of 'hard power', while at the same time what helped contain Iraq were its deficiencies in the tangibles and consumables of military power. A renewal of interest in the correlates of power at least ought to assert the key importance for any country of possessing, and then using, the proper 'mix' of material *and* intangible components and the artful orchestration of diplomatic persuasion with physical coercion.

Linkage theory

Publication in 1969 of Rosenau's edited book of essays[29] marked the heyday of studies into the convergence of national and international systems; also the interplay between domestic politics and external behaviour. Since then, however, the notion of a shrinking world in which the structure and functioning of sovereign states can be the direct result of events in remote parts of the world, and vice versa, has become a commonplace. With the Gulf as a prism, though, there should be a revival of scholarly interest into exactly how linkages take place, blurring the boundaries between national and international systems. Stimulating in particular is the matter of democratization: not only the assumption that democratic societies and regimes are less prone to make war, but whether they are conducive to achieving a new, peaceful 'system-dominant' world order.

Subordinated themes

Conventional deterrence

For over forty-five years the nuclear debate which predominated strategic planning has been carried over as well into academic circles, assuming both the recognition and the mystique of an autonomous if somewhat esoteric and highly specialized branch of international relations, with a language of its own and beyond the comprehension of the uninitiated layman. Whether it is the literature on war-gaming and simulation, military technology transfers and arms proliferation, or arms control negotiations, the single overwhelming impression is of an almost obsessive preoccupation with the nuclear dimension, to the exclusion and subordination of the conventional level. Nowhere is this asymmetry more noticeable than in the area of deterrence theory, frequently mistakenly assumed to be a nuclear age and superpower phenomenon.[30] Now, for the first time really since 1945 conventional deterrence can be liberated from the tyranny of the balance of terror and applied to confrontation scenarios of 'multilateral deterrence', involving preparedness against Third World countries, small states and non-nuclear powers, and where the identity of one's enemy may not be known in advance.

The small and regional powers

Similarly, too much attention has been given at the interstate level to two relationships: (a) the US–Soviet superpower rivalry, and (b) superior-subordinate or patron-client patterns. Neither the struggle between Iran and Iraq nor the Kuwaiti situation fit these moulds. With these cases as inspiration and with the demise of Cold War bipolarity, the way is clear once again to probe more intensively other relationships, in particular those involving two and more small states or local powers competing for regional hegemony, and no longer perceiving themselves constrained from above.[31]

Reinstatement

Two previous fields of study long out of favour within the profession may experience something of a comeback that traces directly to the Gulf. One is political geography; the other international law and organization.

Political geography

Writing in late 1990, Halliday cautioned that the 'oldest of international issues, the fusion and fragmentation of states, is once again with us'.[32] For the better part of this century the analysis of geography as a basic (if not *the* basic) determinant of political behaviour has been de-emphasized, its believers pushed on the defensive by the combined force of three nearly fatal blows. The post-Enlightenment view of modern man and of the modern state expresses confidence in the ability of both to master impersonal environmental forces through harnessing science and technology. A second blow was the widespread conviction that spatial barriers were now neutralized and possibly altogether nullified, as symbolized by the advent of air power, then followed by intercontinental ballistic missiles and transoceanic communication. But the final death-knell for political geography as a respected science was thought to have been the distorted use by the Germans of *geopolitik*, which cited *lebensraum* as the pretext for aggression and racial superiority as justification for the extermination of entire peoples.

Yet our attention throughout the Gulf ordeal was riveted to the map of the Middle East region, it geopolitical features and peculiarities. Suddenly topography, borders, distance, land, sea and air routes, and resources – what the Sprouts categorized as 'man–milieu relationships'[33] – once again became of critical, abiding importance. Political geography hereafter merits reinclusion as a required course in any comprehensive undergraduate programme of international studies, touching as well upon the political impact of science and technology.[34]

International institutions and law

Also likely to enjoy a revival of scholarly interest under the impact of the Gulf War are the two cognate areas of international legal procedure, and the study of regional groupings, international organizations and world government. Criticized by the realist school as normative, impractical and peripheral for real world politics, both international law and organization fell out of vogue during most of the 1960s, 1970s and 1980s, and were downgraded in university programmes. But then the UN became a central arena for shaping the collective response to Iraqi aggression, and for legitimizing Security Council Resolutions 678 (authorizing 'all necessary means' to secure Iraq's immediate withdrawal from Kuwait) and 688 (labelling persecution of Iraqi Kurds a danger to world peace and security) in the name of firm legal doctrines like state sovereignty and the inadmissibility of territorial conquest.

This success, in turn, raises renewed expectations about the rule of law and its robust application under the UN Charter, as well as for revising procedures to encourage peaceful settlement of disputes. This vision of an international society of common values also calls for a revitalized UN world body playing a role in the future on behalf of global peace while also serving common security concerns. It is not by accident that the UN and respect for international norms are two main pillars of the new world order blueprint.

The Gulf contributes directly to the potential of international law and organization, and to their appeal for prospective students of international relations, by having opened up a number of theoretically and politically challenging 'grey areas'. Among these are: the silence of international law about the responsibility of other states in the event of bloodshed, coups or anarchy within a neighbour's domestic domain; the lack of consensus on how and to what extent the Security Council should address threats to international security arising from such internal disorders, what with aid to Iraq's Kurds now established precedent;[35] the legality of 'delegated enforcement', carrying with it the danger that the licensing of a few countries to use force in the name of the UN could be regarded as unrepresentative of the world community; and concern that accepting such an activist, interventionist role could 'overload' the UN organization with its already-existing budgetary and structural problems.[36] Clearly, efforts at bridging the gap between law, justice and global order must be moved forward on the international relations agenda.

DIPLOMATIC HISTORY

The same needs to be said for the history of international relations. If reserved for last in this discussion it is only because diplomatic history most regrettably may fit all three categories: fallen out of favour, subordinated and at other times simply taken for granted; whereas it deserves to be ranked first in any revised core curriculum.

The present estrangement between history and political science is needless and harmful in equal measure. Yet in any reconciliation each party brings to the renewed partnership complementary assets: an ability to generalize and attention to detail, a quest for commonalities and patterns tempered by a sensitivity towards the uniqueness of events.[37] For what stronger message has the Gulf crisis sent through the medium of Persians, Arabs and Kurds than the warning that instead of celebrating history's end we in international relations had best brace ourselves for its return – and with a vengeance. Consequently, those presently responsible for charting the discipline's future course would be remiss were they to fail in providing students with the historical perspective so indispensable for keeping on top of current events . . . and not solely in the Middle East!

PROCESSING INTERNATIONAL RELATIONS

An otherwise disruptive Gulf tremor can make a fourth positive academic contribution. It affords an opportunity to take old-new themes like those just discussed and to rearrange them under fresh headings. The one I favour is 'International political processes'.

For one thing, the study of process offers a useful counter (or, if one prefers, supplement) to the prevailing school of institutionalism,[38] emphasizing formal structures: states as organizational-bureaucratic decisional units, as international actors; or regime theory, hegemonic systems and modelling world orders. Process analysis, by contrast, emphasizes the dynamic, fluid quality of world politics at all levels and at all times. The distinction, if you will, is between the *balance* of power and the *balancer* of power as, respectively, a static type of situation (symmetrical or uneven, favourable or unfavourable) and a fixed role in search of a pivotal actor, versus the constant manoeuvre and readjustment that is the *balancing* of power.

For another thing, this procedural side of international affairs advertises basic properties common to all political processes. If better understood, these features might prepare the student of world politics for the sudden crisis and for the unanticipated 'wild card' development – that one option or scenario no one thought of; but even more, for the all too predictable and recurrent forces of opposition to systemic change and reform.

Among the insights are the following:

- A process, by definition, is organic and ongoing; in principle, most are unending; some in fact are cyclical owing to constant feedback.
- Processes unfold over time; no matter how brief, each can be traced through several distinct stages punctuated by one or more signposts and turning-points.
- The longer and more open-ended any process, the greater its prospects for being deflected from a pre-designed course by outside influences or by the element of surprise.
- Resistance to change may be formidable, yet change is an 'iron law' of international relations that makes permanent equilibrium a sheer impossibility and the status quo a chimera, an improbability. What truly matters, therefore, is the pace and the direction of change.
- Depending upon particular circumstances, the pace of change may vary from slow and incremental to crisis-induced and accelerated in the extreme.
- Each process is subject to setbacks and possible reversal since it bears within itself the push and pull of competing, even contradictory forces. Similarly, in the real world of world politics two or more processes will always be taking place simultaneously and in fairly close proximity to each other. When this happens any one of four relationships may ensue:

  - Unlinked but tending to move in the same direction, which may or may not suggest a pattern or ground swell (war weariness in Angola, in Cambodia, in El Salvador, in the western Sahara entirely independent of each other);
  - Interconnected and mutually reinforcing (defence economics and the process of 'drawing down' conventional forces);
  - Parallel and unconnected, but moving in opposite – clockwise and counter-clockwise – directions (Iraqi regional irredentism and Syrian direct influence over Lebanon, in the face of American global ascendancy);

– Interlocking but mutually exclusive (once US and Iraqi aspirations collided in a direct clash of wills).

In the last analysis, therefore, what governs these single or multiple process configurations are the instruments available to any state or international system for *regulating* change and for *adapting* to it.

Finally, it is suggested that the study of processes is profoundly relevant – even more than institutions and hierarchies – to the central theme of international relations today: continuity versus discontinuity. As Hoffmann admits, we still have no satisfactory, complete or integrated theory of change in world politics.[39] International processes in general and particularly those concerned with political change may not produce the comprehensive theory we wish to have. Still, the process-oriented approach has much to offer because of its receptivity towards change as both dynamic and inevitable. Whatever else, it cannot but help to aid in furthering our understanding: (a) of traditional, recurrent processes, and (b) of basic transformation rules which apply within state units, between states and at the level of an evolving global system.

DOMESTIC PROCESSES

International relations as a process applies to the state-centred paradigm in several useful ways, the two most promising expressions perhaps being decision-making and the integrative process. Both are inspired by the premise of strong linkages between domestic and external politics; both figure prominently in the Gulf sequence and recent international affairs. Likewise both relate to the fashionable theory which argues that democracies are peace-prone by nature and hence make for more responsible, desirable members of the international community[40] – a theory which, if taken at a yet higher level of abstraction, implies that in the end regime type outweighs in importance the nature of the state to pursue maximizing goals and self-aggrandizement.

Under this sub-heading of 'decisional process' we call for supplementing the existing body of work on foreign policy-making by further investigation of such procedural issues as: how personal and state preferences are formed, adopted, coordinated, implemented, reassessed and then re-formed; how the processing of information may differ in open and closed societies (could Saddam really have doubted American resolve to use the force painstakingly assembled in the Gulf?); how the 'ends–means' dilemma of matching national interests with national power is reconciled when the very definition of power and the relative weight of the various components is undergoing change; the extent to which techniques for coping with crisis situations have improved thanks to the accumulated experience in managing crises now augmented by the Gulf case.

The Gulf states before, during and since the war are relevant also for the integrative process. Ernest Renan once likened nation-building to 'a daily plebiscite'.[41] States are far from monolithic, rational or purposive owing to divergent policy views within the ranks of government policy-makers, but also because of a national unification process going on all the time parallel with the state's pursuit of foreign policy goals beyond its borders. In a post-Gulf world of countervailing forces and contradictory influences our narrow 1980s preoccupation with only one side of the integrative process, inspired by the early, apparently successful, take-off of the European Community model, will need readjustment. For unification is never one-directional; nor is it ever completed. Rather, this ongoing process, too, has to be treated as a continuum – a continuum that features union and separatism, consolidation and fragmentation, internal pressures no less centrifugal than centripetal. Where an Iraq, a Lebanon, a Syria or any other country is located along this continuum at any given moment will provide us an important clue as to its international standing and degree of influence in relations with other states.

INTERSTATE PROCESSES

Once foreign policy, the domestic process, becomes foreign relations, additional international political processes command our attention. For the sake of brevity, they divide basically into two: war-making and peace-making. The former, in turn, involves two related areas of concentration:

1 Arms-racing, or what has also been termed the 'weapons succession process',[42] with its own distinctive cycle of military build-up (procurements, arms research and development) – proliferation (arms export, technology transfers, co-production) – restraint (conversion to civilian manufacture, arms limitation accords). Surely one lesson taught by the Gulf War is that conventional arms persist as this century's 'weapons of mass destruction' and therefore merit as much, if not greater attention than nuclear and non-conventional weaponry that have preoccupied strategic studies for so long.

2 War-making, being the actual as opposed to threatened use of

force, with the Iraqi offensive and allied counter-offensive certain to provide the raw material for a good many military studies that will hopefully incorporate diplomatic moves as well.

Peace-making, on the other hand, shifts the focus from the enmity curve in interstate relations to that of amity, with persuasive diplomacy replacing coercion and war as the central focus of research. Here, three processes need to be refined, whether in the aftermath of actual conflict or as an alternative to belligerency. These are: first, channels for communicating, both with enemies and allies but also with neutral third parties, including warnings, signals and secret confidences; second, the negotiating process, with its special repertoire of bargaining techniques; third, conflict resolution and the range of legal and political means available to warring ethnic groups as well as states for terminating disputes. Doubtless the 1991 US-brokered Arab–Israeli diplomatic initiative, one of the by-products of the Gulf crisis, will enrich our understanding of peace-making processes for years to come.

SYSTEMIC PROCESSES

If Gulf-induced renewed interest in strengthening the global community is not to be short-lived and confidence restored in the UN organization, then greater effort must go into evaluating how system-wide functions might best be performed on behalf of international society as a whole. Carrying out these duties in a new world order will involve rudimentary processes like: building consensus on a North–South agenda, enacting and enforcing legislation, protecting global assets, more equitably allocating and more efficiently distributing natural resources, employing economic sanctions against recalcitrant members and financing as well as expanding the use of observer forces in trouble spots around the world.

One of the most interesting processes brought out by the Gulf though is political realignment. Demonstrating once again that international politics do truly make for strange bedfellows, the most remarkable alignments in recent memory were stitched together during the 1990 confrontation, with Iraq, Libya, Jordan and the Palestinians (otherwise at loggerheads) pitted against a vastly more complex and incongruous amalgam of the USA and the Soviet Union, Egypt and Syria, Saudi Arabia and Israel, Turkey and Japan, NATO, one-time Warsaw Pact members, Europeans together with Afro-Asian personnel. We submit that the process whereby this coalition of forces from twenty-eight countries on six continents was assembled, employed in active or passive roles but above all somehow orchestrated holds the key to both alliance politics and collective security in the future.

So, too, is Iran's manoeuvring throughout the crisis and ability to reposition itself particularly noteworthy in regard to realignment dynamics. Saddam's folly was most opportune for Iran, and represented an unexpected windfall. Teheran joined in condemning the Iraqi invasion of an Arab state and adhered to the UN economic embargo, thus easing tensions with its Arab neighbours in the Gulf and beginning on the road to normalizing ties with the USA and the West. Which tells a great deal about the process whereby a revolutionary-revisionist state actor can be encouraged to trade some of its ideological zeal for a more pragmatic diplomacy that reintegrates it into the shifting regional and extra-regional alignments. Moreover, the political realignment process will become far more critical in the post-Cold War and Gulf War era as the emphasis moves from rigid, permanent blocs resting on doctrinal allegiances back to fluid relationships motivated by short-term, utilitarian considerations and pragmatic interests.

The prospectus therefore calls for a return to classic 'balance of power' diplomacy.[43] Realignment, in other words, is really an expression of an even larger, truly systemic process which mandates the careful, unrelenting calibration of power that features both balancing and 'bandwagoning'.[44] Already in the early eighteenth century European statesmen and political theorists grasped the fact that the balance of power is less a mechanical model than an evolving process which seeks to merge the dominant 'simple' two-power contest with regional 'inferior' balances into a general balance that covered the whole European continent. At the close of the twentieth century our work is really cut out for us in tracing this enduring process of equilibrating power in a diffuse system composed of multiple power centres.

New instabilities are bound to be introduced by the growth or decay of states, by the rise and decline of great powers, by the crafting and breaking of alliances, by emerging industrial and military technologies, by an international economy in the making and by other changes within as well as between states. Nevertheless, the balancing of power will surely remain a symbol of historical continuity and quite likely the central fulcrum for governing an untidy and still-divided world.

Power alignment and balancing at the macropolitical level are thus as good a starting point as any in entering upon the final process inspired by the informative Gulf and Middle East experience: the internal professional process of reordering and refining the scientific study of international relations. If the challenge is taken up in ways consistent with the spirit and realities of the times our individual labours within the discipline may yet offer guidance to a transforming international system and society poised somewhere between anarchy, hegemony and harmony.

NOTES

1 A comparative study of pre-crisis in Kuwait and in Korea (1950) would be instructive, given the close parallel that in both instances an ambiguous US commitment may have encouraged misperception by the potential aggressor about the American definition of a vital national interest to be backed by military force. See David Ross, *Korea: The Limited War*, London: Macmillan, 1964; Glenn D. Paige, *The Korean Decision*, New York: Free Press, 1968; and the congressional testimony by US ambassador to Baghdad, April Glaspie (see *Washington Post* 19 March 1991 and *New York Times* 22 March 1991. A verbatim transcript of Ambassador Glaspie's testimony before the House Subcommittee on Europe and the Middle East on 21 March 1991 was issued by the Federal News Service.); also Efraim Karsh and Inari Rautsi, 'Why Saddam Hussein invaded Kuwait', *Survival*, vol. XXXIII, no. 1, January/February 1991, pp. 18–30.
2 The literature on crisis behaviour and crisis management is quite extensive. Any survey ought to begin with Charles F. Hermann's by-now classic article, 'International crisis as a situational variable', in James N. Rosenau (ed.), *International Politics and Foreign Policy*, New York: Free Press, 1969, pp. 411–16; before proceeding to more theoretical works like Charles F. Hermann (ed.) *International Crises: Insights from Behavioral Research*, New York: Free Press, 1972; with an Appendix of 311 empirically testable propositions, and then culminating in the encyclopaedic two-volume handbook edited by Michael Brecher, Jonathan Wilkenfeld and Sheila Moser, *Crises in the Twentieth Century*, Oxford: Pergamon Press, 1988.
3 One possible indication was that at the eighty-seventh annual meeting of the American Political Science Association in Chicago on 29 August – 1 September 1991 only four panels of over 200 were devoted to the Gulf event. Of these, one dealt with the public law aspect of constitutional war powers in the USA, two others addressed the Middle East and Arab angle, while only one even attempted to look at the Gulf crisis in terms of international relations theory.
4 James N. Rosenau, *Turbulence in World Politics: A Theory of Change and Continuity*, New York and London: Harvester Wheatsheaf, 1990, p. 37. He goes on to raise the proposition that because 'the parameters of global politics are undergoing profound and permanent transformation' analysts are challenged to be open 'to making corresponding alterations in

the conceptual premises with which they organize and interpret the course of events'.

5 John J. Mearsheimer, in his rejoinder to criticism of his essay, 'Back to the future: instability in Europe after the Cold War' (*International Security*, vol. 15, no. 1, Summer 1990, pp. 5–56) by Stanley Hoffmann and Robert O. Keohane *International Security*, vol. 15, no. 2, Fall 1990, p. 199.

6 Fred Halliday, 'The Pertinence of IR', *Political Studies*, vol. XXXVIII, no. 3 (September 1990), pp. 502–16.

7 One of the most recent attempts at satisfactorily defining 'international crisis' is offered by Brecher, Wilkenfeld and Moser: 'a situational change characterized by two necessary and sufficient conditions: (1) distortion in the type and an increase in the intensity of *disruptive interactions* between two or more adversaries, with an accompanying high probability of *military hostilities*, or, during a war, an *adverse change* in the *military balance*; and (2) a *challenge* to the existing *structure* of an international system – global, dominant or subsystem – posed by the higher-than-normal conflictual interactions'. *Crisis in the Twentieth Century*, vol. 1, p. 3 (see Note 2).

8 US Secretary of State James Baker, remarks made on 18 October 1991 during a press conference in Jerusalem on the eve of the Middle East peace conference in Madrid – text courtesy of the United States Information Service, Tel-Aviv.

9 Hedley Bull, *The Anarchical Society: A Study of Order in World Politics*, London: Macmillan, 1977.

10 See, for example, Lawrence Freedman, 'The Gulf War and the new world order', *Survival*, vol. XXXIII, no. 3, May/June 1991, pp. 195–209, and the author's 'Gulf Crisis and new world order: the perils of linkage', in the volume of papers contributed by a study group of the Jaffee Center for Strategic Studies, *War in the Gulf: Implications for Israel*, Boulder, Colorado: Westview Press, 1992.

11 A good illustration is Lawrence Freedman and Efraim Karsh, 'How Kuwait was won: strategy in the Gulf War', *International Security*, vol. 16, no. 2, Fall, 1991, pp. 5–41; Stephen M. Walt, 'The renaissance of security studies', *International Studies Quarterly*, vol. 35, no. 2, June, 1991, pp. 211–39, in which Walt describes security studies as becoming 'more rigorous, methodologically sophisticated, and theoretically inclined' (p. 211). Arguing from the opposite direction is Kenneth Thompson – writing in the wake of the Gulf War, he urges 'the restoration of international politics to the center of international studies' because the study of 'how nations acquire, maintain, and employ power' remains crucial to our understanding of recurrent problems of peace and stability – Kenneth W. Thompson, 'The decline of international studies', *Ethics and International Affairs*, vol. 5, 1991, p. 245.

12 Gabriel Garcia Marquez, *The General In His Labyrinth*, New York: Penguin Books, 1990, p. 78.

13 Robert Keohane and Joseph Nye (eds), *Transnational Relations and World Politics*, Cambridge, Mass.: Harvard University Press, 1971.

14 John Mueller, 'The essential irrelevance of nuclear weapons: stability in the postwar world', *International Security*, vol. 13, no. 2, Fall, 1988,

pp. 55–79, further elaborated upon in his book, *Retreat From Doomsday: The Obsolescence of Major War*, New York: Basic Books, 1989.

15 Graham T. Allison, *Essence of Decision: Explaining the Cuban Missile Crisis* Boston: Little, Brown, 1971.

16 One of the first and best attempts at questioning traditional principles against the Gulf experience is James Mayall, 'Non-intervention, self-determination, and the "new world order",' *International Affairs*, vol. 67, no. 3, July, 1991, pp. 421–9.

17 This is the thesis underlining all of the essays in Nicholas X. Rizopoulos (ed.) *Sea-Changes: American Foreign Policy in a World Transformed*, New York and London: Council on Foreign Relations, 1990, completed just prior to the invasion of Kuwait.

18 With specific emphasis on the succession crisis brought on by the rapid dissolution of the Soviet Union following the abortive coup in August 1991.

19 On the Middle East as a distinctive sub-system, see: Michael Brecher, 'The Middle East subordinate system and its impact on Israel's foreign policy', *International Studies Quarterly*, vol. 13, no. 2 1969, pp. 117–39; and Louis J. Cantori and Steven L. Spiegel, *The International Politics of Regions*, Englewood Cliffs, New Jersey: Prentice-Hall, 1970.

20 One of the better efforts is by Lawrence Freedman in his essay on 'The Gulf War and the new world order' (see Note 10).

21 Greater attention to the deeper forces behind the revival of Islam thus might have spared Fukuyama from claiming a premature end to the ideological struggle of ideas (and religious faiths) taken by Hegelians to be the driving force of history. Francis Fukuyama, 'The End of History?', *The National Interest*, Summer, 1989, pp. 3–18.

22 Robert L. Rothstein, 'The Middle East after the war: change and continuity', *Washington Quarterly*, vol. 14, no. 3 (Summer 1991), pp. 139–60; David Garnham, 'Explaining Middle Eastern alignments during the Gulf War', *Jerusalem Journal of International Relations*, vol. 13, no. 3 (September 1991), pp. 63–83; insightful as always on Arab politics is Fouad Ajami's article on 'The end of Arab nationalism,' in *New Republic*, 12 August 1991, pp. 23–7, and also 'The summer of Arab discontent', *Foreign Affairs*, vol. 69, no. 5 (Winter 1990/91), pp. 1–20.

23 See Fred Halliday, 'IR: is there a new agenda?', *Millenium: Journal of International Studies*, vol. 20, no. 1 (Spring 1991), pp. 57–72. In his lecture given at the London School of Economics on 29 November 1990, Halliday identifies a new set of political problems centring on the environment, internationalization, weapons proliferation, migration, international cooperation on human rights, drugs and AIDS, as well as delinking Islam and terrorism. These are supplements to the old agenda items of nationalism, war and the inequality of wealth.

24 Adam Roberts, 'A new age in international relations?', *International Affairs*, vol. 67, no. 3 (July 1991), pp. 509–25.

25 The treaty of Westphalia, not only put an end to the Thirty Years War, but established norms and principles which have served as the basis for the modern international system, including: the notion of the nation-state; the legal concept of state sovereignty, including territorial inviolability, as well as reciprocity and equality in interstate relations.

26 The terms were coined by John Herz in his book, *International Politics in the Atomic Age*, New York: Columbia University Press, 1959, to contrast seventeenth century claims to absolute sovereignty with state vulnerability in this century.

27 Mayall, p. 427 (see Note 16).

28 Joseph S. Nye, *Bound to Lead: The Changing Nature of American Power*, New York: Basic Books, 1990.

29 James N. Rosenau (ed.), *Linkage Politics*, New York: Free Press, 1969.

30 Gordan A. Craig and Alexander L. George, *Force and Statecraft*, New York: Oxford University Press, 1983, esp. ch. 13, 'Deterrence', pp. 172–87.

31 Carsten Holbraad, *Middle Powers in International Politics*, New York: St Martin's Press, 1984.

32 Halliday, 'IR: Is There A New Agenda?', p. 27 (see Note 23).

33 Harold and Margaret Sprout, *The Ecological Perspective on Human Affairs*, Princeton: Princeton University Press, 1965.

34 The economic and environmentalist approaches are both expressions of this renewed sensitivity, and are represented, respectively in Edward Luttwak, 'From geopolitics to geo-economics', *National Interest*, Summer 1990, pp. 17–23, and Jessica Tuchman Mathews, 'Redefining security', *Foreign Affairs*, vol. 68, no. 2 (Spring 1989), pp. 162–77.

35 Alluding to this 'new international interference', *The Economist* on 9 November 1991 editorialized: 'National sovereignty be damned: The UN is already involved in Iraq' (pp. 13–14).

36 These issues are raised in a thoughtful statement by US Ambassador to the United Nations, Thomas Pickering, before the Senate Foreign Relations Committee on 13 November 1991, 'Pickering foresees new types of global conflict' – text courtesy of the United States Information Service, Tel-Aviv. Also useful is Bruce Russett and James S. Sutterlin, 'The U.N. in a new world order', *Foreign Affairs*, vol. 70, no. 2 (Spring 1991), pp. 69–83, which is devoted primarily to the UN's peacekeeping function.

37 See: Ernest R. May, *Lessons of the Past*, Oxford: Oxford University Press, 1973; Paul Gordon Lauren (ed.), *Diplomacy: New Approaches in History, Theory and Policy*, New York: Free Press, 1979. Gordon A. Craig put the point well in his presidential address before the American Historical Association in December 1982, when he told his professional colleagues 'we may gain in analytical sophistication if we overcome our congenital distrust of theory and our insistence upon the uniqueness of the historical event', and called for 'collaboration between disciplines, to the benefit of both' – 'The historian and the study of international relations', *American Historical Review*, vol. 88, no. 1 (February 1983), p. 9.

38 On the institutional approach, see Robert O. Keohane, *International Institutions and State Power*, Boulder, Colorado: Westview Press, 1989, and Stephen D. Krasner (ed.), *International Regimes*, Ithaca, New York: Cornell University Press, 1983.

39 Stanley Hoffmann, 'The future of the international political system: a sketch', in Samuel Huntington and Joseph S. Nye, Jr. (eds), *Global Dilemmas*, Lanham, Maryland: University Press of America, 1985, pp. 280–1.

40 An early version of the theory appears in an article by Melvin Small and J. David Singer, 'The war-proneness of democratic regimes, 1816–1965',

Jerusalem Journal of International Relations, vol. 1, no. 4 (Summer 1976), pp. 50–69.

41 Ernest Renan, 'What is a nation?', a lecture delivered at the Sorbonne in 1882 and reprinted in Arend Lijphart (ed.), *World Politics*, Boston: Allyn & Bacon, 1968.

42 Mary Kaldor, 'The weapons succession process', *World Politics*, vol. 38, no. 4 (July 1986), pp. 577–95.

43 A debate over the applicability of balance of power theory is found in Herbert M. Levine (ed.), *World Politics Debated*, New York: McGraw-Hill, 1983, pitting Hedley Bull (pro), 'The present relevance of the balance of power' (pp. 86–8) against Stanley Hoffmann (con), 'The balance of power' (pp. 88–94).

44 Stephen M. Walt, *The Origins of Alliances*, Ithaca, New York: Cornell University Press, 1987, in which he raises the prospect of states occasionally allying with the threatening power ('bandwagoning') rather than against it in order either to share in the spoils or to divert the aggressor's attack away from themselves. This may be the insight needed, for example, to explain the behaviour of Jordan's King Hussein, who allied himself with Iraq during the Gulf crisis. On the ever-changing balancing process, see Andrew C. Goldberg, 'Soviet imperial decline and the emerging balance of power', *Washington Quarterly*, vol. 13, no. 1 (Winter 1990), pp. 157–67.

Part I
Middle East tremors

2 Continuity and change in the inter-Arab system[1]

Bruce Maddy-Weitzman

For decades to come, declared Morocco's King Hassan in the fall of 1990, Iraq's invasion, subjugation and attempted incorporation of Kuwait as Iraq's '19th province', will be a dividing line in modern Arab history.[2] Indeed, never in the chequered and conflict-ridden history of the Arab League had the tenets of Arab solidarity and good neighbourliness embodied in the League's 1945 founding charter and the Joint Defence Pact of 1950 been so blatantly violated. Moreover, the decision to invade was preceded by months of diplomatic activity culminating in frenzied mediation efforts of a kind that had scored considerable successes in past inter-Arab wrangles. The shock of actual conflict was therefore that much greater, and the departure from established norms that much more pronounced.

Saddam's act prompted similar unprecedented responses by his Arab neighbours. Saudi Arabia abandoned its traditional squeamishness over the presence of Western forces on its soil, even at the risk of creating an affront to Muslim sensibilities. Egypt forsook the traditional modus-operandi of the Arab League – adopting resolutions on the basis of consensus – and fashioned an anti-Iraqi majority coalition from among the twenty-one League members which both endorsed the mustering of Western forces in the Saudi desert and gave the green light to Arab military participation in the anti-Saddam international coalition.

At the same time, the crisis contains many enduring themes of inter-Arab affairs over the last half century: a particular country bidding for regional hegemony, in the service of which it invoked a combination of patriotic, pan-Arab and Islamic themes; the banding together of other Arab countries to act as a counterweight; and peripatetic efforts by various Arab parties to mediate a solution. One is also reminded of numerous past instances in which Arab countries turned to global powers for both overt and covert help in confronting inter-Arab challenges.

The immediate outcomes of the crisis are, of course, now part of the historical record. What remains to be seen is the extent to which King Hassan's dictum is proving to be accurate or whether the Gulf crisis will turn out to have been more of an aberration in inter-Arab history and of limited effect.

In discussing the Gulf crisis this chapter seeks to enumerate and analyse elements of both continuity and change in the system of inter-Arab relations in order to provide a more reliable road map for understanding the ever-changing course of Middle East politics.

BACKGROUND TO THE CRISIS

By the end of the 1980s, inter-Arab relations seemed to have reached a level of equilibrium not attained previously. Over the course of eight years of war between Iraq and Iran, an Egyptian–Iraqi alliance had served as the linchpin of a large, loosely grouped majority bloc of Arab states, which also included Saudi Arabia, Jordan, Morocco and the smaller Gulf principalities. Its *raison d'être* was to contain the geopolitical and ideological-cultural threat posed by Iran's Islamic Republic. Most of the group also shared a general desire for a political resolution of the Arab–Israeli conflict.

Both Egypt and Iraq had derived important tangible benefits from the alignment. In return for extending its support in the way of surplus weaponry and more than two million workers, Egypt was able to break down the walls of inter-Arab isolation which had been built up around it as punishment for concluding a contractual peace with Israel. Moreover, in the latter stages of the war, as the Iranian threat mounted, so did Egypt become increasingly identified as an important factor in maintaining the security and well-being of the Gulf Arab states and the overall regional balance of power. Egypt's full return to a pivotal position in the Arab firmament was consecrated at the 1989 Casablanca Arab summit conference. By the end of the decade, every Arab country except Libya had reopened its embassy in Cairo (although Egyptian–Libyan relations were fully restored in all but name).

Ironically, it was Iraq that had taken the lead in 1978–79 in imposing sanctions on Egypt. However, once it became clear to Saddam Hussein that he had overextended himself in Iran, he shifted course and aligned Iraq with Egypt and the conservative Arab oil-producing monarchies. Thanks to both Arab and Western assistance, the war ended with Iraq in a position of what can be termed 'triumphant survivalism'.

For a time after the Iran–Iraq war, it appeared a new era of stable inter-Arab relations was in the offing. The durability of multiple, independent Arab states had been proven; continuous confrontation with Israel and Iran had produced a feeling of collective exhaustion; and the end of the Cold War promised to have a major strategic impact on the Middle East. Moreover, pressing domestic needs in the face of falling oil-generated revenues, skewed development, rapidly increasing populations, and growing Islamic fundamentalist movements all seemed to necessitate an Arab political order which would place a premium on economic development and interstate cooperation. In addition, the imminent EC economic union reinforced further the notion that if the Arab world was to avoid being marginalized in the international system, it needed to create new cooperative structures.

To these ends, two new regional blocs were created in 1989. The first, the four-member Arab Cooperation Council (ACC), was composed of Egypt, Iraq, Jordan and North Yemen, and marked the formalization of the war-time Egyptian–Iraqi alliance. The second was the Arab Maghreb Union (AMU), composed of the five Arab states of North Africa. The six-member Gulf Cooperation Council (GCC), composed of Saudi Arabia and the smaller Arab principalities along the Gulf, had been created in 1981. With the addition of the two new groups, fifteen of the twenty-two members of the Arab League were now parties to more compact regional organizations based on geographical proximity, mutual affinities, and common economic and political interests, and thus were presumably better equipped and more motivated than the unwieldy and historically ineffective Arab League to promote economic and political coordination.

Syria was the only major state standing apart from these developments, thanks to the long-standing contentiousness between Syria and Iraq. Their dispute was underpinned by geopolitical considerations and bitter personal and ideological rivalries between their respective wings of the Ba'th Party which dated back to the mid-1960s, and was fuelled by Syria's active support for Iran against Iraq. In 1989, the continued bitterness between Damascus and Baghdad seemed to be the only dark cloud in an otherwise increasingly 'purified Arab atmosphere'. At the end of the year, Syria restored diplomatic relations with Egypt after a twelve-year hiatus, in part in order to create a counterweight to an increasingly assertive Iraq.

For Egypt, normalization of ties with Syria seemed to place it squarely in the centre of regional affairs. So did the decision by the Arab League Council in March 1990 to return the League's headquarters to Cairo from Tunis, where it had been transferred as part of the anti-Egyptian sanctions in 1979. To be sure, the League could count few achievements during its forty-five-year existence. Achieving its professed goals of greater Arab solidarity and 'joint Arab action' in the service of a common Arab future had proven most often to be a chimera, foundering on the shoals of very real disparities in social structures, regimes, histories and economies. Nonetheless, even if the League was mainly a debating society, its return to Cairo signified for Egyptians that the inter-Arab centre of gravity had been restored to its rightful place. Concurrently, however, Saddam Hussein had begun making the most concerted bid for all-Arab leadership since the days of Gamal Abd al-Nasser.

The first signs to that effect came at the four-way ACC summit conference held in Amman, Jordan, on 23–24 February 1990. The sharp contrast in tone and content between Hosni Mubarak's calls for peaceful resolution of regional disputes and Saddam Hussein's fiery declarations pointed to serious differences between them over how to best ensure 'the Arab future'. Behind the scenes, their differences were even sharper. One bone of contention was the persistent effort by both Iraq and Jordan to give the ACC a military dimension. Another centred on Saddam's efforts to enlist ACC leaders on behalf of his demands for massive financial aid from the Gulf Arab states, which reportedly prompted an angry exchange between Saddam and Mubarak during one of the conference's closed sessions.[3] Their differences would be played out again at the all-Arab summit conference in Baghdad three months later. Still, both President Mubarak and Saddam would avoid direct confrontations with one another right up until 2 August, the former in the hope that Saddam's good behaviour could best be ensured by cajoling him, the latter so as not to rock the inter-Arab boat prematurely.

The issue on which both Arab leaders and the media were expressing themselves most forcefully in early 1990 was that of Soviet Jewish emigration to Israel, the dimensions of which had only recently become apparent. For Saddam, the alleged threat posed by a strengthened Israel was an ideal tool through which to assert his brand of regional leadership. His uncompromising statements at the ACC meeting and subsequent boasting of Iraqi capabilities to incinerate half of Israel marked the recycling of an old, and somewhat neglected inter-Arab theme: adopting a militantly anti-Zionist posture to distract attention from actual designs by legitimizing one's status as defender of a sacred Arab cause.

Saddam also foreshadowed his later actions by insisting that the

USA withdraw from the Gulf and warned the Gulf Arab states of American dominance if they were 'not careful'. Finally, he suggested that the oil-producing Gulf states think of using their assets to advance overall Arab interests (as defined by him) in order to create a new international balance of power based on Arab strength, like-mindedness and a well-defined plan of action.[4]

Hosting an all-Arab summit conference in Baghdad on 28–30 May was Saddam's next step. For it to take place, he had to overcome reluctance in Cairo and Riyadh. Leaders in both capitals were by this time uneasy with Iraq's more aggressive posture and concerned that a stridently anti-American and anti-Israeli posture would be ineffective as well as deleterious to their relations with the West. Egypt, in particular, was waiting to see if an American-led initiative to convene an Israeli–Palestinian meeting in Cairo would bear fruit. Moreover, the Egyptians and Saudis also believed that a Baghdad summit would merely reinforce inter-Arab divisions unless it was preceded by a Syrian–Iraqi reconciliation. By the second week of May, however, prospects for either an Israeli–Palestinian meeting or a Syrian–Iraqi reconciliation had dimmed, and Baghdad had its way.

The Baghdad summit was boycotted by Syria (with Lebanon in tow as well). Ironically, Syria's absence gave Saddam a freer hand in demanding consensual resolutions backing Iraq against the Western and Israeli 'threats'. Both President Mubarak and Saudi Arabia's King Fahd were on the defensive throughout the gathering, and the summit's final resolutions were more suited in tenor to Iraq than to Egypt. In particular, Iraq received unequivocal support against the 'threats, hostile tendentious political and media campaigns, and the scientific and technological ban' being imposed on it by the West.

Moreover, Saddam delivered a not-so-veiled warning on the last day of the summit against 'some of our Arab brothers' for ignoring OPEC production quotas and thus sending oil prices plummeting. Billions of dollars had been lost by Iraq, he said, and tens of billions by 'the Arab nation' as a result of this 'unjustified mistake'. Whether intended or not, the result was that war was being waged against Iraq by economic means, something to which Baghdad could no longer turn a blind eye.[5]

In retrospect, Saddam's warning was the opening shot in the campaign to take Kuwait. While Egypt and the GCC states were aware of the need to appear to be placating him in the short term, they grossly underestimated Saddam's true intention to radically alter the regional status quo.

The final countdown to the invasion began on 16 July. It was on that day that Iraq's Foreign Minister Tareq Aziz dispatched a long memorandum to Arab League Secretary-General Chedli Klibi which starkly detailed the alleged crimes committed against Iraq by Kuwait and the United Arab Emirates (UAE): conspiring to create an oil glut; Kuwait's 'theft' of oil from the Iraqi share of the al-Rumaila oil field astride their common border, physical encroachment on Iraqi territory, and refusal to forgive Iraq's wartime debts.[6] The next day, the anniversary of the Iraqi Ba'th party's takeover of power in 1968, Saddam Hussein went public, condemning the two Gulf states' 'subversive policy' in support of the campaign being waged by 'imperialism and Zionism' against Iraq's 'scientific and technological advancement. . . . Instead of rewarding Iraq (for defending the GCC states against the Iranian threat), they have . . . thrust their poisoned dagger into our back'.[7] Reports of large scale Iraqi troop movements towards the Kuwaiti border indicated that this might not be a purely verbal exercise.

Responding to the sudden escalation of tension, the wheels of inter-Arab diplomacy quickly spun into high gear, spearheaded by President Mubarak and King Fahd, and assisted by Jordan's King Hussein and Arab League Secretary-General Klibi. In this instance, too, both Arab leaders and Western observers were confident Middle East mediation would again be successful. Indeed, the crisis seemed on its way to a peaceful resolution on 25 July, when President Mubarak issued an upbeat statement announcing that senior Kuwaiti and Iraqi officials would hold bilateral discussions (Iraq insisted that no third parties attend) in Saudi Arabia's port city of Jeddah on 28 or 29 July. As it happened, the Jeddah meeting was held on 31 July, only to have the Iraqis claim it was a meeting of protocol only. The talks ended in confusion, and no date was set for their resumption. Chances of achieving the much sought-after yet perpetually elusive 'Arab solution' to the crisis died at Jeddah, for Iraq's behaviour there indicates the decision to invade had already been taken.

THE GUNS OF AUGUST: CHALLENGE AND RESPONSE

As is often the case in inter-Arab politics, personalities played a key role in determining Arab responses to the invasion. Saddam Hussein had in essence thrown down the gauntlet; Hosni Mubarak took it up. Believing he had obtained an unconditional commitment from Saddam to refrain from the use of force, President Mubarak felt deeply insulted, even humiliated by the invasion. Moreover, he was now well aware that his previous strategy of trying to contain Saddam had produced the opposite effect. Consequently, in consultation with the Saudis, President Mubarak took the lead in mobilizing an anti-Saddam coalition.

In doing so, he found himself working at cross-purposes with King Hussein. In previous years, the two had evolved a pattern of almost bimonthly meetings. Now, however, they stood in sharp disagreement with one another. On the afternoon of 2 August, the two leaders met in Alexandria. The next day, King Hussein informed President Mubarak that Saddam Hussein agreed to the idea of a 'limited summit'. However, the King could give no assurances that Saddam was ready to commit himself beforehand to withdrawing his forces and restoring Kuwait's legitimate government. As a result of what the Egyptians and Saudis viewed as Saddam's stalling tactics, the Arab League Council met in emergency session in Cairo that evening and sharply condemned Iraqi 'aggression' against Kuwait. The Council also called for the 'immediate and unconditional withdrawal' of Iraqi troops.[8]

The vote on the resolution provided the first concrete indication of inter-Arab divisions over the Iraqi invasion. Six League members of the twenty present (Libya did not attend) refused to endorse it: Iraq, Yemen, Jordan, the PLO, Sudan and Mauritania. Together with Tunisia, Algeria and occasionally Libya, this group would constitute a loose, minority alignment throughout the crisis, even at the expense of their own bilateral relations with the anti-Saddam majority coalition, spearheaded by Egypt, Saudi Arabia and Syria and backed by the smaller GCC states.

That same evening, Iraq proclaimed the establishment of a 'Provisional Free Kuwaiti Government,' with a withdrawal of troops to begin on 5 August 'unless something emerges that threatens the security of Kuwait and Iraq'.[9]

Saudi Arabia's initial reaction to the invasion was one of extreme caution, to the point where American officials were concerned Riyadh would undercut its efforts to force a total withdrawal from Kuwait.[10] However, Saudi Arabia's inability to clarify Iraqi intentions, plus American determination in fully committing US forces to protect the Kingdom resulted in Saudi Arabia's abandonment of a long-held preference for keeping the American defence presence 'over the horizon', that is, off of Saudi soil.[11]

At the last all-Arab summit held in Cairo in 1976 a model for Arab consensus had been fashioned out of the conflicting views of Egypt, Saudia Arabia and Syria regarding the future of Lebanon and the Arab–Israeli peace process.[12] Fifteen years later, these three countries now found themselves on the same side of the inter-Arab fault line created by the Iraqi invasion. Thus, instead of a consensual summit celebrating Egypt's renewed pride of place in the Arab League, the emergency meeting in Cairo, which convened on 10 August at President Mubarak's initiative, only further deepened inter-Arab divisions, especially as the Iraqis came to Cairo in a combative mood, and their sympathizers anxious to soften anti-Iraqi sentiment. President Mubarak was now forcefully taking the lead in combating Saddam Hussein's bid for regional hegemony. Doing so marked the renewal of an enduring pattern in Arab and Middle Eastern history: the competition between Mesopotamia and Nile Valley-based power centres for regional pre-eminence.

The Egyptians and Saudis mustered only a bare majority of twelve states behind Arab League Resolution 195, whose operative parts denounced Iraq's 'threats' to the GCC states and its concentration of troops on the Saudi border, and then expressed support for the steps taken on behalf of Saudi Arabia's 'right of legitimate defence'. This right was anchored in the League's Joint Defence Pact of 1950, Article 51 of the UN Charter, and Security Council Resolution 661 adopted four days earlier. In addition, Clause 6 of the resolution declared the summit members' intent to comply with the request from Saudi Arabia and the other Gulf states 'to dispatch Arab forces to help them defend their territories 'against any foreign aggression'.[13]

The twelve states favouring Resolution 195 were: Egypt, the six GCC states, Syria, Lebanon, Morocco, Somalia, and Djibouti. Three participants voted against – Iraq, Libya and the PLO (which on the following day officially changed its vote to one of abstention); Algeria and Yemen abstained, and Jordan, Sudan and Mauritania expressed reservations. Tunisia had already expressed its position by not attending.

Never before in the forty-six-year history of the League had such a controversial resolution been adopted in the face of opposition by almost half of the member states. True, since the early 1980s, there had been repeated talk – but only talk – regarding the need for Arab majorities to take operative decisions even when an Arab consensus was lacking. Various proposals to amend the League's Charter invariably included a clause for making League decisions binding on all members. Usually, this view had expressed frustration over Syria's repeated ability to block decisive action on a wide variety of issues,[14] whereas Syria was ironically now part of the majority aligned against Iraq. In praising President Mubarak's decision finally to push through such a strong resolution, one Egyptian journalist declared that the summit's results were not a sign of division but a 'form of resolution' which had always been required.[15]

President Mubarak wasted no time in dispatching forces to Saudi Arabia. The first Egyptian soldiers began arriving on 11 August. Morocco followed shortly afterwards with what King Hassan termed a 'symbolic contingent' of between 1,000–1,200 soldiers (a 5,000 man unit had been stationed in the UAE since 1986). The arrival of Syrian troops was especially significant in political terms. Given Syria's traditional posture as the standard bearer of pan-Arabism and leader of the resistance to American pre-eminence in the region, its participation made the anti-Saddam coalition more than a club of conservative, pro-Western regimes. By the end of the year, the breakdown of Arab armed forces deployed in Saudi Arabia under a Saudi-headed unified command was as follows: Egypt 30,000; Syria 17,000, Morocco 1,000–1,200, Kuwait 3,000–5,000 and the four smaller GCC principalities approximately 3,100 soldiers. Token Egyptian, Moroccan and Syrian contingents were also deployed in the UAE. With Saudi Arabia's 45,000-man force included, the total number of Arab ground combat troops taking part in the international coalition against Iraq was approximately 100,000.

As for those opposed to the Arab League's resolution, while most emphasized support for the principle of Iraqi withdrawal from Kuwait, a common theme running through their statements insisted the crisis was being exploited by the West to impose economic and military hegemony in the region.

Apart from these common threads, each Arab party was acting according to more specific considerations. Saddam Hussein's depiction of himself as hero of the poor Arab masses and defender of Islamic and Arab sanctity against corrupt regimes and the villainous, imperialist West resonated in a number of Arab countries. In Algeria's intensely competitive political environment, the Gulf crisis became an important issue around which both the Islamic fundamentalist and secular opposition groups and the increasingly vulnerable ruling Front de Libération Nationale (FLN) tried to mobilize supporters. Tunisia's reluctance to oppose Iraq was also partly due to government concern at not giving Tunisian fundamentalists political ammunition. The presence of similar sentiment in Morocco compelled King Hassan, a member of the anti-Saddam coalition, to tread lightly as well.

Jordan, more than any other Arab country, found itself caught between competing currents. Like Algeria, Jordan was in the midst of a significant opening up of its political system, a process which had already witnessed the emergence of a strong Islamic fundamentalist movement now utterly opposed to Western intervention. Moreover, the Palestinian 'street' in both the East and West Banks was extremely vocal in support of Saddam. In fact, only two days after the Cairo summit, Saddam sought to capitalize on this sentiment by linking any solution to the Gulf crisis with a resolution to the Palestinian question and, for good measure, Syria's domination of Lebanon. Given the favourable reaction among Palestinians, King Hussein believed he could ill afford even to appear to be swimming against the tide of his own public opinion.

Other factors were at work as well. Jordan had been one of Iraq's most ardent supporters during the Iran–Iraq war, deriving considerable economic benefit from the relationship, particularly in the realm of overland trade and transit which had come to constitute 25 per cent of Jordan's GNP. The imposition of UN economic sanctions against Iraq would cause severe damage to the Jordanian economy. Similarly, during the previous year, the King had broadened cooperation between the two countries to the military field as well, in seeking to bolster Jordan's strategic posture *vis-à-vis* Israel. The risks entailed in too tight an embrace of the much stronger Iraq could not have been lost on the King. Nonetheless he deemed it prudent to forge friendly ties with the growing power to the East, even while maintaining good relations with his other Arab neighbours. With the onset of the crisis, however, this familiar straddling of political fences became untenable.

No one was more angered with King Hussein's position than Saudi Arabia. Thus, Saudi aid, which had amounted to 15 per cent of the annual budget, and Saudi shipments of oil ceased. Moreover, a number of Jordanian diplomats were expelled from Riyadh, the Saudi–Jordanian border was closed for a time, and the Saudis even reportedly began extending more active support to major tribes and clans in the southern part of Jordan contiguous to Saudi Arabia.[16] The crisis in Saudi–Jordanian relations also carried echoes of what had been another central thread of inter-Arab relations for more than half a century, up until the end of the 1950s: competition between the Saudi and Hashemite royal houses. King Hussein's directive to the Jordanian media that he be referred to as Sharif (a reminder that as a Hashemite he was a true descendent from the family of the Prophet Muhammad) particularly irked the Saudis, already sensitive to Iraqi charges they had forfeited the right to serve as protector of the holy sites of Islam by allowing the 'infidels' to trample on Saudi, and therefore sacred Islamic ground. Moreover, the title immediately evoked the memory of Hussein's great-grandfather, Sharif Hussein, who had ruled Mecca and Medina until being ousted by the Saudis in the mid-1920s. Could King Hussein's tilt towards Iraq and renewed emphasis on his sharifian lineage be a prelude to a grand scheme to wrest the Arabian peninsula from Saudi hands and restore the Hijaz to the Hashemites? This conspiracy argument was not entirely dismissed by the Saudis.

Although less vulnerable than Jordan, newly unified Yemen shared some of the same dilemmas. Like Jordan, it had derived economic benefits from its support for Iraq during the Iran–Iraq war. Like Jordan as well, it had hoped to benefit, both economically and politically, from membership in the ACC, which held out the promise of much needed development aid and political support from Iraq and Egypt. With the imposition of UN sanctions, Yemen, again like Jordan, found itself torn between international pressures to toe the line and Iraqi inducements and blandishments to avoid compliance. Finally, like Jordan, Yemen's tilt towards Iraq enraged the Saudis, who were already concerned over the potential long-term threat to their southern border posed by a unified Yemen,[17] and not dismissive of the possibility that Yemen too was part of an Iraqi-led conspiracy to dismember the Kingdom.[18] To punish the Yemenis, the Saudis imposed strict residency regulations on Yemeni nationals working in the Kingdom, necessitating the exodus of an estimated one million persons. Their departure carried the bonus of easing a potential threat to Saudi Arabia's internal security. The Saudis also acted to mobilize Yemeni tribal leaders on their behalf and against the central government, a time-honoured pattern.[19] Like Jordan, Yemen had been put on notice by the Saudis that there was no middle ground in this most divisive of inter-Arab conflicts.

Singularly untenable, however, was the PLO's situation. Having lost much of his freedom of operation in Lebanon and with Tunisia a poor centre for training and operations, Yasser Arafat had transferred much of his activities to Baghdad during the previous four years. Now, with the Gulf crisis unfolding, Saddam was calling in his chips, and to a receptive audience. Within the PLO, as well as the Palestinian rank and file in Jordan and the Israeli-controlled territories, the image of Saddam as a latter-day Saladin ready to punish Israel with the sword had great appeal. No amount of verbal twists and turns could undo the image of Yasser Arafat embracing Saddam projected on television screens across the Middle East and the world at large.

The Cairo summit thus consecrated the new lines of division in the Arab League which had been forming in the previous weeks and months. A number of questions remained, however. How much like-mindedness would the key parties of the anti-Saddam coalition –

Egypt, Saudi Arabia and Syria – demonstrate? What would be the attitude of the anti-Saddam coalition in the event the Iraqis remained steadfast against international pressures to withdraw from Kuwait? Would the Arab countries support a military option? Would they participate in it, and to what extent? Conversely, how would they react in the face of Iraqi flexibility? Would new life be breathed into mediation efforts? Would developments in the 'Arab street' compel policy reassessments? And what role would Iran play in the crisis?

The answers to these pertinent questions can be summarized briefly. The anti-Saddam coalition remained firm throughout the countdown to 15 January 1991, the deadline set by the UN Security Council for Iraqi withdrawal from Kuwait. Iraq's unwillingness to accept any compromise formula both made it easier for the Arab members of the anti-Saddam coalition to maintain their position and strengthened their resolve to participate in the approaching military operation to expel Iraq from Kuwait.

As the party most traditionally opposed to Western domination of the region, Syria was thought to be a weak link in the international coalition opposing Iraq. However, Syria reaped numerous tangible benefits from remaining in the anti-Saddam camp. Its alliance with Iran was newly appreciated by the GCC states, so much so that Syrian President Hafiz al-Assad could break a long-held taboo in late September by making his first official visit to Tehran to personally coordinate their stands. US President George Bush's meeting with President Assad in Geneva further symbolized this end to Syrian regional and international isolation; and the Saudis immediately came forth with much needed financial aid, estimated at $2 billion. Most important, perhaps, Damascus received a green light from the Saudis and the US in Lebanon to remove rebel General Michel Awn and impose a Pax-Syriana, based on the 1989 Ta'if Accord.[20]

To be sure, Saddam's Robin Hood stance against wealthy Arab sheikhs and evil Western imperialists did resonate in the 'Arab street', among Palestinians, and in Yemen and North Africa, where the Gulf crisis was wound up with domestic political considerations. Nevertheless, even though Saddam's message may have had some appeal in Egypt as well, the government made sure to place efficient limits on the expression of pro-Iraqi sentiment. He had far less public appeal than Gamal Abd al-Nasser during the 1950s and 1960s and a record of brutality and opportunism almost unmatched in the Arab world. Moreover, his Arab opponents possessed far greater means to maintain internal stability. Finally, there was his undeniable aggressive actions against a fellow Arab state, Kuwait. Thus, Saddam's invoking of pan-Arabism and Islamic piety could not generate a response sufficient to reverse the steadily tightening circle around Iraq. Consequently, the bottom line is that Saddam's appeal to the 'Arab masses' to rise up and punish his opponents was never heeded.

As the 15 January deadline approached, King Hussein lamented the 'great tragedy' about to result from the impending 'destructive war', unless it could be avoided by ending the 'embargo on dialogue' and giving Arab mediation a chance.[21] But the middle ground that the King had been seeking since the start of the crisis did not exist. Saddam showed no inclination to negotiate his withdrawal from Kuwait. Besides, his brazen act on 2 August 1990 had torn the Arab world apart, leaving little room for would-be rebuilders of the shattered vessel of Arab consensus.

THE DENOUEMENT AND BEYOND

The swiftness of the war and the decisive defeat of Iraq was gratifying to Saddam's Arab adversaries. Their fear of widespread domestic unrest had proved unfounded; Iraq's formidable military machine had been decimated; Israel's restraint had allowed the anti-Saddam Arabs to avoid the potentially embarrassing situation of fighting on the same side with Israel against another Arab country; Iraq's defeat did not result in its dismemberment, a matter of some concern to both the Saudis and the Egyptians; and aligning with the victorious USA promised to result in future tangible benefits.

Initially the war's results even held out prospects for significant modification on two issues: collective security in the Gulf and progress in Arab–Israeli negotiations. These changes were expected to be underpinned by sober-minded, hard-headed attitudes shorn of the debilitating illusions of pan-Arab grandeur so damaging in the past.

President Bush's talk of a 'new world order' was mirrored by Saddam's Arab opponents. A 'new Arab order' was in the offing, declared GCC Secretary-General Abdallah Bishara. It would be based on 'legality, mutual respect, non-interference in internal affairs, and the primary role of the economy to create mutual interests'.[22]

In this spirit, on 6 March the foreign ministers of six GCC states, plus Egypt and Syria issued the 'Damascus Declaration', their blueprint for the post-war era. Its guiding principles were those Hosni Mubarak had been trumpeting in collective Arab forums for years: good neighbourliness, respect for each member state's unity and territorial integrity, the inadmissability of seizing territories by force, non-intervention in each other's internal affairs and a pledge to settle outstanding disputes by peaceful means. Another key goal was bolstering inter-Arab economic cooperation through an Arab economic grouping able to keep pace with international developments, most notably the imminent economic unification in Europe. The declaration emphasized the importance of respecting 'each Arab state's sovereignty over its natural and economic resources'.

Gulf security also figured prominently in the declaration. The presence of Egyptian and Syrian forces in the Gulf, it declared, constituted 'a nucleus for an Arab peace force' which would guarantee the security of the GCC states and 'the effectiveness of the comprehensive Arab defence order'. With Iran in mind, the 'Damascus Eight' made sure to stress their programme was not directed against anyone and could serve as the basis for dialogue with 'Islamic and international parties'. One week later, following an unprecedented meeting with US Secretary of State James Baker, their eight foreign ministers repeated the essence of the declaration, with accompanying praise for America's role in liberating Kuwait and President Bush's remarks on the need to solve the Palestinian question. A new era thus seemed to be imminent, in which inter-Arab, regional and Arab–Western security arrangements might be knit together.

Crucial matters, however, remained unsettled: the size and composition of the Arab peace force, the nature of the Arab–Iranian relationship, and the extent and length of the US presence. The Iranians were said to be strongly opposed to the continued presence of any non-Gulf Arab forces in region. The Egyptians, for their part, felt unappreciated for their contribution to the war effort, were piqued by what they considered to be an inadequate share of contracts for Egyptian companies to participate in Kuwait's reconstruction, and were uneasy about the GCC's eagerness to include the Iranians in security discussions. In a calculated move to draw attention to their grievances, Egypt brought most of its armed forces home in mid-May, with Syria following suit, although both reiterated their willingness to participate in a security framework for the Gulf.

Consultations among the GCC states, between the GCC states and Iran, and among the Damascus Declaration signatories continued into the summer months, with the intent of ironing out details for a security system and for institutionalizing their alliance. Ironically, the defeat of Iran against Iraq, Iran's slow shift towards greater pragmatism in foreign affairs, and the popularity in Kuwait of the Western, as opposed to Egyptian and Syrian, troop presence had combined to lower the sense of urgency surrounding Gulf security.

The slow pace of forging a regional security system was paralleled in the Arab–Israeli sphere. While an explicit military linkage between events in the Gulf and the Arab–Israeli conflict had been steadfastly resisted by the anti-Saddam coalition throughout the Gulf crisis, there was considerable hope in the Arab world that the end of the Gulf War would lead to renewed Western efforts to promote an Arab–Israeli peace process. To be sure, neither the GCC states, nor Syria, nor Israel for that matter, were themselves eager to undertake bold diplomatic initiatives alone. On the other hand, by Secretary of State Baker's fifth visit to the Middle East since the cessation of the Gulf War, it was clear all parties to the conflict were just as anxious to avoid being branded as the primary obstacle to a peace process. There was thus enough operating room for the US Administration to keep Arab–Israeli diplomacy alive; and by mid-summer, the US had narrowed procedural gaps between Israel and its Arab neighbours sufficiently to be able to issue invitations for a regional peace conference in Madrid.

As for the Arab 'losers', those who had either listed towards Saddam or were perceived as such, the post-war period was a time of both stock-taking and attempting to repair the damage to relations with the anti-Saddam group. The PLO, in particular, was faced with both internal rumblings over its tilt towards Iraq and an increasingly assertive and restive Palestinian constituency in the West Bank and Gaza desperate for tangible progress after three and a half years of the Intifada.

King Hussein, for his part, emerged from the war largely unscathed politically, although the economic devastation wrought by the crisis would take a long time to repair. The USA, Israel and even Saudi Arabia apparently developed a renewed appreciation for Hashemite Jordan's role as a moderate, buffer state. Moreover, the King's standing among the Palestinians on both banks of the Jordan River has never been higher. Thus, he was able to reduce the influence of Islamic fundamentalists in his cabinet, to speak of the need to break old taboos regarding direct, above board meetings between Arabs and Israelis, and to make himself available as an interlocutor for Palestinians, should they so desire.

It is clearly too soon for a definitive evaluation of the long-term impact of the Gulf crisis on regional and domestic Arab politics. But preliminary observations may nevertheless be of some value. In geopolitical terms, Saddam Hussein's Iraq was unabashedly revisionist. Thus, his withdrawal from Kuwait and the partial destruction of his armed forces both restored the territorial status quo ante and insured the continued survival of the Gulf Arab states. On the other hand, Saddam's continued survival lingered on as a cause of concern, and explained Kuwait's preference for a continued Western military presence. One important, related lesson of the war was that the US demonstrated its willingness to commit forces to the defence of regional allies and vital economic interests. How that will effect the course of future regional disputes cannot be known, but the perception of American resolve will undoubtedly be factored into the calculations of policy-makers in the region.

Iraq's defeat provided post-Khomeini Iran the opportunity to resume its geopolitical pre-eminence in the Gulf. As for Iraq's western flank, Hafiz al-Assad could take great satisfaction in the destruction of the armed might of Saddam Hussein, and the accompanying political benefits for his standing from both in the West and in Lebanon. But it also meant that the chance of reviving the eastern military front against Israel was now even more remote.

In ideological terms, Saddam's failed bid to drape himself in the mantel of militant pan-Arabism demonstrated anew that Arabism could no longer compete with *raison d'état* as a workable, practical ideology. The triumph of *raison d'état* also means that alliances and/ or informal agreements with non-Arab countries, both in the region and beyond, will be considered more legitimate. The implications for the long-term evolution of Arab–Israeli relations should not be underestimated.

The Arab world is now truly multi-polar, with the unabashed defence of national prerogatives an overriding principle. To be sure, inter-Arab relations will always have a special cast, owing to common linguistic, cultural and historical bonds as well as common problems. But the golden days of a charismatic leader leading the Arab world against the West has seemingly passed. For the foreseeable future the only workable mode of pan-Arabism seems to be the forging of limited functional cooperation between independent states on the basis of mutual interests.

This was in fact supposed to have been the rationale for the ACC. Its collapse has not discredited the model of regional groupings *per se*, but does compel examining most closely the underlying motivations of potential partners in future Arab coalitions. Ironically, the triumph of the regional status quo leaves room for the continued survival of the venerable and much-maligned Arab League as a collective Arab umbrella, even if its effectiveness in promoting closer inter-Arab ties remains limited.

For all of his cynical manipulation of Arab and Islamic symbols on behalf of self-aggrandizement, Saddam Hussein's attempt to appear as a self-styled Robin Hood and Saladin all rolled into one possessed at least transitory appeal in the Arab world. As such, the crisis pointed to the underlying acute issues confronting Arab governments and societies: huge disparities between Arab 'haves' and 'have-nots'; failures to develop productive economies; large numbers of young, politically mobilized, but politically disenfranchised youth; and the continued appeal of Muslim fundamentalist movements. Arab intellectuals have redoubled their calls for building real democratic institutions as the only way out of their economic, social and political malaise. Indeed, questions of democratization, political participation and even human rights are in the air, from Algeria to Jordan to Kuwait to Iraq itself. So far, however, those who have benefited most from liberalization steps have been Muslim fundamentalist movements, which too often view the democratic process as an expedient way to attain power but without a commitment to genuine democratic politics.

In a diverse, multi-polar system inter-Arab alliances will thus continue to be formed, dissolved and reformed according to momentary exigencies. The primary challenge for the ruling élites in each Arab country is to juggle the conflicting demands imposed by internal, regional and international factors in order to ensure their continued survival and achieve a modicum of progress for their populations.

NOTES

1 The description of events during 1990 draws heavily on my chapter, 'Inter-Arab relations', in Ami Ayalon (ed.) Middle-East Contemporary Survey, vol. XIV, Westview Press, Boulder, San Francisco and London, forthcoming). The author is a Research Fellow at the Moshe Dayan Center for Middle Eastern and African Studies, Tel-Aviv University, and was a Visiting Fellow of Middle East Programs at the Carter Center and Visiting Assistant Professor of History at Emory University, Atlanta, Georgia, 1990–91. Special thanks to Ken Stein, Directory of the Carter Center's Middle East Program for his incisive input into this paper, and for his gracious hospitality during the year.
2 Speech to the Moroccan parliament, Rabat TV, 12 October – Foreign Broadcast Information Service, Near East and South Asia, 16 October 1990.
3 Judith Miller and Laurie Mylroie, *Saddam Hussein and the Crisis In the Gulf*, New York: Times Books, 1990, pp. 12–13.
4 Iraqi News Agency, 19 February; Amman TV, 24 February; *FBIS*, 20, 27 February 1990.
5 Radio Baghdad, 18 July – FBIS, 19 July 1990.
6 Text of Aziz's letter to Klibi in Iraqi News Agency, 18 July – FBIS, 18 July 1990.
7 Radio Baghdad, 17 July – FBIS, 17 July 1990.

8 Middle East News Agency, 3 August – FBIS, 6 August 1990.

9 Radio Baghdad, 3 August – FBIS, 6 August 1990.

10 Thomas L. Friedman, *New York Times*, 5 August 1990.

11 On Saudi Arabia's inability to obtain reassurances from Iraq that its forces were not being deployed to threaten Saudi Arabia, see the comments by Saudi Ambassador to Washington, Prince Bandar ibn Sultan, as relayed to US Congressman Steven Solarz, *New York Times*, 4 October 1990; on Defense Secretary Cheyney's visit, a different version of Saudi Arabia's decision to accept American troops and Prince Bandar's role in the process, see Bob Woodward, *The Commanders*, New York: Simon & Schuster, 1991, pp. 239–77.

12 Daniel Dishon, 'Inter-Arab relations', in *Middle East Contemporary Survey*, vol. I, 1976–77, (Colin Legum and Haim Shaked, eds), New York: Holmes and Meier, 1978, pp. 147–50.

13 For the text of the resolution, see Middle East News Agency, 10 August – FBIS, 13 August 1990.

14 Daniel Dishon and Bruce Maddy-Weitzman, 'Inter-Arab Relations', in Middle East Contempory Survey, vol. VI, 1981–82. (Colin Legum, *et. al.*, eds), New York: Holmes and Meier, 1984, pp. 227–9.

15 *Al-Ahram*, August 1990.

16 *Financial Times*, 1 October 1990.

17 According to Yemen's President Saleh, the Saudis had actively tried to thwart the union by bribing PDRY officials; *New York Times*, 20 October 1990.

18 *Al-Wafd*, 15 October 1990.

19 *'Ukaz*, 2 September; *al-Bilad*, 17 September; *al-Quds-al-'Arabi*, 21 September – FBIS, 25 September 1990.

20 The Ta'if Accord provides a framework for the reconstruction of central Lebanese authority, on the basis of national reconciliation and constitutional reform, with heavy consideration given to Syrian strategic requirements. It was endorsed by some, although not all of the various Lebanese political factions. Its implementation remains, up until now, only partial.

21 Radio Amman, 9 December – FBIS, 10 December 1990.

22 Interview in *La Republica*, 24–25 February – FBIS, 28 February 1991.

23 Radio Damascus, 6 March – FBIS, 7 March 1991.

3 Survival at all costs
Saddam Hussein as crisis manager

Efraim Karsh

It is a commonplace among politicians to substitute the national interest for personal designs, and Saddam Hussein is no exception to this rule. The annexation of Kuwait to Iraq on 8 August 1990, like numerous of his previous acts, was therefore portrayed as 'a dear pan-Arab goal, through which we would comprehensively, eternally and radically rectify what colonialism had imposed on our country'.[1]

This presentation of the invasion struck a sensitive chord with the Iraqi people. Since its inception as an independent state in 1932, Iraq had persistently challenged Kuwait's right for sovereign existence and demanded its incorporation into Iraq. Although this claim was based on the (somewhat dubious) argument that, as part of the *velayet* (province) of Basra under Ottoman rule, Kuwait belonged to Iraq, Baghdad's interest in the emirate had less to do with legal niceties over historical rights than with strategic and economic realities. As a tiny state in possession of mammoth wealth, with a large natural harbour, and some 193 miles of Gulf coastline, Kuwait constituted a greatly coveted prize for greedy neighbours.

And yet, notwithstanding Iraq's longstanding interest in Kuwait, the actual cause of the invasion, as well as the ensuing crisis and war, was Saddam's deep anxiety over the future of his personal rule. In the permanently beleaguered mind of Saddam Hussein, politics is a ceaseless struggle for survival. He perceives the world as a violent, hostile environment in which the will to self-preservation rules. In such a setting one must remain constantly on the alert, making others cower so that they do not attack, always ready to kill before being killed.

In the summer of 1990 two main factors converged to convince the ever-wary president that unless he took immediate action against Kuwait, his indefinite stay in power was no longer a foregone conclusion. The first was the fear that the eight-year war against Iran had eroded the efficacy of his repressive system in general, and the loyalty of the military to his personal rule in particular. Underscored by several abortive attempts on his life by military officers,[2] this fear was magnified several-fold by the collapse of the communist regimes in Eastern Europe, especially the fall of the Romanian dictator, Nicolae Ceausescu, who, like Saddam, had predicated his rule on a combination of fear and personality cult. Under these distressing circumstances, Saddam apparently reasoned that a successful foreign venture would be the safest way to shore up his regime against possible dissent.

But the foremost cause driving Saddam to invade Kuwait was his desperate need for funds to reconstruct Iraq from the havoc left by the Iran–Iraq War. Having presented the end of the war as a momentous Iraqi (and Arab) victory over the 'Persian enemy', Saddam created a wave of popular expectations for a more tangible improvement in economic fortunes which he found impossible to deliver. Since he believed that his political future hinged on the economic reconstruction of Iraq, the incorporation of the Kuwaiti richness, in one form or another, into the depleted Iraqi treasury had become, literally, a matter of life or death.

THE RULE OF FEAR

Like other absolute leaders, such as Stalin and Hitler, whose power base resided in a formidable apparatus permeating every facet of their respective societies, Saddam Hussein has predicated his personal rule on the Ba'th Party. His logic has been strikingly simple: since the Party possesses the organizational infrastructure and ideological basis for controlling people's actions and minds, while he controls the Party it would control the masses and the state machinery.

To this end, the Ba'th has been transformed from a tiny party numbering a couple of thousand full members with little popular basis, to a mass organization boasting some 25,000 full members and 1.5 million supporters. This impressive growth in the Party's numerical strength, however, has been matched by a steady decline in its hold on the real reins of power. During his years in power – both as de facto leader under President Bakr and in the top spot – Saddam fully subordinated the Ba'th to his will, sterilizing its governing institutions and reducing the national decision-making apparatus to one man, surrounded by a docile flock of close associates. He has done this by pre-empting any and all dissent through systematic purges, and by subordinating all domestic and foreign policies to one overriding goal: his own political survival.

Saddam considers that the road to national servility must begin with the education of the young, who have not yet been 'corrupted by backward ideas'.[3] Hence, from their first days at kindergarten Iraqi children are introduced to Ba'thi terminology and, of course, learn to adulate their glorious leader. As they grow up they join the Party's various youth organizations where they are thoroughly brainwashed with the xenophobic 'anti-imperialist' mentality of their President. They are not only taught to distrust everybody, even their parents, but to serve as the Party's extensions in the family, keeping a vigilant eye on their parents' behaviour, always ready to report them to the authorities, should they 'misbehave'.

Having laid the ideological foundations for unquestioning submission to the Party from early youth, the next step is their incorporation into the Party's organizational infrastructure. Consequently, Party membership has become essential for public career, with non-Ba'thists being removed from their positions to make room for dedicated Party members and supporters. All state organs – the army, the bureaucracy and even trade unions and the mass organizations – have come under the Party's complete domination.

Party service, though, may be demanding. While low-level membership is open for all, entailing few privileges and multiple obligations, full membership is limited to an exclusive club of 'chosen few' who have reached a high level of 'maturity'. Not everyone can reach this level which, in any case, requires five to ten years of dedicated work and absolute commitment. Those who fail this sacred duty face the ominous spectre of Article 200 of the Iraqi Penal Code which entails a death penalty for such 'crimes' as leaving the Ba'th and joining another political party, concealing previous political affiliations upon joining the Ba'th or maintaining contacts with other political organizations.

The methods employed to ensure absolute loyalty within the ranks of the Ba'th pale in comparison with the Party's treatment of political dissidents. With one in seven Iraqis a Party member of one rank or another, the common definition of Iraq as a state of informers can hardly be considered an exaggeration. No ordinary Iraqi is immune to the regime's arbitrariness or to the vindictiveness of disenchanted neighbours, friends or even family members. Eavesdropping, spies and informers are a constant threat. A joke or derogatory comment on the President or the governing Party and state institutions can cost people their life according to a state decree of November 1986.[4] Sentences of long-term imprisonment or even execution, as reports by Amnesty International indicate, are likely to be issued by state officials rather than judges.[5]

The notorious security services have been the main means through which Saddam has kept his house in order. With responsibility for the Party's security apparatus entrusted to him as early as the mid-1960s, Saddam has transformed it into the central agent promoting his political interests. In order to prevent his creation from rising against him, Saddam has resorted to a strategy of *divide et impera*, making sure that all of his security services operate independently and report directly to him. As a final security valve Hussein has placed his relatives and kinsmen at key positions within the security apparatus.[6]

With the Ba'th Party reduced to a rubber stamp, Saddam has ruled the country through a small clique of long-time Party associates and family members, as well as more distant relatives from his home town of Tikrit. Their unconditional loyalty and obedience to the ruler in return for political prominence and economic advantages. Yet the footing at the top of the pyramid is treacherous. Should a member of the ruling élite find his loyalty called into question, or should he become too popular, his political career would quickly go into decline, whatever his former standing or performance.

Saddam's closest dependants have thus found themselves between Scylla and Charybdis. These are the people who made Saddam's rise to absolutism possible, and who form the foundations of the regime. Having staked their political future, indeed their lives, on the success of Saddam's policies, they have also reaped abundant rewards in his service. And yet, despite their political prominence and material affluence they exercise virtually no influence on Saddam's major decisions. At most, his inner circle serves as an echo chamber, amplifying his wishful thinking and backing those political options he is believed in any event likely to adopt.

SADDAM AND THE MILITARY

In particular, Saddam has spared no effort to transform the Iraqi military into an 'ideological force' loyal only to him. Accordingly, scores of Party commissars have been deployed within the armed forces down to the battalion level. Organized political activity has been banned; 'unreliable' elements have been forced to retire, purged and often executed; senior officers have been constantly reshuffled to prevent power bases from arising. The social composition of the Republican Guard, an élite corps within the army which made the Ba'th 1968 takeover possible and ensured its survival ever since, has been fundamentally transformed to draw heavily on conscripts from Tikrit and the surrounding region.

In addition, Saddam has sought to counterbalance the military through a significant expansion of the Party's militia, the Popular Army. Established in the late 1950s as a para-military organization, the militia was reorganized in the late 1960s by Saddam Hussein as part of his comprehensive security apparatus. Transformed since then into a more orderly military force, the Popular Army has never been subordinated to the armed forces. Rather, it serves as the Party's main vehicle for rallying the masses behind the regime and for suppressing actual and potential opposition. In 1979, less than a year after Saddam seized absolute power, the Popular Army was more than doubled – from 100,000 to 250,000. During the Iran–Iraq War it was to become an ominous force of some 1,000,000 strong, equipped with heavy weaponry and participating in some of the war operations. This by no means puts the Popular Army on a par with the professional military; yet, by denying the latter monopoly over the state's means of violence, it does widen the regime's security margins against potential coups.

Thus, through sustained effort, Saddam has created a docile and highly politicized military leadership, resting on the principles of personal loyalty and kinship rather than on professional excellence. Consequently, when the Iran–Iraq War broke out in September 1980, the military was no more courageous than the politicians, challenging neither Saddam's war strategy nor his conduct of tactical operations. Only in 1986, when a series of Iraqi setbacks (particularly the fall of the Fao Peninsula in February 1986 where Iraq lost 10,000 soldiers in one week) put the Iranians at the gates of Basra, did Saddam confront for the first time in his career what nearly amounted to mutiny. Fortunately for him, the generals neither demanded political power, nor sought to overthrow the leader who had intimidated them for nearly two decades. All they wanted was to force Hussein to win the war despite himself by permitting them to run military operations according to their best professional judgement. Granted their demand, they restricted their efforts narrowly to waging the war, producing a series of Iraqi successes that culminated in Tehran's agreement to a ceasefire after eight years of fighting.

In retrospect it can be seen that the generals missed an ideal opportunity to rid themselves of Saddam at one of the lowest points in his career. When they failed to seize the moment, he instead moved swiftly to reap the fruits of victory and wipe out any traces of his 'indecisiveness'. The end of the war was presented as yet another product of his great leadership whereas those who had actually made it possible, faded into obscurity, if not into physical demise.

Nevertheless, in retrospect, this episode ushered in a new stage in Saddam's relations with the military. The belief, common among the military, that avoiding any taint of political activity provided certain safeguards against the whims of the Saddam regime was shattered by the purges of the heroes of the war against Iran. Conversely, Saddam's concessions to the military in 1986 proved that even he was not invincible. This combination of fear and hope on the part of the military, which accounts for the growing number of reported *coup* attempts in the wake of the Iran–Iraq War, convinced Saddam that the repressive system he had so laboriously constructed over a long period of time might still crack.

By 1990 one such means of control could be the engagement of the military ranks in a riskless venture abroad that would satisfy their yearning for national gratitude (for saving Iraq from the Iranian threat), while keeping them at a safe distance from the locus of power in Baghdad. And what constituted a more suitable target for such a venture than Kuwait, Iraq's tiny neighbour to the south, whose independence had been repeatedly contested by Baghdad.

A NEED FOR MONEY

If the desire to keep his repressive system intact constituted a powerful incentive for the invasion of Kuwait, a far more paramount consideration was Saddam's deep anxiety over the economic reconstruction of Iraq. Although the general view in the summer of 1988 was that Baghdad had won the long-drawn conflict, it quickly became evident that Iraq had emerged from the war a crippled nation. The economy was wrecked. Economic estimates put the cost of reconstruction at \$230 billion.[7] Even in adopting the most optimistic (and highly unrealistic) assumption that every dollar of oil revenues would be directed to the reconstruction effort, it would clearly require nearly two decades to repair the total damage. As things stood a year after the termination of hostilities, Iraq's oil revenues of \$13 billion were not sufficient to cover ongoing expenditures: with civilian imports approximating \$12 billion (of which \$3 billion was for foodstuffs), military imports exceeding \$5 billion, debt repayments totalling \$5 billion, and transfers by foreign workers topping \$1 billion, the regime needed an extra \$10 billion per annum to balance its current deficit, before it could embark on the Sisyphean task of reconstruction.[8]

By 1990, having failed to find the magic formula to solve Iraq's economic plight, Hussein probably began to suspect that 'in terms of his political survival, the war may have ended but the battle has only just begun',[9] given the potential risk of arousing the Iraqi people against him, should he fail to deliver the promised fruits of the 'historic victory'. On paper, the cure for Iraq's economic plight was strikingly simple: a decisive reduction in expenditures and a significant increase in revenues. In practice, however, the attainment of these goals was a far more difficult task requiring heavy reliance on coercive diplomacy. During the Iran–Iraq War he had already pressured the Gulf states, Saudi Arabia and Kuwait in particular, to forgive their loans to Iraq, and these pressures were significantly intensified in the postwar era. During a summit meeting of the Arab Cooperation Council in Amman in February 1990, Saddam asked King Hussein of Jordan and President Mubarak of Egypt to inform the Gulf states that Iraq was not only adamant on a complete moratorium on its wartime loans but urgently needed an immediate infusion of additional funds, say, some $30 billion. The message was immediately passed on to Saudi Arabia by the Jordanian monarch.

Bullying the Gulf states into writing off their loans and raising further contributions to the Iraqi treasury was only one aspect of Saddam's strategy. The other involved manipulation of the world oil market to accommodate Iraq's financial needs. Following the war, Iraq (as well as Iran) demanded that other members of the Organization of Petroleum Exporting Countries (OPEC) reduce their respective output in order to allow for increased Iraqi production without decreasing oil prices.

This demand, however, was completely ignored. More than that, some OPEC members, most notably Kuwait and the United Arab Emirates (UAE), continued to exceed further their quotas, putting a downward pressure on world oil prices. Since Saddam was intent on pushing oil prices up without relinquishing his plans for enhanced production, an immediate change in Kuwaiti and UAE policy became a matter of great urgency.

In May 1990, after three months of futile attempts to convince the two Gulf states to reduce their oil quotas, Saddam tabled his grievances against the two in the harshest possible manner. In an extraordinary closed meeting in Baghdad with the heads of Arab states, he accused Kuwait and the UAE of 'robbing' billions of petrodollars from the Iraqi treasury by violating their production quotas, going so far as to define this act as *a declaration of war on Iraq*. He told his startled guests, that 'we have reached a point where we can no longer withstand pressure'.[10]

Surprisingly enough, Kuwait and the UAE were unmoved by Saddam's uncharacteristically candid admission of weakness and his consequent blatant threat. While replacing his Oil Minister in a clear attempt to appease Saddam, the Emir of Kuwait refused to reduce oil production; he neither forgave his wartime loans to Iraq nor extended to Baghdad additional grants. Even a direct attack by Saddam on this policy as a 'conspiracy against the region's economy which serves Israel directly' left no discernable impact.[11] It was only on 10 July during a coordination meeting of the Gulf oil ministers in Jeddah that the two states succumbed to combined Saudi, Iranian and Iraqi pressure and agreed to abide by their oil quotas.[12]

This concession came too late and offered too little. Although he probably had not yet made up his mind to invade the tiny principality, Suddam was certainly determined to extract substantial grants in addition to a complete moratorium on war loans. Nothing less than that would satisfy him. Consequently, on 16 July pressure on Kuwait stepped up decisively. In a letter to the Secretary-General of the Arab League, the Iraqi Foreign Minister, Tareq Aziz, accused Kuwait and the UAE of 'implementing an intentional scheme to glut the oil market with a quantity of oil that exceeded their quotas as fixed by OPEC'. To add insult to injury, Kuwait had directly 'stolen' from Iraq by 'setting up oil installations in the southern section of the Iraqi al-Rumaila oil field and extracting oil from it'. In this self-serving assessment, the value of the oil 'stolen by the Kuwaiti government from the al-Rumaila oil field in this manner that conflicts with fraternal relations' amounted to $2.4 billion.

In order to rectify this behaviour and to help Iraq recover from the dire economic plight that it now faced due to its heroic defence of 'the [Arab] nation's soil, dignity, honor and wealth', Aziz presented several demands: the raising of oil prices to over $25 a barrel; the cessation of Kuwaiti 'theft' of oil from the Iraqi al-Rumaila oil field and the return of the $2.4 billion 'stolen' from Iraq; a complete moratorium on Iraq's wartime loans; and, the formation of 'an Arab plan similar to the Marshall Plan to compensate Iraq for some of the losses during the war'.[13]

A day later Saddam escalated the situation further by accusing Kuwait and the UAE yet again of conspiring with 'world imperialism and Zionism' to 'cut off the livelihood of the Arab nation'. He cautioned, 'if words fail to afford us protection, then we will have no choice but to resort to effective action to put things right and ensure the restitution of our rights'.[14]

By stating in public what had hitherto been said behind closed doors, Saddam had effectively crossed the Rubicon. He had committed himself to certain objectives in such a way that any compromise on his part would have been seen as a humiliating capitulation.

Unfortunately, the Kuwaitis failed to grasp the seriousness of their situation. However startled they may have been by the harsh Iraqi rhetoric, they remained amazingly complacent, interpreting Saddam's demands as a bargaining chip rather than an ultimatum.[15] The prevailing view within the Kuwaiti leadership was that surrender to such extortionist methods would only lead to unlimited demands in the future. They suspected that some concessions might be necessary but were determined to reduce them to the barest minimum. They felt military action could not be ruled out altogether but believed it was extremely unlikely, and that in the worst case it would be confined to a small disputed area such as the al-Rumaila oil field and Bubiyan and Warba islands which Iraq had consistently sought to lease in the past. Thus, less than 24 hours from Saddam's speech, Kuwait dispatched to the Secretary-General of the Arab League a strongly-worded memorandum refuting the Iraqi accusations, and expressing strong indignation at the Iraqi behaviour.

This defiant response was the last nail in the Kuwaiti coffin. Not only was it taken by Saddam as a vindication of his longstanding perception of Kuwait as a parasitic state thriving on Iraq's heavy sacrifices, but it was viewed as a personal affront by a minor neighbour. In Saddam's opinion, the Kuwaitis did not treat him (i.e. Iraq) with due respect, or take his word seriously. They were playing their devious game of procrastination, in the belief that they could yet again evade their responsibilities to Iraq – but not for much longer. As friendly persuasion would not make Kuwait recognize its fraternal obligations, Iraq had no choice but to take by force what belonged to her.

From this stage onwards, the road to the invasion was clearly paved. On 25 July Saddam summoned the US Ambassador to Baghdad, Ms April Glaspie, to what was to become one of the most crucial, and controversial, milestones on the path to crisis and war. Whatever the actual content of their conversation, Saddam emerged from the meeting confident of America's neutrality towards the possible occupation of Kuwait. Still, he projected an appearance of Iraqi moderation in order to deflect any potential opposition to such a move. On 31 July Iraqi and Kuwaiti representatives met in the Saudi city of Jeddah in a last-ditch attempt to sort out their differences. Although the outcome of the meeting was probably irrelevant for Saddam, having already decided to invade Kuwait, the Kuwaitis certainly played into his hands by remaining as defiant as ever in regard to Iraq's financial demands.[16] On 1 August the negotiations collapsed amidst mutual recriminations. A day later Kuwait was no longer a sovereign state.

WHY WAR?

If the seizure of Kuwait was indeed an outcome of Saddam's overriding preoccupation with his personal survival, why did he decline the various face-saving formulas offered to him to withdraw from Kuwait, thereby averting a war that could be his undoing? The answer is that unconditional withdrawal, even one with a cosmetic face-saving formula added, was totally unacceptable to Saddam from the outset, because it would not address his fundamental twofold predicament. He had not occupied the emirate for reasons of power-seeking or political aggrandizement. Rather, the invasion had been a desperate attempt to shore up his regime in the face of dire economic straits, created by the Iran–Iraq War. Nor did he apparently plan to annex the emirate to Iraq but rather to satellite it, so as to make it fully subservient to his financial (and strategic) wishes.

Once events did not take the course he planned, with the invasion putting Iraq on a collision course with almost the entire international community, Saddam's script had to be re-written. Withdrawal after the instalment of a puppet regime in Kuwait was one thing, but an unconditional pull-out due to American pressure would be another, an admission of weakness and failure which Saddam felt unable to afford. Iraq's economic plight not only remained untangled but was significantly aggravated by the international sanctions imposed on Iraq following the invasion, and Saddam therefore felt that any loss of face at this precarious moment, particularly one caused by an 'infidel' Western power, would damage his position beyond repair.

Furthermore, until late December 1990 or early January 1991 Saddam apparently believed that war could be averted. The 'Vietnam syndrome' in the United States, the vociferous peace camp in the West, and the variety of would-be intermediaries visiting him in Baghdad – all these were expected to help prevent the outbreak of war. He accordingly interpreted President Bush's 30 November offer of direct talks as proof the Administration could not stomach a war and was ready to compromise. 'Bush's initiative is a submission to Iraq's demand, which it has insisted and is still insisting', gloated the Iraqi media, 'namely, the need to open a serious dialogue on the region's issues'.[17]

During this period Saddam reached two decisions that undermined his military position and must have reflected some optimism that a settlement could be reached or, at least, that war could be delayed. The first was to release all Western hostages on 6 December 1990. Saddam appears to have been persuaded by visiting elder statesmen from the

West, such as Edward Heath and Willy Brandt, that holding hostages was detrimental to his image, and that their release would be taken as a serious gesture of reconciliation generating a momentum towards a negotiated settlement. On balance, the release of the hostages turned out to be a strategic mistake, as Saddam himself was to admit later, with uncharacteristic frankness.[18] It did not weaken the coalition's resolve to dislodge Iraq from Kuwait; and if anything, it facilitated military planning. For once the hostages were out, the US Air Force added many facilities to its target list having excluded them previously because of the hostages.[19]

The second indication of Saddam's disbelief in war was his decision not to pre-empt by attacking coalition forces in Saudi Arabia, a move which could have disrupted and confused the coalition's own military preparations. From the beginning of the crisis he vehemently denied American allegations of Iraqi intentions to attack Saudi Arabia, and took great pains not to threaten the coalition with pre-emption.[20]

Saddam remained defiant even when realizing that the Administration would not budge from the demand for Iraq's unconditional withdrawal from Kuwait. Caught between the hammer and the anvil, between the (perceived) certain demise attending an unconditional withdrawal and the hazardous opportunities and possible rewards offered by an armed confrontation, the choice seemed self-evident. Were he to succeed in holding out against the coalition for some time, war would not only offer Saddam the best chance for political survival but might actually enable him to emerge victorious. Just as Egyptian President Gamal Abd al-Nasser had managed to turn Egypt's military defeat in the 1956 Suez crisis into a resounding political victory, so Saddam hoped that the loss of Kuwait in a war with the allies would make him a hero, to be lauded by the Arabs as a new Nasser, a leader who defied 'world imperialism' and yet survived.

RIDING THE STORM

When war came, Saddam fought with one eye set on his personal rule and postwar survival. Kuwait, the Palestinian cause, Iraqi lives were all important only as long as they served the perpetuation of Saddam. So was his military strategy and deployment: key units had been held back from the start for this purpose and he was clearly anxious that as many units as possible return intact to save the regime rather than make a gallant last stand. Cautious when it came to initiatives and reluctant to hazard his air force, he did not want to commit the Republican Guard, Iraq's élite force, to an offensive move that could decimate them, because he needed them to deal with the postwar climate, as illustrated by their brutal repression of the Shi'ite uprising in southern Iraq in the wake of the war.

Saddam did not have an obvious strategy for war termination other than inflicting such discomfort that the coalition would develop an interest in a ceasefire on terms favourable to Iraq. He strongly believed that the Achilles heel of the United States' was its extreme sensitivity to casualties; thus his strategy became to draw the coalition into a premature ground offensive in Kuwait exacting heavy casualties and driving a disillusioned Western public opinion to demand an early ceasefire.[21] Even were this scenario not to materialize, a quick but honourable withdrawal from Kuwait in the course of a bloody encounter could still allow him to emerge victorious from the conflict.

Missile strikes against Israel were Saddam's foremost attempt to lure the allies into this premature ground assault. Striking at Israel's main population centres would not only be cheered by the Arab masses and put the Arab members of the coalition in a difficult position; it would also lay the ground for Israeli retaliation. This, in turn, could be expected to force the coalition to move earlier than planned to a ground offensive in Kuwait.

Almost simultaneously with the attack on Israel, Saddam sought to put pressure on the allies through another tactic: oil. On 19 January Iraq began pumping oil into the Persian Gulf from the Ahmadi loading complex, south of Kuwait City, creating the worst-ever oil slick. Two days later Iraq set fire to Kuwaiti oil fields and storage facilities, creating large amounts of smoke.

While this action made some military sense by creating a smoke screen that could complicate allied operations, and might also have been in retaliation for attacks on Iraqi oil installations, its main aim was to underline to the coalition the devastating consequences of a protracted war for the world oil market and the region's ecology.

Unfortunately for Saddam, the coalition did not fall for his various ploys and appeared content to carry on with an air campaign, gradually unravelling Iraq's military infrastructure.[22] Consequently, when it eventually began in late February the ground offensive led to Saddam's defeat, rather than being his opportunity. Recognizing this fact, Saddam next sought to get through this stage as quickly as possible with whatever might be salvaged of his military power. As the allied offensive developed, Iraqi political concessions came steadily and rapidly. Within less than 48 hours after its start, around midnight of 25 February, Saddam publicly ordered his troops to withdraw 'in an organized way' from Kuwait. Two days later, he agreed to honour all relevant UN resolutions. On 28 February President Bush called a halt to all war operations. Saddam was saved.

SURVIVAL IN DEFEAT

Paradoxically enough, it was the ignominy of Iraq's military undoing which accounted for Saddam's survival of the Gulf War. Had the Iraqi leader succeeded in carrying out his threats and sent thousands of body bags to the member states of the war coalition, he would have aroused their wrath to such an extent that his position would have most probably been made untenable. As things turned out, with the 'mother of all battles' becoming a humiliating defeat, President Bush felt unable to continue what increasingly came to be seen in the West as a one-sided slaughter of helpless Iraqis.

This decision not only saved Saddam from certain destruction by leaving the hard core of his personal rule, the Republican Guard, largely intact, but it sowed the seeds of his future survival. Having lost the demonic aura that surrounded him during the crisis, Saddam overnight was reduced in Western perception from the 'most dangerous man in the world' to a pathetic figure, a typical brutal Third World leader struggling for his personal and political survival. Having anxiously followed his every word and move for six tense months, people throughout the world were immensely relieved by the actual outcome of the crisis and redirected their attention elsewhere. Mindful of this shift in public mood, President Bush felt no obligation to follow up his 15 February call to the Iraqis to remove Saddam Hussein.

Saddam's survival was also helped by the intensity of Iraqi resentment of his Kuwaiti adventure, illustrated most vividly by the eruption of the first popular uprising against an unelected ruler in Iraq's modern history. Taking observers in the region and beyond by complete surprise, this development was received by the US Administration with grave concern. As evidenced by President Bush's 15 February address, which was targeted more at the military than at the Iraqi people at large, he expected the mortal blow at Saddam to be dealt by a 'conventional' *coup d'état* rather than a popular revolution. Such expectations, to be sure, were not out of line with the general course of twentieth-century Iraqi history: all changes of regime in Baghdad, including the 1958 'revolution' which overthrew the monarchy, had been effected by armed groups of sorts, with the Iraqi people acting as a spectator – normally passive, rarely enthusiastic. Hence, once the unprecedented mass uprising substituted for the anticipated standard scenario, the Administration appeared to be recoiling from the process it had set in motion.

Ever since the Iranian revolution of 1979 and the ensuing 'hostage crisis' Shi'ites have been associated in American consciousness with avowed anti-Westernism and unbridled fanaticism. The spectre of a Shi'ite takeover in Baghdad was, therefore, an anathema to American political thinking. The socio-political diversity of the Shi'ite community, the wide divide between Iranian and Iraqi Shi'ites (who had just fought each other ferociously for eight years), the gratitude felt by Iraq's Shi'ites to the United States for its debilitation of Saddam and their assurances that 'an Islamic government in Baghdad does not necessarily have to be similar to the Iranian system',[23] all these were conveniently glossed over by the Administration which seemed to have retreated into the commonplace demonization of the Shi'ites and, in consequence, into the belief that a defeated Saddam might, in the final account, be the lesser evil.

CONSEQUENCES

This change of heart in Washington is not difficult to understand. If the alternative to the Iraqi leader is yet another 'strong man' in Baghdad, then Saddam may well be the least of all evils. For all his brutality and strategic miscalculations, Saddam is no madman, let alone 'a new Hitler'. He might drive his people to great misery and sacrifice but has always sought to avoid irreparable damage to himself and, by extension, to Iraq. Moreover, while Saddam's excessive paranoia and total amorality can hardly be questioned, he has been largely a captive of the political system in which he has operated, and in which naked force has constituted the sole agent of political change.

When in July 1958 the Hashemite dynasty, which had ruled Iraq since its inception in 1921, was overthrown by a military coup headed by General Abd al-Karim Qassem, the mutilated body of the Iraqi regent was dragged by a raging mob through the streets of Baghdad before being hung at the gate of the Ministry of Defence. When dissenting officers in the northern city of Mosul tried, but failed, to oust Qassem in March 1959, he subjected the city to one of the bloodiest retributions in Iraq's modern history. Four years later, Qassem's bullet-ridden corpse was screened on Iraqi television to the entire nation. His successor, the Ba'th Party, was no kinder in its treatment of political opponents.

The truth of the matter, therefore, is that in the politics of Iraq (and the Middle East at large), where conflicting loyalties, disputed boundaries, religious, ethnic and tribal conflicts abound, either one subdues the system or is devoured by it. Saddam has managed for the present to subject the system to his will, at the exorbitant cost of domestic repression and external aggression. Yet, even this stark approach can last only as long as one's ceaseless surveillance and tyrannical control of the country's governing mechanisms. Unless democracy emerges in Iraq, there will be no solution to the fundamental predicament confronting the person at the top of the political pyramid. Whether Ba'thist or Islamic fundamentalist, military or civilian, he will continue to confront dissent and disaster at every turn, and will be constantly preoccupied with personal survival. In these circumstances, a crippled Saddam reduced to a precarious existence, may prove better than an equally ruthless but unknown successor.

This, in turn, means that the only possible cure to Iraq's fundamental predicament lies in the overall restructuring of its political system, with the minority Sunni group surrendering the leading role in Baghdad to the majority Shi'ite community, three times its size. It is true, of course, that such transition of power is likely to be accompanied by widespread violence, but its chances of success now are better than ever before. The uprising against the regime in the wake of the Gulf War has set a crucial precedent for the future by breaching the wall of fear shielding Saddam from his own people.

This is neither to say that a predominantly Shi'ite regime in Baghdad does not entail potential risks to Iraq's neighbours, nor to suggest that it will inevitably turn Iraq into a liberal democracy. However, by reflecting the 'general will' to a substantially greater extent than its Sunni predecessors, such a regime can be expected to be more confident and less paranoid and, hence, less brutal in its ways and means. The Shi'ite solution is not a panacea. But the continuation of Saddam's personal rule, or for that matter the rule of the 'Tikriti clique' or even the Sunni community, is an assured prescription for domestic repression and external aggression in the future.

NOTES

1 Baghdad Radio, 8 August 1990.
2 On these attempts see, Efraim Karsh and Inari Rautsi, *Saddam Hussein: A Political Biography*, New York: Free Press, 1991, p. 207.
3 See, for example, Saddam Hussein, *For Youth Nothing is Impossible*, Baghdad: Dar al-Ma'mun, 1984.
4 *Guardian* (London), 8 June 1990.

5 See, for example, Amnesty International, *Iraq: Evidence of Torture*, London: Amnesty International Publications, 1981.

6 The best available account of the Iraqi security apparatus is offered in Samir al-Khalil's *Republic of Fear: The Politics of Modern Iraq*, London: Hutchinson Radius, 1989.

7 *Independent* (London), 20 July 1988.

8 *Economist* (London), 30 September 1989, 4 August 1990; *Independent* (London), 20 July 1988, 16 March 1990.

9 Charles Tripp, 'The Consequences of the Iran–Iraq War for Iraqi Politics', in Efraim Karsh (ed.), *The Iran–Iraq War: Impact and Implications*, London and New York: Macmillan and St Martin's Press, 1989, p. 76.

10 Baghdad Radio, July 1990.

11 Iraqi News Agency, 19, 26 June 1990; Saddam's interview with *Wall Street Journal*, 26 June 1990.

12 Judith Miller and Laurie Mylroie, *Saddam Hussein and the Crisis in the Gulf*, New York: Times Books, 1990, p. 15.

13 Baghdad Radio, 18 July 1990.

14 Baghdad Radio, 17 July 1990.

15 Personal interview.

16 See a statement by a Kuwaiti official to Radio Monte Carlo in Arabic (Paris), 1 August 1990.

17 Baghdad Radio, 4 December 1990.

18 Saddam's interview with CNN's correspondent in Baghdad, Peter Arnett, 28 January 1991.

19 *International Herald Tribune*, 14 December 1991.

20 See, for example, Iraqi News Agency, 3, 7 August 1990; Baghdad Radio, 6 August 1990.

21 He openly stated this objective at the start of the war. See, Iraqi News Agency, 18 January 1991.

22 Other ploys of Saddam included the armoured attack on the Saudi border town of Khafji in late January, and the castigation of the allies for the collateral damage caused by their strategic bombardments.

23 Muhammad Baker al-Hakim's interview with *Anatoliya* (Ankara), March 1991.

4 Saudi Arabia's Desert Storm and winter sandstorm

Jacob Goldberg

Saudis at the time described the Iraqi invasion of Kuwait and the stationing of American troops as a watershed in Saudi history. The sense was one of 'mortal danger to our very existence', and a cataclysmic event which shook the kingdom's entire foundations and jolted its society. The magnitude, longevity, and seriousness of the event was even said to have triggered a metamorphosis in the thinking of the ruling family both on domestic and foreign policies.

Astonishing therefore is the rapidity with which Saudi society and politics resumed their traditional patterns once the war was over, as if the crisis had never taken place. The phenomenon was further remarkable because it encompassed broad aspects of domestic, security and foreign policies. This chapter addresses five areas in which basic changes and lessons learned during the crisis evaporated gradually after the immediate crisis to the kingdom passed.

THE CRISIS

The feeling in Riyadh was that the crisis was bound to revamp the Middle East and Saudi Arabia's role in it. For the geostrategic arena surrounding the kingdom seemed to have changed radically. Neighbours who were former allies – Iraq, Jordan, Yemen and the PLO – turned overnight into arch-enemies. Moreover, 'a new Arab political and economic order' was to be created, predicated on the manpower of Egypt and Syria, the money of Saudi Arabia and the Gulf states. It was designed to provide a new security structure in the Gulf, distribute Arab wealth more equitably, reorient Syria away from radicalism, and lead towards a peace settlement with Israel.

Implications for Saudi foreign policy were momentous. The kingdom for years had performed a remarkable balancing act between its Western interests and Arab and Islamic constraints by pacifying Arab and Muslim adversaries – real, potential or perceived – with generous gifts of cash, while maintaining close, if discreet, ties with Washington. The Iraqi threat forced King Fahd to portray himself openly as a firm friend of the USA, totally dependent on America for his survival. This unequivocal reliance on Washington was accompanied by abandonment of the protective umbrella of the Arab consensus.

While in the past Saudis reacted to threats with fear-induced appeasement, such an approach was now seen as compromising national security and affecting independence. This time they stood up to Iraq and the new adversaries, displaying a new kind of decisiveness and a determination to react vigorously. A previously reticent government now sent emissaries around the globe to influence and even put pressure on governments to come to its aid. Thus, Japan and the Europeans, for example, were told that 'if they did not contribute to our defense, we would reconsider all future contracts with their companies; I think they got the message'.[1]

The kingdom appeared electrified. Its economy was jolted by huge expenditures and unstable oil prices, its society exposed to unprecedented Western influences. Above all, there was a sense that Saudi Arabia faced perhaps painful, certainly disruptive choices about its future. The shock of Kuwait's easy conquest and the transparency of Saudi Arabia's own military impotence induced an accelerated process of self-evaluation. Many influential Saudis, indeed, wished to capitalize on the crisis in order to liberalize society: 'We are part of the world and the whole world is changing'. The question was whether 'this theocracy could accommodate the material changes and sophistication of its people'. It seemed obvious the royal family would open up the system and institute political reforms.[2]

But if the crisis tested basic Saudi beliefs, it also found them wanting. As Prince Abdallah ibn Faisal said: 'We are shocked. We never thought it could happen. Each day we say "maybe it's all a bad dream." ' Prominent Saudis admitted that strangely, they were actually pleased with what happened: 'We were living in a cloud-cuckoo-land. Our false security has been blown out like a candle.' Subsequently, there was a consensus that 'this place will never be the same again', because 'things cannot be allowed to proceed as they were before August 2'.[3]

GULF SECURITY

The annual Gulf Cooperation Council (GCC) meeting declared that 'Iraq's invasion upset all realities regarding the concept of Gulf security. It is incumbent upon us to review and reassess long-held beliefs'.[4] Wealthy and well-armed, the bedrock of the Gulf monarchies' security, Saudi Arabia had proved powerless to deter an invasion of a sister state. The GCC, wrote Saudi editors, was 'an inadequate organ, unable to shoulder Gulf security because it lacked any credible military defense'.[5]

But the sense of urgency for Saudi Arabia were rooted in the assessment that the ten Iraqi divisions in Kuwait were really poised there for one reason: forced entry into the Saudi oil heartland. Saudi generals calculated that Iraqi forces could capture the entire Eastern Province in six hours or, if Saudi troops had in 12 hours extensive air cover, taking the entire country in three days. 'That's when we asked for American help,' Ambassador to the USA Prince Bandar ibn Sultan said. 'Saudi Arabia is not going to emulate Kuwait by rejecting American help', he explained.[6]

Given the impotence of the 10,000-strong GCC 'peninsula shield', the major item on the future agenda became the creation of a unified force of 100,000 that would draw 50 per cent of its troops from GCC states and the rest from other Arab states. Egypt and Syria were expected to provide the Gulf states with the core might to ward off future predators.[7]

Consequently, in mid-February 1991, at the height of the war, the foreign ministers of Egypt, Syria, Morocco, and the six GCC states met in Cairo to devise both a permanent Gulf force composed of Egyptian, Syrian and Saudi troops and a regional economic development plan. The 45,000 Egyptians and the 20,000 Syrians already stationed in the Gulf were to constitute the nucleus of the Arab force, which was to be backed up by Western navies, stationed 'over the horizon' to avert protest by other Arabs of a permanent Western presence. But the plan did envision logistical provisions and weapons, ammunition and medical storage areas for a rapid deployment of Western troops in the event of an emergency with which the Arab force could not deal.[8]

In early April, Under-Secretary of Defense Paul Wolfowitz told a Senate committee that 'our Gulf friends have learned the risks of waiting too long before requesting our help. Therefore, they would agree to prepositioning, regular exercises and deployments, which will make it possible for us to come back faster if our help is ever needed again'.[9]

Gulf security, based on Egyptian and Syrian troops, was closely tied to a more equitable re-distribution wealth – 'a new Arab economic order'. The rich GCC states, primarily Saudi Arabia, were to devise major economic development plans for those defending the Gulf –

Egypt and Syria. Both were in desperate need for hard currency and eager to strike a long-term, grand bargain with the Gulf states providing financial rewards for their defence of the Gulf.[10] The stage was thus set for the implementation of what was to mark a milestone in Gulf security: an historic accord making the populous, poor but strong Arab centres of Egypt and Syria protect the rich, but vulnerable Arabs in the Gulf.

MILITARY DRAFT

While growth characterized all other segments of society since the early 1970s, the Saudi armed forces had remained relatively small and compact. Failure to enlarge the army is puzzling in view of the expanding spectrum of strategic challenges and the priority accorded to massive military buildup. Of the ten biggest world military spenders, Saudi Arabia had the smallest ratio of military personnel in comparison to its defence spending.[11]

By 1990, the Saudi armed forces numbered 72,000, an increase of only 10,000 in two decades. Of these, only 52,000 were ground forces in armoured, artillery and infantry units; 17,000 were in the air force; and 3,000 were in the tiny navy. Some 40,000 Saudis served in the National Guard, Frontier Force and Coast Guard.[12] These figures should be compared to the goal of the planned draft, first promoted in 1980, which envisioned 300,000 troops by 1985.[13]

The royal family was consistently reluctant to enact a draft for any number of reasons. It feared that a large army would lead to a *coup d'état* and an overthrow; it always had sought to disarm most of Saudi society as means of ensuring internal unity and stability.[14] It was just as anxious lest a draft antagonize the younger generation; similarly, it feared a large army might arouse suspicions of Crown Prince Abdallah and 'his' National Guard. The leadership always accorded priority to cohesion among royal family ranks, even at the expense of higher national interests. Finally, the size of the army reflected traditional Saudi concepts of the sources of dangers: the two Yemens, Jordan and Kuwait. Remarkably, no contingency plan ever conceived an Iraqi invasion. Thus, the failure of the royal family to impose a draft left the army as small as ever.

Iraq's invasion of Kuwait lent urgency and priority to the debate over compulsory conscription. Though a draft could not counter Iraq's threat, the issue emerged forcefully in the context of the long-term lessons of the crisis. The trauma of only 50,000 Saudi soldiers facing hundreds of thousands of Iraqis, coupled with the demonstration of Saudi vulnerability and defencelessness shook the self-confidence of the Saudis in Saudi wealth being used to build a credible military deterrent. The need to rely on foreigners in order to survive evoked widespread criticism of the traditional reliance on a small army and a well-equipped air force that had proved ineffective in August 1990.

The invasion, in addition, discredited the Saudi national security doctrine. Having an arsenal of highly-modern armaments is one thing; predicating national security on weaponry, without a large body of military personnel, is quite another. Particularly so in the Saudi case, in view of its vast territory, long boundaries, and a chain of adversaries, two of which – Iran and Iraq – respectively could field a million troops. Moreover, as noted, the Saudis had never prepared themselves for an Iraqi invasion. For one, they were certain that with Iran and Iraq neutralizing each other, Iraq would not move against its Arab neighbours in the Gulf. For another, having based their foreign policy on 'Arab solidarity', the Saudis never imagined that the source of protection would turn into the threat.

In retrospect, there was an intoxicating element in the strategy of procuring huge amounts of highly-sophisticated arms. However, in the absence of a sizeable army, they thought that the only way to impress and deter opponents and make up for the shortage of manpower was by showcasing large amounts of sophisticated major weapons systems. It was designed primarily to project an image of power, enhancing Saudi confidence in the ability to deter military challenges.[15]

The bankruptcy of the security doctrine has since prompted tough questions: 'Where did our money go? Why haven't we got an army? Why do we need the US to protect us? How could Saudi military power be a false dream?'[16] In a most unusual article in the *Washington Post*, published during the war, a prominent Riyadh lawyer, Abd al-Aziz Fahad, poignantly asked Saudi rulers why Syria, with a comparable population and considerably fewer resources, posed credible military deterrence, while rich Saudi Arabia, 'has to scramble for the aid of friendly nations to protect it from Iraqi aggression?'[17]

Aware now that the new hostile arena includes not only Iraq and Iran but also Jordan and newly-unified Yemen, Saudi leaders were determined not 'to be so vulnerable and so dependent on foreign powers again'. The Commander of the Arab forces in the Gulf General Prince Khaled ibn Sultan stated that 'in increasing our force, we should think 360 degrees'.[18] The leadership, thus, resolved to impose a draft and expand the ground forces immediately to over 120,000, eventually reaching 300,000 men. So, too, is the National Guard to increase to 100,000 troops, in order to bring the total figure to 400,000.[19]

General Prince Khaled ibn Sultan in his first interview after the war, explicitly confirmed the large increase in troop strength. 'I can't say 100,000 or 150,000; that has to be studied carefully. But I certainly feel that we should have at least eight divisions.' With reservists, this triples the ground forces to about 200,000.[20]

The realization that Saudi resources might inevitably tempt some of its neighbours, coupled with deep suspicions about the long-term reliability of outside assistance, do seem to have prompted the leadership to reverse its long-standing reluctance to enact a compulsory draft. Fears of Bedouin anarchy were no longer valid, while Jordan and Morocco demonstrated that monarchies could build strong military machines and survive.[21] With a draft merely a question of time, and with young Saudis more ready to volunteer to service, the expansion of the army seems a foregone conclusion.

FOREIGN POLICY

The royal family tried to appease Saddam up to the moment of the invasion. Yet this did not stop him from threatening the kingdom. The Saudis were shocked that Saddam, to whom 'we gave billions of dollars, was pointing missiles at us', and asked their leaders to admit that 'he was the same bloody dictator when you aided him that he is now'.[22]

Appeasement having proven 'fallacious', King Fahd confronted Iraq, abandoning discreet diplomacy in favour of militant resolve. He demanded not only a full Iraqi withdrawal but 'guarantees against future aggression by Iraq's ruler', which meant that 'Iraq's army must be neutralized'. Saudi officials spoke about a 'consensus from the king on down that Saddam has to go, and that the only way to safeguard our existence is . . . to do away with the entire Ba'th regime through a decisive military victory'.[23]

The crisis forced the Saudis to abandon their longstanding adherence to the sacred principles of Arab unity and discreet diplomacy. 'We don't care any more about Arab unity, which never existed anyway; other Arabs are not dependable allies. We are less concerned about Arabs' opinions and about respecting the niceties of Arab politics'.[24] Such a self-assured state of mind enabled the royal family to invite in American troops, and to declare an alliance with Washington, thereby abandoning in one stroke both its longstanding rejection of a US military presence and its discretion in relations with the USA.

There are peculiar twists in recent Saudi political alignments. While former allies – Iraq, Jordan, Yemen and the PLO – turned overnight into foes, a powerful Saudi–Egyptian–Syrian bloc was created against Iraq. The Saudi–Egyptian full-fledged alliance was reinforced by Cairo's status as the largest Arab contributor to the multinational force. In October 1990, President Mubarak and King Fahd also discussed the feasibility of a permanent Egyptian military presence in the Gulf.[25] Far more problematic are Saudi–Syrian relations and the deployment of Syrian forces on Saudi soil, given that Riyadh and Damascus had been poles apart for two decades, with divergent views on almost every regional issue. Whereas Riyadh perceived a long-term commonality of interests with Cairo, the alignment with Damascus was viewed as *ad hoc* and tactical. Saudis were reported to have 'strong reservations about the Syrian presence; they don't trust them'. Also noted was that President Assad did send troops, but only after receiving hefty Saudi payments estimated at $2 billion.[26]

The Saudis viewed their allies-turned-enemies – Jordan, Yemen and the PLO – as an integral part of Saddam's plot to control Saudi Arabia and the Gulf states. The conspiracy envisaged King Hussein seizing the Saudi Hijaz, with Mecca and Medina, and incorporating it into Jordan. Yemen was to take over parts of southern Saudi Arabia, while the Palestinians were to attain a major portion of Kuwait.[27] Following the crisis there remains profound resentment towards Jordanians, Yemenis and Palestinians; in Prince Bandar's words: 'All who stood up for Saddam will go under with him. We will make supporters of Iraq pay dearly for their betrayal.'[28]

Indeed, Riyadh suspended entry visas to Jordanians and stopped oil deliveries to Jordan. Most Jordanian diplomats were told to leave, and the two ambassadors were recalled.[29] Calling King Hussein a 'goner', Saudi officials stated their unwillingness to see him as a part of the 'new Middle East order'. Having received $400 million annually, 'Husayn should know that his Saudi lifeline has been severed forever'.[30] The Saudis likewise abolished Yemeni workers' privileges, and by the end of 1990 about one million Yemenis had to leave. The Yemeni diplomatic staff was cut from eighty to four, and the annual $400 million subsidy was suspended. Deploying thousands of troops along the Yemeni border, Riyadh warned Sanaa that any attempt to exploit the crisis would be dealt with by 'massive attacks on Yemeni strategic, military and oil facilities'.[31]

The Saudis viewed the PLO alignment with Iraq as a turning point in Saudi–Palestinian relations, and vowed to cut the PLO down to size. They cut off aid to the PLO, which since 1989 had reached $6 million monthly, and expelled thousands of Palestinians. Saudi leaders explained that if the PLO wanted normal relations and financial aid, it would have to replace its leadership, because 'Arafat is finished here. We kissed him on the cheek for years. No more. He is a thug and a clown.'[32]

The Iraqi challenge, on the other hand, created a convergence of Saudi and Iranian interests, replacing the bitter confrontation between the two. Creating a 'new security system' implied that Iran had to be made a part of any future joint structure. Indeed, GCC officials soon began talks with Iran designed to create just such 'a post-crisis, new regional security system'. In addition to the common Iraqi threat, the Saudis viewed the election of President Rafsanjani as proof that 'Iran of the 1990s will be different from the Iran of the 1980s'.[33] The road was, thus, open for the resumption of diplomatic relations and for Iranian participation in the 1991 *Hajj*.

The 'steadfast Soviet stand' on Kuwait impressed Riyadh, 'proved Gorbachev's credibility', and attested to 'the thorough transformation in Soviet orientation'. Within weeks following the invasion, the Saudis agreed to establish diplomatic relations with Moscow at the ambassadorial level. Saudi officials singled out Moscow's Iraqi stand as crucial because it could 'thwart Saddam's calculations, reinforce his international isolation, tighten the blockade and embargo, enhance the UN role and forge an international consensus'.[34]

POLITICAL REFORMS

At home the crisis evoked dormant aspirations for political and social change. Offering inspiration were:

1 The unprecedented openness and unrestricted flow of information;
2 Hopes that the presence of 500,000 US troops would bring some change toward democracy;
3 Expectations that for its rescue operation, Washington would pressure the royal family into political reforms;
4 Reverberations from a similar demand for democractic reforms in Kuwait; and
5 Hopes that the sight of US service women and 100,000 Kuwaiti women driving cars would change the regime's view of Saudi women's role.

Euphoric at the ability to discuss sensitive issues publicly in an atmosphere of *glasnost*, the middle class sought to exploit the crisis as a catalyst for political change. These were not radicals seeking to overturn the system but rather prominent members of the new establishment who praised the regime for 'turning us into an island of stability and individual liberty in a regional sea of repression and violence'.[35]

These businessmen, professionals and academics rejected the notion that democratization meant betraying Islam or undermining the royal family. But they claimed that the educated population would no longer accept an absolute monarchy in which the Qur'an dictates policy, and where crucial decisions, such as the request for US help, are made behind closed doors. They publicly called for three major reforms:

1 The formation of a consultative council, *Majlis al-Shura*;
2 Codification of freedom of information – a free Press and end to censorship – and the right of free speech without fear of penalties; and
3 Social reforms, allowing for an easier mingling of the sexes.

Fundamentalist jurists viewed with horror such political changes, however, and compelled the authorities to cancel a planned legal reform by branding it 'secular'. They also opposed the consultative council, viewing it as a liberal tool that could diffuse their own influence. Explained a religious scholar: 'Democracy depends on people's will which can change. Islam relies on Allah, and his laws don't change.'[36]

Caught between the liberals and the fundamentalists, the royal family employed its traditional balancing act. Nevertheless, it was aware of growing criticism of the political immobility and of the expectations for reforms, the realization grew that some promises for change had to be made. As a senior prince said: 'The royal family cannot escape its responsibility as an instrument of change.' Consequently, King Fahd relayed to Saudi press editors in November 1990 his plan for three political reforms: 'a basic system of rule [a semi-constitution], a consultative council and a new administration for the provinces'. All, to be sure, were 'within the Islamic framework'. Aware that the same reforms had been promised in 1980, King Fahd argued that 'the drafts are now in the final stages'.[37]

A WAY OF LIFE

Though the regime strove to insulate the population from the impact of the crisis, the massive influx of foreign troops prised open an almost hermetically sealed society. Saudi editors observed that the crisis evoked 'unprecedented activism and assertiveness', resulting in hundreds of letters to the editors and in Saudis speaking freely to reporters.[38] In an atmosphere of openness, the government-controlled Press suddenly became lively, and officials spoke of political reform.

Saudi liberals sought to enhance exposure to the West, hoping that the American presence would loosen the fundamentalists' grip. Anxious lest the openness erode religious practices, Islamic militants attacked 'secularism, modernism and immorality'. The religious police adopted three new measures: raiding private homes and diplomatic residences, using lethal weapons, and displaying a high profile even in the more open city of Jeddah.[39]

Here, again, the regime reverted to its balancing act. It gave the religious police broader authorities to fight all transgressions. But it also named a well-known moderate to head the police, and it cooperated with established religious figures in a bid to limit the influence of the radicals. At the same time, it moved to implement long-overdue political reforms, relaxing its total control over the media.

Reformist Saudis seized on the crisis in particular in order to loosen the regime's grip on the media. Hungry for information, Saudis turned to the Egyptian radio, BBC and VOA, with people saying things like 'Nobody listens to Saudi radio or TV: we know these are all lies.' However, once Fahd announced the Western airlift, the Saudi press itself changed markedly. It carried foreign reports by Reuters, AP and other wires. Editors vehemently condemned Saddam, breaking a long-standing ban on attacks on Arab leaders. Information, censored in the past, now flowed almost freely. Photographs of US servicewomen appeared on front pages. The crisis prompted soul-searching in the media, which concluded that 'we ought to face and print the truth'. The editor of *al-Madina* confessed that 'we have been conservative journalists; now we are driven into an open era'.[40]

The new attitude of the regime resulted in the presence of 240 foreign reporters during the crisis and 600 during the war. They had free access and could discuss sensitive issues with officials in a way unthinkable in the past. Many Saudis tended to go further and wanted to ensure that foreign reporters be allowed into the country on a regular basis.[41]

The government, however, was less tolerant when some Saudi groups seized the crisis to challenge well-established traditions over women's rights. In November 1990, forty-nine Saudi women were detained by the religious police after having driven a convoy of cars in Riyadh. The issue went beyond driving: this first public protest by women was a symbol of their desire for equal opportunities and a rare reflection of public sentiment in conservative Riyadh. The new sense of openness, the acquiescence of the religious police in American and Kuwaiti women driving, and the presence of hundreds of foreign reporters, all led the women to think that their actions would be tolerated creating a precedent. In order to dispel this notion, the fundamentalists went on the offensive, using the protest as proof that the Islamic way of life was threatened and pressing for drastic punishment of the women.[42] Some of the women lost their jobs, six professors were suspended from their teaching positions and others were subjected to harassment.[43]

REACTIONARY COUNTER-ATTACK

Gulf security

First indications of a Saudi change of heart appeared by March 1991. Senior officials said they did not favour proposals to station a pan-Arab military force in the Gulf, adding that they preferred to expand their army and depend on 'over the horizon' US logistical and military help. Subsequently, the Saudis adamantly rejected any foreign troops, American or Arab, or pre-positioning of American arms and equipment on Saudi soil.[44] The idea of an Arab force dwindled into nothingness in April when the GCC dumped the plan, and the Saudis and Kuwaitis formally asked Egypt and Syria to remove their troops. Justifying the shift in policy, a Saudi editor wrote that 'the plan resulted from hasty ideas raised during the war'.[45]

What accounts for Saudi reluctance to depend on other Arabs for defence? First, the Saudis feared that Arab troops might get involved in domestic disputes that had imperiled the royal family so often in the past. In times of crisis, these troops could not be trusted to protect the monarchy. Second, the Saudis feared that Egypt and Syria might use their troops to try to dominate the GCC politically. Third, the Saudis felt that given the fighting abilities of Egyptian and Syrian troops, their presence was not worth the billion-dollar payoff expected by Cairo and Damascus. Fourth, Saudi Arabia sought to avoid the political pressures bound to come with Arab troop presence. Fifth, the Saudis preferred to enlarge their own army and deal directly with their old ally, the USA. Sixth, Riyadh did not wish to alienate Iran, which had condemned the Damascus declaration, seeing no role for non-Gulf states in its security.

The Saudis also reversed their stand on the US role in the security of the Gulf. In May 1991, Secretary of Defense Dick Cheney presented

Riyadh with a draft of a 'Memorandum of Understanding on Gulf Security'. While not envisaging US troops on Saudi soil, the plan contained the following elements:

1 Stationing of senior US Central Command officers in the Gulf;
2 Storing tanks and hardware in Saudi Arabia equal to an armoured division;
3 Rotating tactical aircraft throughout the region;
4 Conducting joint military exercises;
5 Moving aircraft carriers in and out of the Gulf; and
6 Shifting an amphibious force to the area periodically.[46]

Alerting the USA to the change in policy, Prince Khaled warned Washington not to expect 'to leave behind a stockpile of arms'. Instead, the US should provide the Saudis with advanced weapons to defend themselves. 'In the future', he said, 'we will take only US military personnel whom we need to train us on new equipment; it depends on how much equipment we take. This will be the only way American troops can stay on Saudi soil.'[47] By late April, however, Riyadh felt that though Saddam survived, Iraq's military capabilities were considerably reduced by the war, and therefore General Prince Khaled could not 'see much of a threat now'.[48]

Wary of being criticized by Muslim and Arab countries for their close ties with the Americans, Saudi rulers also feared religious resentment at home. They were anxious lest the US role be seen as an admission of Saudi incapability to handle future threats. Finally, Riyadh felt confident that in any future emergency the USA would rescue the Saudis because of American interests in the region, regardless of any future security structure. So why enter into an arrangement fraught with costs whose benefits the Saudis were likely to enjoy anyway?

Thus, the Saudis turned down the proposed Memorandum. Unwilling formally to institutionalize defence relations with the USA, King Fahd indicated that he would be happy to rely on Western military help so long as it remained invisible. With a nod to Saudi sensitivities, Cheney promised all information on troop presence and arms storage would remain classified, stating that the GCC states 'tentatively approved the US plan for new security arrangements'. The Saudi refusal, however, remained intact as late as October 1991, causing 'growing strains in US–Saudi relations'.[49]

This Saudi stand is diametrically opposed to Kuwait's position, which actually boasts of close ties with the USA, and the physical presence of American troops, as provided for in the ten-year American–Kuwaiti defence treaty of September 1991.

Thus, within two months after the war, the Saudis reversed their acceptance of three changes introduced as a result of the Gulf crisis: Egypt and Syria were excluded from any plan for the Gulf's security, which also aborted all talks of 'a new Arab order'; there was no agreement of the presence of US troops nor on pre-positioning of American weapons; and plans for a 100,000-man GCC force were put off.

Military draft

Contrary to all expectations that a draft was imminent, once the war ended King Fahd struck a distinctly different note. In a public speech he promised 'our armed forces shall be . . . equipped with state-of-the-art military equipment and advanced technology', and added 'we shall improve the efficiency of our armed forces, double recruitment efforts and protect this precious country and its territory'.[50]

It was obvious that the king felt compelled to respond to public criticism of bankrupt security doctrine and of poor military preparedness. He was clearly trying to avoid the issue of a draft, never mentioning the size of the army. His speech focused on improving the quality, not quantity, of the military, in keeping with a previous pattern, whereby each crisis threatening national security elicits plans for a formal draft which fade away once the crisis is over.

Likewise, King Fahd's plan 'to double recruitment efforts' reflected adherence to the old system, with an effort to improve its effectiveness, rather than a readiness to introduce the 'revolutionary' change of conscription. Finally, the promise to supply the armed forces with 'state-of-the-art military equipment and technology' marked a return to the policy of massive arms procurement.

Thus, by the end of 1991, it appeared that not even the traumatic Kuwait crisis and the mortal Iraqi danger had the power to force long-term changes in Saudi security policies. Essentially it was back to 'business as usual'.

Foreign policy

Senior Saudi officials claimed the victory over Iraq reinforced Saudi resolve to play a more assertive role in Arab politics as an ally of the West and an opponent of radical Arabs. They were determined not to re-embrace the traditional policy of appeasement of adversaries and they wished in particular to strengthen bonds to Egypt and the tactical alliance with Syria.[51]

The most pronounced shift was in 'stopping our policy of handing out money to friends or foes to shore up their economies or appease their hostile intent', said a senior official. 'We will now expect much more for our money, at the very least not betrayal, as we got from Iraq, Jordan, Yemen and the PLO.'[52]

The Gulf crisis was also said to have effected something of a sea-change in Saudi attitudes towards the Arab–Israeli conflict, in the direction of greater moderation, flexibility, and readiness to play a role in the peace process. Indeed, as peace efforts resumed after the Gulf War, King Fahd promised Secretary Baker that Saudi Arabia would be 'active' in the search for an Arab–Israeli accord.[53] These signs of intent are extremely significant because, if true and sustained, they could lend Islamic legitimacy to any peace settlement with Israel.

Saudi help was particularly intended to create an alternative Palestinian leadership from the West Bank and Gaza Strip which would abandon its attachment to PLO chairman Yasser Arafat and agree to participate in the peace process. The Saudis were reported to have set up a mechanism for their funds to flow into economic projects in the territories without passing through the PLO. Saudi officials warned the Palestinians that if they continued to adhere to Arafat, Riyadh would endorse a 'step by step' approach involving Syria and not the Palestinians.[54]

But expectations for an active Saudi role all but evaporated on 21 April when King Fahd told Secretary Baker to count Saudi Arabia out of any Arab–Israeli peace process. The blow to US efforts to convene a peace conference prompted President Bush personally to pressure the Saudis. Fearing that failure to partake in the peace process would adversely affect future arms sales, the Saudis made a concession designed to preserve US–Saudi relations rather than to stake out a Saudi role in an Arab–Israeli settlement.[55]

Accordingly, in mid-May, the Saudi foreign minister announced the GCC states would participate in a peace conference. The Saudis, however, imposed key limits on their role:

1 Representing the Gulf states in the opening session would be the GCC secretary general, and even this as an 'observer' only;
2 Individual countries would send delegates only to the multilateral meetings; and
3 No national envoys would attend talks on peace terms, i.e. Saudis

intended to be conspicuously absent from meetings on sensitive issues of peace and recognition.[56]

This arrangement was crafted to satisfy the USA, by attending the conference, while not offending militant Arabs by peace talks with or recognition of Israel. Saudis described it as 'getting through the door in the softest way; because this really is not bilateral but regional discussions'.[57]

The shift in Riyadh's stand was manifested also in the attitude towards the PLO. After a twelve-month boycott, Fahd wrote to Arafat in late July, urging him to compromise on Palestinian representation in the peace conference. He implied that this might improve Palestinian–Saudi relations. In September, for the first time since the invasion, Saudi Arabia resumed forwarding to the PLO the 5 per cent surcharge imposed on all Palestinians employed in the Kingdom.[58]

The reversal of convictions held during the crisis was reflected also in post-crisis attitudes towards Iraq. During the conflict the consensus in Riyadh was that Saddam and the entire Ba'th regime had to go. But the Saudis changed their mind immediately after the war when they realized that the alternative to Saddam's regime might be the disintegration of Iraq, which posed the dual danger of a Shi'ite threat in southern Iraq and the absence of a counterbalance to Iranian power.

The return to pre-crisis thinking was demonstrated in yet another field. In late September, when the USA considered bombing Iraq for its refusal to cooperate with the UN mission, Saudi Arabia rejected the US request to base bombers on its soil. The reluctance emanated from fear that a major Saudi role in a new attack on Iraq would poise the Arab world against the Kingdom.[59]

Thus, the record of Saudi foreign policy by the start of 1992 was very mixed. Some of the new elements introduced during the crisis remained unaltered, specifically relations with Russia and Iran, the axis with Egypt and Syria, and the hostility towards Jordan and Yemen. However, on other issues Saudi attitudes were gradually reverting to traditional, pre-crisis features: low profile, back-stage roles, appeasement and financial aid, the politics of Arab consensus, non-alienation of radicals, and invisible relations with Washington.

Political reforms

Domestically, and external affairs aside, Saudi liberals renewed their demand for reforms, assuming that Fahd's enhanced position after the war would enable him to institute changes. In April the king repeated his pledge to form a consultative council, leading Saudis to believe that action was likely after the June *Hajj*.[60] However, the royal family's dilemma was this time more difficult because both liberals and conservatives had each heightened expectations that at the moment of truth after the war, their agenda would prevail. Some experts predicted that 'having to respond either by opening up or cracking down, the regime would crack down'.[61]

Instead, the king was back at striking a balance between the two forces. King Fahd reined the fundamentalists on some issues and relented on others, perfecting the art of manipulating diverse interests in order to preserve power and stability. The balancing act ended in scrapping any major political reform. All that changed was a modest cabinet shuffle in August 1991 which filled two vacant posts. The three promised reforms were relegated to oblivion. Alluding to the lack of need for a consultative council, the King stated that 'Saudi leaders always consulted with qualified religious and liberal men'.[62]

In his balancing act, King Fahd realizes that the religious establishment carry a lot more weight: more organized, visible and vocal, they have the vast network of mosques as a tool of mobilization. He accorded priority to their wishes because they remain a central pillar of the Saudi state and a source of legitimacy for the House of Saud. Articulating this stand, Fahd pledged not 'to borrow any principles which vary from the Qur'an or the Sunna to which we are permanently committed equally as a faith and a political basis and from which there is no deviation'.[63] Political considerations also figure prominently. King Fahd seems to have struck a deal with the religious groups: they would acquiesce in the pro-Western orientation and he would refrain from any political reforms. Finally, the royal family must always fear that any reform might prove to be a contagious virus, which would eventually undermine the entire system.

In view of their exaggerated crisis expectations, one can appreciate the magnitude of the disappointment of most Saudis. Once conditions return to normal, promises are largely forgotten.[64]

Ways of life

Saudis, by 1992, were struck by how quickly life had returned to normal and by the lack of substantive change. The lively political discussions, cassettes and pamphlets that had characterized the crisis disappeared. Saudis who had offered their views freely were once again fearful of being quoted by name. Censorship over newspapers was restored and applied vigorously. Only a handful of Western reporters remained in the kingdom. CNN was no longer available at major hotels and thousands of satellite dishes were abandoned. Finally, after a ten-month suspension in consideration of the sensitivities of foreigners, the regime reinstituted public executions by beheading.

The royal family was back at its balancing act. The king met with some of the forty-nine women drivers and promised to restore their jobs. The religious police were given an $18 million budget increase to improve employee training. But simultaneously, the government warned fundamentalist leaders not to use schools or mosques for political indoctrination. As a Saudi official explained: 'The government lets them speak out as long as they function inside the system. But if they go beyond the line, they will be stopped.'[65]

CONCLUSION

In retrospect, the Saudi royal family at the height of the acute threat understandably viewed the Gulf crisis as an earthquake. Its behaviour from 2 August 1990 till 1 March 1991 represented temporary crisis management and expedience which had to be terminated as fast as possible. This led to a formula of 'normalization': the need to restore the pre-crisis status quo in every aspect. Ironically, the goal of 'eliminating the consequences of the Iraqi aggression' applied not only to Kuwait's liberation but also to the liberation of Saudi politics from the 'deviations' of the crisis.

During the crisis the key word was 'change', deemed irreversible. After the war, the key word was 'restoration'. The kingdom that opened its doors to the West when it needed protection against 'Desert Storm' since then has been engaged in the process of shutting the doors again once the giant winter sandstorm had passed. It is a peculiar Saudi paradox.

NOTES

1 *New York Times*, 22 September 1990.
2 *Washington Post*, 6 September 1990
3 Saudi TV, 9 August; *Daily Report*, 9 August; *Financial Times*, 16, 25 August; *New York Times*, 23 December 1990.
4 *New York Times*, 23 December 1990.
5 *Al-Riyad*, 14 August, 8 November; *Los Angeles Times*, 23 August; *al-Madina*, *al-Yawm*, 24 August 1990
6 Middle East News Agency, 11 August; *Daily Report*, 13 August; *Wash-*

ington Post, 5 September; *Ha'aretz*, 28 September; *New York Times*, 4 October 1990.

7 *New York Times*, 23 December 1990; *Economist*, 7 September 1991.

8 *Al-Jumhuriyya*, 12 February; *New York Times*, 13 February 1991.

9 *New Republic*, 6 May 1991.

10 *New York Times*, 13 February 1991.

11 Arab Press Service, 'Strategic Balance in the Middle East', 31 December 1985.

12 The Military Balance 1989, The International Institute of Strategic Studies, London; and The Military Balance 1989, the Jaffee Center for Strategic Studies, Tel Aviv University.

13 Saudi News Agency, 28 April; *Daily Report*, 30 April; *al-Riyad*, 14 March, 22 June; *al-Watan al-Arabi*, 6 July; *Washington Post*, 14 July; *Newsweek*, 29 July 1979

14 *International Herald Tribune*, 13 February 1991.

15 For a study of the issue, see Jacob Goldberg, 'The Saudi military build-up: strategy and risks', in *Middle East Review*, vol. 21, no. 3 (Spring 1989), pp. 3–13.

16 *International Herald Tribune*, 5 September, 11 October 1990.

17 *International Herald Tribune*, 13 February 1991.

18 *Washington Post*, 21 April 1991.

19 *Los Angeles Times*, 15 September; *Jerusalem Post*, 5 October; *Middle East Economic Digest*, 19 October; *New York Times*, 22 October 1990; *Ha'aretz*, 22 April 1991.

20 *Washington Post*, 21 April 1991.

21 *International Herald Tribune*, 13 February 1991.

22 Saudi Press Agency, 28 July; *Daily Report*, 30 July; *New York Times*, 1, 2, 3, 4, 5 August, 5 October 1990.

23 *Al-Riyad*, 14 August; *Washington Post*, 24 October; *New York Times*, 24, 27 October; *International Herald Tribune*, 25 October, 5 December; *al-Sharq al-Awsat*, 3 November 1990.

24 *Jerusalem Post*, 6 August; *New York Times*, 7 August, 22 September, 20 October; *Washington Post*, 6 September 1990.

25 *Al-Sharq al-Awsat*, 5, 24 September; *New York Post*, 14 September; Middle East News Agency, 27 September; *Daily Report*, 28 September; Saudi TV, 22 October; 23 October; *al-Madina*, 7 October; *al-Mustaqbal*, 31 October 1990.

26 *Ha'aretz*, 16 September; *New York Times*, 22 September; Agence France Presse, 4 November; *Daily Report*, 5 November; *International Herald Tribune*, 6, 19 December; *Washington Post*, 18 December 1990.

27 *New York Times*, 25 August; *Ukaz*, 8 October; *al-Wafd*, 15 October; *al-Sharq*, 18 October 1990.

28 *Los Angeles Times*, 22 February 1991.

29 *New York Times*, 5, 26 September, 3 October; *al-Sharq al-Awsat*, *Ha'aretz*, 24 September; *al-Dustur* (Amman), 27 September; *Daily Report*, 2 October; Radio Monte Carlo, 6 October; *Daily Report*, 9 October 1990.

30 *New York Times*, 20 October; *al-Riyad*, 23, 26 October 1990; *Los Angeles Times*, 22 February 1991.

31 *Al-Ahram*, 16 September; Radio Riyadh, 21 September, Radio Monte

Carlo, 22 September, Radio Sana'a, 23 September; *Daily Report*, 24 September; SPA, 6, 8 October; *Daily Report*, 8, 10 October; Agence France Presse, 8 October; *Daily Report*, 10 October; *New York Times*, 22 October 1990.

32 *Al-Akhbar, al-Jumhuriyya* (Cairo), *al-Ahram, al-Fajr*, 12 August; Agence France Presse, 13 August, 8 September; *Daily Report*, 15 August, 10 September; *New York Times*, 14, 25 August, 22 September; *Economist*, 14 September; *Ha'aretz*, 16 September 1990; *Los Angeles Times*, 22 February 1991.

33 Radio Tehran, 1 October; *Daily Report*, 3 October; Kuwaiti News Agency, 2 October; *Daily Report*, 4 October; *Al-Sharq al-Awsat*, 10 October; *Mideast Mirror*, 30 October; *Washington Post*, 2 November; *International Herald Tribune*, 3 November; Gulf News Agency (Manama), 23 December; *Daily Report*, 24 December 1990.

34 TASS, 23 August, 17 September; *Daily Report*, 25 August, 20 September; *Los Angeles Times*, 16, 18 September 1990.

35 *Washington Post*, 7 November 1990.

36 Salah al-Hasan, quoted in the *Wall Street Journal*, 2 May 1991.

37 Saudi Press Agency, 8 November; *Daily Report*, 9 November; *Financial Times*, 10 November 1990.

38 *Arab News*, 4 September; *New York Times*, 5 September 1990.

39 *New Republic*, 28 January 1991.

40 *Financial Times*, 20 August; *New York Times*, 24 August; *Arab News*, 25 August; *al-Madina*, 27 August; *Los Angeles Times*, 6 September; *International Herald Tribune*, 11 October 1990.

41 *Financial Times*, 20 August; *Los Angeles Times*, 6 September 1990.

42 *New York Times*, 7 November 1990.

43 *New York Times*, 7, 17 November; *Financial Times*, 13 November; *Los Angeles Times*, 15 November 1990.

44 *New York Times*, 2 March, 29 April, 12 May 1991.

45 *Al-Sharq al-Awsat*, 21 June 1991.

46 *New York Times*, 7 May 1991.

47 *New York Times*, 29 April 1991.

48 *New York Times*, 9 March, 29 April, 7 May 1991.

49 *New York Times*, 7, 12 May, 13 October; *Los Angeles Times*, 5 August 1991.

50 *Los Angeles Times*, 17 April 1991.

51 *New York Times*, 2 March 1991.

52 *New York Times*, 2 March, 8 May 1991.

53 *New York Times*, 9 March 1991.

54 *New York Times*, 2 March; *Ha'aretz*, 27 March; *Los Angeles Times*, 12 April 1991.

55 *New York Times*, 22 April, 12 May; *Los Angeles Times*, 11 May 1991.

56 *Los Angeles Times*, 11 May; *New York Times*, 12 May 1991.

57 *Los Angeles Times*, 11 May 1991.

58 *Ha'aretz*, 31 July, 29 September; Agence France Presse, 28 September; *Daily Report*, 30 September 1991.

59 *Daily Telegraph*, 29 September 1991.

60 *New York Times*, 8 May 1991.

61 Kiren Chaudhry, quoted in the *New York Times*, 10 March 1991.

62 Saudi Press Agency, 1 August; *Daily Report*, 3 August; *New York Times*, 6 August 1991.
63 Saudi TV, 5 March; *Daily Report*, 6 March 1991.
64 Saudi Press Agency, 8 November; *Daily Report*, 9 November; *Financial Times*, 10 November 1990.
65 *Los Angeles Times*, 30 April; *New York Times*, 8 May 1991.

5 The PLO

From Intifada to war and back

Menachem Klein

'With the end of the war, the Arab world enters a new era . . . The new reality in the Arab region is that there can be no return to the status quo ante'.[1] Thus did Dr Abdul Hadi Mahadi, one of the leading intellectuals in East Jerusalem, evaluate the situation at the beginning of 1991. How did the PLO enter the war? How did its spokesmen evaluate the war? And what was its influence upon the organization's internal structure and external policy? Using these questions as guidelines, I will try to examine in the following pages whether such a dramatic turnabout in PLO policy and outlook has in fact transpired.

The Gulf crisis occurred at a time when the Intifada, the uprising initiated by the inhabitants of the West Bank and Gaza in December 1987, had bogged down and faced its own crisis. Since the start of this century, when the Palestinian national movement first took shape, it has shown an ambivalence towards whether to emphasize internal Palestinian strength and self-reliance as opposed to relying upon broader outside support. Since the organization's liberation from Egyptian stewardship in 1968, the principle of self-reliance has served as the cornerstone of PLO policy, as further underlined by the initial stages of the uprising in 1987–88. In addition, the Intifada reinforced the trend of a more pragmatic orientation by the PLO, highlighted the distinctive Palestinian identity of the inhabitants of the territories, and strengthened their bond with the PLO. Symbolic of these developments is the 'Declaration of Palestinian Independence', adopted by the nineteenth session of the Palestine National Council (PNC). As long as the Intifada retained its momentum, the uprising fortified the self-image and standing of the PLO, while also building up the organization's expectations and hopes. However, from the second half of 1989 when the Intifada lost altitude and was beset by difficulties on the ground, further compounded by dissatisfaction at the limited support given by the outside world, the PLO organization entered a phase of radicalization, and, in seeking some sort of a breakthrough, fastened its hopes upon an external force, namely Saddam Hussein.

Among the possible reasons for this shift away from self-reliance in favour of an outside leader: a perceptible decline in mass public participation on the part of local Palestinians as well as in media coverage of the Intifada-related activity; Israel's success in mitigating the level of violence directed against her; the failure of the 'Popular Committees' to set up the foundations for an independent government; and finally, the absence of any political process since the end of 1989. Particularly worrying was the inability of the Palestinians or of the PLO to impose uniform rules of operation. There was a marked failure to establish basic institutions acceptable to the various Palestinian factions within the community and possessing the authority to determine (a) who is permitted to act against parties suspected of collaboration with Israel, and (b) the nature of the punishment. Such clarification is so necessary in the case of a civil uprising precisely because of the fact that out of the several hundred executions enacted by *ad hoc* 'shock committees' against 'collaborators' a high percentage were groundless and justified by 'confessions' made under duress and torture in settling old personal accounts and disputes. Taken together, these phenomena provoked the wrath of the population and generated criticism against Yasser Arafat and the PLO.

In this setting of acrimony and disarray, a strong leader could yet reinspire the Intifada and force the Palestinians to regroup. Such a person might disabuse those who were coming to believe the PLO and the Palestinians had no choice but to abide by the dictates of Israel and the United States. Similarly, he would be able to mobilize masses and governments in support of Palestinian rights – in the name of Arab solidarity, and on behalf of a common Arab identity and fate.

Saddam Hussein's ascendance in the second half of 1990 as an Iraqi leader with pan-Arabic designs thus seemed most fortuitous. His threats to deploy non-conventional arms against Israel, his bold invasion of Kuwait in August 1990, and his direct confrontation with the USA, seemed on the surface to supply the PLO leaders and the Palestinian public at large with the very exemplar they had been looking for and so desperately needed. Accordingly, seizure of Kuwait was offered as confirmation of the Intifada's success in breaking beyond the limited confines of Palestine, and as a symbol of the Arab awakening for which they, the Palestinians and the PLO, had provided the spark.

With but two exceptions, the PLO was unanimous in its initial support for Saddam's unilateral initiative.[2] PLO spokesmen insisted that with Iraq's help the organization could end Israel's domination, and possibly even attain political parity with her. This new balance of power in the region, backed by the military option Iraq now conferred upon the Arabs, would, in their view, bear fruit in the political sphere by diminishing at one and the same time both the power of Israel and of the USA.[3]

Based on this line of reasoning, therefore, from the beginning the PLO sided with Saddam Hussein, calling for linkage between the settlement of the problem in Kuwait and the Palestinian problem. No less important was the PLO's demand that the West enact measures against Israel comparable to those enacted against Iraq, 'the putative aggressor'. The PLO viewed failure by the West to condemn Israel as an aggressor and occupier in her own right as proof of a double standard traceable to classical imperialism's anti-Arab prejudice. Spokesmen for the organization even went so far as to praise Saddam Hussein for having wiped out Kuwait's 'reactionary' leadership, a leadership which abstained from supporting wholeheartedly the Intifada in a manner proportionate to Kuwait's ample resources and assets.[4] This rationalism is seen in the words of one spokesman who explained his organization's commitment to the 'creation of a new geopolitical map in the region . . . and to the creation of a new military map' replacing the existing order wherein 'Israel is the regional power, and our people lack bona-fide Arab depth'.[5] PLO policy during the Kuwait crisis was therefore guided in some measure by instrumentalist–rational considerations.

Also, more than at any other time in the recent past, or at least since the start of the Intifada, use was made of symbols of identity, self-identification and belonging. Borrowed from radical Palestinian-Arab national mythology, this expressive search for 'real Arab depth' in Palestinian identity and in the opposing conception of the Americans as 'modern crusaders'[6] was distinctly evident in the manifestos that circulated support for Yasser Arafat, Saddam Hussein, and the deeds of the PLO's leaders.

These expressions of collective Arab identity, of mythical images and of past tragedy, on the other hand, cast a dark shadow upon alternative conceptions of distinctive Palestinian identity and upon the rational-instrumental foundation of policy. In the expressive-Arab solidarity model, the world was divided into two poles: 'us' versus 'them', and 'good' versus 'bad'. Here could be found at least a partial answer to recent Palestinian despair and weakness, as well as a source of strength and of hope. Inspiration, in other words, could be found emotionally in perceiving one's self belonging to a good and just collective. With the advent of the Kuwait crisis, therefore, the mainstream PLO sought to balance two alternative approaches: the rational-instrumentalist view, and the expressive-solidarity view. Regarding the former, it also tried to juggle between pragmatic and radical tendencies.[7]

Since the war, the PLO has had to face a different set of pressing problems demanding immediate answers. These include the perilous status of Palestinians still in Kuwait, or the plight of those thousands forced to leave in the wake of the fighting and anti-Palestinian discrimination. How to cope with the economic damage caused by the war and the halting of financial help previously extended the PLO by the Gulf states is another urgent matter. So, too, the organization's need to respond to the Madrid peace conference and US–Arab–Israel initiative. Equally vexing for the PLO are two other longer-term, retrospective questions. First, how to assess PLO and Palestinian achievements, but also failures during the Gulf War? Second, to what extent the Gulf War was really terminated with the ceasefire? or whether it might be continuing today, even years later, but in a different version with they, the Palestinians, having become the main target for American highhandedness and aggressive behaviour? In other words, have the Palestinians been forced back into their own restricted war, the Intifada, and without any outside Arab patronage; or, because the Gulf War introduced fundamental change to the Middle East as a whole, has the Intifida possibly taken on a different character and altogether new dimensions?

WAS IT A MISTAKE?

Since the war, Palestinian spokesmen have willingly addressed themselves to positions adopted at the time of the crisis. Their commentary points to a significant contrast. In the late 1980s, virtually every PLO policy measure tended to stir controversy among organization members and the Palestinian public; whereas, since August 1990, there has been little if any such internal split. Unity between the people and its leaders was steeled in the test of war, such spokesmen claim. Putting aside factionalism, the PLO and the Palestinian public are depicted as having stood as one with Iraq in opposition to the USA and Israel. Moreover, in this uncritical view, Iraq is claimed to have achieved genuine military gains.

First, despite the heavy casualties and damage, and while confronted by ultra-modern technology, it was not entirely routed. Second, the American goal of repressing Iraq, the most promising

Arab military threat to American–Israeli hegemony in the region, was not achieved. The term 'mother of wars' (*Um Al-Maarik*), coined by Saddam Hussein, is used repeatedly by PLO analysts when discussing the war. In their estimate, a third international war in effect had been conducted against Arabs and Muslims; but:

> For the first time in Arab history in the modern era, and perhaps for the first time in world history, a small Third World state withstood a political and economic siege without collapsing totally, and endured threat after threat. Iraq survived these threats and an alliance of over thirty states. It taught the world a double lesson: the meaning of national self-respect, and the meaning of strategy.[8]

Third, and not to be disparaged, the Scud missiles had deflated Israel's security conception emphasizing the strategic value of Judea and Samaria, while damaging Israeli deterrence. A fourth plus for Palestinians is the definite linkage, despite American and Israeli attempts to the contrary, established between finding solutions to the Gulf Crisis and the Palestinian problem. In the final analysis, therefore, organization spokesmen are convinced that supporting Iraq was not a mistake.[9] One thus reviews the Palestinian press and literature in vain for expressions of regret.

Immediately after the war, the PLO line continued to describe American action during the conflict in terms consonant with the classical portrait of imperialism. The USA aspires to set up a new order in the Middle East: to take control over the region, divide it, transform it into a prime market for American military products, guarantee for the West oil at cheap prices as well as military bases, and perpetuate Israel's proxy position. Consistent with this interpretation, in the course of the crisis the USA dominated the UN and managed, by intimidation or enticement, to harness to its side well-entrenched Arab regimes. By its behaviour, America resembled imperialist Britain during World War I, when it mobilized the Hashemite family and the ibn Saud dynasty. The Gulf War thus exposed the true extent to which the USA threatens the Arabs, and the degree to which America is prepared to intervene in Arab internal affairs. The United States is portrayed as having established a satanic alliance (*Hilf Al-Taghut*) against the Arabs, a coalition of modern Tartars that wrought destruction on Iraq. Worth mentioning are the pains PLO propagandists take to avoid attributing the damage inflicted on Iraq to Saddam Hussein or to his misguided policies; instead, they put the full burden solely upon the West.[10]

WHICH WAR IS BEING WAGED NOW

By way of contrast to this consensus, in the second debate over which struggle the Palestinians ought to commit themselves to at present, two opposing streams in the PLO are evident: one emphasizing the Gulf War and the Iraqi cause, the other the Intifada. Both schools of thought have urged the establishment leadership to adopt their respective positions.

The 'hawkish' opposition of the 'Popular Front for the Liberation of Palestine' led by George Habash, segments of the 'Democratic Front for the Liberation of Palestine' led by Secretary-General Naif Hawatme, and the radical wing of Fatah directed by Faruq al-Qadumi were all convinced that while Iraq was the principal target of the war, it was not the only target. Ultimately, the war was directed against the Palestinians and the PLO because of the support Iraq had been giving the PLO and its claims that the USA was determined to liquidate Iraq's military strength. Hence, the war continues in a new phase. Furthermore, radical elements in the PLO insisted the war had exposed a grave schism in the Arab world marked by a pivotal Arab state, Syria, joining the American-Zionist enemy. So long as Syria did not revert to its previous 'nationalist' Arab position, the PLO should not embark on the political path opened by US Secretary of State Baker, which under existing circumstances, meant nothing less than national and political suicide. In their view, it is unrealistic to expect the USA to compel Israeli withdrawal from the occupied territories in a manner similar to what was forced upon Iraq; the USA, these radicals claim, clearly distinguishes between Iraq and Israel. The USA sides with Israel, whereas she is hostile toward Iraq and the Arabs. So, too, is it naive to trust the United States, as America wishes to split the 'internal' Palestinians (inhabitants of the occupied territories), from 'external' parties (members of the PLO establishment in Tunis), just as it had consciously divided the Arab countries during the Gulf War, or as it had forced them to accept the Camp David formula which ignored the national rights of the Palestinians.

From this analysis and interpretation, it now followed that the PLO must veto American political directives, while strengthening ties with Russia. By the same reasoning, the PLO is advised to strengthen the organizational rank and file, by reforming its structure and operations (see below); by strengthening the Intifada; by establishing a tactical alliance with Palestinian Muslim fundamentalists, Hamas and the Islamic Jihad, against the Western enemy and its Israeli partner; and by waiting until the Arab world undergoes a transformation, and

Syria resumes a role of leadership in the 'nationalist camp'. In the opinion of the 'hawks', the full impact of the Gulf War on the region has not yet been felt. Just as the Palestinian War did not end with the Six-Day War in 1967, the glorious chapters of the Gulf War are still to unfold, and will be written only in the future.[11]

Pitted against this school of thought was a 'dovish' opposition comprised of moderates in the Fatah under the charge of Haled al-Hassn and Nabil Shath, and a section of the 'Democratic Front', led by Yassir Abed Rabbo, Naif Hawatme's former number-two man. It was their primary contention that the Gulf War had passed them by. Iraq was vanquished, meaning the Palestinians could not rely any longer on Baghdad's leadership or military strength. While the Gulf War had certainly left its mark, the Palestinians now had no choice but to return to their own parochial cause and local war, the Intifada.

The 'doves' are also convinced that the USA demonstrated it is the only global superpower. In their view, the Americans are sincere about their intention to establish a permanent settlement in the region; adding that, if the Palestinians do not make a stand at this point of time, it is more than likely that they will be excluded from the new regional order. The 'doves' do not appraise the international situation as grave and gloomy; unlike the 'hawks', they are not convinced of the Palestinians' inability to determine their future. On the contrary, the 'doves' maintain that the war put the Palestinians and the PLO in an excellent position to enter the political process. Linkage, after all, has been established between the problem in the Gulf and the Palestinian problem; making it possible to compel Israeli withdrawal in a manner similar to the Iraqi evacuation.

Encouragement also derived from President Bush's statement before the US Congress on 6 March 1991, declaring that the USA supports the principle of territories for peace, recognizes the legitimate political rights of the Palestinians, and is inclined to believe that Security Council Resolutions 242 and 338 ought to be applied to the West Bank and to the Gaza Strip. The 'doves' reason that a determined President Bush will be able to impose his position on Israel with no significant opposition from a defensive Jewish lobby. They are even convinced that for all its failures the Intifada has accomplished a number of successes; most importantly, the uprising transferred the confrontation with Israel to the territories, enhancing the independent decision-making ability of the PLO. Today, due to the Intifada, the PLO is liberated more than before from Arab world schemes or dictates; nor can the pact between the USA and Egypt, Syria and Saudi Arabia be allowed to weaken its hand.

Nevertheless, optimism by the 'doves' is not unrestrained. Along with their effusions of optimism in the international sphere, they express a large measure of pessimism in regard to the Palestinians' ability to oppose Israeli actions. In their view, Israel's strength has increased as a result of the infusion of Soviet Jews to Israel, and Jerusalem has acted vigorously to expand the Jewish presence and settlements in the territories. Thus, in May 1991, Haled al-Hassn argued at the central council meeting that the Palestinians must leap out and grab any proposal and capitalize upon any possibility that might result in Israel's withdrawal from the territories; indeed, only in this fashion would it ever be possible to save the homeland.[12] In the opinion of the 'doves', the PLO must adopt a dynamic foreign policy in order to regain Western sympathy and renew pressure on Israel. The organization is called upon to outline its political programme since November 1988, defining exactly how the Jordanian–Palestinian confederation is to function, and precisely how the PLO can be incorporated into the Baker peace initiative and longer negotiating process initially as part of a joint Jordanian–Palestinian delegation, and later as an equal actor with full rights.

Where does the PLO mainstream, Arafat-led establishment stand in this argumentation? In an emotional, political and intellectual sense, it was difficult for the mainstream to distinguish clearly between the policy of the United States during the war and her political behaviour towards the Palestinians both before the war and after it. This difficulty was exacerbated by the fact that the top leadership had itself orchestrated and encouraged the flow of Palestinian support towards Saddam Hussein.

From March to May 1991, the mainstream found itself closer to 'hawks' who were openly hostile to the USA than to 'doves' who were suspicious of America yet believed only Washington could bring about a full Israeli withdrawal.[13]

In May 1991, however, the argumentation changed. In a style akin to the orientation of the 'doves', spokesmen of the PLO mainstream stopped addressing the actions of the USA during the war, and started focusing on America's likely postwar policy towards the Palestinians. Editorials began to ask questions such as: 'will the American programme bring about peace?' 'what are the parameters of the American effort to foster a just peace?'[14] This notable change in the nature of the ideological and strategic debate derived, first and foremost, from the new reality. Iraq was vanquished, Secretary of State James Baker's proposal for the convocation of a regional peace conference had been put forward, and the majority of the leaders in the occupied territories joined forces with establishment 'doves' in the PLO in insisting they be allowed to respond to Secretary of State Baker's April 1991 proposal, and be permitted to meet with him and discuss their participation in the proposed conference. Yasser Arafat's consent was given because the pressure upon the establishment was great, and because a green light for such meetings did not involve an unacceptable political price. In subsequent Arab–Israeli-related conversations, leaders from the territories appeared as representatives of the organization, not as alternative leaders; and, the PLO could claim that a renewal of the dialogue between them and the USA, suspended in May 1990, had now resulted from these meetings with Secretary Baker. Conversely, Syria's positive response in July 1991 to the American-proposed initiative for the convocation of a regional peace conference, coupled with Soviet support for the initiative, significantly upset calculations of the 'hawks'. Moreover, with Syrian participation in the conference, the danger that the political process might begin without the PLO became quite palpable.

THE ESTABLISHMENT AGAINST THE OPPOSITION: NEW LINES OF DIVISION

The polarized division of opinion over external policy among the two principal hawkish and dovish opposition factions becomes less significant once the context shifts to internal PLO affairs. An interesting unanimity of opinion exists between the 'Popular Front', the two factions of the 'Democratic Front', the moderate and radical opposition in Fatah, and the majority of representatives of the 'internal' Palestinian public in the occupied territories: all call for reform of PLO institutions and in the organization's working procedures. The gist of these demands can be summarized as follows.

1 The 'fronts' demand that the establishment respond to their call for rebuilding institutions on an egalitarian basis compatible with the structure of the 'United National Command' in the occupied territories, replacing the current arrangement in which Fatah, the foremost entity among PLO organizations, enjoys wide prerogative powers. While the opposition to Yasser Arafat among the Fatah ranks may not be all that enthusiastic about this trend of reducing Fatah's share of authority, still this group is supportive of the fronts' criticism of Arafat's 'Napoleonic' brand of leadership; and, together with the fronts, this group is searching for a way to lessen his authority.

2 Most opposition groups believe that the composition of the Palestinian National Congress (PNC) should be changed by means of a general election in which all Palestinians, wherever they are, would participate. Alternatively, should such elections be impractical, as the PLO establishment and the 'popular front' charge, then members of the Council should be appointed (a practice since the PLO was founded in 1964) but with the main criterion for appointment the candidate's standing with the public, and not his organizational or personal loyalty. The Abed Rabbo section of the 'Democratic Front' even proposes to treat committees of the PNC as permanent, and calls for reducing the national council from about 400 to 100 members, thereby converting it into a fully-functioning parliament supervising the actions of the PLO executive committee. However, the 'Popular Front' and the PLO establishment counter by claiming that the idea of elections is not feasible, since the necessary organizational foundations for elections, such as electoral lists, population registration, electoral laws and a citizenship law, are still not in place. In addition to this logistical problem, also cited is a more basic difficulty: are Palestinian inhabitants of Jordan or Israel to be allowed to vote? A negative decision would contradict fundamental PLO values, for it would mean giving up authority for major segments of the Palestinian people and consenting to their separation from the homeland.

3 Not satisfied with the 1988 decision of the PNC which delegated the powers of a provisional government to the PLO executive committee, with the exception of the 'Popular Front', the opposition demands that the establishment create a provisional government with both representational and operational authority. The reasons compelling the opposition groups to demand this differ from group to group, as do their specific proposals regarding the provisional government's composition. The 'doves' favour these changes because they want to incorporate the PLO in the political process, and they want to bring about some erosion in Yasser Arafat's power; Naif Hawatme, the 'hawk', favours the changes only because of the latter. As a member of Fatah, Haled al-Hassn proposes the establishment of a 'mixed' government composed of 'inside' representatives (within the occupied territories) and 'outside' representatives, but still dominated by the present establishment in which Fatah retains final authority.

In contrast, Hawatme and members of the Abed Rabbo group support a government whose members will come mostly from 'inside', whose decisions will be enacted on a majority basis rather than a consensus verdict (as the case stands today within the PLO executive committee), and which will be entrusted with administering civilian matters concerning West Bank and Gaza inhabitants. At least two wings of the 'Popular Front' hope this structure can be utilized to prevent Fatah from attaining unchallenged status in the territories. The 'Popular Front's' opposition derives from its doctrinal approach and tactical constraints. It aims at damaging Arafat and Arafat's camp, yet without impairing the PLO's ability to function as the central ruling power. In its view, attaining ultimate PLO aspirations depends on the existence of an authoritative central leadership, which prevents it from striking against the establishment even when disagreeing with specific policies.

4 Apart from the 'Popular Front', all of the opposition groups, and especially leaders from the occupied territories, call for a change in the existing pattern of relations between leaders from the 'outside' and leaders from the 'inside'. In their view, 'inside' leaders must take a far more central part in determining PLO policy, and not merely settling for a consultative role. Moreover, the PLO is called upon to grant a larger degree of freedom of activity to people and institutions in the occupied territories. Several spokesmen for the 'inside' forces even call for a transformation of the 'United National Command' by which it will become a 'popular government' entrusted with operational powers. In response to these demands, spokesmen for the establishment claim that relationships between the 'outside' and the 'inside' have already changed as a result of meetings between representatives of the territories and Secretary Baker that preceded convening of the Madrid conference.

5 While the opposition as a whole is satisfied neither with the administration of the Intifada nor with the PLO's part in it, here, too, opinion is divided over the alternatives. The 'Popular Front', Naif Hawatme's faction in the 'Democratic Front', and the radicals in Fatah endorse an increase in the 'armed struggle', be it in the framework of the Intifada uprising, or under the PLO's direct command. On the other hand, the Abbed Rabbo faction in the 'Democratic Front', the moderates in Fatah, and leaders of the Palestinian public in the occupied territories demand less emphasis on demonstrative, outward-oriented activity, and more effort towards the goal of spreading practical self-help institutions and establishing an independent economic base.

In their view, everyday life should be normalized, the frequent trade strikes and general strikes causing huge economic losses should be brought to a halt, local production should be enlarged, and strong professional unions and trade boards should be established along with social and educational institutions and elected regional councils – even in collaboration with Israel. 'Here [in the occupied territories] it is, at last, understood that insofar as the Intifada stands apart by its own powers as an isolated event, it will never bring the Palestinians independence. The war and the defeat [in the Gulf- M.K.] transpired while the Intifada was in the throes of a difficult stage'.[15] These groups believe an independent economic base will allow inhabitants of the territories to separate themselves from Israel while forming the indispensable infrastructure for a Palestinian state.[16]

The argument and viewpoints are not new. They have been found in their present form really since the beginning of the 1980s; the agonizing and debate, have however, increased since the outbreak of the Intifada.[17] Like the Intifada preceding it, the Gulf War did not cause a turnabout in PLO positions; but it has certainly accelerated intellectual and political processes begun earlier. In the past also there were clear distinctions between the ruling establishment and those in opposition, but, these lines were primarily organizational. Fatah was identified with the establishment, and the opposition was identified with the 'Fronts'. After the Gulf War, however, the traditional divisions between different organizations, as well as the gap between 'the inside' and 'the outside', narrowed considerably. Instead of these lines of division, a new distinction between a conservative establishment and a reformist opposition emerged.

At first, the response made by the PLO establishment to the opposition claims was defensive. The establishment deferred by insisting each proposal be considered very carefully, also its practicality examined; the claim was also heard that in any case several of the demands had already been met. As long as external developments were not urgent and did not force unequivocal choices, the establishment remained defensive. But when Syria, Jordan, and Israel gave positive responses to the Baker initiative the PLO was finally compelled to make some difficult choices, and to make them quickly, about whether, and how, to accept terms put before it: no direct PLO participation in the peace conference, non-inclusion (at least during the first stage of the discussions) of a representative from East Jerusalem, and subsuming Palestinians within a joint delegation with Jordan. Forced to concentrate exclusively on the diplomatic front, questions of internal reform were pushed off the top of the agenda; and in the process, the previously repressed split between 'doves' and 'hawks' within the ranks of the PLO was suddenly exposed. In an atmosphere of policy disarray the twentieth session of the PNC was convened in September 1991. Its discussions were largely devoted to formulating the PLO's affirmative position towards convocation of a Middle East regional peace conference. Various proposals tabled for reforming the structure, composition and authority of the council were left unaddressed, nor were operational aspects of PLO armed activity and resistance considered with any measure of seriousness.

While it might seem, on the surface, that PLO matters have returned to their familiar course, it is nevertheless reasonable to expect that the PLO has been undergoing a quiet process of gradual politicization that is nonetheless far more accelerated and profound than similar processes in the past.

From an historical point of view, the PLO's main achievement since its inception, beyond sheer survival, has been the marked success in rebuilding a political centre that had all but collapsed in the period between 1939–49, and the equally impressive success in winning Palestinian, pan-Arab and international recognition. Fostering a national identity in the case of the Palestinian national movement has preceded the process of building a society and its institutions; similarly, the process of politicization in the PLO has been based, in the main, upon the organization's record of achievement in the sphere of foreign relations. PLO gains in cultural, economic, and social spheres pale by comparison with its political attainments.

In the final analysis, the PLO may have created a national consciousness and assured a political focus; but it did not, however, build a society made up of fully developed, diverse institutions. The Gulf War and the decline in the PLO's political status in the pan-Arab and international arenas needs to be seen as having harmed the organization precisely in the one sphere where it prided itself in having attained the largest number of goals.

True, the decision taken by the twentieth session of the PNC to 'honor the present peace efforts and to relate to them positively'[18] improved the PLO's status and the personal standings of leaders in the PLO establishment. However, the need for institutional and political reforms was merely deferred, not nullified. To the extent the veteran establishment does not learn to integrate leaders from the occupied territories, it can expect to lose a large measure of its power and political authority. In addition, the organization may become little more than a reserve for purely symbolic leadership that enjoys a kind of moral standing founded exclusively on past historical achievement.

Present and future political developments dictate internal reorganization; so, too, must the areas of activity widen and the operational ability of its centre be improved. While the motives behind the claims of the various opposition groups are obviously political and expedient, there is nevertheless a foundation to their demands. Whatever the exact nature of the reform of the PNC, the call for internal reform is founded upon objective necessity: a state cannot be built only from the top. The difficulties with the Intifada uprising, the collapse of the support-base in Iraq *during* the Gulf War, and the political process inaugurated in the Middle East *after* the Gulf War further aggravate this necessity, making it more urgent now than ever before. Future conflicts within the PLO, therefore, can be expected to centre on the two following questions. The first is the extent to which the process of politicization, the establishment of institutions and the decentralization of powers will be administered and controlled by the existing establishment. The second is the degree to which the current opponents of the mainstream will succeed in constricting the political power of Chairman Arafat and his existing establishment, or perhaps whether new faces and forces might emerge to join the top echelons of the PLO and to change its power structure.

THE PRICE OF MESSIANISM

The majority of Palestinians viewed the Gulf War as something of a political, messianic event necessitated by the general climate of distress and disillusionment. Far from a catastrophic mentality or a martyrology, this was a distinctly optimistic brand of Messianism.

But like any other Messianic form, Palestinian Arab Messianic politics have exacted a high price from its adherents, especially when they experienced such a crushing defeat. The difficulties experienced in the Intifada and the Gulf War have created in the traditional PLO leadership a sharp measure of cognitive dissonance. The arguments traced in the discussion above can be seen as their attempt to choose the least costly way of coping with this dissonance. Should misguided positions that the organization took during the war continue to be denied, along with the bitter results of the war? How should the events that transpired be interpreted as historical experience? Should the political behaviour, and the structure, of the PLO be altered for the purpose of minimizing the damage? There can be no doubt that this process of awakening to sober realities is painful, once the true dimensions of the post-Gulf War political reality really thrust themselves upon the PLO, as is attested to by the acute internal soul-searching that took place in the PLO during the months March–September 1991, and the quasi-official statements of Palestinians in support of the conspiracy attempt perpetrated in the USSR during August of the same year.

The limited extent to which the Gulf War events succeeded in transforming the consciousness of the PLO and of Palestinians in general can be gleaned from the discussions and the decisions of the twentieth session of the PNC. During the last week of September 1991, the period of the convocation of the session, the Iraqis were engaged in frustrating the efforts of a UN inspection team that had come to search for evidence of nuclear weapons programmes, in compliance with the terms of the ceasefire agreement of the Gulf War, to which the UN delivered an ultimatum to Iraq and the USA sent Patriot missile launchers to Saudi Arabia. Yet the council's discussions proceeded uninfluenced by the increase in tension in relations between the USA and Iraq; nor did council decisions in any way reflect these larger exigencies. As far as the Palestinians and the PLO were concerned, the Gulf War had ended; in 1992 and beyond, Palestinian preoccupations as well as expectations of outside support were sharply narrowed in a process of turning inward.

NOTES

1 Dr Abdul Hadi Mahadi, 'Post Gulf War assessment: a Palestinian assessment of the Gulf War and its aftermath', *Palestinian Assessments of the Gulf War and its Aftermath*, Passia, Jerusalem, 1991, p. 122.
2 Haled Al-Hassan, who opposed vociferously, and Mahmud Abbas (Abu-Mazin), who opposed in a more muted manner.
3 *Al-Siyasa* (Kuwait) 26 October 1990.
4 *Filastin al-Thaura*, 26 October 1990, pp. 20–4.
5 Ibid., pp. 21–4.
6 Ibid., p. 20.
7 For an extended discussion, see my monograph: 'The PLO and the Intifada: from euphoria to trouble', Dayan Center, Tel-Aviv University, 1991 (in Hebrew).
8 *Filastin al-Thaura*, 3 March 1991, p. 17.
9 *Rayat al-Istiglal*, 1 April 1991, pp. 15–21, 69–71; *Filastin al-Thaura*, 17 March 1991, pp. 4–7, 12; Ibid., 3 March 1991, pp. 10–11; Ibid., 17 February 1991, Arafat's letter of 9 February 1991.
10 *Rayat al-Istiglal*, April 1991, pp. 4–6, 7–11, 21–2; *Filastin al-Thaura*, 17 February 1991, pp. 6–7; The Central Council of the PLO in its declaration of 23 April 1991, Ibid., 28 April 1991, pp. 4–5; Ibid. 27 January 1991, 3 February 1991, 10 February 1991, in which the term 'mother of wars' is deployed frequently.
11 *Rayat al-Istiglal*, April 1991, pp. 28–32; *Filastin al-Thaura*, 3 March 1991, pp. 10–11, 16–17; 17 March 1991, pp. 10–11, 14–15.

12 *Rayat al-Istiglal*, June 1991, p. 27.

13 *Filastin al-Thaura*, 28 April 1991; 24 March 1991; 17 February 1991; The Central Council of the PLO in its Declaration of 23 April 1991; Ibid, 28 April 1991.

14 *Filastin al-Thaura*, 12 May 1991; 19 May 1991; 28 July 1991; 9 June 1991.

15 Ghasan al-Hatib in *Rayat al-Istiglal*, April 1991, pp. 33–4.

16 For discussions of the economic damage incurred by residents of the occupied territories during the war, and the significant drop in their incomes and standard of living, see Hulaileh Samir, 1991 (Note 1) pp. 35–52; Rayat al-Istiglal, April 1991, pp. 28–32; 39–57; 59; 4–6; June 1991, pp. 26–30; *Filastin al-Thaura*, 21 April 1991, p. 13.

17 Klein, 'The PLO and the Intifada', See Note 7.

18 *al-Quds*, 29 September 1991.

6 Migrants and refugees
The human toll[1]

Elizabeth N. Offen

INTRODUCTION

The Iraqi aggression against Kuwait triggered a devastating chain of sequences, including one of this century's largest and most widespread migrations. By some accounts more than 5.5 million people from forty countries were temporarily or permanently displaced by the Gulf War of 1990–91.

The human toll of the war includes thousands of lives lost, not just soldiers but thousands of Kurds, and some Asian and Arab refugees.[2] The costs, however, cannot simply be counted in lost lives. The uprooting of millions of people wreaked havoc on the economies of the world, domestic and international. Fleeing migrants lost wages, savings, property, and suffered the extreme psychological and physical trauma of being displaced. Few returning migrants have job prospects, given high unemployment in their countries of origin, and many will seek to return to the Gulf or elsewhere in order to earn a living. With millions of families dependent on remittances, the sudden return of migrants caused enormous social upheaval, including ethnic conflict threatening the stability of states from India to Turkey to Egypt.

MIGRATION OVERVIEW

The waves of migration from the Gulf War of 1990–91 can be broken down into three phases which roughly represent the periods before, during and after the war. During the first phase from Iraq's 2 August 1990 invasion of Kuwait until the US-led coalition's military response in January 1991, nearly 2 million people fled countries in the Gulf region, including: 750,000–1 million Egyptians; 380,000 Kuwaitis; 250,000–300,000 Palestinians/Jordanians; 350,000 Asians. This figure does not include those, particularly Asians, stranded at borders. In addition, an estimated one million Yemenis left Saudi Arabia under political pressure and returned home to Yemen (the remainder left later on and apparently not during this first phase).

The second phase of migration occurred shortly after Saddam relinquished control of Kuwait. During this time an estimated 65,000 people fled the region, including: 35,000 Iraqis who went to Iran, and 28,000 Asians and Arabs returning to their native countries. Other foreign workers continued to stream out of the region over the next few months; the thousands still stranded at borders and in refugee camps unable to leave the region are not included in these figures. A considerable number of foreign workers chose to wait out the war in Iraq and Kuwait, particularly labourers from Lebanon, which reduced the numbers during this second migration phase.[3]

The third phase of migration occurred from mid-March to early April 1991, the period of Iraq's civil strife. During this time an estimated 1.5–2 million Kurds left Iraq for Turkey and Iran. In addition, 100,000 Iraqis (non-Kurds) also fled the area, and an estimated 700,000–800,000 Iraqi Shi'ite Muslims were also reported to have entered Iran or established camps on the border.

Migration flows out of the region divided into the above phases can also be analysed as outflows from a particular country. This allows one to examine the particular exit (and entrance) policies of a particular country. Also, migration from Kuwait was very different in character from the flow out of Iraq where exit was restricted for highly political reasons and thousands were held as hostages inside the country. And both of these outflows contrast with the virtual expulsion from Saudi Arabia of ethnic Arab migrants whose governments held differing political views of the war. Similarly, the flood of migrants into Jordan was quite different from the flow into Turkey, due to disparities in volume and absorptive capacity.

MIGRATION FLOWS BY COUNTRY

The massive displacement of people as a result of Iraq's invasion of Kuwait is arguably the most striking effect of the crisis. Over 1.5 million people were displaced from Kuwait, another 2 million from Iraq, and, in addition, the domino effect in Saudi Arabia and elsewhere dislocated approximately 2 million people. This uprooting of 3.5 million people between 2 August 1990 and January 1991 has vast economic as well as geopolitical significance, because they constituted the majority of the foreign labour force in Iraq, Kuwait and Saudi Arabia. Indeed, more than half of the residents in Kuwait were of foreign origin.

Kuwait

Prior to the occupation, Kuwait had a population of 2.2 million, of whom an estimated 750,000–800,000 were ethnic Kuwaitis. Fortunately, at the time of the occupation it was the holiday season, and an estimated 200,000 Kuwaitis were holidaying abroad. Of those 550,000–600,000 Kuwaitis in Kuwait, approximately a third to a half left the country very quickly when Iraq invaded, taking up exile in Saudi Arabia, Egypt, Bahrain, the UAE, Oman, and Qatar, where they were joined by Kuwaitis on holiday returning to the region to monitor the situation more closely. Thus the migration of Kuwaitis into neighbouring Gulf countries was greater than the emigration spawned by the crisis itself. The second type of outflow of Kuwaitis resulted from their forced removal into Iraq. These Kuwaiti prisoners of war returned to their country in slow streams from late February 1991 through mid-May, many on foot. The majority of Kuwaitis in other Gulf countries and in Europe did not return to Kuwait, however, until the end of summer 1991, in part because the government needed time to restore sewerage, electricity, telephone and other basic services and requested that only skilled workers return immediately. In addition, given their comfortable financial positions, most chose to stay abroad while reconstruction took place in Kuwait.

Kuwait relied heavily on foreign labour for its workforce, from doctors, teachers and engineers to carpenters and household servants. In return, Kuwait offered many attractive opportunities and was one of the few Gulf countries to allow families to migrate together. Also part of the second crisis outflow from Kuwait, the emigration of Asians was considerable.

Hundreds of thousands of Bangladeshis, Sri Lankans, Filipinos and Indians fled Kuwait after the occupation. Table 6.1 shows the number of migrants in the region before 2 August 1990, those still stranded by 22 September, and those stranded in the region as of 7 December 1990. On 22 September there were still 70,000 Indians in Kuwait, and by December only 16,000–18,000 remained. In September 80,000 Sri Lankans remained, in December, 65,000 were still stranded due to limited resources which restricted their ability to leave. Of an estimated 15,000 Filipinos in Kuwait by 7 December all but 3,500 had left.

How particular Asian populations left the region, which border they fled to and the timing of their departure was determined by reports they received about open borders and the capability of their respective governments to bring them home quickly. As the numbers show, the

Table 6.1 Stranded foreigners in Kuwait (Estimates from foreign embassies and the US State Department)

Country	Before 2 August 1990[1]	22 September 1990[2]			7 December 1990[3]		
		Kuwait	Iraq	Total	Kuwait	Iraq	Total
Australia	127	50	44	94	50	26	76
Austria	140	1	3 or 4	4 or 5	1	3 or 4	4 or 5
Bangladesh	110,000	20,000	10,000	30,000	N.A.	N.A.	15,000
Belgium	59	7	38	45	5	0	5
Brazil	450	N.A.	N.A.	N.A.	N.A.	N.A.	40
Britain	4,000	1,000	430	1,430	590	720	1,310
Bulgaria	N.A.	N.A.	N.A.	N.A.	N.A.	N.A.	370
Canada	800	50	50	100	11	31	42
China	10,000	4,800	N.A.	N.A.	N.A.	N.A.	4,800
Cyprus	35	N.A.	N.A.	20	N.A.	N.A.	20
Czechoslovakia	470	6	157	163	6	40	46
Denmark	100	35	41	76	0	16	16
Egypt[4]	1.6 million	N.A.	N.A.	288,000	N.A.	N.A.	1.2 million
Finland	46	4	21	25	2	3	5
France	560	100	260	360	most have left		–
Germany	1,000	N.A.	N.A.	N.A.	0	15	15
Greece	127	29	36	65	N.A.	N.A.	3
Hungary	178	0	32	32	0	32	32
India[5]	190,000	70,000	125–150	70,150	16,000–18,000	6,000	22,000–24,000
Ireland	380	N.A.	N.A.	N.A.	34	130	164
Italy	540	10	300	310	6	200	206
Japan	790	10	348	358	8	200	208
Lebanon	60,000	45,000	10,000	55,000	45,000	10,000	55,000
Netherlands	200	13	160	173	N.A.	N.A.	150

Country							
New Zealand	36	11	8	19	N.A.	N.A.	9
Norway	46	1	26	27	1	5	6
Pakistan	130,000	N.A.	N.A.	100,000	3,500	N.A.	90,000
Philippines	93,000	5,000–15,000	2,300	7,300–17,300	4	2,300	5,800
Poland	3,300	N.A.	N.A.	N.A.	0	473	477
Portugal	89	34	40	74	0	8	8
Romania	3,055	N.A.	N.A.	N.A.	9	300	300
South Korea	1,327	9	184	193	0	140	149
Soviet Union	10,000	0	5,000	5,000	0	3,232	3,232
Spain	183	5	19	24	65,000	6	6
Sri Lanka	150,000	80,000	125–150	80,150	N.A.	125	65,125
Sweden	200	5	80	85	N.A.	N.A.	5
Switzerland	168	0	70	70	0	8	8
Thailand	8,150	30	1,000	1,030	20	300	320
Turkey	4,000	40	60	100	40	60	100
United States	3,500	930	170	1,100	600	305	905
Venezuela	38	N.A.	N.A.	N.A.	N.A.	N.A.	28
Vietnam[6]	15,000	N.A.	N.A.	N.A.	N.A.	14,000	N.A.
Yugoslavia	7,000	300	1,000	1,300	10	300	310

Notes

1. *Source*: Associated Press, reprinted in *New York Times*, 7 December 1990.
2. *Source*: Associated Press, reprinted in *New York Times*, 22 September 1990.
3. *Source*: Associated Press, reprinted in *New York Times*, 7 December 1990.
4. It appears that the numbers of stranded Egyptians shift from 1.6 million to 288,000 and rise again to 1.2 million as of 7 December 1990. There may have been political reasons that would account for the over-stating or under-stating of these numbers at the particular time at which they were reported.
5. Some reports suggest that India has 65,00 people en route from Iraq or in refugee camps as of 22 September 1990. Other reports indicate this number of Indians had not yet managed to leave Iraq by 22 September 1990.
6. Figures are for Vietnamese in Iraq only; number of those in Kuwait are not available.
7. NA = not available.

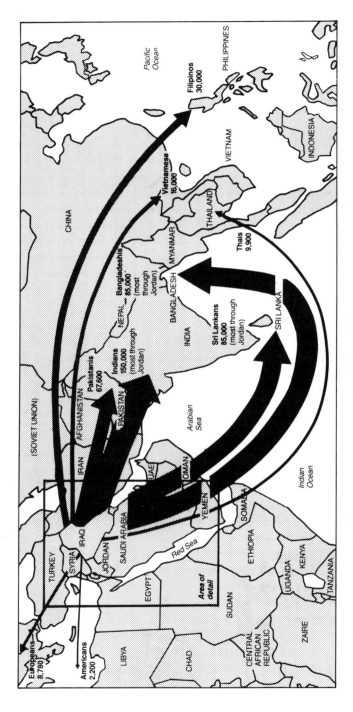

Figure 6.1 Gulf War migration to Asia, Europe and North America
Source: New York Times, 16 June 1991, p. E-3.

Indians migrated out of Kuwait in the greatest numbers in the shortest period of time. India quickly arranged for daily flights, and was also the first country to receive permission to ship food into the region for their nationals. In contrast, the Sri Lankan and the Bangladeshi governments had no capabilities for airlifting their workers, and had to rely entirely on other nations and the international relief effort, which seriously delayed the departure of their nationals.

Asians leaving Kuwait, unlike those migrating out of Iraq, were more likely to travel by foot or by car to whatever borders were open. Some reports suggest it is these refugees who took the longest to be repatriated, spending more time stranded at borders and in refugee camps. At no time during the crisis could planes land in Kuwait City as they could intermittently in Baghdad. Nor were ports near Kuwait open to transport, as were those in Iraq. And because governments had such difficulty communicating with workers in Kuwait, migration and repatriation efforts were more haphazard than those from Iraq.

Asian refugees at first crossed primarily into Jordan, until closure of its border redirected the later flow of migration into Turkey. Forced to leave their earnings behind in the Iraqi takeover of the banks, they came without possessions; and in addition suffered many indignities en route, with extensive reports of Iraqi soldiers raping Pakistani and Filipino women.

Within a month of the invasion, more than 130,000 Asian refugees remained at the border or in Jordanian camps. To ensure that none infiltrated the towns where other Asians had work and residence permits, and totally overwhelmed at the immense task, the Jordanian authorities refused to allow the Asians to leave the desert. This policy kept thousands of people exposed to harsh desert conditions, and lacking water, electricity or adequate shelter. The final numbers show between 350,000–400,000 Asian refugees crossed the Jordanian border from Iraq and Kuwait. Their poor treatment owes to the fact that Western governments airlifted their nationals more quickly, and Arab refugees mostly passed briefly through Jordan to the port of Aqaba, whereas the Asian nationals were forced to wait for weeks and months for their governments to work out plans for repatriation.

Egyptians were the second largest group of foreigners in Kuwait. An estimated 200,000 Egyptians fled Kuwait during the occupation; an estimated 850,000 Egyptians left Iraq. Most travelled through Jordan to the port of Aqaba and from there on to Cairo.

Since President Hosni Mubarak was among the first Arab leaders to join the multinational coalition, the Egyptians fled early in the crisis, fearing Iraqi reprisals. Yet Saddam Hussein's outmigration policy

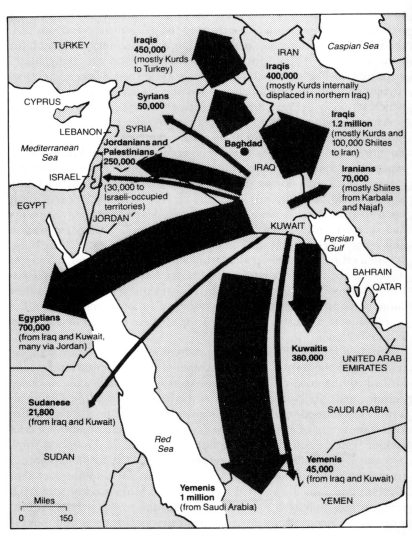

Sources: U.N. Disaster Relief Organization; U.S. Committee for Refugees; State
Department; General Accounting Office; International Organization for Migration

Figure 6.2 Gulf War migration within the Middle East
Note: While the numbers shown in this map (and Figure 6.1) may differ from some
other reports they are helpful in illustrating the enormity of the migration that resulted
from the Gulf War.
Source: *New York Times*, 16 June 1991, p.E-3.

allowed the Egyptians to leave Kuwait and Iraq freely, as a gesture of pan-Arabism, and also because he hoped to appeal to the masses in Cairo for support. However, in truth Egyptians had begun fleeing Iraq even *prior* to the invasion. Since 1988, Iraqis returning from the war with Iran had reportedly harrassed and stolen from Egyptians – an estimated 1,000 Egyptians were killed. Again, en route out of Kuwait in August–September 1991, more Egyptians were assaulted and robbed by the Iraqis, and like the Asians many Egyptian women were reportedly raped by soldiers. As a result, the Egyptian masses did not join Saddam's cause.

Once inside Jordan, the Egyptians were treated very badly by the indigenous Palestinian and Jordanian populations due to ethnic and political tensions. Exhaustion, delayed departure and the trauma of dislocation appear to have culminated for the Egyptians at the port of Aqaba, where rioting was reported by hundreds of Egyptians for several days. By mid-September there were still 300,000 Egyptians in camps on the Jordan/Iraq border awaiting evacuation, their transfer delayed until those already in Aqaba could be repatriated to Egypt.

The fourth migration flow from Kuwait occurred in the months immediately following its liberation in February 1991. If the Palestinian population of Kuwait before the war had approximated 400,000, one year after the occupation no more than 40,000 remained.[4]

Some Palestinians working in Kuwait had lived there for two or three generations. Although denied right of citizenship, Kuwait was their home. Others held Jordanian passports, and still others were from the West Bank. While Palestinians in Jordan, Tunisia, the West Bank and Gaza were united in support of Iraq's linkage of the Gulf War to the Palestinian cause, many of those in Kuwait had a divided loyalty, and were doubtful whether Iraq's attack was the best means for securing their homeland. A majority remained in Kuwait during the occupation, many out of concern for the country, and to safeguard their businesses, their homes and the homes of Kuwaiti friends or employers who had fled. Others, to be sure, actually worked on behalf of the Iraqi army, some even bearing arms against the indigenous Kuwaiti population, fuelled by anger and old resentments over unequal treatment and lack of legal rights accorded Palestinians in Kuwait.

When Kuwait was liberated, the Palestinians as a whole then became targets of retribution, with Kuwaitis unwilling to distinguish between those who assisted Iraq in dismantling the country and those who committed no acts of disloyalty. Many Palestinians were executed as collaborators and others forced to stand trial for war crimes; the majority were expelled. For those residing in Kuwait all their lives there was no other home to go to, and they became *de facto* stateless people.

Some initially migrated to Jordan. But with the border camps already filled by other refugees, and few job opportunities inside Jordan, they sought to return only to discover they were no longer able to re-enter Kuwait because of new entry rules excluding all non-citizens. The majority of these Palestinians returned again to dim prospects in Jordan.

Those with Egyptian travel papers trekked through Jordan to Aqaba, only to learn they would not be allowed to enter Egypt either. Basically, since they were on different sides of the crisis, the Egyptians regarded the Palestinians as politically undesirable. In addition, Egypt was trying to cope with its own immigration of displaced workers from the Gulf.

Those Palestinians trying to enter Israel in order to return to the West Bank or Gaza found the process difficult as well. And for them, perhaps more than for some others, that option of return migration held no prospects for future employment at all, given the already existing high unemployment rates on the West Bank. As of September 1991, an estimated 35,000 Palestinians returned from Kuwait to the West Bank out of the estimated 65,000–70,000 Palestinians who were working in Kuwait with Israeli residence permits.[5] The remainder, by and large, joined the other Palestinians expelled from Kuwait and fled to Jordan. Furthermore, according to one source, a preliminary estimate indicates that 20 per cent of the 35,000 Palestinian returnees to the West Bank subsequently left Israel for Jordan.[6]

The majority of the 250,000 Palestinians in Saudi Arabia and those in the other Gulf states were reportedly left alone. An estimated 40,000 Palestinian families were expelled from Saudi Arabia, or denied re-entry, but this figure is a small outmigration in comparison to the outmigration of the Yeminis.[7] Additionally some Palestinian diplomats were expelled from Qatar and Saudi Arabia.

Iraq

Emigration from Iraq is shaped by three characteristics: (1) those used as human shields by Saddam pending their release via diplomatic channels; (2) those transferred to hotels who could move freely but were unable to leave the country; and (3) those free to leave and who fled on their own, primarily crossing the border by foot or car. In total 10,000 Westerners were prevented from leaving the country. Several hundred of them were used as hostages and placed at military sites – chemical factories, military bases, defence industry plants, airfields, and Kuwait's desalinization plants – ostensibly as deterrents to international military intervention or bombing of those facilities. Simultaneously, tens of thousands of primarily non-Westerners – Indians, Bangladeshis, Sri Lankans, Thais, Filipinos, Egyptians, and Pakistanis – fled, crossing into Jordan or Turkey.

One of the most distinguishing factors of Iraq's behaviour was this overt use of foreigners as military shields, especially as the Geneva Convention expressly forbids the use of civilians as obstructions in military conflict. Moreover, Iraq's cynical detention of these foreign nationals gave excessive publicity to their plight. Saddam made direct appeals via televised broadcasts to the families of the few hundred American and British nationals held as hostages in pressing the USA and other governments to meet his demands. Thus he insisted any killing of foreigners would be the fault of the governments that bombed the sites, not the Iraqi government.

Those unable to leave, but not placed at military sites as human shields, were the second group of refugees in Iraq. The Iraqi government repeatedly refused to grant landing rights to planes from other nations throughout the first four months of the crisis. And then, when the war did break out the airports in Iraq were closed immediately. Some flights did leave sporadically, but typically a government would announce that it had received approval to land and return with passengers, only to then have the flight cancelled due to an Iraqi change of heart.

In time what emerged were rules of the game, so to speak, created by Saddam Hussein, which brought exit migration policies to an all-time nadir. First a country would request landing rights for an airlift evacuation of a few hundred men, women and children. Saddam would initially agree, with much publicity, only then to add conditions, such as food, medicine or the cessation of counter-military action, or recognition of Iraq's annexation of Kuwait. Iraqi politicization of the removal of foreigners prolonged the departure of foreign nationals for weeks, and effectively tied the hands of the international community.

Saddam's attempts to use this second group of foreigners to break the UN-sanctioned economic boycott against Iraq ultimately failed. Nevertheless, there was a point at which his manoeuvring did appeal to popular sentiment. When Iraq declared food rationing and announced that foreigners would be treated the same as Iraqi families who had limited supplies of food, fresh water and milk, people throughout the world sought to relieve the situation with humanitarian aid. Consequently when individual mediators sought the release of nationals held hostage in exchange for medical supplies and food, it was virtually impossible for their own governments to criticize this discreet diplomacy which more often than not secured the release of hundreds of people.[8]

By thus conducting negotiations with primarily unauthorized or non-government personnel, Saddam successfully circumvented the authority of governments pledged not to negotiate for hostages. And while he failed to divide the international coalition, he did drive a wedge between, on the one hand, the allied governments and, on the other hand, a percentage of their citizens; especially in the case of Japan, Germany and France. By 1 December 1990, 2000 Westerners were still detained in Iraq, even while over 430,000 soldiers with the international military force were being deployed to the Gulf. Given that the repatriation of all hostages was a pre-condition to a peaceful solution, as was complete withdrawal from Kuwait, Iraq's intentional protracted release of foreign nationals forced extensive dialogue among the parties. The forced relocation of hundreds of Westerners and Japanese to military installations and other vulnerable strategic sites initially may have delayed an immediate military counter-response, but ultimately it helped to coalesce much of the international community against Iraq.

The third type of emigration from Iraq was by far the largest: some 1.9 million people. When it was reported in September that tens of thousands of people were reaching the borders without food or water after having experienced harrowing flights across the desert, attention shifted from Westerners held as human shields to the nearly 2 million foreigners internally displaced in Iraq, mostly from the Third World.

Saddam Hussein's policy cleverly provided that nationals from countries not sending military or support forces to the Gulf were free to leave. This included Austrians, Finns, Portuguese, Swedes, and Swiss nationals, Argentinians, Chinese and Yugoslavs. Many of the European nationals were fortunate to receive flights directly from Baghdad. Also, Indonesians, Indians, Bangladeshis, Pakistanis, Filipinos, Thais and Sri Lankans were for the most part free to leave the country by whichever means they could arrange. Emigration arrangements for all of them were politically complicated. For example, plans for the Indians to cross into Iran from Iraq where they would be airlifted were repeatedly stalled by the Iranian government; consequently, the majority of Indians crossed the border into Jordan in order to be airlifted. Similarly, Iraq delayed release of Soviet nationals as a means of preventing the Soviets from sharing information about

USSR-supplied military equipment, or about Iraq's defence capability. Baghdad adopted the opposite ploy with regard to the exit of resident Egyptians. Even though Cairo had sent forces to Saudi Arabia, its nationals were free to leave Iraq and Kuwait in a move intended to appeal to Egyptian popular sentiment.

In general, Iraq implemented arbitrary and often capricious exit requirements at its borders, favouring some foreigners over others. In some cases, those who travelled days to reach a border were turned back for lack of a special exit permit or failure to pay an automobile registration tax or to obtain special licence plates. In numerous instances, migrants had their passports confiscated, while some were forced to pay exorbitant exit fees; and many were killed trying to cross the border from Iraq or Iraqi-controlled Kuwait.

Several countries carefully avoided condemning Saddam given the vulnerable situation of their citizens, including India, the former USSR and Pakistan. India all along had been seeking a non-military role for itself and the 105-member non-aligned movement. And when Iraq demanded supplies in exchange for people, India was the first country to receive UN clearance to deliver 10,000 tons of food to stranded Indian refugees.[9] The Pakistanis, by contrast, reported harsh treatment by Iraqi soldiers. Indeed, ethnic tensions in India and Pakistan (and between the migrating groups) flared because the Indians were seen as receiving better treatment than the Pakistanis, whose government had strained relations with Iraq.

Saudi Arabia

Saudi Arabia was the source of a significant Yemeni emigration during the War. Vulnerable to Iraqi military invasion, the Saudis were concerned about domestic security as well, given the enormous number of foreigners in the country. In particular, Riyadh had become displeased with the resident Yemeni population, against the background of previous tensions over the unification of North and South Yemen.

The Saudi government knowingly changed its residency policy in the midst of the War in order to encourage emigration. In reality these changes applied only to the Yemenis. For example, the Saudi government enacted a series of residency limitations, prevented Yemenis from owning businesses by insisting they be lesser partners with Saudis, and required all Yemeni workers to have Saudi sponsors. While permitted to take out their money and possessions (though many valuables were confiscated at the border) those unable to acquire Saudi partners were forced to abandon their businesses. In addition the Saudi policy separated many Yemeni families, since some members had acquired citizenship while others had not. These measures saw the hasty departure of an estimated 750,000 Yemenis within the first weeks. In total, an estimated 1–1.5 million Yemenis out of the 2 million working in Saudi Arabia fled the country during the War.[10]

This massive return migration has had a detrimental effect on the newly united Republic of Yemen, one of the poorest and most densely populated countries in the region. Estimated at $2 billion a year, remittances from workers in Saudi Arabia had been the nation's largest source of income.[11] Those returning to the country have few prospects for employment and will likely seek work in other countries of the region. Prospects for their return to Saudi Arabia, however, appear quite bleak; by early February 1991 the Saudi government had promised jobs to nearly 1 million Egyptians to replace the Yemenis. From the perspective of the Saudi government, the more Egyptians working in the country, the more likely Egypt will continue to provide a military deterrent.

Indonesian workers in Saudi Arabia felt their security to be jeopardized, being so close to the Iraqi border. An estimated 100,000 sought to leave but were prevented from doing so by their government's inability to finance repatriation.[12] Instead, Djakarta sought assurances from Riyadh about the safety of its nationals given previous incidents of pilgrims being poorly treated, including 500 killed at the Mina Tunnel disaster.

Turkey

There were two types of migration to Turkey during the Gulf War: Asians fleeing Iraq and Kuwait after the invasion, followed by inmigration of the Kurds during the Iraqi civil war.

A few thousand Chinese passed through Habur but were quickly shuttled on buses to Istanbul where they were housed in hotels until the Chinese government arranged for their passage home. Tens of thousands of other Asians, mostly Pakistanis and Bangladeshis, fled Kuwait and Iraq for Turkey once Jordan announced its borders to be closed. Many Bangladeshis travelled on foot from northern Iraq, while Pakistanis drove their own cars, a likely reflection of economic disparities. Pre-existing facilities for serving Turkish Muslims on their annual pilgrimage to Mecca were put at the disposal of these migrants in the Habur tent city on an emergency basis. The Turkish Red

Crescent provided tents, food and water. But not all migrants could be housed there and many were located in makeshift camps along the border.

Given their experience with pilgrims, the Turks were far more organized than any other country in responding to the migration flows, but still found themselves imposing limits to prevent their facilities from being overwhelmed. As applied to the Asian refugees, Turkey's inmigration policy required most to wait outside the border until those within could be repatriated. At one point, about 45,000 Bangladeshis, Pakistanis and Indians were forced to wait on the Iraqi side of the border until the 8,000 already in Turkey could be airlifted to their countries of origin. At that time 35,000 had been successfully repatriated. Flights were sponsored by the EC, since most Asian countries could not finance the evacuation themselves, leading to delays in flying refugees to Dhaka and Delhi.

Migration into Turkey reached its peak in numbers and drama during the period of Iraq's civil war, when over 1 million Kurds are estimated to have entered Turkey or camped outside its border. As many as 500,000 Kurds also went to Iran during this period of enormous upheaval and devastation, when an estimated 6,700 Kurds died from starvation and exposure.

It is the extensive media coverage which sets this migration apart from others. Already in 1988 some 60,000 had fled Iraq for Iran and Turkey. Having also recently accepted 310,000 ethnic Turks escaping persecution in Bulgaria in 1988, Turkey's hesitant response to accepting more migrants was shaped by the current large population of Kurds and others already in their border camps, and by the need for a permanent solution to the persecution and dislocation of the Kurds. Terrain and climate also made relief efforts difficult. At the point when hundreds of Kurds started to die, continuous media coverage relentlessly depicting the atrocities and death of thousands of Kurds in effect forced the international community and particularly the US military to become directly involved.

Implications of the Kurdish Migration Experience

The migration of Kurds was markedly different from others during the War. It did not stem from Iraq's invasion of Kuwait, but resulted from the on-going Kurdish struggle for independence. Nevertheless, the military assaults against the Kurdish rebels, their armed resistance and exodus need to be viewed as part of the domino effect the Gulf War has had. Extreme fear of Iraqi reprisals stimulated a massive flow of

Kurds seeking to leave, with UN estimates suggesting between 1.5–2 million Kurds were in transit from Iraq. While other wars have produced refugees, the Kurdish migration may well be the single largest refugee flow in the shortest period of time, and made all the more extraordinary by the inhospitability of both climate and land-scape.

The Turkish government, no matter how reluctant, was simply unable to prevent hundreds of thousands of Kurds from amassing on its border and relocating within the rugged mountain terrain. By early April, Turkey had accepted over 200,000 Kurds out of the estimated 1 million en route or already encamped on the Turkish border. There were also an estimated 1 million Kurds seeking to enter Iran.

Unlike the emigration of the Arabs (except some Palestinians) and the Asian nationals who were eventually repatriated to their country of origin, the Kurds sought temporary asylum within the two border countries until genuine autonomy or a permanent independent homeland could be politically established for them to return to. The EC and President Ozal of Turkey jointly sought to create protected enclaves for the Kurds in northern Iraq – a proposal later condemned by Iraq as prejudicial to its domestic security and sovereignty. At heart a political struggle, the Kurdish plight nevertheless has been portrayed by the media as a humanitarian crisis. Even so, long-term resettlement could not simply be addressed by an outpouring of international aid. The Kurdish migration flow poses genuine problems for Iran and Turkey, for Iraq and for international relief workers in the region struggling to cope with shortages, thousands of deaths and the threat of military attack by Iraq.

Turkey is concerned at the massive Iraqi military build-up on its border as part of Baghdad's thirty-year struggle with the Kurds, particularly given Iraq's past use of napalm and other chemical warfare against the Kurds in 1988. Furthermore, Turkey has its own population of 20 million ethnic Kurds, and fears resettlement of more Kurds might increase international pressure on Turkey to create a Kurdish state within its borders. So much so that Ankara requested internationally-donated food and supplies be dropped exclusively on the Iraqi side of the border to discourage border-crossing by refugees. Both Iran and Turkey fear the Kurdish movement will attempt to fight its battle against Iraq from within their side of the borders. Even Syria, with its own Kurdish minority, is sensitive lest extreme nationalist expression create domestic discontent in their country.

Turkey asked the USA, the EC and other countries in 1991 formally to admit some Kurdish refugees. Alternatively, the UN estimated it would cost $480 million to care for the Kurds for a three to five-month period. But efforts to raise international aid were initially slow. By 10 April 1991 the EC had pledged $187 million, Britain pledged an additional $35 million and $67 million was guaranteed from other countries. France, the USA, Japan and others sent food, tents, blankets, water and medical supplies. But topography, rain and mud greatly delayed relief efforts. An estimated 6,700 Kurds died, primarily from starvation, dehydration and exposure but also attributable to the delay and disorganization of the relief effort, while the UN debated its responsibility towards the Kurds under international law. Moreover, it was only after persistent and graphic international media coverage that most countries committed aid and resources. Hence, Kurdish migration represents the clearest example of the tragedy of dislocation during the Gulf War.

ECONOMIC IMPACT ON BOTH SENDING AND RECEIVING COUNTRIES

The economic impact of these migration flows is equally profound. The most obvious are billions of dollars in lost remittances experienced by forty different countries. Combined with the return of hundreds of thousands of nationals and the social upheaval it has caused, this has over-extended domestic economies. Also worthy of consideration are: the vast sums of international aid made available; oil subsidies and oil price hikes; extensive reconstruction; and the long-term effect of ecological devastation caused by the oil fires and bombing of the region. Taken together, these factors inevitably affect the climate to work and live in a given locale – and will clearly affect prospects for return migration into the Gulf for years to come.

The scope of economic issues

The aftermath of Kuwait has created public awareness of the vast economic disparities between Arab states, between different ethnic populations residing in the Middle East, and between wealthy Middle East countries and poor Arab and Asian countries. Many misconceptions were shaken by over a million workers made instant refugees when Kuwait was invaded, by a million more refugees fleeing Iraq and later over one million more Kurds. The economies of Middle Eastern countries like Egypt, Jordan, Yemen as well as the Palestinians lost billions of dollars in lost wages (see Table 6.2), as did the Asian countries of Pakistan, Bangladesh, Sri Lanka and India (see Table

Table 6.2 Remittance of Asian workers in Iraq or Kuwait prior to 1990

Country	Number of workers ('000)	Annual remittances home (US\$ million)[1]
India	200	260
Bangladesh	105	250
Pakistan	100	350
Sri Lanka	100	60
Philippines	63	40
Vietnam	16	N.A.
Thailand	12	15

Note:
1. These estimated numbers are likely based on official reports and therefore are likely to under-represent the actual figures, since the greatest proportion of remittances are not captured by official statistics. Remittances dollars in large measure are part of the 'hidden economy' in most countries.
Source: *Far Eastern Economic Review*, 30 August 1990, p.8.

6.3). The Asian countries also experienced the compounded economic loss of exports to the region such as rice, tea and textiles. Turkey lost millions of dollars in revenues when the Iraqi oil pipeline was shut down; and, Jordan's economy was simultaneously burdened by the refugee flows across its border, the return migration of nationals and the loss of jobs and trade in the region.

Remittances

Given the large presence of Asian workers in the Gulf, Asian domestic economies experienced a staggering financial loss. By some estimates each Bangladeshi in the Middle East had supported eleven people at home; each Indian worker three in India; and each Pakistani or Sri Lankan seven family members back home[13] – not to mention regional differences within countries. For example, very poor villages had a greater dependency on monies sent from the Middle East, and perhaps double the average number of dependants actually relied on remittances. In regions where workers have particular skills or trades they were over-represented in the migrant labour force: in Kerala an estimated 700,000 Indians were economic migrants working in the Middle East – the largest proportion of any Indian state. Clearly the impact of the Gulf War, massive return migration, and loss of jobs and remittances has been far greater in Kerala than other communities.

Arab states experienced an economic fallout similar to that of the Asian states. More than half of the displaced workers were indigenous to the region. In the case of Egyptian workers, they supported on

Table 6.3 Lost remittance earnings from Arab workers

	US$ billion
Egypt[1]	2.5
Jordan[2]	0.6
West Bank/Gaza[3]	0.14
Yemen[4]	2.00
Total	5.24

Sources:
1. *New York Times*, 26 August 1990, p. 18.
2. *Foreign Affairs*, Winter 90/91, vol. 69, no. 5, p. 24. This figure includes remittances of Palestinians from Jordan.
3. *New York Times*, 27 August 1990, p. 8. This figure represents lost remittances only for those West Bank and Gaza Palestinians who had been working in Kuwait. It is a net figure and does not include the $120–125 million from remittance earnings which the Palestinians would have otherwise paid in taxes to the PLO. *Economist*, 22 September 1990, p. 48.
4. *Economist*, 1 December 1990, p. 36.

average six or more relatives with wages sent home.[14] While Egyptians anticipated losing $1 billion in remittances from workers in Kuwait, the Saudi offer of one million work permits to Egyptians (replacing Yemenis) has helped to offset the original loss. Nevertheless, it is unlikely that the same workers displaced by the Gulf War will receive these Saudi jobs. Consequently, while new opportunities may offset aggregate economic losses, they do not stabilize personal income losses of individual workers displaced in the Gulf.

The total loss to the Palestinian economy from displacement, including lost international financial aid (from Qatar, Kuwait, UAE, Saudi Arabia), was estimated as high as $10 billion. Prior to the crisis, Palestinian family members received an estimated aggregate total of $80 million a year from relatives in Kuwait, in addition to the $125–175 million paid to the PLO and related projects, diminishing its administrative capacity.[15] Political tensions between Gulf states and Palestinians also dramatically reduced Palestinian export revenues, making it a prime example of the ripple effect of economic conditions initiated by a migration flow that leads to domestic economic and political instability as well as external security risks.

One final note about the effect of the War on remittances and economic opportunities. Whereas Arabs in search of employment opportunities previously travelled freely throughout much of the Middle East, the Iraqi invasion has caused countries to restrict entry and residency based on citizenship requirements. Kuwait expelled Palestinians, Saudi Arabia expelled Yemenis, and in both cases lifelong residents were considered part of the foreign labour force without the benefit of political rights or citizenship. These restrictions on movement highlight the changing economic climate in the region, despite the interdependence of nations on labour and workers, as much as the vulnerability of economic migrants.

Reconstruction

Kuwait and Iraq face extensive reconstruction needs. Reconstruction in Kuwait is estimated at $50–100 billion, in Iraq, at $100–150 billion. This does not include $1 billion in lost Kuwaiti export earnings, and the added $100–125 million costs to Kuwait for US and other allied military support. Nor do the costs to Iraq include hundreds of billions of dollars of output/production losses and the loss of lives. And none of these costs address the immeasurable damage to the environment and the hazardous effects to the ecosystem throughout the world.

Reconstruction in the region already has created new economic opportunities for local residents and foreign labourers. Kuwait, for example, promised Egypt they could receive up to 13 per cent of projected costs estimated at $800 million to rebuild Kuwait. Many American companies such as AT&T, Caterpillar, Motorola and Raytheon received lucrative contracts as early as February 1991. Reconstruction labour needs, however, are short-term, perhaps no more than five years. And to date, contracts are being awarded in large measure based on allied military connections during the War. Thus, economic opportunities in the region over the long run may not reach pre-war levels. Also, both Kuwait and Saudi Arabia are re-evaluating industrial policies with the aim of reducing dependence on foreign labour. Clearly a reduction in the number of jobs and changes in the residency requirements will have far reaching consequences for the post-reconstruction economic climate in the region, which will greatly influence domestic economies and economic migrants throughout the world.

International aid

International aid relating to the Gulf War either addressed acute crises arising when foreigners were unable to be repatriated quickly, or was intended to offset longer-term instabilities upon domestic economies. The former was met largely by humanitarian aid offers, the latter by grants, loans, debt forgiveness and oil/trade commitments.

One example of other indirect international aid are teams from the UK, Iran, China, Romania, the former USSR, Scandinavia and the

USA who put out the oil fires. Only after nine months were all of Kuwait's 700 oil fires finally extinguished, in November 1991. Another example is when Saudi Arabia supplied Pakistan with 50,000 barrels of crude oil a day at no cost to offset their other losses. And many countries participated in the massive airlift of the stranded migrants by covering costs and donating planes.

Saudi Arabia, financed several flights of Egyptians from Aqaba to Cairo; the EC chartered a Soviet jet to make ten trips to Dhaka in order to evacuate 500 Bangladeshis trapped in Amman; and another forty-five flights were chartered by the EC, at a cost of $7 million, using Soviet planes to airlift Sri Lankans who, like the Bangladeshis, had no domestic resources to facilitate repatriation. Japan was very active in evacuating refugees from Mideast countries, running flights into Baghdad, Amman, Damascus and Cairo. They also facilitated the repatriation of 1,000 Vietnamese workers who fled Iraq and escaped as far as Egypt, before being flown home.

Still, international aid clearly will not offset the deeper disruptive economic impact of migration flows, internal displacement and war in the Gulf region. Aid cannot cover the loss of human lives, the psychological trauma or the destruction of natural resources, though it can cushion the destabilizing economic impact of the War.

On the other hand, despite the delayed response, countries ultimately shared responsibility for feeding, sheltering and airlifting hundreds of thousands of displaced people. And while the institutional response was largely the provision of military support to the region, that was not exclusively the case. Furthermore, hundreds of non-profit agencies throughout the world, like Food for the Hungry, American Near East Refugee Aid, the International Rescue Committee, Refugees International, World Relief and the American Friends Service Committee collected private donations that most certainly can be credited with saving tens of thousands of lives. This feat of humanitarian concern alone bodes well for the future.

CONCLUSION

Much can be learned from this war about the way conflict shapes population movements. Clearly, while some of the outflows were unintended consequences of military conflict, other emigrations were deliberate expulsions of a particular group of people as in the cases of the Kuwaitis from Kuwait, later the Palestinians from Kuwait, and the Yemenis from Saudi Arabia.

These outflows have had enormous influence on the social

structures of both the sending and receiving countries. Most of these countries relied on migrant labour without extending the rights of citizenship or the political privileges accorded the indigenous population, as highlighted by the unequal treatment accorded particular groups depending on their ethnic background. This earlier practice institutionalized the disenfranchisement of hundreds of thousands of people, many of whom spent their lifetime in a particular country without being able to make any claims (social, political or otherwise) on the society. Without labour organizations or unions, the fleeing workers had to fend for themselves, losing savings, wages, pensions and company-held titles to homes and cars.

The complexity of issues around migrant labour forces requires more comprehensive political and economic strategies. In the wake of the war new policies will emerge, but it is likely that some may only further restrict the rights of migrants. The uneven response by the international community to the dislocation of millions of people also points to the lack of institutional preparedness in responding to a crisis of this magnitude. In the end, the have countries were far more successful in evacuating their nationals then the have-not countries whose nationals languished in border camps for weeks, making economic disparities of states once again readily apparent. Clearly, however, the response of the international community with guarantees of loans, subsidized trade exchanges and new offers of employment will help to cushion the social, economic and political instabilities caused by these mass migration movements.

Yet, despite the unity of the international coalition in 1991, in analysing the consequences of wartime migration on the stability and security of states, it must be clearly understood that the hundreds of thousands of people fleeing to the borders under the threat of military attack did so because of government and diplomatic failure to secure their safety in the region and failure to secure their safe departure either home or to an identified host country.

A post-war scenario has begun to show a new flow of foreign labour into the region. In time there may be as many foreign workers in the region as before the War, particularly given the level of reconstruction to be completed. The interdependence of states on labour and remittances makes the role of jobs critical to the economic stability of the Third World. It is therefore essential that the vulnerability of these economic migrants be addressed.

As we saw, Middle East destabilization has had a resounding effect across the world, and posed a security threat of one type or another to dozens of countries. After Kuwait it is now certainly obvious that an act of military aggression and the displacement of massive numbers of people can quickly escalate into an international security crisis both outside and within the borders of states.

NOTES

1 A larger version of this paper was prepared for the Conference on the Impact of International Migration on the Security and Stability of States at the Massachusetts Institute of Technology's Center for International Studies, 5 and 6 December 1991.

2 As foreigners fleeing a temporary place of residence the UN saw the Asians and most other migrants as evacuees and not refugees, arguing that they did not meet the legal UN definition of refugees fleeing from fear of persecution in their native land. This chapter, however, uses the terms refugees, evacuees and migrants interchangeably when referring to those fleeing upheaval during the Gulf War, because many of the individuals fleeing resided long-term and even for generations in the countries they were forced to leave.

3 Many of the Palestinians who left Kuwait, are reported by the *New York Times* (16 June 1991) as migrating during the first phase, though other accounts indicate they may actually have left during the second phase from January to March. Therefore, migration during this time period may actually be higher. Some of the specific data reported in this chapter are inconsistent with other data also reported here. There are many obvious limitations in securing precise documentation of population movements, nevertheless it is important that existing data be presented even when it varies considerably from source to source. Discrepancies primarily concern numbers of migrants and the level of remittances. Both factors have hidden numbers not captured in official government statistics. With regard to the numbers of migrants, these statistics should be treated as estimates, since there are inconsistencies from country to country in their counting methods (e.g. some include dependants, some include those on travel visas, and other statistics only reflect the number of work permits issued).

4 *Middle East Economic Digest*, 9 August 1991.

5 It has been difficult to locate statistics to indicate the number of Palestinians who returned from the Gulf to Israel. It is also difficult to identify the precise number of Palestinians who fled to Jordan, since many hold Jordanian passports and most statistics do not distinguish between Jordanians and Palestinians. These figures are from Nusseibeh (1992, p. 12).

6 Ibid., see Note 5.

7 USCR *World Refugee Survey*, 1991, p. 102.

8 The list of former heads of states and celebrities who travelled to Iraq seeking the release of foreign nationals includes: Austrian President Kurt Waldheim; Former German Chancellor Willy Brandt; French politician Jean-Marie Le Pen; Soviet official Yevgenii Primakov; Former New Zealand Prime Minister David Lange; Former Danish Prime Minister Anker Joergenson; Former British Prime Minister Edward Heath; American politician Jesse Jackson; Former Japanese Prime Minister Yasuhiro

Nakasone; Bulgarian Vice-President Atanas Semerdzhiyev; and several members of the British, Canadian and Swiss Parliaments.
9 *Economist*, 22 September 1990.
10 The Yemenis were not the only Arab nationals who emigrated from Saudi Arabia during this time. However few statistics indicate the number of Palestinians, Jordanians and others who fled. There was some indication, however, that these numbers were low and the majority of those living and working in Saudi Arabia were left alone.
11 *New York Times*, 26 October 1990.
12 *Far Eastern Economic Review*, 31 January 1991.
13 *New York Times*, 15 September 1990.
14 *New York Times*, 4 September 1990.
15 *Economist*, 22 September 1990.

REFERENCES

Addleton, J. (1991) 'The impact of the Gulf War on migration and remittances in Asia and the Middle East', *International Migration* XXIX(4).

Chouchri, N. (1986) 'A new view of migration and remittances in the Middle East', unpublished paper prepared for the Annual Meeting of the Population Association of America, Cambridge, MA: MIT.

Chouchri, N. (1990) 'Impacts and prospects of return migration in the Middle East', unpublished paper prepared for the International Labor Office, Cambridge, MA: MIT.

International Organization for Migration (1991) *Annual Report 1990*, Geneva: International Organization for Migration.

Nusseibeh, S. (1992) 'Consequences for labor mobility of Arab Israeli peace initiatives'. Paper prepared for the Institute for Social and Economic Policy in the Middle East. Cambridge, Mass.: John F. Kennedy School of Government, Harvard University.

Reed, S. (1990–91) 'Jordan and the Gulf Crisis', *Foreign Affairs*, Vol. 69, no. 5.

United Nations (1991) *World Populations Trends and Policies: 1991 World Monitoring Report*, New York: UN Population Division.

USCR (US Committee for Refugees) (1991) *1991 World Refugee Survey*, Washington, DC: US Committee for Refugees.

Weimner, H. (1990) 'Security, stability and international migration', unpublished paper, Cambridge, MA: MIT Center for International Studies.

World Bank (1991) *World Development Report*, Washington, DC: World Bank.

Part II
Israel in the post-Gulf era

7 Society and politics in war

The Israeli case

Gad Barzilai

The Gulf War brought into sharp relief the interactions which tend to occur between a country's internal politics and its international relations, on the one hand, and between wars and a society's relationship to its regime, on the other. Thus, for example, even though a large majority of Israeli society found no fault in its government's reluctance to approve military response to Iraqi missile attacks on its cities, it nevertheless revealed itself to be a society fully prepared to do battle with the enemy if need be. Again, although (within its Green Line, pre-1967, borders) certain democratic features were temporarily suspended, no significant impairment of democratic principles was permitted to take place. Moreover, though the events of the Gulf War did much to reinforce the views of those elements in Israeli society who have always advocated most vociferously the resort to arms, the latter stopped short of articulating any express demand that military force be implemented against Iraq, leaving the country as a whole essentially passive over that issue. In other words, the manner in which Israel comported itself during the Gulf War resulted from the interplay of many more factors than the professional literature thus far published would have led one to expect.

Conventional wisdom argues that political regimes, and the way they react to severe crisis situations, can fairly neatly be divided into two distinct, non-overlapping types: aggressive, non-democratic and militaristic societies with an ingrained tendency towards initiating wars and military operations; versus civilian, democratic societies, which merely engage, when forced, in acts of self-defence against outside threats to their existence.[1]

This article rejects that brand of topology as being insufficient to explain all cases and will attempt to demonstrate that Israel, though democratic within its pre-1967 borders, can be defined as exhibiting militaristic features which constantly push it towards preparing for war.

THE CREATION OF CONSENSUS

The political polarity which characterized Israel during the Intifada[2] underwent a considerable upheaval following Iraq's invasion of Kuwait in August 1990. Saddam Hussein's threats to inflict great damage on Israel's population centres, the rumours circulating about his possession of ballistic missiles armed with chemical (and, possibly, biological) warheads and Iraq's attempts to develop nuclear weaponry, all vastly heightened Israel's apprehension over the vulnerability of its civilian population. So did the possibility of an 'Eastern front', encompassing Iraq, Jordan, Syria, other Arab 'rejectionist' states and the PLO. As the self-imposed deadline for a US attack on Iraq drew closer, the Israeli Press delivered itself of the estimate that Iraq was capable of targeting Israeli urban centres with as many as 50 Scud missiles. It was believed that this would not result in any mass extermination, but still remained an alarming prospect. In consequence, unprecedented measures were taken to protect the civilian population. Special kits were distributed to the civilian population against possible effects of Iraqi bio-chemical attack, a mass information campaign was launched instructing the population how to take shelter, preparing 'sealed' rooms and setting up special regional crisis headquarters. The entire Israeli population rapidly became a military-like community.

The literature dealing with 'disaster' studies has suggested that, in these sorts of situations, societies have a tendency to develop consensual attitudes and the nature of their political debates undergoes a drastic change.[3] But, since the nature of political debates in Israel, unlike in Western democracies, tends to be security-oriented at the best of times, it was not that particular issue that underwent change. What happened, instead, was that certain aspects of the security were suddenly accorded far more attention than previously. In that respect, the Gulf War produced repercussions somewhat different from those created by Israel's inter-communal conflict, in the form of the Intifada. The latter, because it had contributed to the surfacing of the intransigence of the Israeli–Palestinian conflict underscoring the fundamental question of coexistence, brought into focus (more sharply than had occurred since 1948) the severe dilemmas being confronted. By obliging the country to ponder over its national identity, to produce an answer to the problem of Arab refugees and to define the geographical location of permanent borders, the Intifada resulted in Israel's political debates focusing acutely on matters highly tinged with ideological overtones. By contrast, the deep apprehension which gripped the country on the eve of the Gulf War had the effect of making politicians address themselves more emphatically to purely military affairs and thereby dictated the content matter of the debates they engaged in.

Most politicians agreed that a resort to arms by Israel might very well become possible. Practically, as all of them were unable to refrain from recalling the saying: 'The friend of my enemy is also my enemy' when contemplating the PLO's overt identification with Saddam Hussein and the support expressed by the Palestinians for Iraq's invasion of Kuwait. A very broad consensus took hold and the style in which the Israeli political game was played temporarily was altered. Whereas, prior to Iraq's aggression, many politicians on the Zionist Left had begun to claim that the PLO had genuinely moderated its stance and had renounced its former intent to destroy Israel, these conclusions were now re-evaluated. It became fairly apparent that their prophecies, concerning the likelihood of Israel, the PLO and the Palestinians being able to coexist, actually had very little to support them. Declarations uttered by leftist leaders gave expression to the changes evolved in their attitudes. Thus, Ratz Party Knesset member Yossi Sarid, one of the leading 'doves' in Israel, gave vent to the dismay with which the Zionist Left viewed the way the Palestinians abandon the path of moderation which appeared to be their chosen way since 1988 onwards:

> If it is permissible to support Saddam Hussein who, without blinking an eyelid, murdered tens of thousands of his political opponents and gassed Kurdish men, women and children, it may not be so terrible to support the policies of Shamir, Sharon and Rabin. In comparison with Saddam Hussein's crimes, those committed by the Israeli government are as white as snow. Were I to support the notion of a Palestinian state – solely because the Palestinians, too, deserve to have a state of their own – I would now renounce such support. But I continue to endorse their right to self-determination and to a state because it is my own right to be rid of the Israeli occupation of the territories, and of the damage that such occupation inflicts. But I do not need the aid of Arafat, Husseini or Darawsha for my supreme effort . . . until further notice, I will not be seeking them out any more. It is they who can now come looking for me.[4]

The new opinions aired by Sarid and by other prominent personalities on the Israeli Left were not entirely accepted by the Zionist Left, and certainly not by the non-Zionist Left. But all dovish Zionist groups were practically unanimous in their realization that, subsequent to the events of the Gulf War, all hope based on coexistence had faded for solutions to the Israeli–Palestinian conflict. They accepted, now, that it would make greater sense to focus on solutions grounded in a separation between the two peoples, based on mutual recognition and self-determination.[5]

Among Israel's Jewish population, a general state of apprehension brought almost everyone, with no regard to individual political views, to start talking the same political language. The ruling élite, the Likud, did whatever it could to encourage that trend, particularly emphasizing the fact that, because Israel would probably always be faced with serious threats to its security, it has no alternative but to rule out any form of withdrawal from the territories. The Likud's task was considerably aided by the fact that the media, both in Israel and abroad, gave considerable publicity to the PLO's unreserved support for Iraq. The fundamental contention put forward by scholars in the field of the sociology of war, like Lewis Coser and George Simmel, to the effect that wars conducted between states produce consensus, was therefore found also to apply accurately to situations of grave security crisis.[6] However, whereas Simmel stressed the importance of an external threat in producing consensus, and Coser attached greater significance to the manner in which different groups and individuals interpret such threat, the Israeli case, clearly demonstrated the extent to which a government's active intervention in citizens' daily lives can play a decisive role in fashioning political order and in developing tendencies to broader consensus.

GOVERNMENTAL INTERVENTION IN SOCIETY

The development of consensus, and the enhanced degree of governmental involvement in citizens' lives, were among the most prominent phenomena which occurred in Israel on the eve of the Gulf War. Governmental interference in daily life became even more pronounced with the landing of the first Scud missiles on urban centres, particularly in the Tel-Aviv area. A special form of emergency regime was declared and the civil defence regulations were activated, to the extent that management of the country's civilian life was taken over by the army and other security forces. In part, this process could be explained by the Lasswellian model, which holds that during severe security crises the military bureaucracy can be expected to take over responsibility for handling key functions within the civilian sector. In contrast to this model, the socio-political changes that took place in

Israel did not derive from any form of surrender by the political echelon to demands issued by the military, but rather from its active desire to obtain the military's assistance (which involved also resort to military legislation) in increasing the degree of governmental control over the public. Such control was considered essential both by the ruling élite, and the army in order to ensure the achievement of the country's defence goals. The consequence was that the political system became characterized by prominent symptoms of what Clinton Rossiter has termed 'constitutional dictatorship'.[7]

For the most part, the country's life was conducted subject to emergency regulations, and all aspects of social and cultural life were affected by the wartime footing adopted. For example, the restrictions announced regarding the working hours, and the ban on holding public gatherings after dark, made it possible for the government to maintain control of the population's movements with minimum disruption effects. It applied such control without seeking the Knesset's approval and failed to heed a High Court ruling on the matter, pursuant to which resort to emergency regulations was never intended to improve the efficiency of the executive branch other than in circumstances where getting a law passed rapidly in the Knesset is simply impossible.

Instead of taking steps to amend the Civil Defence Law, which would have enabled the Knesset to exercise a reasonable degree of public control over its emergency legislation, the government authorized the Minister of Defence simply to institute emergency regulations. He activated them within two weeks of the outbreak of the Gulf War vesting him with the authority to declare the onset of a special period of civil defence, to restrict freedom of movement and to oblige all citizens to take refuge either at home or in a public shelter. As a matter of actual fact, most members of the public gave little thought to the legality of these regulations and, being so occupied with fears for personal survival and so swept up by the general inclination to consensus, would most probably not have protested over them even if suspecting them to be not entirely legal. Their behaviour thereby lent further credence to Noam Chomsky's claim that people's fears are typically exploited by political systems, and to the observation made by Jurgen Habermas, to the effect that the 'rule of law' consists of a means for increasing governmental control over the mechanisms of a state and a society. All things considered, the situation created by the Gulf War constituted yet another example of the phenomenon, indicated by the social historian, Martin Shaw, whereby wars have the effect of extending the degree of governmental intervention in the lives of a country's citizens.[8]

Since the content of political debates became so very circumscribed during this period, almost no one, was prepared to take the risk of challenging the national security policy being pursued for concern over being branded as disloyal to the state. Stohl, the American scholar, has drawn attention to the fact that, in periods of war, political institutions become more inclined to proceed violently against groups of potential or actual demonstrators.[9] And, indeed, Israel's indigeneous Arab population was very severely warned by police minister Roni Milo not to try to show any signs of active political support for Iraq (as, for example, via demonstrations) or to interfere in any manner with Israel's preparations for dealing with the military threat it was facing. This served to widen still further the chasm which existed between the country's Jewish political administration and the demographic reality, which features two separate peoples, Jewish-Israeli and Palestinian-Israeli.[10]

An indication of where Jewish–Israeli national boundaries lie was provided when the country began distributing gas masks to its civilian population. Israeli Arabs received the masks only after applying to the High Court of Justice, while Arabs living in the occupied territories never received them. After making their own, frantic, appeal to the Court, a mere few days prior to the war's outbreak, Palestinians residing in East Jerusalem and in a limited number of villages in the Jerusalem area were eventually provided with gas masks too.[11] If, in periods of 'no war and no peace', the boundaries of nationality in Israel were defined in terms of religion and the manner in which the country's Arab-Palestinian population was to be related to, these boundaries suddenly became particularly pronounced given the arousal of general suspicion that the Arabs in Israel and in the territories might identify very closely with Iraq and take advantage of the war to commit acts of sabotage. But what happened, in reality, was that after a short time Arab Israeli leaders announced their dissociation from Iraq's invasion, declaring that they would remain loyal to the state indicating their intention to obey any decision issued by its governmental institutions.

Nevertheless, both the government and the army issued statements to the effect that, in the event of an attack, Israel's urban areas would probably suffer the severest war damage and that its rural areas, in their entirety, would therefore have to accept being placed in second position of priority in respect to the distribution of gas masks. They claimed, accordingly, that the Arab agricultural settlements were in no way discriminated by comparison with Jewish settlements in rural areas. But their assertions rang a somewhat suspicious note given the general spirit of intolerance in attitudes towards Israeli Arabs at the time. Moreover, since the Arab population, overwhelmingly, resides in agricultural areas while the Jewish population predominantly occupies urban ones, it is fairly obvious that the procrastination conducted in distributing gas masks to the agricultural sector was bound to discriminate principally against the Arabs.

The national state of anxiety was exploited to achieve certain internal political aims, especially in regard to Palestinians residing in the occupied territories. One example was the attempt made to subdue the Intifada by creating problems for its leaders. Particularly significant was the placing of one of the Palestinians' leaders under house arrest – Seri Nuseiba – incarcerated by order of the Minister of Defence. That order was issued on the strength of the allegation that Nuseiba had cooperated with Iraq by faxing messages concerning the arrangements which Israel had made to defend itself against Iraqi missile attacks. If possessing any evidence to substantiate these charges, the government refused to disclose it, claiming that any such disclosure would occasion serious damage to state security.

The intolerance characterizing the government was also clearly expressed by its decision, on 5 February to bring the Moledet party into the coalition, thereby granting an appreciable degree of legitimacy to that party's 'transfer' policy. In acting to bring Moledet into the government, the Likud aroused serious suspicions, among Zionist and non-Zionist parties alike, that its policy thenceforth might include forcible expulsion of Palestinians living in the territories and possibly also of Israeli Arabs. As a result, and for the first time since the Gulf War began, stormy debates took place in the Knesset and severe criticism was levelled at the government and at the Prime Minister, Yitzhak Shamir. Nine years previously, in 1982, the Likud had similarly exploited the fact that the public's attention was riveted on national security issues (the Lebanon War) to take the controversial step of bringing the Tehiya party into the government. This time, however, by virtue of Moledet's 'transfer' platform, the Likud's act aroused even more furious controversy than before. Where the Arabs were concerned, it presented a very serious signalling. Their spokesmen in the Knesset delivered themselves angrily of the view that Moledet's accession to the government was likely to cause the political system to deteriorate drastically, even to the point of civil war.[12]

The government did all that it could to avoid responding to public criticism. Only a limited number of its cabinet ministers – chiefly members of the ministerial committee on security matters – were provided with data and informed about decisions taken on national security issues. In fact, it was the prime minister and defence minister who took most of the important decisions on their own, without really consulting with any of their colleagues in the government, and very often even without informing them of what had been decided. But this type of decision-making process is quite typical of Israel, particularly in wartime and when exceptionally serious security crises arise.

During the Gulf War, just as happened during previous wars, various politicians proposed the establishment of new political structures, to serve as special decision-making forums. Among the proposals was that of reinstating the 'national unity' government. But personal rivalries – especially between Yitzhak Shamir and Shimon Peres – as well as the still-unhealed wounds inflicted by the crisis attending the national unity government's fall in March 1990, put a halt to that notion fairly quickly. And, in any case, partly by virtue of having further consolidated his power base with the inclusion of Moledet, Prime Minister Shamir had succeeded in establishing a government sufficiently strong to survive even the pressures of war, so replacing it by a national unity government would have hardly been worthwhile from the Likud's point of view. A proposal which did manage to earn some genuine attention, however, was that of setting up a national security council – an idea that had already risen many times in the past in the national agenda.

But the general public was essentially incapable of appreciating the significance of the suggestion and the two political élites, Likud and Labour, quickly made it clear that they were each basically against the formation of an additional body of that variety, whose impact on future policy-making might undermine that of any major party currently in power.

During the war, the government scarcely bothered to report its activities to the Knesset and the Prime Minister abstained from providing information either to the Knesset or its committees. The Knesset Foreign Affairs and Defence Committee, whose duty is to supervise the activities of the security forces, found itself helpless in the face of the obstinate refusal, witnessed by ministers and senior officials alike, to supply it with any valuable information over and beyond what was published in the mass media. On their part, the media became wholly subject to military controls, particularly those imposed by the army spokesman's office and the military censors. The country's two radio stations were temporarily merged for the duration of the war, so that even the limited degree of pluralism which characterized the electronic media during less hectic times became restricted even further. The more militant elements in the society accepted it as wholly understandable that, during a period of crisis, such as Israel was undergoing, all matters related to national information efforts, such as the provision of information and the instructing of the public of how to conduct itself should be placed in the hands of the military authorities.

Public opinion surveys, conducted during the period, indicate a high degree of consensus. About 90 per cent of the public concurred with the consolidation of the radio stations.[13] The astonishing fact, that the public was prepared to cede its right to receive more than a single source of news about what was going on, can be attributed to the extraordinary degree of importance which people attach to various national symbols during wartime and security crises. For a month and a half, Israel's civilian population, found itself protected by practically no real air coverage against salvoes of ballistic missiles, but nevertheless suppressed almost every inclination to question the wisdom of instructions that they take shelter in 'sealed' rooms which really offered very little protection, particularly in the event of a direct hit. Even while the war was still in progress, rumours began to spread about the defectiveness of many of the gas masks distributed, but they were rapidly and effectively silenced. The army and other security forces issued energetic, and somewhat pretentious, denials of any defect, claiming that the population had been provided with very effective protection against possible chemical or biological attack.

Censorship restrictions meant that the public was given only very limited information, while the reports issued by the army spokesman's office were usually very general in nature and provided, at best, a severely fragmented picture of the real situation. The ban imposed on army generals granting any form of press interview provide a clear indication to the lengths of which the government was prepared to go in increasing its control over the amount of information imparted to the public. The very distribution of civil defence kits to each citizen made a considerable contribution towards establishing consensus. This was because it reinforced the fears already sensed by the public and gave the impression that the government was ostensibly adopting efficient measures for defence. Even political parties as dovish as Ratz, which had up to then severely criticized the government on a whole variety of issues, supported its policy of military passiveness and praised Prime Minister Shamir on the way in which he was leading the nation.

Convincing evidence that many civil defence kits and gas masks were actually either entirely or partially defective was made available to the public only after the war ended. The reports prepared by the State Comptroller's Office, published soon after the end of the war, pointed at the fact that many such kits would have been incapable of furnishing even the minimal degree of protection required in the event of a chemical or biological attack. This constituted yet another piece of evidence supporting the claim that, contrary to what is commonly alleged in the theoretical literature to the effect that consensus is a positive political phenomenon, the phenomenon of close identity in public thought risks sometimes serious damage occurring.

THE PUBLIC DISCOURSE DURING THE GULF WAR

During the war the Israeli public generally conducted itself with considerable discipline. In most of Israel's previous wars, a large proportion of the population had been drafted into the army – a fact which had made it difficult for extra-parliamentary opposition to those wars to gather support. Where the call-up was restricted in scale (as during the Lebanon War), protest groups could organize themselves more easily. In the Gulf War, recruitment took an entirely different form. In fact, most of the reserves were not called up, instead, about 200,000 workers, employed in various vital fields, were informed that they would temporarily be working subject to the special emergency regulations invoked.

In democratic societies, the public generally does not pose any opposition to its government during the early stages of that government's conduct of a war. This is because the collective assumption is made that the government deserves a certain period of grace to prove the correctness of its war management policy. Also because people have a tendency to shun controversy at a time when their country faces serious security dangers. It was precisely this form of 'permissive consensus' to come to light during the Gulf War and enable the expansion of the State into the society.

Although the civilian population suffered direct missile hits, casualties were relatively low and, the whole time, the government managed to convey the impression that its handling of the crisis was firm and efficient. Few people asked themselves what might have happened to the repeated vows, uttered by the defence authorities and the Prime Minister, to the effect that Israel would be making an appropriate military response and would not make do purely with measures of self-defence, as facilitated by its Patriot batteries. About

94 per cent of the public was of the opinion that the government was 'taking care of the security situation', either 'well' or 'very well'.[14]

The army, in contrast, was somewhat better informed on the real situation, and some senior officers demanded military action against Iraq. However, since the army was, as always, entirely controlled by the political echelon, its disagreements with the government over this issue were not permitted to spill over into the public arena. Furthermore, since so much genuine anxiety was rife and since the army was of the opinion that Israel would certainly resort to arms when its national interests were truly threatened, a sufficient degree of consensus within the military was preserved.

Israel's traditional confidence in its ability to vanquish any aggressor singlehandedly – a trust which had already previously begun to erode – gave way to a more realistic appraisal. The entire population, including all political groups, seemed to accept without protest, and even to support, the situation where it was precisely a government as nationalistically oriented as Shamir's which chose to veer from time-honoured tradition by allowing a military threat to Israel to be thwarted by reliance on foreign intervention, and by calling in foreign forces (to protect Israel's skies and its population generally) for the first time since the Suez Campaign of 1956.

What actually took place, was a shift in the manner in which an external threat had hitherto generally been perceived. Many more people than ever before began to accept the assumption that Israel's military power was actually very limited. The fact that thousands of citizens displayed Israeli flags and affixed 'We Are All Patriots' stickers to their vehicles is an evidence of the rapid formation of a sense of solidarity rarely seen in periods of relative calm. But this solidarity was derived from a particularly acute case of national nerves: about 40 per cent of the public testified that, during the war, they suffered either 'often' or 'sometimes' from attacks of anxiety. Towards the end of January 1991, 36 per cent admitted their worry that they might not be able to cope with the war's stresses if Scud missiles were to continue to fall on Israeli population centres.[15] Naturally enough, tension was at its highest in areas hit by missiles – Tel Aviv and Haifa. It was a clear indication, and the clearest ever witnessed during the history of Israel's many wars, of an unmistakable decline in the public's ability to withstand pressures and external threats. Some of those who expected to buckle under the strain travelled overseas, either permanently or temporarily, so as to seek much-needed respite. Others (around 100,000 in number) remained in the country, but abandoned their homes, at least during the fateful night hours. Nevertheless, as stated, most of the public supported the government's stance.

The Gulf War represented the first occasion, since 1949, in which the country's civilian population suffered hostilities, standing in the front line and bearing the brunt of the enemy's onslaught. In place of the euphoria which engulfed victorious little Israel in 1967, in place of the dilemmas aroused by Israel's 'goliath-like' strength since 1967, in place of the doubts about the country's identity created by the growing importance of the struggle with the Palestinians – far more basic and fundamental thoughts, about identification with one's ethnic origins, with one's community, and with one's society which was fighting for its survival, began once again to occupy Israeli minds. This was not by any means a process grounded in military necessity in the narrow Lasswellian sense. It was, instead, one which quite consciously strove to reduce political divisions within the society at the same time as altering the position and the nature of boundaries developed over time separating the country's citizens from their government.

One expression of what was happening to Israeli society during the Gulf War related to the matter of defining 'Who is an Israeli?'. During most of Israel's previous wars, the criterion for measuring people's 'patriotism' was whether they either fought, or volunteered in some other manner, to assist the country towards victory. In the Gulf War, by contrast, the criterion was consent to take the necessary steps to survive, people's readiness for passive acceptance of whatever fate might bring and their preparedness to stay put and not flee from the missile barrages arriving. The fact, that slogans such as 'We'll get through this, too' appeared on street corner posters and were repeatedly heard on the radio, testifies convincingly to the nature of the consensus which developed while providing also evidence of a certain measure of passivity, grounded in a general recognition that no alternative was in sight. The night curfews, to which a large proportion of the population was subject for about a month and a half and which brought most cultural life and entertainment to a standstill, reinforced the atmosphere of reluctant submission to the grey reality imposed on the country and intensified people's sense that Israel was paying a very high price for being dragged unwillingly into an international confrontation.

It was for these reasons that even political groupings on the Left, who engaged in considerable actions of protest during the Intifada, looked on in relative silence when very stiff curfew conditions were applied in the occupied territories. Groups like 'Peace Now', as well as clusters of intellectuals, issued calls to peace movements throughout the world to support Israel and its policies during the crisis. Their message was that occupying another country by force had to be politically opposed, and that, once the war was over they would redouble their demands that the Intifada be solved through the granting of political self-determination to the Palestinians. But, at the same time, they stressed that, as a first step, Saddam Hussein's regime of 'genocide' had to be crushed. Overall, their stance was that Israel, had ceased temporarily to be an all-powerful conqueror and was, instead, only a victim.

What was revealed yet again, was that involvement in war has a habit of strengthening considerably the symbols of the state, at the expense of its basic democratic values. In the case of Israel, it reinforced the regime's Jewish elements, while the problems faced by its minorities were thrust aside, as attempts during the war, to deal with their solution would have been regarded as contradicting the nation's 'logic'. This general rule, though, was broken by the Israeli Association for Civil Rights whose appeal to the High Court, when the War was terminated, succeeded in lifting the general curfew in the territories. In addition, a certain amount of relatively marginal activity was undertaken by a small leftist groups and by Jewish and Arab intellectuals, who called on the USA to cease its military operations in the Gulf immediately and to recognize the solution of the Palestinian problem as comprising Israel's principal task. The most prominent of those groups was one which, prior to the outbreak of the Gulf War, had called itself 'A Moment Before War' and which, during the course of the war, was given the name 'Enough' by a number of its members. It declared the need to establish a linkage between ending the Gulf and the Palestinian crises. Their expressions of protest diverged appreciably from the general consensus and produced no results whatsoever, largely because the rules of the political game, as played by Israel's traditionally fighting society, were simply far too powerfully entrenched.

A comparison with the Six-Day War (1967) indicates the extent to which permissive consensus played a significant role during the Gulf War. In 1967, the national consensus had been in favour of a pre-emptive strike while, in the Gulf crisis, it was precisely the opposite. Whereas in 1967 the danger was considered to be very close to Israel's borders, in 1991 it was regarded as being very far from them. Another reason was that the public was aware of the fact that, this time, a super-power had taken on itself most of the military burden involved. Furthermore, and probably most important of all, the Israeli civilian population was inclined to identify with its government on matters of national security. Notwithstanding the damage occasioned to residential areas, 80 per cent of the public felt that Israel 'ought to stay in calm control and not react for the moment'.[16] And this expression of national forbearance occurred despite the fact that most of the people interviewed were aware of the possibility that the war might well endure for a relatively protracted period, as long as two months in duration, and that population centres were quite likely to sustain severe damage.

That this phenomenon of permissive consensus came into being within a traditionally combative society does not necessarily mean the society is militant in nature and inevitably and unreservedly supportive of the idea of going to war. In the case under review, it demonstrated a preparedness to be disciplined and obedient to its government. That obedience, translated into a readiness to have Israel's military wait and do nothing, was especially noteworthy given the fact that senior army officers, including the chief of military intelligence, had issued repeated warnings that Iraq possessed chemical and even biological weapons,[17] and taking into account the declarations, issued by Iraq's leaders, that they intended to strike Israel a lethal blow.

The Gulf War, as everyone is aware, was an international rather than an inter-communal war. In complete opposite to the Intifada, which had exposed the difficulty involved in defining the Israeli national identity, the Gulf War strengthened tendencies within Israel to unite around a national identity determined by the criterion of Jewishness. A danger deriving from a source, lying external to the system, Iraq, assisted in the crystallization of that identity. In actual fact, the Gulf War diverted the Israeli public's attention from the painful Palestinian aspect of its country's protracted struggle. The energetic support given by Yasser Arafat to Saddam Hussein provided Israel with a convenient pretext for evading the necessity to define its permanent borders.

The Palestinians, yet again, were conveniently branded by the political élites, and also by most of the public, as a satanic enemy, working hand in hand with elements bent on bringing Israel to ruin. This occurred despite the fact that, while the war was in progress, a few manifestos were published, and a few hesitant voices raised, against the Iraqi aggression, giving expression to the fear that Saddam Hussein's occupation of Kuwait might result in damage to Palestinian interests. It occurred, too, despite the fact that several Palestinian leaders publicly accused Iraq of engaging in a forced transfer of

Palestinians from Kuwait. But these phenomena of protest, limited in number, made practically no impression on the Israeli political system.

AFTER THE STORM

With the end of the Gulf War, Israeli society returned once more to 'normal'. State control over the broadcasting stations was somewhat reduced, the economy resumed its regular course and most citizens resumed their former lifestyles. The rules of the democratic political game, it became apparent, did not have to face any particularly grave challenge because, at least on the surface, the regime managed to demonstrate reasonable efficiency in dealing with a crisis situation of considerable proportions. Coping with the arrival of waves of new immigrants, a matter which the war had temporarily shunted aside, rose again to the top of the national agenda.

The extent to which the Gulf War proved to have exerted any particularly significant long-term impact over basic attitudes within the political system remains questionable. The political élites did not exhibit any fundamental change in respective postures on matter of implementing military force. Once the war was over, for example, debates over the issue of how much strategic depth Israel requires resumed, but no alteration in any of the various parties' former positions became apparent. If anything, they seemed to have become even more entrenched in them. The Likud asserted that the Iraqi 'blitz' assault on Kuwait, as well as its resort to firing ballistic missiles, offered fairly conclusive proof of what would likely happen if a Palestinian state (probably a pro-Iraqi entity) was to come into existence alongside Israel, no more than 15 km (around 9 miles) from Israel's western border, the sea. By contrast, the Labour party claimed that the Gulf War proved clearly how vital a stable Jordan was to Israel's security and the extent to which that Hashemite kingdom was capable of granting Israel the real strategic depth so needed. Shimon Peres, Labour's chairman, expressed his opinion that it was time to return to the notion of solving the Israeli–Arab conflict on the basis of territorial compromise with Jordan, including a Palestinian delegation in the process. Political 'doves', both within the Labour party and on its left, argued that the Gulf War provided further evidence proving the idea of strategic depth to be no more than a myth and that, in an era of advanced military technology, no strategic advantage could be gained by holding on to the Jordan river's west bank. The best form of strategic depth that Israel could hope for, they stated, would be achieved by entering into a stable peace agreement and granting the

Palestinians their rights to political self-determination. The parties situated politically on the right to the Likud, in extreme contrast, were quick to point out that the PLO's unreserved identification with Iraq served to prove how vital, *de facto*, is to take urgent measures which would effectively produce massive settlement activity in Judea and Samaria – and that it was equally necessary to deny, firmly and categorically, the idea of granting the least legitimacy to the notion of letting any independent or autonomous Palestinian political entity come into being.

No noticeable change occurred in the attitudes held by the public at large, however, and instead it appeared that the Gulf War had made the public entrench itself even more firmly in the views it had maintained before the Gulf crisis ever broke out.[18] All the same, the possibility became apparent that Israelis would thereafter be more suspicious than before of the effectiveness of having their country rely on its military might as a means of establishing an unshakable presence in the Middle East. It became perfectly possible, in fact, that even Israel's political élites would rapidly become obliged to moderate their previous postures in unprecedented fashion, given their awareness of the following developments: the massive acceleration in the regional arms race, the growing likelihood (probably unavoidable) that nuclear weapons would become part of the Middle East scene, the determination evidenced by the USA to neutralize the Middle East as a factor capable of upsetting its vision of a new, international 'world order', and Israel's relative vulnerability to ballistic weapons. If that did not occur, indeed, it looked very much as though the democratic bases of Israel's political regime would be forced to confront some very serious challenges, largely because the country might not be capable of withstanding an indefinite situation of national emergency and the bleak prospect of one war after another.

NOTES

1 See, for example, H.O. Lasswell, 'The garrison state', *American Journal of Sociology*, 46 1941, pp. 455–68.
2 G. Goldberg, G. Barzilai and E. Inbar, *The Impact of Intercommunal Conflict: The Intifada and Israeli Public Opinion*, Policy Studies No. 43, Jerusalem: Leonard Davis Institute, 1991.
3 A.H. Barton, *Communities in Disaster*, New York: Anchor Books, 1969, pp. 63–322.
4 Yossi Sarid, 'Let them come look for me', *Ha'aretz*, 17 August 1990, p. 13.
5 For repercussions of this change on the non-Zionist Israeli Left, see interview with retired general Matti Peled, formerly one of the leaders of

the non-Zionist 'Progressive Party for Peace', *Hadashot*, Supplement, 8 February 1991, pp. 18–19.

6 G. Simmel, *Conflict*, New York: Free Press, 1955; L. Coser, *The Functions of Social Conflict*, New York: Free Press, 1956, pp. 92–5.

7 C. Rossiter, *Constitutional Dictatorship*, New York: Harper & Row, 1963.

8 M. Shaw, *War, State and Society*, London: Macmillan Press, 1984; J. Habermas (ed.) *Observations on the Spiritual Situation of the Age*, Mass., MIT Press, 1985, pp. 1–28; For Chomsky's ideas, see: M. Blatt, *et al.* (eds) *Dissent and Ideology in Israel*, New York: Ithaca Press, 1975, pp. 1–7; also see: A. Giddens, *The Nation-State and Violence*, Cambridge: Polity Press, 1985.

9 M. Stohl, *War and Domestic Political Violence*, Beverly Hills, California: Sage Publications, 1976, pp. 82–95.

10 For an expanded treatment of this topic, see G. Barzilai and Y. Shain, 'Israeli democracy at a crossroads: a crisis of non-governability', *Government and Opposition*, vol. 26, no. 3, Summer 1991, pp. 345–67.

11 High Court of Justice, *Miladi Murcus* vs. *The Minister of Defence et al.*, not yet published.

12 See: Knesset debates over Member of Knesset Rehavam Zeevi joining the government, 2 May 1991, *Protocols of Knesset Debates*, pp. 2030–55.

13 Zeev Segal, Gad Barzilai, 'An administration bereft of goodwill', *Ha'aretz*, 14 February 1991, p. 2b.

14 Shlomit Levi, 'Support for the government: like during the Six-Day War', *Ma'ariv*, 1 February 1991, p. 7. The author reports on the surveys run by the Institute for Applied Social Research, Jerusalem; see, also, the report on a telephonic survey run by the same institute: *Ha'aretz*, 28 January 1991, p. 3a.

15 Note 14.

16 Note 15.

17 See, for example, the declaration by the Chief of Military Intelligence, Gen. Amnon Shahak, *Yediot Aharonot*, 15 February 1991, p. 3.

18 See the report by Roni Shaked on the survey conducted by the Institute for Applied Social Research, Jerusalem, dated June 1991, published in *Yediot Aharonot*, 7 June 1991, p. 4; similar conclusions emerge from a research study, edited by Dr Ephraim Inbar and Dr Gad Barzilai, and compiled on the basis of questionnaires distributed to Knesset members and public opinion surveys; see: Gad Barzilai and Efraim Inbar, 'Do wars have an impact?: Israeli public opinion after the Gulf War', *Jerusalem Journal of International Relations*, vol. 14, no. 1 March 1992, pp. 48–64.

8 Strategic consequences for Israel

Efraim Inbar

Many Israelis at first regarded the conquest of Kuwait by Iraq and the international developments that followed as 'manna from heaven'.[1] International attention had been diverted from the intractable Arab–Israeli conflict and the difficult Palestinian question serving as a source of criticism against Israel from many countries, including friendly ones. Less gratifying, however, was Saddam Hussein's attempt at involving Israel in the Gulf conflict in order to burden Washington with its link to Jerusalem. Furthermore, America's long deliberations on which steps to take against Iraq caused considerable apprehension in Jerusalem lest Saddam end up as a winner after all.

The receptiveness of many in the international community to linking a solution of the Gulf Crisis to a peace initiative for the Arab–Israeli conflict, as Iraq insisted, represented yet another additional reason for worry in Israeli policy circles. When the war began it was thus welcomed as assuring ultimate Iraqi defeat; less so once Iraqi missiles landed in Israel's populated centres.

A careful analysis of developments leading up to the war and deriving from it, as well as their implications for Israel, suggests a mixed strategic balance sheet. This chapter traces the conduct of the Israeli government from the invasion of Kuwait to the end of the Gulf War, and then proceeds to analyse the deeper ramifications for Israel. Finally, the consequences of the war for national security are evaluated.

ISRAELI BEHAVIOUR

The invasion of Kuwait caused profound concern in Jerusalem, and for good reason. The Iraqi army, after all, was ranked the fifth largest in the world, with some 950,000 men under arms, and an arsenal ncluding over 5,000 tanks, nearly 4,000 artillery pieces and close to 700 combat aircraft. Iraq, a self-proclaimed enemy of the Jewish state, also had at her disposal missiles capable of reaching Israeli territory, and openly threatened to arm them with chemical warheads. The takeover of Kuwait, its oil and wealth, was an additional important asset in sustaining Iraq's quest for regional hegemony. Therefore American determination to restore the status quo ante and curb Iraqi influence was welcomed no less in Israel than in the capitals of Egypt, Syria, Saudi Arabia and the Gulf states.

Washington's attempt to force Baghdad to withdraw from Kuwait by forging an international coalition under the mantle of UN legitimacy was a main factor in the moulding of the Israeli reaction to the events in the Gulf. The 'low profile' policy adopted by Prime Minister Shamir's government was primarily intended to facilitate this American endeavour. Worth noting in this regard is that it was only in June 1990, after several months of byzantine political manoeuvring, that the Likud Party under Yitzhak Shamir had succeeded in establishing a rightist coalition government. Despite the fact that confirmed hard-liners were members of this government, Israel would behave with remarkable restraint throughout the period under discussion.

Despite complementary interests, Israel was not a welcomed partner in the American led-coalition. Traditional Arab reluctance to be formally associated with Israel was evident when Saddam Hussein, championing the Palestinian cause, tried immediately to divert Arab energies away from its invasion of Kuwait by linking its occupation to Israel's rule in the territories and to a solution of the Arab–Israeli conflict. Nevertheless, the Arab coalition partners refused to fall into the trap of formally accepting this mischievous linkage, legitimizing Iraq's invasion, though they undoubtedly expected a more active American role (namely pressure on Israel) in the Arab–Israeli context with the end of the Gulf crisis. Under such circumstances, Israel obviously preferred to attract as little attention as possible in order to circumvent the proposed linkage.

What counted most in Israeli decision-making of course was the American preference for an Israeli low-key approach. While it had the potential of undermining Israel's claim to being a strategic asset, Jerusalem wanted above all for America to succeed in administering a blow to Iraq without further antagonizing the Bush administration. In other words, Israeli leaders were interested primarily in preserving a working relationship with the USA hoping to capitalize on its 'good behaviour' once the crisis ended. Refreshingly, for a change, Israel was in the American administration's good graces and received favourable coverage in the international media.

Furthermore, so long as they were not under direct attack, Israelis had little appetite for allowing their military units to fight in Iraq. Minimizing Israeli involvement was also regarded as prudent in reducing chances of an Iraqi missile attack. As the occupation of Kuwait came to be perceived not just as a regional problem, but as threatening Western oil supplies as well as international order and stability, the situation lent itself to intervention by the USA. Even the hawkish minister Rafael Eitan, an ex-Chief of Staff and leader of the right-wing Tzomet, warned not to interfere with the 'hornets' nest' in the Gulf.[2]

The low-key approach also proved instrumental in denying political ammunition to radical elements in the Arab world, especially the fundamentalists, that might have succeeded in undermining the pro-American, and anti-Iraqi stance of their governments. Stability in Jordan, always a vital Israeli interest, in particular weighed on Israeli minds during the crisis. For Israel wanted to prevent Iraqi troops from entering Jordan, with or without King Hussein's expressed consent, and showed real apprehension at the growing political influence of Islamic elements in that country. Consistent with the 'low profile' strategy, the Shamir government sought to assure the King of not harbouring any plans to topple his regime or to invade his country.[3] Unclear, however, is how reassuring such messages were in Amman in light of the conviction among the Likud leadership that ultimately Jordan is the Palestinian state!

The 'low profile' policy certainly reflects the cautious temper of Israel's Prime Minister, Yitzhak Shamir. His known reluctance to engage in risk-taking neatly dovetailed with Israeli traditional interests in refraining from 'rocking the boat' in Middle East politics. This time, in particular, the patient Israeli policy preference of wait-and-see in preserving the status quo seemed to be exquisitely appropriate under acute crisis circumstances.

However, immediately after the war started, this strategem came under severe duress when Baghdad aimed its Scud missiles at Israel's heartland. Hoping to deter such attacks, Israeli leaders had already issued stern warnings at the end of August 1990, when Shamir declared that if those planning to attack Israel 'will dare to do so, they will pay a terrible price'.[4] Similar threats were voiced by the Defence Minister and the Chief of Staff. Deterrence has always been a central concept in Israel's strategic thinking, as the best way of discouraging irresponsible and provocative Arab military initiatives, notwithstanding the fact that several Arab–Israeli wars had been fought, coupled with the persistence of the terror campaign against the Jewish state.[5] In the winter of 1991 Israeli deterrence failed again. The use of force to lend credibility to deterrence being an article of faith and almost instinctive in Israeli strategic thinking,[6] the Israeli government did indeed seriously weigh taking independent military action against the Scud missile launchers deployed in western Iraq.

Still, as we know, the unilateral retaliatory strike by Israel failed to materialize. The principal explanation is that the main consideration in Israeli crisis management was to maintain its dependability and standing with the Americans. In service to this overriding goal, other objectives, including credible deterrence and the inviolability of Israeli territory and citizenry, were subordinated. The USA also made great efforts to discourage the contemplated Israeli retaliatory strike. Two senior officials, Lawrence Eagleburger and Paul Wolfowitz, spent hours in Jerusalem pressing their government's point of view on Israeli leaders and military strategists. Even timely presidential messages were needed to dissuade Israel from acting on its natural inclination. By way of tangible, demonstrative support the USA airlifted batteries of Patriot surface-to-air missiles to provide a limited missile defence capability; hunting missile launchers in west Iraq was given a higher priority by the US-led military coalition; and real-time intelligence on incoming missiles was provided to Israel. Finally, vague promises of future material and political support were made, with the European allies adding similar pledges and seeming to be more sympathetic to the Israeli stand on the Arab–Israeli conflict than before. Israel thus awoke to the possibility of parlaying military self-restraint into diplomatic benefits.

Furthermore, clearly no Israeli punitive action against Baghdad could be conducted without the risk of heavy casualties; nor could an Israeli Defence Forces (IDF) air strike equal in thoroughness and scale what the Americans were already doing in Iraq's interior. The sheer complexity of any planned commando strike combining land and air forces evoked apprehensions about either possible failure or the human toll. Crossing Jordanian airspace likewise posed dangers, both military and political.[7] In sum, considering the heavy American pressure, coupled with the risks involved in any military option plus anticipated political benefits resulting from restraint, the 'low profile' policy had to be a satisfactory, albeit less than ideal response, and one worth maintaining for as long as possible.

The war ended prematurely for Israel in the sense that Saddam Hussein still remained in power and in possession of a diminished but not insignificant conventional military arsenal. The USA, for its part, felt victorious. Its efforts to stabilize the Gulf region lost momentum, even as the belief that the time was now ripe for a mediation effort in the Arab–Israeli conflict.[8] Nevertheless, following the war, Washington and other international actors did accept Israel's preference for a process centring on the Arab states rather than focusing on the Palestinian issue alone. This and the weakening of the Iraqi adversary would become the main achievements Israel had to show for its 'low profile' policy.

ISRAEL'S CHANGING STRATEGIC SETTING

The Gulf crisis has also once more demonstrated for Jerusalem the significance of systemic factors in regional stability. Decentralization of the international political system, which had been heralded in many quarters as the beginning of an era of peace, has direct if mixed effects on the Middle East.[9] Unlike the European sub-system, this region had never been under rigid bipolar control by the superpowers. Soviet decline by 1990 further decreased Moscow's ability to constrain its Arab allies, thereby allowing countries like Iraq and Syria greater freedom of action. One factor accounting for the timing of the Iraqi action in Kuwait was Gorbachev's reluctance to be drawn into Middle Eastern affairs. Another systemic factor further explaining the Iraqi move was the deterioration of the local balance of power in the Gulf. In the wake of the long Iran–Iraq War, a weakened Iran had no longer been able to deter an Iraqi Anschluss of Kuwait.

Growing freedom of action by regional actors and changes in the regional balance of power are both developments working to Israel's long-term strategic detriment. The emergence of a strong Iraq capable of manipulating Gulf oil and petrodollars for imperial schemes is as dangerous for Israel as for its Arab neighbours. Indeed, what we in Israel may have witnessed, was, *inter alia*, an attempt by several Arab actors to prevent Iraqi hegemony in the Gulf region, with wider implications for the future Middle East politics and alignments.

One corollary of events in the Gulf concerns Israel's immediate rival, the Palestinians, and the long-term possibility that the Palestinian issue may lose some of its presumed salience. The Arab–Israeli conflict is a 'compound conflict', a term denoting two interrelated aspects: an interstate struggle and intercommunal strife.[10] In the previous decade and a half, because of PLO success in becoming a visible international actor, the interstate aspect of the conflict had come to be widely perceived of as less threatening, allowing for

Palestinization' of the conflict and emphasis of its intercommunal dimension. The Gulf crisis, which generated a high level of threat perception from an Arab state, served to redress the balance by reasserting the external Arab states factor.

Indeed, both conventional and unconventional Arab state capabilities pose a military threat to the existence of Israel in the absence of a broad regional peace framework. While unpleasant, Palestinian subconventional activities like terrorism or Intifada-related acts of violence, viewed in perspective, are after all a problem of 'current security'[11] or regular, ongoing and unexceptional precautionary measures. Despite the fact that ruling over Palestinians is potentially damaging to the fabric of Israeli society, from a purely military point of view it is secondary. Furthermore, the Palestinians are seen in some Israeli circles as clear losers in the Gulf War, particularly the PLO, which makes addressing their claims less urgent.

Nevertheless, in truth it is doubtful whether the Palestinian issue can be marginalized for long. As a matter of fact, the Gulf crisis has prompted yet another wave of Palestinian refugees, some finding a haven in Israeli-ruled territories, others in East Bank Jordan. In addition, the flow of money from the Gulf states to Palestinian institutions and individuals has been cut back drastically, creating economic hardship both in Jordan and in the territories. These developments must have a negative effect on Israeli and Jordanian attempts to maintain minimal quiet among the Palestinians.

Despite the setbacks, the low-key Intifada is definitely not over. Through soul-searching discussions by Palestinians in the territories about the direction of their struggle, possibly a more assertive and hopefully more pragmatic Palestinian local leadership will emerge.

Another troubling development for Israel was the Jordanian alliance with Iraq and the domestic difficulties experienced by the Hashemite regime. A possible massive Iraqi military presence in Jordan, which serves as a buffer zone between Israel and Iraq, has long been viewed with great concern in Jerusalem. Iraqi troops may constitute an indirect, distant threat to Israel, but an immediate, direct one to King Hussein and his country's sovereignty. The Likud, in spite of occasionally toying with the idea of endorsing Palestinian statehood to the east of the Jordan river at Hussein's expense, realized that stability of the Hashemite regime is a strategic asset, at least in immediate terms. Which lends credence to the old Jewish saying, never pray for a new king'. Israel quite understood that anything less than Iraqi defeat in the Gulf would have put Jordan on the next Iraqi list for possible annexation. Iraq dispatched seven divisions from camps near Baghdad to Kuwait with impressive speed, whereas Amman is the same distance from Baghdad and not very far from the Jordan river – Israel's eastern border. Iraqi troops in Jordan would be a most unwelcome and destabilizing development, for it would require a higher level of IDF preparedness as well as a far greater redeployment along the river.

Weapons technology available to Iraq, Syria and other Arab actors even before the crisis had made an attack with conventional and unconventional warheads on Israel's population centres a plausible contingency. Such a scenario receives greater cogency since February 1991. Distributing gas masks to the Israeli public has lowered the threshold on the use of chemical weapons, even though a chemical attack on Israel may not necessarily be devastating or decisive.

Yet the fact remains that attacks of missiles armed with conventional warheads did almost paralyse the whole country for a number of weeks. Many civilians left the Tel-Aviv area for the duration of the war, disrupting life, commerce and industry. Obviously, Israel's extraordinary sensitivity to casualties increases the perceived utility in Arab eyes of a conventional or chemical assault even were its results to be limited. The Scud missiles, in other words, have created a window of vulnerability for Israel. Until the Arrow system (the decision on its completion preceded the crisis) becomes operative sometime in the late-1990s, Jerusalem has no adequate defensive response in case deterrence once more fails. The experience with the Patriot surface-to-air missiles shows it offers but a partial answer to incoming missiles. No foolproof defence for the civilian population is technologically feasible. Furthermore, investments in aerial defence must also come at the expense of the IDF's offensive capability.

Part of the new strategic equation is that the option of hitting Israel's population centres with missiles is now in the hands of more distant enemies as well, giving Muslim states like Iran and Pakistan a greater say in any subsequent Arab–Israeli confrontation. Nor does Israeli hesitancy and restraint in 1991 augur well for deterring missile attacks in the future. The possibility of far away countries involving themselves in an Arab–Israeli encounter by firing missiles on Israel complicates the strategic equation, adding uncertainty to an already volatile situation.

Worth noting is that vulnerability of the home front is not a new phenomenon in the Arab–Israeli conflict. In 1967, Israeli authorities prepared 20,000 graves for expected civilian casualties. In 1973 Migdal Haemek was hit by a Syrian missile and Egyptian airborne missiles were fired at Tel-Aviv. A clear implication of the Gulf crisis is that Israel has to relearn to live with the possibility of civilian casualties in future military encounters, just as it has to adjust to a higher level of losses in the military forces. Belated revelations about Iraqi progress on the path to nuclear capability further indicate the Middle East as a region faces a very serious threat in the employment of weapons of mass destruction.

During the Gulf crisis, in response to the looming chemical and ground threats, Israel for all intents and purposes reactivated its earlier system of *casus belli*, muted during the years of Yitzhak Rabin's tenure as Defence Minister (1984–90). This revival became necessary in order to give new substance and credence to a weakened Israeli deterrence posture with the advent of missile warfare. The struggle against the local Intifada, diverting IDF attention from a general war, had a share as well in diminishing deterrence. So, too, a reduced defence budget that mandated a smaller order of forces.

An explicit *casus belli* approach, positing clear cautionary 'red lines' no Arab opponent could dare cross with impunity, when enunciated by a government perceived as ready to act, certainly stands to strengthen deterrence. A heightened threat perception on the part of Israel, coupled with awareness that the USA prefers Israel to adopt a low profile, also contributed to this return to the doctrine of *casus belli*. It serves to diminish Arab misperceptions, but also to signal Washington that Israel will not be able to tolerate certain life-threatening scenarios.

Whatever interpretation is offered to the end of the Gulf War, one thing seems certain: the Arab states – Syria and Saudi Arabia in particular – are anxious to complete major weapon procurement plans. The USA, too, is interested in further expanding the military forces of at least Egypt and Saudi Arabia. Both considerations resulted by 1992 in extremely high American arms transfer figures. Increased military strength in some Arab armies may indeed deter certain types of aggression, though the extent to which such weapons assure internal political stability is less evident. At the same time, massive arms transfers pose the greatest military threat to Israel, for high-tech American weapons in Arab hands stand to erode Israeli margins of security and qualitative superiority.

Jerusalem has little chance of successfully opposing the flow of American or European high-tech weapons to the Arab world. A direct consequence of the 1990–91 Gulf crisis is, if anything, the dramatic increase rather than decrease in arms transfers to the Arab countries in the Middle East, which in preceding years had actually begun to slow down. Higher defence expenditures in the region are not welcome as far as Israel's troubled economy and contracted IDF are concerned. Even transfer of American arms free of charge to Israel does not alleviate the situation. Weapons need maintenance and spare parts, both of which must come from the Israeli budget.

Prospects for an arms control regime in the Middle East are slim, despite the lip service paid to this concept by all parties concerned. The decline of Soviet power seemed on the surface to augur well for Western coordination in controlling the arms transfers to this region in the spirit of the 1950 Tripartite Declaration. Yet, such coordination has been and will continue to be a problem. We can expect domestic pressures, coming primarily from the arms industries, to sell indiscriminately. Furthermore, in contrast to the 1950s, when arms producers were few, in recent decades this market has seen considerable growth with producers such as Brazil, North Korea and China offering remarkable products. These newcomers have little incentive to cooperate in limiting arms procurement in the Middle East. The discoveries by UN missions to Iraq in the fall of 1991 clearly indicate that the International Atomic Energy Agency's inspections are still not effective in preventing violations of international agreements.

Imports of the latest military products to the region can only erode Israel's qualitative superiority. Though the Gulf War has little direct application to Israeli military doctrine, the utility of smart weapons was clearly demonstrated.[12] In order to maintain such an edge – an imperative for Israel – more indigenous production is required. For example, in light of the US refusal to sell a surveillance satellite or initially to supply real-time intelligence received from its own satellites, the building of an Israeli satellite seems now more justified than ever.[13] The new tasks to be given the Israeli arms industries, many of them uneconomic, becomes an additional burden on the Israeli budget stemming from the post-Gulf arms race.

The American military presence in the Gulf in time may still acquire some form of greater permanence. As seen from Jerusalem, such presence can have a mixed effect upon Israeli national security. While acting to curb Iraqi ambitions, an American presence probably limits Israeli freedom of action against those Arab countries where American troops are stationed. A comparable effect on Arab states hosting American personnel is not equally evident, particularly at moments of tension between Jerusalem and Washington. American military deployment on Arab soil would also neutralize the tacit pledge to come to Israel's aid in case of need. In any case, an American military effort to help Israel, if in existential danger, following American guarantees to Israel's security, does not appear terribly convincing.

The ability to reach the Middle East in time and to fight-side-by-side with Israel against a concerted Arab invasion is still not demonstrated by the Gulf crisis. It took the Americans over two months to bring their troops to the Gulf. Furthermore, the political will to intervene militarily on Israel's behalf is far from certain. Actually, officials in the Bush Administration studiously refused to confirm that were Israel to be in trouble it would evoke an effort similar to the one in the Gulf.

Is Israel still a strategic asset? Taking into consideration the great dependence on the USA this is a most troubling question for Israel. As a matter of fact, the changing status of Israel as an ally started with the loosening of the bipolar system. The reduction of the Soviet or Russian global threat has obviously reduced the American need for 'coal stations' around the world. At the strategic level 'Desert Storm' has demonstrated American hegemony in an emerging unipolar system. Under such circumstances small allies have a more difficult time to extract support from the world power, while the possibility of international estrangement does exist.[14] Indeed, present circumstances are not conducive to Israeli leverage in bilateral relations with the USA. In addition to the unfavourable international systemic configuration, Israeli requirements of American economic aid to finance the absorption of Soviet immigrants and to defend the cost of the developing regional arms race if anything, are increasing since the Gulf crisis.

During the Gulf crisis itself, when Arab cooperation was needed, the Israeli alliance took on the appearance of a political burden for Washington strategists. The war has created fresh American commitments to Arab friends, and Israelis are fearful that the political bill will be sent to Jerusalem. Until summer 1992 President Bush denied governmental guarantees for the $10 billion loans Israel sought, after the administration first tied financial support to a freeze in the settlement policy of the Israeli government. Basic differences concerning the contours of a Middle East settlement, which were to a great extent muted in the days of bipolarity, inevitably have resurfaced. As the United States is determined to reach a settlement on the Arab–Israeli conflict, its perspective clashes with Israeli preferences.

Though problematic, Israel unquestionably remains the most stable and reliable American ally in the region. It is the only 'natural' ally in the region by virtue of being a democracy with a clear pro-American orientation, both political and cultural. In contrast to Arab political systems, its regime is stable; also Israel obviously has military capabilities that are reassuring for the USA.

How this perceived relative value of Israel translates into political relations has never been very clear. Israel probably can benefit in the near future more because of its nuisance potential, than for its value as an ally. Stressing such potential for making trouble is clearly problematic; but no less counter-productive is a pliant Israel simply taken for granted in US and Western planning.

In the final analysis, the USA reacted in the Gulf because vast oil reserves, huge sums of petrodollars and the international economic order were at stake. An oil-thirsty world is surely no good omen for Israel. Such a state of world affairs would require showing greater sensitivity to Arab desires than to Israeli insecurity. Seen in this vein, adjustments in the 1992 world economy to an oil market without Iraqi oil could be interpreted as good news for Israel.

Effective international cooperation in implementing economic sanctions and the international consensus in allowing the use of force in imposing the economic blockade has been another, more encouraging surprise for Jerusalem. This is definitely a sign of the leadership potential of the USA in world affairs in a changing international scene, and Israel therefore has good reason to be satisfied with the improved fortunes of its American ally. Yet, even this indication of international cooperation has a worrisome side. Since its establishment Israel has been subject to an Arab attempt at waging economic war against it. Despite some success the Arab boycott has failed to secure widespread international cooperation for this attempted economic strangulation of Israel. But under certain circumstances greater international cooperation against Israel in the economic sphere, begins to look plausible as part of a concerted effort at imposing political conditions on Israel to end the long Arab–Israel–Palestinian dispute once and for all. A more assertive Europe might well lead such a campaign of economic sanctions against Israel.[15]

The USA, indeed, lauded Israeli leaders for their low-key approach, because it best suited Washington's own strategy for coping with Iraq's provocation. Differences between the two countries were kept under wraps for the duration of the crisis, but then resurfaced as it ended. As noted, preserving close relations with the USA was defined as a strategic objective for the Shamir government, which accordingly shied away from an open confrontation with the American administration, such as over modalities in the peace process or the delay of government guarantees. However, it showed itself less compromising on the cardinal issue of West Bank settlements.

Apprehensions about the weakness of the Hashemite regime have been a sobering experience for supporters of 'Jordan is Palestine' and for the idea of enthroning Yasser Arafat instead of King Hussein in

Amman. The possibility for ever engineering a regional order conducive to Israeli interests was already shown to be problematic in 1982 after the invasion of Lebanon. Renewed concern in 1991–92 for the well-being of King Hussein suggests a similar conclusion.

On the other hand, the timing of the Gulf crisis did suit the Likud, sparing it having to make difficult choices on Shamir's own peace initiative of May 1989. There is nothing wrong in principle with buying time or hard bargaining in negotiations with Americans and Arabs in order to get better results. Yet, in the absence of a clear commitment to make changes in the status quo, such a strategy is internally problematic for a war weary society. Analysis of Israeli public opinion indicates that the status quo is no longer acceptable even as an interim arrangement.[16] Indeed, the Shamir government was virtually dragged by Washington into participating in the Madrid regional conference. Therefore, regardless of how the current American peace initiative ends, the domestic pressures for progress, however defined, will continue undiminished and in all probability only increase with time.

In the economic area we are already witness to the beginning of higher defence spending in Israel. Expanding the defence budget will severely tax already limited resources for spending in other economic and social areas, and will compete with taking care of the great wave of immigrants and problems of housing and unemployment.

CONCLUSION

When all is said and done, however, Israel was lucky to see the power of a formidable Arab opponent, Iraq, significantly reduced through the combined efforts of the USA and its allies. Yet, 'Desert Storm' did not eliminate other known potential threats to Israel's security, while it also generated new, unfamiliar and ominous dangers for Israel. A possible rupture in its relations with Washington would be a most unwelcome consequence of the whole crisis exercise. Similarly, a Palestinian state is feared more in Israel and elsewhere today than before August 1990. Nonetheless, marginalization of the Palestinian issue will be difficult, even though domestically the Israeli Right seems generally to have come out better from the crisis ordeal.

The Iraqi conquest of Kuwait, the ensuing international crisis and the war itself were presented in the Israeli media in highly dramatic, almost apocalyptic terms, with much talk of the emergence of a new Middle East. American performance as the only superpower left in the international arena may have contributed to such expectations;

whereas, empirically speaking, there was little unusual in the behaviour of Middle Eastern actors before or after the war. A famous French saying captures my evaluation – 'plus ça change, plus c'est la même chose'. Israel's Arab neighbours are adjusting to an international arena in which the USA is the leading actor. Israel is, of course, concerned primarily in the concessions that it may be asked to pay in smoothing the way for such an American-sponsored regional order. Exactly how Israel and its government will be able to secure American support without compromising its narrow margins of security remains to be seen as the original Gulf destabilizing influence and Scud missile experience further recede in time.

NOTES

1 For an analysis of the reasons for the invasion, see Efraim Karsh and Inari Rautsi, 'Why Saddam Hussein invaded Kuwait', *Survival*, 32, January/February 1991, pp. 18–30.

2 See his statement in *Ha'aretz*, 15 August 1990, A-2.

3 For the exchanges between the two countries, see the statement of the Jordanian Prime Minister, Mudar Badran in *Ha'aretz*, 13 January 1991, A-1.

4 *Ha'aretz*, 23 August 1991, A-2.

5 For an analysis of Israeli deterrence see Avner Yaniv, *Deterrence Without the Bomb: The Politics of Israeli Strategy*, Lexington, Mass.: Lexington Books, 1987; Jonathan Shimshoni, *Israel and Conventional Deterrence: Border Warfare from 1953 to 1970*, Ithaca, New York: Cornell University Press, 1988; and Efraim Inbar and Shmuel Sandler, 'Israeli Deterrence Revisited,' forthcoming.

6 See Yitzhak Rabin, 'Israel's security policy after Desert Storm', in *Thoughts on the National Security Concept of Israel*, (Hebrew) Ramat Gan: Bar-Ilan Center for Strategic Studies, August 1991.

7 For the deliberations of the Israeli leadership, see Yuval Neeman, *Ha'aretz*, 2 February 1991, B-2. Neeman, a cabinet member, was the leader of the right-wing Techiya party.

8 For a critique of this shift of focus see Alvin Z. Rubinstein, 'New world order or hollow victory', *Foreign Affairs*, 70, Fall 1991, pp. 53–65.

9 For a serene view of the international changes taking place, see John J. Mearsheimer, 'Back to the future: instability in Europe After the Cold War', *International Security*, 15, Summer 1990, pp. 5–56.

10 For this term, see Shmuel Sandler, 'The protracted Arab–Israeli conflict: a temporal–spatial analysis', *Jerusalem Journal of International Relations*, 10, December 1988, pp. 55–6.

11 In Israeli strategic parlance this term refers to threats to the daily routine of Israelis, without constituting a threat to the mere existence of the state or its territorial integrity, which is termed 'basic security'.

12 For a sober analysis of the technological and organizational dimensions of the Gulf War, see Gene I. Rochlin and Chris C. Demchak, 'The Gulf War:

technological and organizational implications', *Survival*, 33, May/June 1991, pp. 260–73.

13 See the statement of Moshe Arens, the Defence Minister, in such a vein, *Ha'aretz*, 16 April 1991, A-2.

14 For the importance of systemic factors in the relations between the US and embattled small allies see Efraim Inbar, *Outcast Countries in the World Community*, Monograph Series on World Affairs, Denver, Colorado: University of Denver, 1985.

15 For an analysis of such a possibility see Ilan Greilsammer, *European Sanctions Revisited*, *Policy Studies* No. 31, Jerusalem: Leonard Davis Institute for International Relations, The Hebrew University, July 1989.

16 Giora Goldberg, Gad Barzilai and Efraim Inbar, *The Impact of Intercommunal Conflict: The Intifada and Israeli Public Opinion*, *Policy Studies* No. 43, Jerusalem: Leonard Davis Institute for International Relations, Hebrew University of Jerusalem, pp. 11–15.

Part III
Great Power realignment

9   Origins of the new world order[1]

Robert W. Tucker

It is striking that at the outset of the 1990s Americans found themselves debating the desirability of a role that only a few years before would have been scornfully dismissed by those charged with the conduct of the nation's foreign policy. For the authors of the Reagan Doctrine, America was the crusader for freedom, not the guarantor of international law and order. The Reagan Doctrine, certainly in its more expansive version, subordinated the traditional bases of international order to a particular version of legitimacy by proclaiming a right of intervention against non-democratic governments and particularly against Marxist–Leninist governments. In doing so, it went well beyond the grounds for intervention sanctioned by the traditions and practice of states. For it declared that even when a state's security interests, conventionally defined, were not in jeopardy and when its support of rebel movements was not a form of counter-intervention, intervention might nevertheless be justified to overturn illegitimate governments. The latter presumably had no rights, legitimacy being defined in terms of conformity to the democratic process.

The Reagan Doctrine cast the nation in the role of extending freedom and not only of defending it, as earlier the Truman Doctrine had done. The essence of the Reagan Doctrine, again in contrast with the Truman Doctrine, was the promotion of freedom even at the risk of greater disorder. In part, the subordination of the claims of order was justified simply by invoking what were proclaimed to be the superior claims of freedom. In part, however, the response to the criticism that the Reagan Doctrine was inimical to the claims of order was that any real semblance of international order had long ceased to exist. International order, the argument ran, must ultimately rest on the promise and reality that the rules comprising such order will be reciprocally observed. Since the communist adversaries obeyed no law other than the law of expediency, we were held to be under no obligation to conform to the norms of the 'old' order which, indifferent to internal forms of legitimacy, rested on the foundation of self-determination, sovereignty and non-intervention. These norms were given their principal institutional expression in the UN. During the years of the Reagan Administration, the relationship between the American government and the world organization reached its lowest point. The Reagan Doctrine in its various articulations reflected a thinly disguised contempt for the UN. The unilateralism that plainly characterized the doctrine was all but a formal rejection of the organization that was seen as increasingly dominated by states hostile to American interests and purposes.

Yet the Bush Administration appeared to have virtually reversed the outlook that informed the Reagan Doctrine. It did so by its insistence in the Gulf crisis that the measures taken against Iraq have a multilateral character and that their legitimacy be based on authorizing decisions of the United Nations Security Council. More significantly still, it did so by virtue of the role that it assigned to the UN and to the principle of collective security in the Administration's vision of a new world order. That vision not only placed principal emphasis on the maintenance of law and order; in assigning to the USA the role of insuring order, it did so by pledging that this role would be undertaken within the institutional constraints of the UN. The change this represented from the position of the preceding administration was striking.

Equally striking was the insistence of the Bush Administration on playing a role the nation was thought to have rejected a generation ago and in circumstances far less exigent than those of a generation ago. In intervening in Vietnam the Johnson Administration ostensibly did so largely for the same reasons that the Bush Administration intervened in the Gulf. In both instances, the interest in and commitment to world order was advanced as a – if not *the* – compelling motivation of American policy. In both instances as well, the interest in world order was considered inseparable from American security. The American intervention in Vietnam was repeatedly justified in terms of the freedom and self-determination of the South Vietnamese. Unless this could be assured in the case of South Vietnam, it was argued, the prospects for world order were slight. If these prospects were diminished, the security of the USA was correspondingly diminished. Were this country to refuse the role of policeman, the Johnson Administration repeatedly contended, world order would be placed in jeopardy and with it America's security. World order, in turn, formed an undifferentiated whole, with the result that a challenge to one part of this order formed a challenge to every part. It followed, in the words of then Secretary of State Dean Rusk that: 'We can be safe only to the extent that our total environment is safe'.

It was the equation of world order and American security upon which the Johnson Administration's defence of Vietnam ultimately had to stand or fall. In the end, we know, the Administration failed to make that equation effective. In the context of a conflict marked by many difficulties, the argument was rejected by the American nation. Yet the contention that was once considered by many as excessive, though in circumstances that gave it a substantial measure of plausibility, was widely accepted in the course of the Gulf crisis. It was so accepted despite the appearance of circumstances that were markedly, even radically, more favourable to American security than those prevailing at the time of Vietnam.

The explanation of this reversion to a role that was so widely rejected as a result of Vietnam may in part be accounted for precisely by the vast change in circumstances that had occurred. It is because the equation once drawn between American security and world order is far less compelling in 1990 than it was at the time of Vietnam that it acquired a new attractiveness. For the fact that it was far less compelling at the time of the Gulf crisis also meant that it was an equation which no longer entailed the risk when acted upon that it once did. It was America's ability to entertain an order-giving role in circumstances which permitted, or at any rate seemed to permit, the implementation of this role to be undertaken without the costs it once imposed that gave it a new attractiveness.

It is also the case, however, that the goals America was to pursue in the Bush Administration's vision of a new world order were those that had long found support in twentieth century American diplomacy. An emphasis on the rule of law and the maintenance of order has been as pronounced as the emphasis on extending freedom. The freedom *of* nations (self-determination) has been seen to be quite as important as the freedom *in* nations (democratic institutions). In the American view, the two have been viewed as mutually supportive, even symbiotic. And if, experience has shown that this is not always so, the point remains that Americans have persisted in believing that it is so. Certainly, President Woodrow Wilson believed that it was so. It was largely what he meant by a world made 'safe for democracy'. Franklin Roosevelt subscribed to it. The same conviction formed an integral part of the Truman Doctrine. Even the Reagan Doctrine did not really reject it. The 'disorder' the Reagan Doctrine sanctioned may instead be explained by the persuasion that a satisfactory and enduring international order can be achieved only if totalitarian power is once banished. A season of disorder is sanctioned so that a true system of international order may be established.

The Bush vision of a new world order, then, was not novel. Nor was the role the nation is assigned to play in that order novel. If the shift in emphasis from defending and promoting freedom to ensuring order represented a marked change when seen against the background of the past generation, this may be largely accounted for by the unexpected events that virtually transformed the international system, above all, the sudden end of the Cold War. It was these events that set the stage for what appeared to be a curious reversion to an earlier period in our history, to the period of World War I. In George Bush's vision of a new world order, we seemed to witness a replay of sorts of Woodrow Wilson's vision of a new world order. For both, the states of the world, great and small, were to be guaranteed the same right of respect for their sovereignty and territorial integrity. For both, the peace of the world was to be maintained and democratic societies to be made safe against the threat of arbitrary power by a universal system of collective security which would create a community of power in place of the age old balance of power (the threat to peace and order being considered general rather than specific). And, of course, for both, the USA was destined to play the role of leadership in the new world order, a role that fell to the nation primarily because it alone had 'sufficient moral force' (Wilson) or 'moral standing' (Bush) to lead the other nations of the world.

In the manner of most historical parallels, however, this one is far from exact. If the similarities between the two visions are striking, the differences are scarcely less impressive. Wilson's new world order implied, and indeed necessitated, sweeping change in the status quo. The international system that prevailed to World War I, with its militarism and imperialism, its great and imposed inequalities, its secret diplomacy and its balance of power, had resulted in the disaster of the Great War. It had to be transformed if peace was to be preserved and democratic institutions to be safeguarded. A just peace, the only peace that would last, required the recasting of borders to satisfy the principle of self-determination. It required as well putting an end to the system of inequality known as colonialism. And it dictated a new diplomacy, a diplomacy the effectiveness of which would rest on the power of public opinion, a power that, when the necessity arose, could be supplemented by economic power. Mediated through democratic governments sharing common purposes and interests, these forms of power, rather than armed force, would provide the foundations of the new world order, and the sanctions provisions of the League of Nations covenant were designed accordingly. Wilson was not the first American statesman to place high hopes on finding an effective substitute for war. A century before, Jefferson had done so. But whereas Jefferson had done so in circumstances of American weakness, Wilson did so when the nation's power was reaching a new level of greatness.

In all of these respects, the contrast with the vision of George Bush is apparent. The new world order proclaimed by the President was not one that either promised or required sweeping change in the status quo. There was little reason for believing that George Bush saw either himself or the nation he represented as the agent of change in the sense that Woodrow Wilson did. To be sure, it could be argued that given the changes that had occurred in the world – the disappearance of the colonial system and of the inequalities it sanctioned, the acceptance and substantial realization of the principle of self-determination, above all, the apparent triumph and vindication of free institutions – President Bush did not feel the need for change that was evident in Wilson's day. Even so, the point remains that for him the new world order was the status quo. The equation that Wilson could not make even had he been disposed to do so, for fear of sacrificing his principal bases of support, President Bush was both disposed to make and found little difficult in making. And while the institutional mechanisms (the League of Nations and the United Nations) through which the respective visions were to be realized are similar, the distinctive means on which primary reliance was to be placed were not. The faith Woodrow Wilson had in the power of public opinion either to prevent or to defeat aggression was lost; and the same must be said of the confidence he placed in the efficacy of economic sanctions. To an extent that Wilson would undoubtedly have been shocked by, Bush accepted and indeed embraced many of the presuppositions of the old diplomacy, particularly the reliance on force, in proclaiming his new world order. The dream of banishing aggression persisted but the principal means for doing so were those which Wilson had largely excluded from his new world order.

Wilson's vision remained just that. The vision assumed a peace that could not possibly be gained in the wake of a terrible war – one so destructive of the very conditions indispensable to democratic development – save by a victor possessed of truly overwhelming power and ready, if necessary, to impose such a peace. Despite the favourable position of the United States at the close of World War I, these conditions were not even approximated (as they were at the close of World War II). Yet in the absence of a peace that left all of the major states satisfied and democratic (or well on their way to becoming so), it was difficult to see how, even under Wilsonian assumptions, the great institutional mechanism for fashioning and employing a community of power, and thus guaranteeing peace, could work. On the other hand, given a peace that satisfied all of the major states, now either democratic or on a democratic course, there would be no real need of a League of Nations to give expression to a community of power. For either the occasions requiring the use of such power would not arise or, if they exceptionally did, the remaining democratic states – with or without a League – would be quite capable of dealing with the errant government.

The Wilsonian vision could not be sought primarily through the mechanism of the League of Nations. The effectiveness of the system of collective security Wilson had championed depended on a community of interest and power which did not exist and which could not be called into existence by incantation. In the absence of such community, Wilson was faced with the choice between attempting to change the international system or to adapt to it. Changing the international system, that is, attempting directly to create what did not exist, required a degree of power well beyond America's capabilities at the time and a commitment to the use of power well beyond America's will. Even had Wilson believed in the need of such a commitment, and urged its acceptance by the nation, he still would have had to persuade the nation that America's security depended on making the commitment. This Wilson would not do because he did not believe it to be true. Nor is it apparent that had he believed it to be true he could have gained the public support required for so momentous a transformation of policy.

The alternative course of adapting to the system rather than attempting to transform it, also required a break from the nation's past. Championed by Wilson's Republican critics, Theodore Roosevelt, Henry Cabot Lodge and Eliahu Root, this course entailed a victor's alliance, an alliance of democratic states designed to guarantee the territorial settlement and to insure a favourable balance of power in the post-war period. But Wilson despite the treaty of guarantee he concluded at Versailles with France and Great Britain (later quietly dropped), would not seriously consider following this course (one that did not preclude American participation in a League of Nations but that would have altered the significance of this participation). He would not do so given his aversion to the old diplomacy and its obsession with equilibrating power by means of alliances and, when necessity arose, the use of armed force. There had to be another way to guarantee peace rather than the way of a balance of power that left peace at the mercy of the competitive process – one which had inevitably resulted in the destruction of all past balances.

Thus America emerged from a victorious war that was to have ushered in a new world order without having committed its power either to the achievement of a new order or to the effective maintenance of the old order. While the American role in the world was not the same after the war that it had been before, neither was it the role that Wilson had cast. The interwar period was anything but a time when, in the words Wilson had once used, America exercised 'the infinite privilege of fulfilling her destiny and saving the world'.

When the United States did finally commit its great power to the task of international order, following World War II, it did not do so on behalf of the system of collective security that succeeded the League of Nations. For that system, given the emerging hostility between the Soviet Union and the West, was stillborn. The community of power and purpose that an effective collective security system presupposes, but cannot simply create, disappeared with the defeat of the Axis states. In its stead emerged a conflict that could be managed only by pursuing the age old strategy of alliance and the balance of power.

In the brief period before the cold war dispensation became apparent, however, the new world order was equated with the international security organization established by the victorious allies – above all, the United States – in the closing stages of the war. It is useful to recall that the UN was initially conceived as a collective security organization in name only. In practice, it was intended to be an alliance of the victorious great powers of World War II, an alliance principally directed against the threat presumably posed by a revival of German and Japanese aggression. In retrospect, that intent may seem inexplicable. But it did not appear so to most in the circumstances of the last year of the war when the Charter was drafted. At that time, the great task was believed to be that of preventing history from repeating itself. Only the continued cooperation of the principal powers that had fought Germany and Japan, it was thought, could ensure that this would not happen. The Charter of the UN was seen as the instrument for preserving that cooperation.

The pre-eminent position thus accorded the victorious great powers in the Charter was justified in part on this basis. In part, though, it simply rested on the familiar claim that power must be commensurate with responsibility. There was little that was novel in the principle of a great power directorate presiding over the peace and order of the world. That principle had been a foundation of the settlement following the Napoleonic wars in the early nineteenth century. Nor had it been absent from the plan of a new world order that was worked out at Versailles following World War I. However great the emphasis placed on the equality of states, they were not equal in the plan of the Covenant. The great power members of the League of Nations enjoyed a distinctive position of power and responsibility, one that was reflected in the provisions respecting the membership and functions of the League Council. Even so, this position paled in significance when set alongside that accorded the principal victors of World War II by the UN Charter. The Charter represented, as supporters and critics alike agreed, the apotheosis of power. 'If the Security Council decided that Utopia must surrender the whole or part of her territory to Arcadia', one critic of the Charter wrote at the time, 'the decision is not only binding upon the parties but all the members of the UN are pledged to assist in carrying it into effect'.[2] The relevant provisions of the Charter confirm this still startling conclusion. Those provisions conferred what amounted to an unlimited discretion in matters of peace and security on the great powers in their role as permanent members of the Security Council, provided only that they remained united in outlook.

What was novel, then, about the new world order that the American government championed at the end of World War II were the lengths to which it carried the principle of great power supremacy. That this principle was to be given so predominant a role only during a relatively brief period of post-war transition, as was occasionally intimated by the Roosevelt Administration, strained credulity. Quite apart from the difficulty so basic a change in the Charter necessarily would have entailed, the position accorded the great powers responded to the belief, held by the president on down, that perhaps the most important reason for the League's failure was that the major states, those bearing the greatest responsibility for peace, had not been given sufficient power in the Covenant. That this reading of the experience with collective security in the interwar period was plainly at odds with the historical record appeared irrelevant. The League had failed to keep the peace, the familiar argument ran, because the great powers had not been given a sufficiently dominant role and, of course, because one great power, the United States, had played no role at all.

The provisions of the Charter which were designed to prevent a recurrence of the interwar experience may be better understood, however, as reflecting the American government's determination not to agree to any security arrangements that would constitute, or that would even be seen as constituting, a marked departure from the past.

There was little in the Charter to upset those who wished to continue a policy that avoided alliances and interventions outside the Western hemisphere and that preserved a complete independence of action. The essential characteristics of an isolationist policy might well be preserved despite membership in the UN. Although the Charter consecrated as never before the principle of great power supremacy and although it conferred on the great powers an almost unlimited discretion in matters of peace and security, provided that they could agree on a given course of action, it obligated them to nothing in the way of guaranteeing the political independence and territorial integrity of the member states of the organization. The veto power possessed by each of the permanent members thus ensured that in matters of collective enforcement the United States retained the same freedom of action – or of inaction – that it had always insisted upon in the past. It was with this understanding that the Senate accepted the Charter. There was no repetition in 1945 of the fight that had been waged in 1919; there was no repetition because, among other reasons, there was plainly no reason for assuming that in joining the UN the USA had in any way compromised its freedom to determine the circumstances in which it would employ forcible measures. The right of veto that formed the essential precondition of the American membership in the UN also effectively ended a dispute that had gone on for more than one generation. It did so, however, by vindicating the position taken by Wilson's great senatorial adversary, Henry Cabot Lodge; for the power of veto was the functional equivalent, and indeed more, of what Lodge had insisted on in 1919.

In retrospect, there is no little irony in the fate of the principal criticism that was initially directed against the Charter. This criticism was not so much that the system of the Charter simply would not work but that it would work only with respect to the smaller powers. Against the great powers possessing permanent seats on the Security Council no enforcement measures could be taken, given the right of veto enjoyed by each. The enemy powers of World War II apart, states that according to a special provision of the Charter (Article 107) could be dealt with at will by any member of the Organization that had been at war with them, only the small powers remained as prospective objects of the enforcement measures provided for in the Charter. But a collective security organization limited to the taking of enforcement actions against only the smaller powers, the criticism ran, was hardly a sufficient guarantee for the maintenance of international peace and security.

What critics once viewed as a grave defect was seen during the Gulf crisis almost as a virtue. In a world that no longer appeared threatened by great power conflicts arising from age-old motives of territorial expansion, there remained only the threat posed by smaller powers whose aspirations and state of development had yet to be reconciled with the norms of a more conventional statecraft. It was in this world that the UN, under American leadership, was once again found to express the community of power that Woodrow Wilson aspired in vain to find in the League. It was so found because that leadership went virtually unchallenged by any other great power. What many saw as an emergent global community of power was inseparable from America's new-found hegemonical position.

In the world of the late 1940s, however, there clearly was no such community of power. Although America's position was in many respects even more ascendant than it was in the Gulf crisis, it did not go unchallenged. The onset of the long conflict with the Soviet Union, a conflict which made irrelevant the order of the Charter, gave rise of necessity to efforts at creating a limited community of power. It was these efforts, occurring roughly over the period 1947–52, that resulted in the great transformation of American foreign policy. In undertaking to create with the nations of Western Europe a partial community of power for the purpose of countering the power of the Soviet Union, the United States abandoned its historic policy of isolation – something it had not done by participating in the UN. Whereas membership in the world organization committed the nation to very little that broke from historic tradition, the creation of the Western alliance broke from the entirety of that tradition, centred as it was on the avoidance of entanglement – above all, permanent entanglement – in Europe's politics. In a period of only several years, American foreign policy shifted from the new politics of collective security – which President Roosevelt characterized in his last address to Congress as 'the end of the system of unilateral action, exclusive alliances, spheres of influence, and balances of power' – to the old politics that had supposedly been left behind in establishing the UN.[3]

This reversion to the old politics, though not easy, was in some measure facilitated by the manner in which the change was perceived. An embrace of the old politics was frequently characterized as a realization of the new politics. Thus the Senate hearings on the North Atlantic Treaty were marked by the care with which the treaty was distinguished from the traditional military alliance which was, as Senator Arthur Vandenberg noted, a 'partnership for power' rather than, as was the case with NATO, a 'partnership for peace'.[4] A State Department memorandum on the differences between the North

Atlantic Treaty and traditional military alliances sought to distinguish between the two by noting that alliances 'were designed to advance the respective nationalistic interests of the parties, and provided for joint military action if one of the parties in pursuit of such objectives became involved in war'. NATO, however, was a pure application of collective security: 'It is directed against no one; it is directed solely against aggression. It seeks not to influence any shifting "balance of power" but to strengthen the "balance of principle" '.[5]

In time, a balance of power diplomacy based in the main on the Western alliance came to be accepted for what it was. Yet what it was did in fact go beyond the vital task of balancing power against power. Although the Western alliance was plainly directed against a specific party, it not only formed a community of power but of ideals as well. What came to be known as the 'free world' had as its essential core the nations that made up the Western alliance. This creation of a partial, not a universal, community of power and value was the great achievement of American foreign policy in the postwar period. It was the principal achievement of the policy of containment.

The post war order was an order inseparable from containment. With some exaggeration, it may even be seen as the order of containment. Although this order brought a remarkable measure of security, peace, and prosperity to the nations of the Western alliance, we were never quite satisfied with the policy that made these results possible. Conservatives criticized containment from the outset for being too defensive and for failing to hold out the solid prospect of bringing the great contest with the Soviet Union to an early and victorious end. Indeed, until the eve of the Soviet Union's sudden collapse as a superpower, the right continued to insist, even more emphatically than in earlier years, that containment, if continued, would issue catastrophe. Liberals, too, though for the opposite reason, came increasingly to believe that the pursuit of containment would lead to disaster. From the time of Vietnam, those who had once been containment's strongest supporters came more and more to equate that policy with the excesses that had led to the nation's involvement in South-east Asia. Caught between these attacks from the right and the left, containment survived only in practice. Even the startling and unexpected vindication of that policy at the close of the 1980s has apparently not been sufficient to rehabilitate it in the nation's memory.

The policy that essentially defined the American position in the post-war world finally came to an end. Containment had come to entail a quite modest price in blood and treasure.

This persistence of belief in the ease with which collective security may be implemented responded to the deeply ingrained American habit of wanting grand ends and only modest means. Though the means President Bush employed against Iraq were anything but modest, they were in fact very modest when measured in terms of American casualties and financial costs to the nation. Moreover, the costs of sustaining the new world order would have to remain modest if it were to have a promising future. For there was nothing in the Gulf experience which set aside the lesson that public support for a foreign policy requiring substantial sacrifice could only be assured provided it could be demonstrated that vital security interests of the nation are at stake. Role would have to be effectively equated with security, and security given, in the first instance, a conventional meaning. It was the failure to make this equation effectively that provided the principal cause of the opposition to the intervention in Vietnam. So, too, the new world order would be doomed unless its implementation avoided the costs of Vietnam.

Whether it would prove possible to enforce the new world order at only modest cost largely depended on whether the experience of the Gulf War established a pattern for the future. Should it establish such pattern, small casualties would result from America's persisting technological advantages while low financial cost would result from the continued willingness of others – above all, our principal allies to pay for America's order maintaining role. Even if the first condition could be safely assumed, the second could not. Burden sharing on behalf of the new world order was unlikely to prove a less contentious arrangement than burden sharing in support of the old order of containment proved to be. Since those asked to share the new burden would feel less constrained to do so, it could be expected to prove far more contentious. The thought might not be long in forming that the United States was using the centre to order the periphery, while using the periphery (above all, the Middle East) to maintain its influence over the centre.

The new world order also rested on the likelihood of the cooperation of the permanent members of the Security Council. Without that cooperation, the United States would be deprived of the legitimacy it had enjoyed in the Gulf crisis. Whether that cooperation would be forthcoming, however, was very uncertain. The instability that marked the domestic politics of the Soviet Union and China might well deprive the United States, in a future crisis, of the support it enjoyed in the Security Council in 1990–91. Whether it could rely, in that event, on the endorsement of the Western alliance was by no means assured. Despite alliance support of the American-led action against Iraq, it was by no means apparent that comparable support could be assured future actions. The alliance support given in the Gulf crisis was given, after all, in the context of UN support. In a future crisis, assuming that it arose in the developing world, an absence of the latter might well give to the former the appearance of renewed North–South confrontation. Whatever their other reservations might be, it seemed safe to assume that at least some alliance members would strongly desire to avoid giving this appearance. That desire might even lead them to withhold endorsement of an American-ed initiative.

The fate of the new world order was necessarily speculative. Yet it was striking that, in the second year of the Bush Administration, the United States had returned to the vision, Woodrow Wilson's vision, with which it began the long odyssey at the outset of this century, only attended by circumstances that appeared to hold out the promise of a more successful outcome. At the same time, that outcome, even if successful, might prove to be irrelevant. For the principal threats to order after the Gulf War stemmed not from the prospect of naked territorial aggression against which the new world order was primarily directed, but from the distinct possibility of the disintegration of existing states as a result of the insistence of peoples on self-determination. The great problem that confronted Woodrow Wilson, and that he sought to address by proclaiming that every people should have its own state, also confronted George Bush. To the extent the new world order addressed this prospective danger, however, it did so largely by dismissing it. The President's new world order was the order of the status quo.

NOTES

Based upon a lecture delivered at the Paul H. Nitze School of Advanced International Studies, Johns Hopkins University, 14 October 1991.

2 H.A. Smith, *The Crisis in the Law of Nations*, Stevens, Institute of World Affairs, London: 1947, p. 90.

3 Address to Congress, Mauhl, 1945, cited in Roland N. Stremberg, *Collective Security and American Foreign Policy: From the League of Nations to NATO*, New York: Praeger, 1963, p. 18.

4 Senate Committee on Foreign Relation Hearings, North Atlantic Treaty (81st Congress, 1st Session), Part 1, p. 145.

5 Ibid., Note 3. pp. 334, 337.

10 A changing American–Israeli relationship

Abraham Ben-Zvi

At first glance, a direct linkage appears to exist between the Gulf War, which clearly demonstrated the American hegemonic role as a leading world power, capable of consolidating a broad and diverse war coalition, and the about-face in basic Israeli perceptions of an international peace conference. This change fully manifested itself in the aftermath of the conflict, thus enabling the Bush Presidency to translate the initial phase of its two-track peace design into an actual policy. Indeed, the fact that the Administration managed to induce Israel to set aside its initial view of *any* multilateral peace-making framework as potentially detrimental to core security concerns and interests in the wake of its impressive performance against Iraq, may be construed as indicative of a causal link between the two consecutive sets of events.

The purpose of the following review is to replace this widespread notion of linkage with a more nuanced and differentiated interpretation. In this context, the Gulf War will be depicted as a prism through which the basic components and tenets of these dynamic relationships can be most clearly illuminated. While providing the impetus for accelerating certain processes and developments within the dyad, it did not alter their basic direction and course. Furthermore, while American diplomacy was provided – during the immediate period following the war (but not necessarily as a result of it) – with an apparent wider margin of manoeuvrability in approaching the Arab–Israeli conflict, it is doubtful whether it ultimately will manage to exploit fully this broader latitude of choice *vis-à-vis* Israel once the deep-rooted origins of the conflict become the subject of negotiations.

THEORETICAL INTRODUCTION

In attempting to shed light on the actual dynamics and patterns of behaviour as they shaped and delineated before, during, and particularly after the Gulf War, the analysis will be closely patterned on the assumption that power resources are situationally specific, and that, consequently, power assets in one policy-contingency framework may lose their effectiveness in a different context.[1] Thus in a variety of situations, frameworks and locations, potential power cannot be automatically translated into actual power. Thus, for all the vast overall asymmetry, which exists between the USA and Israel in terms of their respective power resources, what may ultimately determine the outcome of a possible intramural encounter between them is the balance of intrinsic interests involved rather than the overall balance of power.[2]

In case of an asymmetry in the balance of the specific interests at stake favouring Israel, it will demonstrate a higher level of resolve than Washington's in defence of these interests. Prepared to take greater risks and make sacrifices, Israel is therefore bound to resist fiercely the pressures exerted, and may ultimately prevail in the confrontation despite its relative inferiority in terms of power capabilities (and near total dependence upon American military and economic assistance).

Consequently, the Gulf War has provided the impetus for a more assertive and forceful American posture in the Arab–Israeli sphere. Ultimate success of this drive is far from certain, and will require an elaborate system of trade-off mechanisms. In the absence of adequate compensation, Israel will remain convinced that it has everything to lose, and that compliance may endanger certain basic principles of its foreign and defence policies. Hence, it will remain defiant and recalcitrant despite the costs involved and its vastly inferior bargaining position.

THE 'SPECIAL RELATIONSHIP' PARADIGM

Turning from the abstract and theoretical level to the concrete historical context of American–Israeli relations, clearly when the crisis in the Gulf erupted, in August 1990, the Bush Administration was on the verge of overcoming – at long last – an entire complex of domestic constraints which, for almost four decades, severely delimited and restricted the parameters, within which American diplomacy could exert influence on Israeli behaviour. Derived from the 'special relationship' paradigm, this domestic constraint consisted of a cluster of broadly-based beliefs and attitudes in American public opinion, which underscored the affinity and similarity between the two states in terms of their pioneering nature and commitment to domestic values.[3] As

William Quandt maintains in describing the essence of the 'special relationship' paradigm:

> The bond between the United States and Israel is unquestionably strengthened because of the congruence of values between the two nations. Americans can identify with Israel's national style . . . in a way that has no parallel on the Arab side. Neither the ideal of the well-ordered Muslim community nor that of a modernizing autocracy evokes much sympathy among Americans. Consequently, a predisposition no doubt exists in American political culture that works to the advantage of the Israelis.[4]

During the period: 1948–81, this basic sympathy – which was not restricted to the Jewish community – was reflected in numerous public opinion surveys. Polls taken during this period showed that whereas sympathy for the Arab nations did not surpass 16 per cent, support for Israel fluctuated between 44 and 56 per cent. Similarly, throughout the 1970s, at least three out of four American polls held a positive image of Israel.[5]

In view of the pervasiveness and legitimacy of the images incorporated into the 'special relationship' paradigm, it is hardly surprising that pro-Israeli groups and organizations were frequently successful in promoting favourable policies, programmes and legislation. To the extent that American Jews were able to advance their interest in Israel, their success depended on the sympathy, or at least acquiescence on the part of their coalition partners and the public at large. This deeply-held and broadly-shared support for Israel's existence, security and well-being, formed therefore the infrastructure or screen through which the activities of influential Jewish organizations were filtered and delineated.

The most effective institutional representative of this pervasive cluster of beliefs and attitudes, which constituted the main bulwark in the face of repeated executive efforts to broaden the administration's margin of manoeuvrability *vis-à-vis* Israel, has been the US Congress. The Symington–Javits resolution of 28 June 1967, which had sixty-three sponsors; the Ribicoff–Scott statement of 25 April 1969, with sixty-eight signatories; the Case–Tydings declaration of 25 February 1970, which had seventy signatories; and the letter to President Ford that was sent on 25 May 1975, to seventy-six senators – these are but a few instances of the sort of legislation activity that reflected widespread and persistent support for Israel in the US Congress, especially the Senate.[6]

Therefore, in attempting to promote a settlement of the compound

Arab–Israeli dispute, various administrations had to cope with an entire complex of domestic constraints – which not infrequently compelled them to scale down, obfuscate, or altogether abandon certain desired courses of action.[7]

THE EMERGENCE OF NEW FACTORS

The 'special relationship' paradigm has been undergoing an incremental and gradual shift in its nature, scope and magnitude in the course of the 1980s (and early 1990s), as it could not remain totally decoupled and insulated from the dynamics of a highly volatile regional environment. The Lebanon War of 1982, Secretary of State George Shultz's abortive peace initiative of 1988, and the Intifada – were the major landmarks or 'triggering events' in a process which witnessed a progressive erosion.[8] Indeed, as the 1980s approached to their end, the cumulative impact of this process significantly eroded the level of public support for some of the premises comprising the 'special relationship' paradigm.

On the very eve of the Gulf War, this growing erosion of the paradigm converged with, and was further reinforced, by such momentous global development as the abatement of the cold war, radical transformation of the global international system from a bipolar-confrontational framework to a much more benign one (in which the United States emerged as the only strategic and political superpower) and the growing disintegration of the Soviet Union, which vastly reduced the importance of Israel as a 'strategic asset' to the United States.

At the beginning of the 1980s, the perception of Israel (which was closely patterned on President Reagan's initial bipolar-confrontational world view) 'as a . . . military offset to the Soviet Union' and 'as perhaps the only remaining strategic asset in the region on which the United States can truly rely',[9] emerged as an increasingly dominant perspective, and as a potential substitute for the eroding complex of sentimental and moral factors, which were incorporated into the special relationship' paradigm. The October 1983 National Security Decision Directive III (NSDD-III), which reinstated the concept of strategic collaboration with Israel, the November 1983 American-Israeli agreement on the establishment of a formal Joint Political-Military Group (JPMG) that would convene every six months in order to discuss such strategic issues as combined planning, joint exercises and requirements for repositioning of American equipment in Israel;[10] the May 1986 decision of the Reagan Administration to affiliate Israel in the Strategic Defense Initiative (SDI) research and development programme, and the conclusion – in December 1987 – of a new Memorandum of Understanding on strategic cooperation which 'formally designated Israel as a major non-NATO ally'[11] – these were the major stepping stones along the path of the continuously expanding and flourishing security ties between the United States and Israel.

However, with the abatement of the global Soviet threat to American security, the need to rely on Israeli military capabilities (particularly in the Eastern Mediterranean) as a deterrent, drastically diminished.

With an embattled and disintegrating Soviet Union abandoning its traditional cold war objectives, and with the Bush Presidency increasingly prepared 'to move beyond containment' in order to integrate Moscow into 'the community of nations',[12] the very premises upon which American–Israeli strategic cooperation was shaped, delineated and institutionalized in the 1980s, became increasingly outdated and obsolete at the turn of the decade.

The outcome of these converging processes was that Israel had to follow the unfolding crisis (and subsequent war) in the Gulf from a position of weakness, disarmed of at least part of its ammunition and infrastructure of support in American public opinion, and deprived of its status as a major strategic bulwark against the threat of Soviet regional expansion and encroachment.

US–ISRAEL RELATIONS IN THE LIGHT OF THE WAR

Since the Gulf crisis was completely decoupled from East–West rivalries, there was no need, in American thinking, to involve Israel in the multilateral effort to cope with the challenge to regional stability posed by Iraq. Furthermore, the fact that President Bush had succeeded in forging a broad inter-Arab coalition against Iraq, further reinforced his desire that Israel maintain 'a low profile' in the course of the crisis. It was feared in Washington that any deviation from this course was bound to superimpose the animosities and tensions related to the Arab–Israeli conflict upon the Gulf encounter, thus making it exceedingly difficult for such parties as Syria to remain members of the anti-Iraq bloc.

Fully committed to its desire to decouple the Gulf crisis from the Arab-Israeli sphere, the Administration continuously insisted that its Israeli ally watch the entire confrontation from the sidelines, even in the face of mounting Iraqi provocation.

Shortly after the war had started, and in view of the Scud missile attacks, which were launched by Iraq against Israel's population centres, this posture became even more salient and explicit when President Bush and Secretary Baker urged the Israeli leadership to refrain from any retaliatory move. Such a retaliation, it was feared in Washington, was bound to threaten the cohesion of the anti-Iraqi Arab front by injecting into it the strains and tensions of the Arab–Israeli predicament. Any deviation from this pattern entailed, in the President's thinking, the risk of the defection of at least the periphery of the anti-Iraqi coalition in the Arab world, thus jeopardizing the entire structure of an alliance, which the Administration had laboured so hard to consolidate.

Even on the tactical level, it became clear that the Israeli contribution to the war effort against Iraq was marginal. Specifically, in such areas as intelligence gathering, repositioning of American equipment and material, and logistical infrastructure, the United States preferred to rely on alternative sources and thus to avoid even the indirect involvement of Israel in the conflict. Similarly, in all discussions on the shaping and desired structure of the post-war regional strategic environment – which took place in Washington throughout the fall and winter of 1990 – the strategic role assigned to Israel remained peripheral. Instead, the Administration focused on the need to institutionalize and further consolidate the anti-Iraqi Arab axis of Saudi Arabia, Egypt and Syria, and thus to ensure that Damascus – the newly recruited regional partner – does not defect into reticence or recalcitrance.

In conclusion, fear of alienating its Arab partners clearly emerged as the administration's major concern, outweighing any consideration related to the vision of Israel as a strategic asset to the United States. Although the deterioration in the value of Israel as a strategic asset to the United States was the product of fundamental changes in the very structure of both the global international system and can by no means be attributed exclusively to the Gulf conflagration, this conflict clearly provided the impetus for exposing and demonstrating the extent of Israel's strategic vulnerability in this vastly revised environment.

THE AMERICAN–ISRAELI DYAD AFTER THE WAR

Turning from the strategic dimension to the 'special relationship' paradigm, it is clear that although the outbreak of the Gulf War provided the precipitant for changing the direction of American public opinion from the pole of increasing criticism of various facets of Israel's operational code to the extreme of renewed identification with

Israel in its hour of suffering and sacrifice, this wave of sympathy and empathy quickly receded into the background of the American–Israeli dyad in the immediate aftermath of the war. Incapable of altering the course of the pre-war public trends and proclivities, it was soon outweighed by increasingly critical – or at least sceptical – images and beliefs.

Notwithstanding the restraint, which Israel exhibited in the face of repeated Iraqi provocation, the American public became increasingly convinced, in the wake of the war that Israel should be economically coerced into acquiescence on such issues as its settlement posture and the applicability of Security Council Resolution 242 to the West Bank and the Gaza Strip. Not only did a majority of American public opinion indicate support, in several surveys conducted in the spring and summer of 1991, for 'decreasing the level of economic assistance to Israel', but a growing number of the interviewed were prepared to link the level of economic assistance to Jerusalem's peace posture.[13]

THE ECONOMIC DIMENSION

It is indeed in the economic sphere that the ongoing changes in the very structure of the American–Israeli dyad were most clearly manifested during, and in the aftermath, of the Gulf War. Similar to what transpired on the strategic level of the relationship, the outbreak and course of the war did not in itself alter drastically the economic rules of the game between Washington and Jerusalem. However, by virtue of converging with such processes as the mounting wave of immigration of Soviet Jews to Israel (which forced the Israeli government to seek from the United States vast amounts of housing loan guarantees), the economic dimension of the war clearly demonstrated the extent of Israel's dependence on American assistance, and the fact that the American–Israeli framework has become almost totally asymmetrical. Once again, then, rather than launching a process, the dramatic events of early 1991 served to amplify, sharpen and in some respects accelerate developments which had already been under way, albeit in a less salient or pronounced form.

Most indicative in this respect was the administration's reaction to Israel's request for emergency economic assistance. Indeed, despite the intensive efforts (which included the missions to Washington of Finance Minister Moda'i and Defence Minister Arens), Israel was originally left out of the Operation Desert Storm special supplemental foreign aid package for 1991. Nor was it included initially among the 'front-line' states which were eligible for compensation by the Gulf

Crisis Financial Coordination Group (of which the United States was the chairman, and which was set up in order to provide assistance for such nations as Turkey and Egypt, which incurred substantial costs as a result of the Gulf War). The Israeli attempt to appeal directly to American public opinion for economic support, and its concurrent lobbying effort to induce its congressional allies (through the American–Israeli Public Affairs Committee – AIPAC) to initiate legislation which would appropriate to Jerusalem large-scale supplemental aid enraged the administration, thus aggravating a situation already permeated with misunderstanding and ambiguity.

On the whole, seeking to link the issue of special assistance to an entire cluster of post-war political and strategic questions (including the Israeli approach toward a renewed peace initiative on the Arab–Israeli front), leading members of the Bush foreign policy entourage remained wedded to the view that any indication of generosity and goodwill in the economic sphere had to be reciprocated by an Israeli willingness to compromise on the parameters of a settlement with Syria or the Palestinians. It was surmised in Washington that any major deviation from the logic of this 'bargaining strategy',[14] would needlessly deprive the administration of a valuable leverage *vis-à-vis* Israel during the post-war era. Thus, whereas Israel pursued a 'strategy of reciprocity' in the hope that its continued restraint in the face of repeated Iraqi provocation will encourage the Bush Administration 'to take a conciliatory action in return',[15] the Administration insisted on a different form of linkage, namely, on an explicit, specific and simultaneous exchange between any such action and a modification of at least some of the parameters which comprise Israel's peace posture.

Since the Gulf War served Israel's most vital security interests by destroying Iraq's war potential and overall military capability, there was little reason – in Washington's view – to reward Jerusalem for its restraint.

In view of this incompatibility in the parties' respective predispositions and expectations, it is hardly surprising that the initial Israeli plea for emergency assistance in loans and grants totalling $13 billion incensed the administration and prompted Secretary Baker to remark to Defence Minister Arens (in the course of their 11 February 1991, meeting) that it was 'inappropriate to request aid at a time when US soldiers were dying in a war beneficial to Israel, especially since the Patriots were largely delivered as grants'.[16]

Not until Secretary Baker's Middle East mission of March 1991, was this 'bargaining strategy' momentarily modified. Seeking to induce the Israeli government to soften its posture on the Palestinian

front and in the Syrian–Israeli sphere, the Secretary decided t
recommend to the Congress the appropriation of $650 million i
emergency military aid for Israel. Although the decision comprised
departure from the Administration's pure and unmitigated 'bargainin,
strategy', it still fell considerably short of the initial Israeli request
Furthermore the Administration made clear that the transaction wa
contingent upon an expressed Israeli willingness to set aside an
additional aid requests until September 1991.

However, when Israel formally submitted – in early September – it
request for $10 billion in loan guarantees for the period 1992–97
President Bush and Secretary Baker adopted a posture of procrastina
tion, in the hope that it would compel Israel to soften its position o
such issues as its settlement activity (formally, Bush and Baker aske
Congress to postpone consideration of the Israeli loan request for fou
months). Incensed by the plethora of reports which suggested tha
Israel did not fully comply with the terms of the February 1991 loa:
guarantees agreement (which required the Israeli government period
ically to update the Administration about the scope of its settlemen
activities), the President and his Secretary of State further implied tha
the guarantees would not be approved at any future date unless Israe
agreed first to establish joint American–Israeli supervision machiner
for ascertaining that the funds appropriated would not be used
directly or indirectly – in the occupied territories.

Regardless of the question as to whether or not this 'bargainin
strategy' will ultimately become the main coercive tool for America:
diplomacy *vis-à-vis* Israel, it is evident that Israel's growing economi
predicament (as a result of both the Gulf War and the wave of Jewis:
immigrants from the Soviet Union), has provided Washington with a
added leverage in its quest to influence Jerusalem's predilections an
preferences. Combined with the growing willingness of America
public opinion to support this linkage as a means of inducing Israel t
negotiate a Palestinian settlement, and with the reluctance of mos
representatives of the 'special relationship' paradigm directly t
challenge the President's 'bargaining strategy' it is this new complex c
strategic, economic and political conditions and expectations whic
may well precipitate an increasingly assertive and ambitious America
posture.

REPERCUSSIONS IN THE AFTERMATH OF THE WAR

For all its scope, magnitude and initial dramatic impact, the Gulf Wa
– which clearly reaffirmed the status of the US as an undispute

hegemonic power – did not provide the only trigger or impetus for reviving the search for peace in the Arab–Israeli zone.

Nor can it be regarded as the only factor, which invariably and directly led to the success of the American effort to convene a regional peace conference for negotiating a settlement on both the Palestinian and Syrian fronts. The linkage between these two policy frameworks is indeed vastly more complex and tenuous than any naive and linear theory implies. However, by merging with and reinforcing several concurrent global and regional processes of great significance (such as the evaporation of the Soviet empire and the growing number of Jewish immigrants from the Soviet Union), it helped underscore the fact that, in approaching the Arab–Israeli predicament, American diplomacy was now provided with a broader margin of manoeuvrability and latitude of choice *vis-à-vis* Israel.

The culmination of these mutually reinforcing processes, most of which preceded the Gulf War, was the administration's success in enticing both Israel and Syria (as well as the PLO) to modify their pre-existing perceptions of the international conference, and thus to agree to participate in the two-track American peace design. The Syrian decision, of July 1991, to set aside its traditional perception of the international conference as the appropriate machinery for imposing upon Israel a settlement and instead to endorse the American view of the planned regional conference as a strictly non-coercive springboard to direct bilateral peace negotiations, (which led to the Israeli decision to attend the conference), derived mainly from the decline in the status of the Soviet Union as a superpower and a patron, and was only tenuously related to the Gulf War. With the abatement of the Cold War, and against the backdrop of Moscow's mounting domestic predicament and inability to provide Damascus with an umbrella of continued political, strategic and military support and assistance, it was only natural for President Assad to resort to 'the American option'.

No less striking was the Israeli about-face in the matter, which reflected the cumulative impact, which the vastly asymmetrical structure of the dyad has already had upon the formation of Israel's peace posture in the aftermath of the Gulf War.

In 1987, faced with King Hussein's demand that the peace conference be conducted within a legitimizing international umbrella, Prime Minister Shamir remained adamantly and irrevocably opposed to the very notion of the international conference as an appropriate peace-making framework. Viewing the idea of the conference as a homo-geneous and undifferentiated entity, he was predisposed to regard even the non-coercive and minimalist version of the proposed multilateral convocation as highly dangerous and as lacking any intrinsic positive qualities. Highly sceptical of Israel's capacity effectively to control the dynamics of negotiation in any multilateral structure, the Prime Minister therefore remained convinced that the very convocation of any international forum was bound – by virtue of its unbalanced composition – to isolate Israel and to intensify pressures for an imposed settlement.[17]

Four years after Shamir had effectively blocked King Hussein's initiative (which was incorporated into the 11 April 1987, London Accords), he was once again confronted with a multilateral peace design, albeit of a regional nature. According to the Bush Administration's postwar design the peace process was initially to unfold under joint superpower auspices and within the formal framework of a regional peace conference. Perceived by President Bush and Secretary Baker as a strictly ceremonial and symbolic 'international event', this international framework was intended to provide 'a legitimizing umbrella' for the Arab parties to the negotiations. Thus, it was expected that the convocation of such a conference would be the prelude to a direct, two-track bargaining process between Israel and a joint Palestinian–Jordanian delegation, as well as between Israel and Syria. In other words, whereas – in the American thinking – the plenary of the regional conference was assigned the function of formally launching the entire peace endeavour (as was outlined in the 1987 London Accords), the actual discussions were to take place within the framework of separate geographic and functional sub-committees, without interference, pressure or coercion from outside.

Notwithstanding the fact that the 1991 outline was closely patterned on the basic procedural premises of the 1987 drive, Prime Minister Shamir decided, in the aftermath of the Gulf War, to set aside his preliminary undifferentiated and acutely menacing perception of the conference, in favour of a more nuanced and heterogeneous view. Specifically, while remaining irrevocably opposed to the maximalist and coercive type of the multilateral framework, the fact remains that the Israeli Prime Minister came around, in 1991, to endorsing the delimited and constrained model of the regional conference as the symbolic and ritual precipitant to the actual peace-making effort. And although the Israeli acceptance of the plan was accompanied by an American letter of assurances, which guaranteed – among other things – that the plenary of the conference would not be assigned any material function during the entire process, that the principle of direct peace negotiations between Israel and its neighbours would not be compromised, and that any initiative to reconvene the multilateral forum would require the consent of all the participants, the fact that Prime Minister Shamir agreed to give his qualified support for a scheme which, four years earlier, had been characterized by him 'an instance and monstrous notion', can at least be partially attributed to this postwar environmental setting, which clearly exposed the growing asymmetry within the American–Israeli dyad. Unwilling to risk a confrontation with Washington under these adverse strategic, economic and political circumstances, Jerusalem therefore adopted, in 1991, an essentially accommodative course on the issue of the structure of the peace-making machinery.

For all its significance, the Israeli decision to abandon its irreconcilable approach towards the international conference is unlikely to fundamentally affect American public opinion, and thus to change the direction of the pendulum of public support for Israel. By comparison, it is the Syrian decision to join the peace process (combined with the decision of the PLO to follow suit), which may be viewed as the potential impetus for exacerbating Israel's predicament by virtue of its anticipated impact on American public opinion. Specifically, Damascus' move may well become the precipitant for eradicating one of the last remaining pervasive and influential premises of the 'special relationship' paradigm, namely, the belief that an unbridgeable gap continues to exist between Israel's desire for regional peace, and the unabated Arab commitment (with the exception of Egypt) to a course of intransigence and belligerence along the Arab–Israeli front.

The central conclusion which emerges from the foregoing analysis that although the Gulf War did by no means trigger the processes of decline and erosion in American–Israeli relations, some of its developments and phases clearly provided the impetus for exposing, amplifying and even accelerating them. With the implicit and subdued becoming fully manifested and explicit, the prospects that the very structure of the dyad will change from an essentially consensual one into a framework which will be permeated with tension, should not be, therefore, underestimated. As a result, disarmed of much of its strategic ammunition (and infrastructure of support in American public opinion), Israel confronts the administration in a vastly asymmetrical setting. At which time it will have to rely almost exclusively on its intrinsic resolve and determination in seeking to soften, defy or abort undesired American diplomatic moves and initiatives.

A clear indication from the postwar era, that the American–Israeli alliance has already become increasingly fraught with animosity and disagreement, is provided by President Bush's frontal attack, of 12 September 1991, or the very essence and legitimacy of the 'special relationship' paradigm. On that date, the American–Israeli disagreement over the question as to whether or not the loan guarantees should be decoupled from any other aspect of the dyad, escalated into an open and bitter dispute. Expressing anger and resentment in the face of the intensive lobbying drive of such pro-Israeli forces as AIPAC, to ensure a rapid congressional approval of the Israeli loan request, President Bush – in a strong and irreconcilable statement – threatened to veto any such legislation. Reiterating Secretary Baker's assertion that the loan guarantees issue and the peace process were in fact inextricably interrelated, the President argued that to reward Israel before the peace process was formally launched, would inevitably excerbate and aggrevate a situation already charged with emotion and uncertainty, and thus doom to failure the entire American peace initiative. Furthermore, by insisting that Israel's supporters on Capitol Hill were exclusively motivated by a narrow and particularistic cluster of 'domestic political considerations' which, in his view, were incompatible with the American national interest, President Bush clearly intended to question the very legitimacy of the lobbying activity in favour of the Israeli request and thus turn the clock back to the Eisenhower era. Indeed, his pointed reference to the 'powerful political forces' with which he was confronted[18] most dramatically demonstrated the fact that the pendulum of American–Israeli relations has indeed accelerated its swing from the pole of unbounded affinity and empathy (reinforced by an intricate network of strategic ties), to the extreme of suspicion and mistrust, with Israel increasingly depicted by Washington's high policy élite, as well as by American public opinion, as an economic and strategic liability.

Four months later, when the administration resumed its consideration of the loan guarantees, it quickly became evident that unless the Shamir government formally and unequivocally agreed to freeze all settlement activity in the West Bank (as well as in the Eastern part of Jerusalem), it could not expect to receive the requested loan. Apparently, in an attempt to exacerbate Prime Minister Shamir's predicament on the eve of the parliamentary elections, the administration embarked – in late February 1992 – on an uncompromising, irreconcilable course.

With American public opinion (including significant segments of the Jewish leadership) highly critical of Israel's settlement policy, the pursuit – by the administration – of a 'linkage strategy' (which consisted of a direct and formal linkage between the suspension of all housing starts in the West Bank and the granting of the housing loans), proved effective. Unwilling to confront the President over the highly controversial issue of Israel's settlement activity, most representatives of the 'special relationship' paradigm (both in Congress and in the Jewish community) gave their support (tacit or even explicit) to President Bush's linkage approach. The result was that the Israeli government found itself (in the course of the abortive negotiations over the specific terms of the guarantee loans, which followed the February 1992 decision) deprived of much of its traditional base of support in American public opinion which, in the not too distant past, had repeatedly and effectively constrained Washington's latitude of choice in the Arab–Israeli sphere. Against this backdrop, it is hardly surprising that the Israeli effort to secure at least a portion of the requested loan guarantees without acquiescing to the new American demand, proved futile. Ultimately, the entire issue was suspended without providing any guarantees to Israel for the year 1992.

Against this backdrop, President Bush's frontal attack of 12 September 1991, on the very essence and legitimacy of the 'special relationship' paradigm, and the growing friction between Washington and Jerusalem in such areas as Israel's settlement activity, may be viewed as the prelude or precipitant for a forceful American effort to bridge the gap still separating the potential from the actual and thus to ultimately redefine the rules of the game within the American–Israeli dyad.

It remains to be seen whether or not the Bush Presidency (or successive American governments) will fully exploit these conducive circumstances in order to accomplish, at long last, an objective which has eluded the architects of American diplomacy for more than four decades.

NOTES

1 David A. Baldwin, 'Power analysis and world politics: new trends versus old tendencies', *World Politics*, vol. XXXI, no. 2 (January 1979), pp. 163–7.

2 Robert Jervis, 'Deterrence theory revisited', *World Politics*, vol. XXXI, no. 2 (January 1979), pp. 314–15.

3 Bernard Reich, *Quest for Peace: United States – Israel Relations and the Arab–Israeli Conflict*, New Brunswick, New Jersey: Transaction Books, 1977, p. 365.

4 William B. Quandt, *Decade of Decisions: American Policy Toward the Arab–Israeli Conflict, 1967–1976*, Berkeley: University of California Press, 1977, p. 14.

5   Eytan Gilboa, *American Public Opinion Toward Israel and the Arab-Israeli Conflict*, Lexington, Mass.: Lexington Books, 1987, passim.
6   Reich, *Quest for Peace*, (see Note 3) p. 374.
7   Abraham Ben-Zvi, 'The limits of coercion in bilateral bargaining situations: the case of the American–Israeli dyad', *Jerusalem Journal of International Relations*, vol. 8, no. 4, 1986, p. 73.
8   Abraham Ben-Zvi, 'American peace-making strategy in the Middle East and the limits of the U.S.–Israel special relationship', *Middle East Review*, vol. XXI, no. 1, Fall 1988, pp. 7–8.
9   Ronald Reagan, 'Recognizing the Israeli assets', *Washington Post*, 15 August 1979.
10 Helena Cobban, 'The U.S.–Israeli relationship in the Reagan Era', *Conflict Quarterly*, vol. IX, no. 2, Spring 1989, pp. 12–13.
11 Cobban 1989 (see Note 10) p. 13; Deon Geldenhuys, *Isolated States: A Comparative Analysis*, Cambridge: Cambridge University Press, 1990, pp. 454–5.
12 Arnold L. Horelick, 'U.S.–Soviet relations: threshold of a new era', *Foreign Affairs*, vol. 69, no. 1, Fall 1990, p. 56.
13 For illustrations see *Ha'aretz*, 3 October 1991 (a report by Ori Nir); *Ha'aretz*, 17 September 1991 (a report by Eytan Rabin and Akiva Eldar); *National Journal*, vol. 23, no. 27, 6 July 1991, p. 1706.
14 Alexander L. George, 'Strategies for facilitating cooperation', in Alexander L. George, Philip J. Farley and Alexander Dallin (eds), *U.S.–Soviet Security Cooperation: Achievement, Failures, Lessons*, New York: Oxford University Press, 1988, p. 693.
15 Ibid, Note 14.
16 *Jerusalem Post*, 19 February 1991 (a report by David Makovsky).
17 Abraham Ben-Zvi, *Between Lausanne and Geneva: International Conferences and the Arab-Israel Conflict*, Boulder, Colorado: Westview Press 1989, pp. 60–71.
18 Quoted by the *Jerusalem Post*, 13 September 1991 (a report by Allison Kaplan and Michal Yudelman). See also *Ha'aretz*, 15 September 1991 (a report by Akiva Eldor and Ori Nir); *Ma'ariv*, 13 September 1991 (a report by Oded Shorer).

11 Soviet policy during the Gulf crisis

Yitzhak Klein

Soviet policy in the Gulf crisis was marked by uncertainty and vacillation, reflecting Soviet decision-makers' difficulties in reconciling their own conflicting motives, as well as portending the breakdown of central authority in Moscow.

On one hand, Soviet leaders viewed the crisis as a challenge, in which they were called upon to confirm their country's continued status as a superpower, capable of pursuing an independent line of policy. This perspective was informed by a sense that the Soviet Union was still in competition with the United States and that an optimal outcome to the crisis, from the American point of view was, partly for that very reason, less satisfactory from a Soviet perspective. On the other hand, the 'new thinking' in Soviet foreign policy introduced by the Soviet President, Mikhail Gorbachev, called for the Soviet Union to maintain a constructive, cooperative profile in international affairs. Indeed, by August 1990, when the crisis began, the Soviet Union could hardly do otherwise. Its position and influence in Europe had disintegrated and its economy was in a steep decline. Overt opposition to American policy risked diplomatic isolation – something the Soviet Union could hardly afford.

All Soviet decision-makers were united in their preference in seeing the Gulf crisis resolved peacefully, by diplomatic means. As time went by, however, it became increasingly evident that the USA was not prepared to countenance such an outcome, at least not in the form envisioned by the Soviet leadership. The Soviet Union's choices were either to fall in with American intentions, or else break openly with the USA and advocate forcefully an alternative policy. President Gorbachev and his closest advisers found the latter unacceptable. However, instead of coming to terms with the consequences, and supporting the Americans consistently, the Soviets did make several abortive attempts unilaterally to promote a diplomatic solution to the crisis. Failing in these attempts only caused gratuitous damage to the Soviet leadership and its prestige.

THE SOURCES OF SOVIET CONDUCT IN THE GULF CRISIS

Soviet dilemmas found expression in divisions among the Soviet élite. Three major Soviet groups, or schools of thought, directly or indirectly, influenced Soviet policy in the Gulf crisis. Each stemmed from a different interpretation of the issues.

A liberal group was led, indeed epitomized, by Eduard Shevardnadze, Soviet Foreign Minister until 20 December 1991. Even after his departure, Shevardnadze's views retained wide currency within the Foreign Ministry and were reflected in a section of the liberal Soviet Press. The liberal group disapproved of what they viewed as the Soviet Union's imperialist past, and held no sentiment about a former client regime such as Saddam Hussein's. If Saddam's invasion of Kuwait confronted the Soviet Union with the need to choose between an old protégé and a new foreign policy, for the Soviet liberal the choice was unequivocal: to denounce the aggression.[1]

Shevardnadze himself, and with him many leading Foreign Ministry personnel, seemed to believe sincerely that the Soviet Union's interests lay in collaborating to create a non-violent, democratic international order ruled by law. Shevardnadze thought Soviet–American cooperation crucial and, more broadly, viewed the action of the UN Security Council against Iraq a promising harbinger of a new world order.[2] Like all Soviet decision-makers, Soviet liberals preferred a diplomatic resolution of the Gulf crisis: a non-military solution in which the Soviet Union might yet play an active role, rather than a military denouement which might leave the United States dominant in the region. In the last analysis, however, they would much rather countenance a military solution than permit Saddam to derive any kind of political benefit from his actions, or risk the Soviet Union being portrayed as Saddam's accessory.

On the other side of the political extreme were those, mainly military officers and political conservatives associated with the heavy-industry sector, the KGB, and the bureaucracy of the Communist Party's Central Committee, who were scandalized by the prospect of the Soviet Union supporting an assault upon an ally such as Iraq and, in doing so, handing political preponderance in the Gulf to America on a silver platter. Conservative commentators suspiciously viewed American policy in the Gulf primarily as an attempt to increase Washington's own influence under the guise of a crusade against the Iraqi malefactor,[3] Conservative assessments of the Iraqi regime ran the gamut from sycophantic praise to open distaste for the invaders of

Kuwait.[4] All, however, felt that the Soviet Union should not assist an American policy which appeared aimed at the destruction of the Iraqi regime, and called for the Soviet Union to oppose in the UN the United States' attempts to obtain sanction for the use of force.

For much of the period Soviet conservatives did not exercise direct influence on foreign policy.[5] However, during these months, a crisis emerged in Soviet domestic politics that came to a head in late November and early December, when it became apparent that conservatives had taken control of Gorbachev, dictating his political appointments. This period saw the dismissal of the liberal Minister of the Interior, Vadim Bakatin, and the resignation of Shevardnadze.

In this domestic crisis, Soviet policy in the Gulf became a political football. The fall of Bakatin and Shevardnadze marked a turn in Soviet attitudes towards the United States' policy in the Gulf. Thereafter, the official Soviet position disapproved of what was viewed as the Americans' unseemly desire for war in the Gulf and, later, of American conduct of the war.

A more 'centrist' position in the Soviet scheme of things hoped to bolster the Soviet Union's standing in the world by mediating a peaceful end to the crisis, preferably by linking it to an imposed solution of the Israeli–Palestinian conflict. The preferred vehicle for such a scenario was an Arab summit conference, rather than the UN, at which Saddam would agree to withdraw from Kuwait in return for an unstated understanding that the Palestinian problem would be next on the international agenda. This formula would permit the Iraqi regime to save face, while enabling the Soviet Union, in effect, to orchestrate and even steal the show. Supported at times by President Gorbachev and some of his personal advisers, this policy was advocated most consistently by his special envoy to the region, Yevgenii Primakov.[6]

Including, as it did, people close to the Soviet President, and possessing the qualified support of Gorbachev himself, this school of thought was well aware of the value to the Soviet leadership of keeping up an appearance of close relations with the United States. An open breach with the Bush Administration on Gulf policy was not contemplated: this meant rejecting, at least rhetorically, any suggestion of a deal with Saddam that would allow him to salvage any political gains from the conquest of Kuwait. Yet as Primakov argued:

[Linkage was to be rejected.] Yet a dual question arose. Why was it absolutely forbidden to attempt to use the Arabs' extreme interest in resolving the Palestinian problem to get Iraq to leave Kuwait? And why not make an attempt to use the political solution of the emergent crisis in Kuwait to impel a resolution of the other conflict important to the region's security – the Arab–Israel?[7]

Unfortunately, such a 'solution' would have required squaring the circle – arranging a face-saving solution for Saddam without forcing an open breach with the United States. Primakov never brought it off, but the Soviet President's consistent support for his recurring missions to and about the Gulf indicate how deeply it was desired.

THE OPENING PHASE: FROM THE INVASION TO THE HELSINKI SUMMIT

The invasion of Kuwait found the Soviet Foreign Minister and the American Secretary of State having just completed discussions in Irkutsk in south-central Siberia. Reconvening in Moscow, the two officials then issued a joint statement condemning the invasion and calling on the Security Council to condemn it as well.[8] The Soviet Union announced the immediate suspension of arms supplies to Iraq, even going so far as to divert shipments already en route.[9] Twenty-four hours later the Security Council passed its first two resolutions on the Gulf crisis, condemning the Iraqi invasion and imposing a comprehensive set of economic sanctions on Iraq.

In the early days of the crisis the Soviet Press and official Soviet statements glowed with enthusiasm at the initial display of rapid and effective US–Soviet cooperation on the Iraq issue. Even elements of the conservative press expressed approval. The glow faded soon and turned to alarm as the extent of the United States' military commitment in the Gulf became evident. Even before the Bush Administration formally declared a naval blockade of Iraq on 11 August, the Soviet Foreign Ministry indicated its apprehensions about this unilateral American move, noting that the Soviet Union itself could not contemplate a similar step, 'or any other measures outside the framework of Security Council decisions'.[10] As American military might began to flow to Saudi Arabia, the Foreign Ministry sounded a note of concern:

The tendency for the confrontation to escalate and for passions to be kindled is unfortunately continuing to gain momentum rapidly. . . . We would like to stress once again that the acuteness and unpredictability of the current situation in the Persian Gulf zone urgently require everyone involved . . . to show respect for the will of the international community and a sense of supreme responsibility for the fate of peace.[11]

In official Soviet jargon 'supreme responsibility' is an attribute of the two superpowers, so this warning was not directed at the Iraqis alone.

The Soviet Press, and not merely its most conservative elements, began to question American motives: was not a power play underway to create a permanent military presence in the Gulf? The Soviets adopted the position that all measures to be undertaken against Iraq had to be previously approved by the Security Council, including any use of force.[12] In this way the Soviet Union hoped to 'capture' the American military effort and place it in a multilateral and institutional framework over which the Soviet Union could exercise some control. On 12 August, Saddam Hussein advanced his proposal to link the issue of Kuwait with the Palestinian issue and the withdrawal of Syrian forces from Lebanon. The United States, unwilling to countenance anything that even suggested of linkage or a reward for Saddam, rejected the proposal out of hand. The Soviets, however, were already looking for some reasonable diplomatic exit from the crisis, and Foreign Minister Shevardnadze, after some delay, stated that the proposals 'deserved careful study'.[13]

Military circles in the Soviet Union viewed with increasing disquiet the American build-up of forces in the Gulf. Particularly unsettling was the transfer of American units from Europe, where the accords on conventional forces in Europe (CFE), then being negotiated, called for sharp cuts in superpower forces, to a new theatre a scant 1,200 kilometres from the Soviet Union's southern border (far closer, if air deployments to Turkey are considered). On 30 August a senior officer, General V. Lobov, Commander-in-Chief of the Warsaw Pact and an important member of the Soviet team on the CFE talks, warned of the dangers posed to Soviet security by this transfer of forces. Lobov stated that by transferring forces out of Europe to another strategically sensitive region the United States was trying to circumvent the spirit of the CFE accords, warning that this could 'wreck' the CFE negotiations.[14]

Almost simultaneously, the official Soviet position began to veer sharply away from that of the United States, towards the adoption of an independent diplomatic initiative to resolve the Gulf crisis. In Vladivostok, five days after Lobov's warning, Foreign Minister Shevardnadze, called for the convening of an international conference on the Middle East.[15] Shevardnadze's statement implied close linkage between the Gulf crisis and the Arab–Israeli conflict. In effect, the

Soviet Union was adopting the essence of Saddam's statement of 12 August. The United States could not but consider this Soviet policy counter-productive. For one thing, it offered Saddam the diplomatic ransom he had named as his price for leaving Kuwait; moreover, as it opened a way for the peaceful resolution of the crisis, it was bound to be extremely attractive to other powers. Even prior to Shevardnadze's statement President Bush had sent a hurried request to the Soviet President proposing a meeting at Helsinki on 9 September.

The Soviet proposal for a conference did not outlive the Helsinki summit. The joint statement issued by the two Presidents at its end made no mention of it, beyond an anodyne statement about the necessity of working – after the resolution of the Gulf crisis – towards the resolution of other Middle East conflicts. The statement, however, *did* mention the possibility of 'additional [steps] consistent with the UN Charter' if existing sanctions against Iraq did not bear fruit. In such a context this could only have meant the use of force.[16] Apparently the only reassurance President Gorbachev received was that the use of force was not imminent. President Bush had managed to hold the diplomatic line, and in the eyes of the world Moscow's attempt at adopting an independent course on the Gulf had collapsed at the first touch of American pressure.[17]

THE PRIMAKOV ODYSSEY

Yevgenii Primakov an orientalist by training and one of Mikhail Gorbachev's closest associates, was hand-picked for a mission to the Gulf area in early October to examine the possibility of achieving a peaceful solution to the crisis.[18] Although Primakov was not a professional diplomat, his appointment by Gorbachev implied an intention to bypass the Foreign Ministry establishment, its liberal views, distaste for Saddam, and desire to cooperate fully with the Americans. Primakov hoped to finesse the question of rewarding Saddam for withdrawing from Kuwait by convincing all the parties involved to go through a kind of charade: Saddam would withdraw from Kuwait, and immediately afterward an international conference would be called to deal with the Arab–Israeli problem. Any formal connection between the two would be denied; nevertheless, Saddam had to be given to understand that the conference would take place if he withdrew, and everyone would know that he knew. Primakov had another mission – to secure the release of thousands of Soviet specialists and their families who, like many other foreigners, were being held at the pleasure of the Baghdad regime.

Primakov arrived in Baghdad on 4 October. On the 5th, in a meeting with Saddam, the special Soviet envoy warned the Iraqi leader that his choices were either to leave Kuwait or be attacked. Yet Saddam refused to be intimidated. He mentioned his proposals of 12 August, linking the Gulf crisis with other Middle East issues, but without acknowledging the possibility of an Iraqi withdrawal. Having to be content with this, Primakov also received assurances that Soviet nationals in Iraq would be released soon, a promise the Iraqis had no intention of keeping at this stage.

Back in Moscow, in a consultation with Gorbachev, Prime Minister Ryzhkov, and KGB chief Kriuchkov, it was decided to send Primakov on a mission to Europe and the United States to gather support for a compromise solution: getting Iraq to leave Kuwait while emphasizing that a 'specific action should take place facilitating the resolution of disputed questions and stabilizing the situation in the entire Middle East'.[19]

After fruitless meetings with the Italian Prime Minister, Giulio Andreotti and President Mitterand, Primakov continued on to Washington and met on the 19th with Pesident Bush, Secretary Baker, Brent Scowcroft, the national security adviser, his deputy Robert Gates, and the President's Chief of Staff, John Sununu. Primakov later claimed to have found the President somewhat hesitant. Bush asked Primakov to report to Saddam that the American position was uncompromising, but that 'if Hussein gives us a positive signal it will be heard by us'.[20] As to whether the Soviet initiative would be endorsed by the United States, Bush promised Primakov an answer within two to three hours, and the latter withdrew. Primakov, in his account, gives the impression that it did not take long for the other men in the room to disuade the President; within the hour a messenger came to Primakov informing him he could go. Primakov's first mission had died in the Oval Office.

Primakov returned to Moscow, where the assessment was gloomy: war was more than likely, aiming to destroy Iraq's industrial and military potential. So unpalatable was this prospect and imperative the need to head it off, that it was decided to send Primakov on yet another assignment, this time to organize a pan-Arab summit at which Saddam would be invited, in the name of the entire Arab world, to accept the basic deal of an international conference linked-but-not-linked to Iraq's withdrawal from Kuwait. Primakov set out on the 24th. The first Arab leader he met with was President Assad of Syria, who supported Primakov's proposal; President Mubarak of Egypt was more sceptical.

On the 28th Primakov met the Iraqi leader again. Saddam still would not accept outright the idea of a pan-Arab conference, however. He insisted that before acting he needed specific assurances: about the lifting of sanctions; about Iraqi access to the sea; and a connection between the Gulf crisis and the Palestinian issue. Thus, what Primakov hoped to leave unmentioned, so that other parties could pretend they did not exist, Saddam demanded explicitly, as a precondition for a conference. Complying with it would have undoubtedly involved an open breach with the United States; more-over, Saddam's response was not sufficiently forthcoming to tempt certain Arab members of the anti-Iraqi coalition, particularly Egypt, to a conference.

Primakov's 'Arab conference' gambit expired in Baghdad. His two missions illustrate clearly Soviet policy, caught between a rock and a hard place. Between Washington's insistence on an Iraqi capitulation and Baghdad's inflexibility, the Soviets could do nothing – unless they were willing to take up the Iraqi cause in opposition to Washington. Had they been the first to do this, others might have joined them; but nobody else was willing to take the initiative. The Soviet government, too, thought that to refrain from doing so was a much wiser course of action.

RESOLUTION 678

Following Primakov's abortive missions in October, once again control over the Soviet diplomatic agenda shifted into Eduard Shevardnadze's hands. Instead of centring on Saddam and the Gulf, the Soviet Union aimed at a longer-term objective: institutionalizing UN regulation of the use of force in similar crises in the future. In an address to the Supreme Soviet in October, Shevardnadze explained his logic:

> The [UN] Charter ensures for each state the right to collective defense. Applied to the present crisis, this means that the United States and other states juridically . . . can use force on the basis of the request by the legitimate government of Kuwait. . . . [Had] any machinery existed for the collective repulsion of aggression, then Kuwait could [have counted] on this machinery, on the Security Council, on the appropriate structures of collective security. . . . This is too cruel [sic] a lesson, comrades, for us to leave unchanged the present structures of maintaining the peace.[21]

In other words, the United States was able to seize the opportunity to increase its influence in the Gulf because no machinery existed for a truly international, UN-based effort in which the Soviet Union would have at least equal say. Towards this end, as early as September Shevardnadze had taken the risky step of proposing to give the UN real teeth, including Soviet teeth if necessary. It was his suggestion that:

> The Security Council . . . should begin by initiating steps to reactivating the work of the Military Staff Committee, and study the practical aspects of assigning national military contingents to serve under the authority of the council. The Soviet Union is prepared to conclude an appropriate agreement with the Security Council . . .[22]

Statements like these raised the possibility of the deployment of *Soviet* forces in the Gulf in conjunction with a multinational force opposing Iraq. They also raised a storm of protest among Soviet conservatives still smarting from the Afghanistan experience.

In a meeting between Secretary James Baker and Foreign Minister Shevardnadze in London on 9 November, the latter apparently gave his consent to the adoption of a Security Council resolution authorizing the use of force against Iraq.[23] This willingness to use force was not immediately shared by President Gorbachev; and as the month of November wore on, it appeared that the deal struck in London was having trouble in remaining viable.[24] American insistence coupled with the futile visit by Tareq Aziz to Moscow at the end of November appear to have convinced the Soviet leader of the necessity of the move. The Soviet Union duly voted for Resolution 678 on 29 November, while claiming that by voting for 678, the Soviet Union was not supporting a blanket authorization of war. Rather, the resolution increased the pressure on Saddam, hence improving the prospects for a peaceful solution to the Gulf crisis.[25] It is hard to suspect that experienced politicians like Gorbachev and Shevardnadze actually believed that any such thing was possible. Perhaps for this reason the Soviet Union did not make any serious attempt to exploit the new opportunities allegedly created by the resolution.

SEA CHANGE IN THE SOVIET PERSPECTIVE ON THE GULF

Internal opposition to the Foreign Ministry's conduct of Soviet policy in the Gulf had been on the rise since October and centred on two issues: the possible use of Soviet troops in the Gulf, and, during

November, attempts to prevent the Soviet vote in favour of Resolution 678. The main source of the conservatives' power was not in the Supreme Soviet or the Press, but in the Communist Party, the KGB, and the army, where it worked behind the scenes. Yet conservative statements in the Press and the Supreme Soviet do illustrate quite clearly the trend of their thought.

Delegates to the Supreme Soviet, particularly from the conservative 'Soyuz' (Union) group, emphasized the fact that only the Supreme Soviet could authorize the dispatch of Soviet troops abroad.[26] In mid-October Col. Nikolai Petrushenko, a leader of 'Soyuz', launched a general attack on Soviet foreign policy under Shevardnadze's guidance in which he criticized the Foreign Ministry for not keeping the Supreme Soviet informed, and for contemplating the use of Soviet forces against a Soviet ally.[27] When in early November Shevardnadze indicated approval for the Security Council resolution authorizing the use of force against Iraq, Yurii Blokhin, a 'Soyuz' leader, pointed out that his faction would demand a debate in the Supreme Soviet before the USSR cast its vote on such a resolution.[28]

Shevardnadze was not fated to realize his goal in making the UN the ultimate authority for the armed resolution of international disputes. His vote for Resolution 678 also proved to be his last significant act as Soviet Foreign Minister. On 4 December the Foreign Ministry felt constrained to deny as 'insinuations'

> Immoral attempts by some . . . circles to interpret the recent statement by [Shevardnadze] as a search for a pretext for Soviet military intervention . . .[29]

Yet the crescendo of criticism continued. On 20 December, Shevardnadze announced his resignation to the Supreme Soviet. From that point on, the Soviet Union began to adopt a much more distant and cool stance towards the United States and its Gulf policy.

Since the beginning of the crisis the Soviet Press carried a drumroll of articles that, while sometimes criticizing the United States and its motives, nevertheless, praised Soviet–American cooperation. But in December the general tenor of the Press began to change. Criticism of the United States became more pronounced, emphasizing the selfish aspects of American policy and the supposed dangers its military policy posed.[30] The American objective was alleged to be, not the liberation of Kuwait, but the destruction of the Iraqi regime:

> The ultimate [American] goal, should war break out . . . will be to

set up a pro-American regime in Iraq, which will immediately alter the alignment of political forces throughout the Arab world . . .'[31]

Other voices were raised to say that it was time for the United States and the Soviet Union to part ways.[32] The Soviet Union had hitherto sacrificed its national interests in pursuit of a chimerical 'universal' policy, a practice that had brought only losses and therefore had to be reversed.[33]

ATTEMPTS TO MAKE PEACE

The thrust of American intentions regarding Iraq had been clear for some months prior to the outbreak of hostilities on 17 January. Soon after the fighting began the Soviet Union engaged in the first of a series of attempts to prevent the destruction of the threatened Iraqi regime. On 19 January, according to Primakov, the Soviet Union offered to mediate a ceasefire in return for a secret Iraqi commitment to evacuate Kuwait. Somewhat to the Soviets' embarrassment, this proposal was rejected publicly by Baghdad Radio two days later.[34] On 22 January, five days after hostilities commenced, President Gorbachev issued a warning to the effect that 'we are duty bound to do everything possible to prevent an escalation of the conflict'.[35]

Soviet attempts to bring about a cessation of hostilities began in earnest on 9 February, as the destruction of Iraq's fighting power became marked and preparations for a ground offensive against Iraq got into gear. On that day Gorbachev issued a statement which said, in part: 'the logic of military operations and the nature of military actions are threatening to *exceed the mandate which is defined in these resolutions*'.[36] Gorbachev thus implied the United States was about to act illegally in the Gulf. Further, he announced his intention once more to send a personal representative to treat with Saddam Hussein. Primakov set off for Baghdad the same day, in an effort to get the Iraqis to capitulate, and thus to forestall the impending allied ground offensive.[37]

Alone with Saddam in the early hours of the 11th, Primakov informed him that Iraqi forces in Kuwait were about to be destroyed. He urged Saddam to announce the evacuation of Kuwait, to be carried out quickly. Saddam began to explore the various possibilities: Would sanctions be lifted if he made such an announcement? Was there a possibility for regime change in Kuwait? Primakov brushed the probes aside, insisting the situation prior to 2 August had to be restored. On the morning of the 13th, Tareq Aziz came to Primakov and announced that the Soviet proposals were under consideration and that Aziz himself would come to Moscow. Two days later Radio Baghdad announced Iraq's acceptance of Security Resolution 660, which called for the 'unconditional' evacuation of Kuwait, but accompanied by a long list of conditions.

Aziz arrived in Moscow only on the 17th. Gorbachev delicately pointed out to him the contradiction between the text of Resolution 660 and the list of conditions in Baghdad Radio's message. Aziz replied that the latter were not conditions, but merely 'a program, as it were, to be realized in the future'.[38] Gorbachev then steered the conversation in another direction: let Iraq evacuate Kuwait, mentioning it by name (as the Baghdad Radio message had not), and commit itself to a firm timetable of military withdrawal. The Soviet Union, for its part, would try at least to secure guarantees that the withdrawing forces would not be attacked. Aziz, who had no authority to make on-the-spot personal decisions, took this proposal, basically the same one Primakov had brought a week earlier, back to Baghdad, and then returned to Moscow on the 21st, bearing Saddam's agreement in principle.

The Soviets were now acting as mediators between Washington and Baghdad. At 4 a.m. (Moscow time) on the 22nd Gorbachev called President Bush to inform him of the progress in his talks with Aziz. During an all-night session with Aziz, the Soviets worked out a proposal, the main points of which were as follows:

1 Iraq to announce the complete and unconditional withdrawal of its troops from Kuwait according to a fixed timetable.
2 A ceasefire to come into effect, with the withdrawal to begin the following day. Simultaneously, all prisoners of war to be released.
3 After two-thirds of Kuwait are evacuated, economic sanctions against Iraq to lapse; all other Security Council resolutions [including that requiring Iraq to pay reparations] to lapse when the evacuation of Kuwait is completed.[39]

These proposals would have preserved the Iraqi regime and released it from any obligations resulting from the invasion of Kuwait. The proposal to lift sanctions against Iraq once two-thirds of Kuwait were evacuated was meant to allow the Iraqis to save face. But, as the Soviet leadership must have known full well, it was asking for trouble in pushing to suspend both hostilities and sanctions while leaving Iraq still in possession of part of Kuwait (including, presumably, Bubiyan Island and the Kuwaiti half of the al-Rumaila oil field). Washington's rejection of the plan, as a 'conditional' withdrawal, was swift.[40]

The Soviet government tried again. On the 22nd, a revised plan was suggested to Baghdad differing from the first chiefly by setting a definite deadline for the Iraqi withdrawal from Kuwait – 21 days from the time a ceasefire was declared, with Kuwait City to be evacuated within four days – and postponing the suspension of sanctions until the full withdrawal from Kuwait was completed.[41] But the American administration took matters in hands before the Iraqis could compose a reply. Peremptorily cutting through Soviet efforts to bring about a ceasefire, President Bush on the 22nd announced his own conditions for a ceasefire: Iraq was to withdraw from Kuwait within seven days. Bush also set a deadline of noon (New York time) on the 23rd for Iraq's acceptance of these terms. An evacuation under such conditions could only turn into a rout, and Iraq's acceptance by the deadline mentioned could only amount to capitulation. By the time the deadline passed darkness had fallen over the Gulf, and the coalition's ground offensive jumped off before midnight. To all intents and purposes, the Soviet attempt to rescue Iraq was over.

Official Soviet opinion maintained that the ground offensive had not been necessary; once the Iraqi government had committed itself to withdrawing from Kuwait, the crisis was essentially over and the details could have been worked out by diplomatic means.[42] In reality, of course, the ground offensive had been necessary to achieve American purposes. The Soviet Union had intervened in order to frustrate those purposes by creating political conditions under which the United States would find it impossible to continue the war.

CONCLUSION

The Soviet Union cut a poor figure in the Gulf crisis. It vacillated between cooperation and opposition with the United States. The mandate to conduct Soviet foreign policy oscillated between the Foreign Ministry and Gorbachev's personal circle, adding to this overall impression of inconsistency and uncertainty. Having squandered its last chance to exert a decisive influence on events by voting for the Security Council Resolution 678,[43] only then did the Soviet Union decide under the influence of domestic political pressure to oppose American policy, the only outcome being a series of diplomatic setbacks echoing round the world.

The actual influence of Soviet policy on the course the crisis took was nugatory. In a broader sense, the Gulf crisis illustrated the difficulty the Soviet Union experienced in general in adjusting its foreign policy to new international circumstances. In its abortive attempts to play a distinctive role in the crisis, i.e. one in opposition to, or at least independent of, the United States, Moscow tried to maintain a firm hold on the title of superpower, but merely succeeded instead in confirming that its days as a great global power were over.

Eduard Shevardnadze pointed the way unsuccessfully to another, potentially more effective policy. According to his alternative crisis strategy, he had hoped to restrain the United States within a formal international legal framework, centred on the institutions of the United Nations, one which would permit other powers to check and limit the sole remaining superpower. Among the secondary powers the Soviet Union was at that point still *primus inter pares*. Under Shevardnadze's guidance it might have formed and led a coalition of nations in meliorating the disproportionate power of the United States. This would have been a long-term policy, extending beyond the immediate issue of the Gulf crisis. Unfortunately, from a narrow Soviet perspective, most Soviet leaders neither understood nor supported Shevardnadze.

In failing to appreciate the Soviet Union's true state of dwindling influence and power, and the less expansive foreign policy agenda it dictated, former President Gorbachev must partially share the blame. Even before Shevardnadze's dismissal, Gorbachev gave him only limited, intermittent support. Had he supported Shevardnadze wholeheartedly, Gorbachev might have turned the issue of foreign policy into a weapon against the conservative cabal that appeared to take control in the autumn of 1990. Gorbachev could have argued with a certain amount of justice that the policies they advocated represented an unsustainable throwback to times and conditions that were no longer obtainable. Instead, Gorbachev allowed the conservatives to use the Gulf crisis as a stick for intimidating the liberals. Ironically, having abandoned the liberals, he was betrayed in turn by the conservatives in the abortive coup of August 1991, emerging as the lame-duck President of a state teetering on the brink of dissolution.

Soviet policy in the Gulf crisis may perhaps be summed up as a lost opportunity from both a domestic and international perspective. By 1992, those conditions which might have permitted the Soviet Union to form and lead a coalition of secondary powers no longer existed. With the Soviet power structure in the throes of disintegration, leaders at the Union level had less time and resources than ever to invest in foreign policy initiatives, while the leadership of the Russian Republic has yet to move decisively to fill the gap. Successor states to the former Soviet Union, cannot return to the path marked out by Shevardnadze in foreign policy until the ever-deepening domestic crisis is at least on the way to being resolved.

NOTES

1 Eduard Shevardnadze, interview with *Yomiuri Shimbun*, Tokyo, 27 August 1990.

2 See especially Shevardnadze's addresses at the UN on 25 September and 29 November 1990.

3 See, for example, Eduard Volodin in *Sovetskaia Rossia* (*Soviet Russia*), 11 January 1990, p. 5; V. Linnik, *Pravda*, 10 August 1990. Criticism in a more moderate tone was expressed by the former Soviet Chief of Staff, Marshal Sergei Akhromeev, in *Pravda*, 21 January 1991, p. 5.

4 Many writers emphasized the close economic ties that had existed between the Soviet Union and Iraq before the outbreak of the crisis. Note Eduard Volodin, in *Sovetskaia Rossia*, 23 October 1990.

5 There is some indication that elements within the Soviet military sought to violate the UN-sanctioned embargo on arms sales to Iraq during the crisis. Some eighty Soviet advisers remained in Iraq after 15 January 1991, allegedly to maintain and operate Iraq's air defences [Radio Free Europe/ Radio Liberty 'Report on the USSR #4, 25 January 1991, p. 27]. On 4 January US naval forces intercepted at sea the Soviet freighter *Dmitrii Furman*, bound for the Jordanian port of Aqaba with military supplies that were not listed on its manifest [Ibid. #3, 18 January 1991, p. 31]. General Al'bert Makashov, a highly placed officer, was rumoured to have visited Iraq before the invasion and possibly to have helped plan it. The Defence Ministry later issued a denial of this rumour [TASS, in English, 23 August 1990]. Makashov, a virulent critic of Gorbachev, opposed Boris Yel'tsin in the elections for the office of Russian President and was later implicated in the August 1991 coup against Gorbachev.

6 See A. Vasiliev in *Komsomolskaia Pravda*, February 1991, p. 5; also Primakov, 'The war that might have been avoided', part I, *Izvestiia*, 27 February 1991.

7 Primakov, 'The war that might have been avoided', part 1, *Izvestiia*, 27 February 1991.

8 TASS, 3 August 1990.

9 TASS, August 2 1990.

10 Yurii Gremitskikh, Foreign Ministry spokesman. Reported by TASS, 9 August.

11 'USSR Foreign Ministry statement', *Pravda*, 10 August.

12 TASS, 15 August 1990 Note also broadcast commentary by TASS military correspondent Vladimir Chernyshov, in English, 14 August 1990.

13 TASS, in English, 21 August 1990.

14 TASS, 30 August. In Soviet jargon the term 'wreck' carries connotations of malicious sabotage.

15 For text of Shevardnadze's statement see Francis X. Clines, 'Soviets suggest conference combining issues of Middle East', *New York Times*, 5 September 1990, p. 17.

16 See text in *Pravda*, 10 September 1990. p. 1.

17 Apparently, President Bush also promised at the summit that American forces would be withdrawn from the Gulf after the end of the crisis – an important consideration from the Soviet perspective.

18 Primakov, 'The war that might have been avoided', part I, *Izvestiia*, 27 February 1991, p. 8. This is the first part of a four-part series by Primakov, appearing in *Izvestiia* 27 February–2 March, describing his diplomatic missions during the Gulf crisis and war. The ensuing account of Primakov's pre-war missions generally follows his account.

19 Primakov, 'The war that might have been avoided', part II, 28 February 1991.

20 Primakov, *Izvestiia*, 28 February 1991.

21 Shevardnadze, live television broadcast on Moscow Television Service, 15 October 1990. In FBIS-Sov-90-200, 16 October 1990, p. 20.

22 Shevardnadze, address to the UN, 25 September 1990. In FBIS-Sov-90-187, 26 September 1990, p. 4. The following day Gennadi Gerasimov, spokesman for the Foreign Ministry, confirmed that the employment of Soviet troops in such a framework, should it be established, was indeed contemplated. Gerasimov press briefing, TASS, 26 September.

23 See M. Yusin, in *Izvestiia*, 9 November 1990, p. 4.

24 A two-hour meeting between Presidents Bush and Gorbachev, in Paris for the signing of the CFE treaty, did not yet result in Soviet agreement vote for a resolution authorizing the use of force. See Andrew Rosenthal, *New York Times*, 20 November 1990, p. 1.

25 This line was consistently maintained by Shevardnadze and the Foreign Ministry. See Foreign Ministry official statement, *Izvestiia*, 4 December, p. 4; Shevardnadze, in an interview the day after the resolution passed, stated that 'the new resolution is being adopted precisely in order to avoid a military solution to the crisis' TASS, 30 November 1990.

26 See, for example, an article by Aleksandr Goltz, in *Krasnaia Zvezda*, 4 October 1990, p. 1.

27 Radio Free Europe/Radio Liberty 'Report on the USSR', #43 1990, 25 ff.

28 Radio Free Europe/Radio Liberty 'Report on the USSR', #48, 1990.

29 Statement by Deputy Foreign Minister Vitalii Churkin, TASS, 4 December 1990.

30 See, for example, Konstantin Geivandov in *Izvestiia*, 11 January 1991, p. 4; Eduard Volodin, *Sovetskaia Rossia*, 11 January 1991, p. 5; Yurii Glukhov, *Pravda*, 15 January 1991; and others. An interesting point is the convergence in tone between papers such as *Pravda* and *Izvestiia*, hitherto considered centrist and identified with the President, with that of right-wing papers such as *Sovetskaia Rossia*.

31 M. Yusin, in *Izvestiia*, 10 January 1991; translation in *Current Digest of the Soviet Press*, v. 43 #2, 13 February 1991, p. 21.

32 See Aleksandr Goltz, *Krasnaia Zvezda*, 4 January 1991, p. 3; A. Shalnev, *Izvestiia*, 5 March 1991, p. 6.

33 See, for example, Mikhail V. Aleksandrov, in *Literaturnaia Rossiya*, 4 January 1991, pp. 4–5; translation in *Current Digest of the Soviet Press*, vol. 43 #2, 13 February 1991, p. 23.

34 Primakov, 'The war that might have been avoided', part IV, *Izvestiia*, 2 March 1991.

35 Presidential press statement, Moscow domestic television service, in Russian, in FBIS-Sov-91-015, 22 January 1991, pp. 3–4.
36 TASS International Service in Russian, 9 February 1991. In FBIS-Sov-91-028, p. 18. Emphasis added.
37 Details of Primakov's mission are taken largely from his series of articles in *Izvestiia*, 'The war that might have been avoided' (see Note 18).
38 Primakov's report of the conversation (see Note 18).
39 *Izvestiia*, 22 February 1991, p. 1.
40 See Maureen Dowd, 'Pressing demands', *New York Times*, 22 February 1991, p. 1, citing President Bush.
41 Serge Schmemann, 'Moscow sends revised plan to Baghdad', *New York Times*, 23 February 1991, p. 5.
42 See briefing by Vitalii Ignatenko, Gorbachev's press secretary, *Izvestiia*, 27 February 1991, p. 1.
43 In a briefing given near the end of the Gulf War, Vitalii Ignatenko, President Gorbachev's spokesman, remarked bitterly that the Soviet Union had 'abdicated' its ability to mediate a conclusion to the war by voting for Resolution 678. See *Izvestiia*, 27 February 1991, p. 1; cited in *Current Digest of the Soviet Press*, vol. 43 #9, 3 April 1991, p. 1.

12 European reactions to the Gulf challenge

Ilan Greilsammer

INTRODUCTION

Iraq invaded Kuwait at a moment when the European Community was preoccupied with its own political unification.[1]

The personal representatives of the EC's twelve foreign ministers, meeting on 25 July, had agreed just a week earlier on a preparatory conference in September 1990, to pave the way for an extraordinary summit of heads of governments, scheduled for 27 October. Italy, then serving as EC president, took the lead in drawing up a detailed memorandum on problems remaining to be worked out: how to reinforce the Community's institutions; what the role of the European Parliament would be; ways for enlarging Community powers in the field of common foreign policy and security, etc. Of course, traditional differences of view among the member-states persisted; such as Great Britain's opposition to greater supranational integration and to any kind of 'federal' development, in contrast to other members, mainly France and Germany, wanting to progress rapidly towards full political union.

Throughout the summer of 1990, the struggle to determine the timing and shape of the European Monetary System (EMS) had intensified, with EC Commission President Jacques Delors proposing, in August, to accelerate the use of the ECU as a single currency. The Commission's blueprint called also for the creation by 1 January 1993 of a European Central Bank modelled on the US Federal Reserve System. In general, the political atmosphere among the Twelve was good, and the hope was that by the end of the summer there would be quiet, businesslike progress towards compromise on all of these proposals in advance of the next meeting of foreign ministers routinely scheduled for the beginning of October.

Also interesting to note is that, on the eve of the Iraqi action, the Community continued to issue 'common declarations' on foreign policy problems in the framework of European political cooperation, as it had been doing for twenty years. But while easily adopted on virtually every crisis, *coup d'état*, and breach of democracy in the world, no real steps had ever been taken to implement these declarations. Only on rare occasion had the Community approved economic or financial sanctions against a guilty state. No precedent whatsoever for concerted European military action had as yet been established.

Indeed, one of the principal questions discussed in the months preceding the Gulf crisis was Europe's own defence and security. Could Europe progress towards political unity while looking indefinitely to the United States for its defence? Might NATO evolve into the keystone for a new pan-European security structure? Was it not imperative to begin moving towards a new European Security Community that would reassure the USA of Europe's long-term approach to the maintenance of its own security?

FIRST EUROPEAN REACTIONS

Given this preoccupation with continental affairs, the twelve governments were entirely surprised by the unilateral Iraqi action that precipitated a full-scale crisis in the Middle East. The general feeling immediately was that annexation of Kuwait constituted the single most direct – and flagrant – challenge to international order since the Second World War. Most Europeans also believed the UN should take immediate action since Saddam Hussein's use of force against a small neighbouring country epitomized what the UN was established to prevent happening. As soon as the news broke, there arose the question of economic sanctions against Iraq, particularly an oil embargo. Circumstances seemed quite favourable for such a measure: first, because the cold war was now officially over. The Soviet Union, now seen as a 'status quo power', joined the USA and Europe in defending the existing international order. Second, Iraq was a heavily-indebted country also dependent on a single export; a credit freeze coupled with a boycott of its oil could quickly render Baghdad's position untenable, provided both measures were universally observed and strictly enforced.[2]

Europe collectively had learned three lessons during the 1970s from its experience with oil crises:

1 Objectively, there was no physical shortage of oil production capacity under the earth's surface now or in the foreseeable future;

2 Temporary price-boosting shortages could be created by OPEC, but only through unified action, which was doubtful;

3 Panic among Western consumers and governments had played a dysfunctional role in creating the past crises and needed to be prevented.

The overall consensus within the Community in August was that the invasion of Kuwait should pose no more of a threat to the world's economy and the financial markets than did Saddam's war against Iran.

Therefore, in this mood of guarded confidence and momentum towards greater EC cooperation, there were immediate calls for an oil embargo on Iraq and occupied Kuwait. If properly orchestrated, sanctions would not only be easily enforceable but, given the state of the world economy and energy markets (with European oil stocks, including government strategic reserves, at near record levels) could also be surprisingly painless for consumers and producers alike. In addition, Saudi Arabia alone could increase exports by 2 million to 2.5 million barrels a day with no technical difficulties. The United Arab Emirates could probably add another 0.5 million barrels and Venezuela 0.7 million.

Everyone, of course, understood the key prerequisite for such economic sanctions: that the integrity of Saudi Arabia and the physical safety of its oil fields be unconditionally guaranteed by the international community. Leading European personalities expressed their concern that Saddam Hussein was capable of escalating the conflict by retaliating militarily against Saudi Arabia. And the truth was that the latter would be especially vulnerable to such retaliation, unless given explicit, iron-clad guarantees, made credible by the presence, either on Saudi soil or nearby, of outside armed forces capable of defending it from Iraqi attack.

The reaction of the Twelve was swift and unanimous: stern condemnation of Iraq for the invasion and insistence upon immediate withdrawal of Iraqi forces from Kuwait. On 4 August, the Community decided on a comprehensive embargo aimed at halting the aggressor. The twelve member countries froze Iraqi assets while taking legal measures at the same time to protect those of Kuwait. In addition they suspended bilateral trade, technical, scientific, and military cooperation agreements with Baghdad; at France's initiative, they halted oil imports from Iraq and occupied Kuwait; and banned arms sales to Saddam Hussein's regime.[3]

These measures were the strongest punitive action ever taken by the

European Community, and were aimed at core Iraqi national economic and military interests. Such a principled and forceful decision was in marked contrast to past crises – during the US hostage affair in Tehran, or following the Soviet invasion of Afghanistan – when EC nations had been divided over whether to impose sanctions, and with what degree of severity.

The strongest EC economic sanction by far was its embargo on Iraqi and Kuwaiti oil, considering that in 1989, oil from the two countries accounted for more than 10 per cent of total EC oil imports, and despite the strong likelihood that some EC members like Denmark, which depended on Iraq and Kuwait for more than 50 per cent of its oil, would be hurt more than others. In Britain, too, the prospect of higher oil prices further threatened a troubled economy with 10.5 per cent inflation a year and clouded the already faltering UK stock market. In Germany there was particular reason to fear an oil crisis, since Chancellor Helmut Kohl had pledged not to boost taxes to pay for German unification. Borrowing on international markets, Germany could feel the direct impact of higher inflation and interest rates.[4] Hence, there were genuine fears of inflationist consequences in some European countries. But this was countervailed, on the other hand, by comforting knowledge that the oil stocks of the EC were at their highest.

Moreover, Europeans became convinced of the embargo's positive results. Iraq was totally dependent on oil for its export earnings, and was selling some 20 per cent of its oil exports to the European Community (the same proportion of its exports were sold to the USA). At the same time, Iraq could lose its assets in Europe (about $100 billion). Of course, attempts to freeze the assets of hostile governments are usually messy and highly contentious affairs.[5] All of which makes the speedy reaction and wide support for European sanctions striking. The primary explanation is that these sanctions were perceived of by Europeans not as an act of retribution against a hostile country, but rather directed specifically at preventing a belligerent regime from seizing the sovereign territory and wealth of a legitimate government. In short, EC measures were aimed at protecting the rightful owners of Kuwait's assets and to punish the wrongdoer.

With specific reference to the arms embargo, as the second largest supplier of weapons to Iraq after the Soviet Union, France was the European country with the most to lose. Of the 24 billion francs owed France by Iraq, 15 billion were for unpaid weapons. Even before the crisis, France had repeatedly asked to be paid for these arms contracts and deliveries, to which the Iraqi government had turned a deaf ear. Besides, there were those experts who felt an arms embargo would have little results, since the Iraqi army had been stockpiling equipment and was prepared for a lengthy war.

The European Community also pledged itself to the legitimacy of the original Kuwaiti government, and from the outset denied recognition to the Iraqi-supported Kuwaiti puppet regime. As for the dispatch of armed forces, the western European countries pledged in a joint statement to support 'mandatory and comprehensive UN sanctions' should the Security Council so decide. Nonetheless, some observers questioned the actual readiness of the Twelve to send troops to the Gulf area in the event of conflict following the UN decision to blockade Iraq.

Initial European reaction was, indeed, so strong and unanimous that it unintentionally caused deception in Baghdad. The Iraqi ambassador to Paris insisted the Twelve had made a terrible mistake, and that Europe's industrial economy could not survive for long without Iraqi and Kuwaiti oil.[6] Clear threats by Saddam Hussein and his ministers against European interests in the Middle East were also issued. Yet, this time the European leadership showed solidarity and resolve; it yielded neither to Iraqi intimidation or blandishments. As a result, the strong European reaction in turn influenced other countries' stand. Japan, for instance, halted all purchases of oil from Iraq, following the US and EC lead. China, too, at least announced it would no longer be selling arms to Baghdad.[7]

The Europeans then proceeded as well to adopt immediate measures for enforcing the embargo. Germany began requiring export licences for any goods destined for Iraq, while Italy announced its intention to strictly apply EC trade guidelines. A move by the Spanish government to protect Kuwaiti assets in Spain mainly affected Kuwait's London-based state investment arm, the Kuwaiti Investment Office, which owned 72 per cent of Gruppo Torras SA, a giant holding company controlling numerous major Spanish companies.

When the Security Council voted to impose a total ban on trade with Iraq, on 7 August the EC took further legislative and administrative measures to enforce the embargo[8] through three separate EC prohibitions: a general embargo on trade, specific measures applying to oil imports already decided on 4 August, and a suspension of trade concessions to Iraq. Humanitarian aid such as food and medical supplies would continue, however. Statistically worth bearing in mind is that in 1989 EC exports to Iraq totalled 2.12 billion sterling, with imports of 2.3 billion – of which 96.7 per cent were oil and petroleum products.

Lest the wrong impression be conveyed, it must be emphasized that, already in the first days of the crisis, European unanimity was far from absolute. There are nuances evident in the reactions by each of the twelve EC members. Britain, for example, was way ahead of the others in adopting an uncompromising, even harsh position. Prime Minister Margaret Thatcher insisted no small country could ever feel safe again and pledged a total economic embargo against Iraq, while calling on the UN to assert its authority. By comparison, the tenor of the other governments' declarations was more moderate.

Similarly, the hostage issue loomed in the forefront of European concerns in the initial phase of the crisis and caused discrepancy among the Twelve. One point of agreement, however, was that the EC nations did not sever diplomatic ties with Iraq or withdraw their ambassadors out of fear it might complicate protecting their citizens trapped in Iraq and Kuwait. Declarations aside, the operative question everybody asked was: what ought Europe really do about Saddam Hussein? The horror of Kuwait lay not so much in the totality of the conquest as in the vital interests at stake and threatened in the strategic, oil-rich Middle East. Both international principles and tangible geopolitical concerns, in short, mandated getting Saddam to acknowledge the sovereignty, territorial integrity and borders of his weaker neighbours, to release foreign nationals and to submit his quarrel with Kuwait to mediation. The options were straightforward: persuasion, compellance, or a combination of both.

THE MILITARY OPTION

Following Iraq's seizure of the Emirate, the United States, France and Britain moved to strengthen their military presence in the Gulf region. However, full military intervention was not as yet seriously considered because most people wanted to believe in the efficacy of economic sanctions, even if the results might not be immediately seen.[9] It was assumed Baghdad would not find enough oil outlets outside of industrialized Europe to provide the revenue needed to pay for the 20 per cent of its food purchased abroad or for other imports. Hunger, in other words, might work best to undermine Saddam Hussein's popularity; starved into submission, the Iraqi people would compel their autocratic ruler eventually to capitulate by restoring Kuwait's rightful sovereignty.

However, two reasons encouraged increasing discussion in Europe of recourse to military force in place of or by way of reinforcing economic measures. First, if trade sanctions were seriously intended to hurt Iraq, they would have to be bolstered by maritime blockade.[10] In which case might it be politically and militarily possible to commit European warships to such a multinational naval force? Britain was the first member of the Community to favour a blockade in direct collaboration with the USA, whereas President Francois Mitterrand discussed a punitive blockade of Iraq with senior French cabinet members alone. Others inclined more towards organizing a blockade within the framework of NATO. In Washington, the National Security Council was already debating missions and roles for US, British and French warships, even as Secretary of State Baker consulted NATO members in Brussels. By this dynamic, purely commercial measures shaded into the military sphere.

Secondly, given the imperative for Saudi Arabia to be a central element in the collective effort at isolating Saddam, both America and Europe clearly had to station substantial forces in the Kingdom. Without waiting for an authoritative European decision, the US unilaterally moved to deploy American forces in Saudi Arabia and to transfer planes from England to Turkey. The two main European states concerned by the US decision were France and Britain.

In his first televised interview on the crisis, President Mitterrand announced on 9 August a strengthening of French military presence in the Gulf.[11] Paris already had three warships in the region; they were to be joined by the aircraft carrier *Clemenceau*. In the recent past France showed little hesitancy about selective military interventions, as in Chad and Lebanon; but it had always been wary of costly open-ended wars against Arab nationalists, particularly those who, like Saddam Hussein, had oil and were considered good customers. To reassure his own party and the Gaullist wing of the opposition, President Mitterrand insisted France would send military material and personnel to Saudi Arabia, only if asked to do so; nor would French forces be put under American command. Compensating for these loopholes in the French military posture was the very strong commitment to economic sanctions. This can be explained by the fact that France was itself in an awkward position. The invasion of Kuwait had jolted the self-satisfaction of the French at the wisdom of French Middle Eastern policy, long centring on France's close friendship with Iraq. For years, governments on both the left and right had professed esteem for Saddam Hussein. Everyone also remembered the links between Paris and Baghdad, especially when Jacques Chirac was prime minister under President Giscard d'Estaing. It was then that France had begun o sell huge quantities of arms to Iraq, and to build its defence arsenal, including the nuclear plant at Tamuz. French business circles bene-ited enormously from these links to Saddam's regime.

Consequently, on the one hand, France, viewing itself as the Arab world's main European ally, was reluctant automatically to follow the US lead in the crisis. On the other hand, neither did it wish to appear an unreliable ally to the West by holding back. Moreover, Mitterrand found most leaders of his ruling Socialist Party extremely reluctant to act impulsively; especially Defence Minister Jean-Pierre Chevenement, known to be a personal friend of Saddam Hussein. On 16 August, Chevenement expressed reservation at any French military involvement when, at the National Assembly's Defence Commission he insisted on 'the continuity of French traditional Arab policy'. A few days later, the gap between Mitterrand and Chevenement surfaced again: Mitterrand adopted a position similar to that of the Americans in that French warships would be authorized to use force in imposing the embargo;[12] this, in contrast to his opponent's demand that force not be employed.

Britain showed less hesitancy. As a former dominant power in the Middle East, and as America's closest European ally, London had been the first European capital to accept the principle of direct military involvement in order that the United States not be left to do the job alone. For the duration of the crisis Britain consistently sought to have the Community participate in every way possible to help sustain the US commitment. Thus British forces in the Gulf were placed under US command. Contrary to French public opinion, the British public saw Saddam Hussein as a new Hitler who had to be stopped by all means. Opinion polls indicated over 80 per cent of the population favoured harsh military measures against Iraq. In augmenting a destroyer already stationed in the Gulf and two frigates soon expected in the area, London sent a squadron each of Tornado fighter planes and Jaguar ground attack aircraft, as well as deploying Rapier air defence missiles, Nimrod maritime reconnaissance planes and three mine hunters.

While wholeheartedly supporting economic sanctions, the other ten members of the European Community were reluctant to consider direct military involvement.[13]

With German reunification expected to take place in October, a major global confrontation in the Gulf was the last thing Chancellor Kohl desired.[14] Subsequently, the German government had trouble making up its mind on the invasion of Kuwait, and statements from the offices of Chancellor Kohl and Foreign Minister Genscher often

conflicted. All German ministers stressed the legal restrictions on th
use of German forces outside German soil. Under the lead of th
Social Democrats and the Greens, opposition to any German militar
involvement grew steadily, contending that German troops had n
business in the Gulf.

Until then, German intervention outside the NATO area had been
moot issue, if only because the need to intervene simply had neve
arisen since West German rearmament in 1955. Moreover, Defenc
Minister Stoltenberg said that on legal grounds his country could no
send ships to support US action, as German troops were not allowe
to operate outside NATO; their one possible function might be to fil
the gap left in the NATO area by shifts of US forces to the Gulf.

As pressure in Europe and Washington intensified, however, on 1
August Bonn reluctantly announced that the Federal Republic woul
be sending five minesweepers and two supply ships to the easter
Mediterranean – not the Gulf – amid indications of sharp disagree
ment within the government.

Italy, as president of the European Community at the time, coul
not decide even whether to support totally a UN embargo on Iraq
oil.[15] Caught between its desire to please the USA and its constan
policy of friendship towards the Arab world, it decided, like Germany
to send some warships to the eastern Mediterranean in place of U!
ships. Rome did add it might consider greater involvement, but onl
under a larger European umbrella such as the West European Union

Spain joined Germany and Italy in adopting a low-profile policy,
only allowing the USA to use base facilities. Spanish public opinio
and political leaders strongly opposed any Western military interven
tion in the Gulf, causing Madrid to argue that the best solution ough
to be in an Arab or regional framework, without Western involve
ment.

Belgium, for its part, adopted a similarly cautious attitude.[17] It sen
three warships to the eastern Mediterranean and insisted, like Italy
that any decision on military coordination had to be taken in th
framework of the Western European Union. All Belgian declaration
insisted on the UN framework, on European solidarity, on diplomacy
on peace.

In fact, the only small country of the Community which did mor
than equivocate was the Netherlands. The Dutch firmly decided t
despatch two war frigates to the Gulf area, rather than only as far a
the Mediterranean, which were under orders from Prime Ministe
Ruud Lubbers to impose the embargo, if necessary by force.

It can only be concluded, therefore, that the show of European unit was rather minimal and primarily rhetorical. Most Europeans were convinced that Saddam Hussein's ambitions would end with Kuwait which was, after all, a non-democratic country. They refused to see Saddam as a dictator wanting to rule the whole Middle East through military threat, political intimidation and economic might.[18] Nor was there much eagerness for a military encounter outside continental Europe, and one promising to involve possibly large numbers of casualties to European military personnel as well as ominous economic dislocation.

INCREASING DISCREPANCY AMONG THE EUROPEANS

The verbal show of European unity continued all throughout the crisis. However the gap between the Community member-states increasingly widened for a variety of reasons as the confrontation intensified. NATO's sixteen members unanimously supported the American decision to provide military support for Saudi Arabia and to help protect Turkey against Iraqi aggression. But since hostilities were taking place outside the NATO theatre there was no direct need to activate or coordinate that organization's integrated military structures. Besides, France adamantly resisted any American effort at extending or redefining NATO's role. The French position argued that each country had to contribute to the collective effort in its own way, with NATO remaining solely a forum for consultation.

If NATO was disqualified as central coordinator, then it was felt the role could be assumed, at least in part, by the nine-nation Western European Union.[19] Formed in 1954, the WEU was made up of the nine NATO members of the EC, and had been revived briefly in the 1980s for the express purpose of conducting military operations outside the North Atlantic area. Most notably, in 1987–88, Britain, Italy, Belgium and Holland had sent ships to the Gulf, encouraging the belief that now the WEU might again achieve greater integration among European forces, and possibly encourage countries such as Italy and Spain to send forces. On 21 August 1990, WEU defence ministers met in Paris for this purpose, with Britain, Germany, France, Italy, the Netherlands, Belgium, Luxembourg, Spain and Portugal in attendance. Denmark, Turkey and Greece sent observers, while Ireland, which was neutral, declined the invitation.

At the end of their meeting, the Nine announced several steps aimed at implementing a coherent military response. Seven WEU countries now agreed to send ships to the Gulf and to execute sanctions by force. Military commanders of the WEU would meet shortly to coordinate naval operations connected with the sea blockade. More assertive rules of engagement would be applied. The 'armada', drawn from half-a-dozen European countries would contain more than twenty warships operating in close coordination with US forces. Viewed in proper perspective, and considering the respective disincentives for each described above, European governments were committing themselves to the strongest economic and military actions witnessed in years. Compared to the European naval presence in the Gulf in 1987, the current European plan involved far greater military coordination, including sharing of intelligence, an attempt to adopt similar operational concepts, a joint stand on when and how to use force to uphold the sanctions, and plans for some forces to operate under integrated command, as in the case of the Belgian and Dutch warships pledged to function as a single unit.

However, if one considers the gravity and implications of the Gulf crisis, the decisions taken by the WEU, nevertheless, do appear rather limited. Germany, after all, agreed only to send vessels to the eastern Mediterranean in an auxiliary capacity and preferred to play a greater role in providing economic assistance to Jordan and Turkey.

Margaret Thatcher, for one, sharply criticized this failure of most European countries to seize the opportunity to demonstrate European unity by supporting strong military action in the Gulf. As she told a meeting of the European Democratic Union in Helsinki: 'We have all this rhetoric about a common security policy as part of political union, yet when it comes to something practical which affects us fundamentally some countries are hesitant. It is not what you say that counts but what you do.'[20] The only countries which had done significantly more than the bare minimum were Britain and France.

The USA, for its part, increasingly exerted pressure on its European partners. Secretary Baker repeatedly lectured NATO members on the cost of the Gulf operation, urging them to send ground forces to join the American forces in Saudi Arabia.[21] Although the USA made clear its wish to have the European allies step up their military contribution, apart from France and Britain, the ten other members of the Community held fast in refusing to deploy ground units in the Gulf conflict zone. At most, they would only consent to supplement the naval blockade already in force with an aerial blockade as well.

Early in the crisis it was entirely obvious that three central Community members – France, Germany and Italy – were extremely anxious to maintain their strong political and commercial links with the Arab world. This motivation was behind their labours at pressing the Community as a whole to have close contact with individual friendly Arab governments, while also offering support for Arab efforts at defusing tension. Distancing themselves from the US–British stand, most Europeans wished to avoid being seen as part of an American crusade against the Arab world. Foreign ministers Dumas and Genscher were adamant on this point, and redoubled efforts at an 'Arab solution' to the crisis. They endorsed sending the 'troika' (the foreign ministers of Ireland, Italy and Luxembourg) to Jordan, Saudi Arabia and Egypt, countries particularly concerned at the disturbing trend of Gulf events. They also urged EC institutions to give Jordan important financial aid that might enable her to comply with the embargo. Their basically pro-Arab attitude was reinforced by the decision of the Arab League on 12 August to condemn the invasion, to honour UN sanctions and to contribute Arab forces to Saudi Arabia's defence.

At French and German initiative, the European Community did decide in principle to extend economic aid to Middle Eastern 'frontline countries' – Egypt, Turkey and Jordan – only to have the united front weakened on 17 September by the conspicuous failure to reach final agreement on the exact terms of the financial assistance to be rendered. With support from the Netherlands, Britain vetoed the initiative by demanding further review of a proposed EC Commission package based on shared funding by the EC and by individual states. Britain took the view that any contribution formula had to take account of the military effort made by the various European members. Not until October did the Twelve agree on a specific plan for 1.5 billion ECU in emergency aid to the three hardest-hit countries.

Despite British reluctance, it was also decided to normalize European relations with two countries long suspected of encouraging terrorism: Syria and Iran. By way of reinforcing participation by Damascus, the Community decided to release 146 million ECU frozen since 1986 because of Syrian terrorist activities.

Cleavage further evidenced itself in evaluating the embargo's effectiveness. Most EC countries, in favouring economic over military reprisal, insisted the embargo had to be given a chance to prove itself. Implicit in this stand, a military solution was regarded critically; a pre-emptive strike against Iraq would be both untimely and undesirable. A minority of only three member-states emphasized the embargo's limitations. Britain, the Netherlands and Denmark expressed the belief all along that prospects for a diplomatic solution were extremely slim.

Another topic on which Europeans reacted differently was that of the Western hostages. A total of 4,700 British subjects remained in

Iraq and Kuwait, along with 560 Frenchmen, 480 Italians, 240 Greeks and 220 Spaniards.[22] European public opinion was unanimous in making safety of the hostages the top priority. Alert to this sensitivity, Saddam tried to use it by way of encouraging divisiveness among his Western opponents, toying with the hostages in a cynical version of psychological warfare. Saddam's tactics, if anything, had the opposite effect. In their strongest joint statement ever, the twelve nations threatened a united response should harm come to any EC citizens held against their will in Iraq and Kuwait.[23] Not only did they defy orders to close their Kuwait embassies, but warned Iraqi citizens that it was they who would be held personally responsible under international law for any damages or injury.[24] Mitterrand's strong reaction to Iraqi threats helped lessen the gap between France, America and Britain once he decided that French warships could use force in order to apply the embargo,[25] as well as sending military advisers and material to various countries in the region.

On these issues and others, the European Parliament became the chief forum, where the various political philosophies current in Europe could express themselves on the crisis. It was only towards the end of August that the political committee of the Strasbourg assembly convened to discuss the Gulf situation. If the Parliament was so slow to react, this owed in part to its being sharply divided: Christian Democrats and Liberals wanted an immediate, total endorsement of sanctions; Extreme Right[26] and Extreme Left groups were against any reprisal; the Socialists split, yet essentially were hostile to any form of military commitment. At the end of the deliberations the enlarged Bureau of the Parliament sent a six-member parliamentary mission to the countries of the Gulf, and on 12 September the Assembly voted decisively for resolving the crisis by diplomatic means and for applying strict sanctions.[27] This action had a strong moral effect, contributing to a climate of opinion against any military action.

Reviewing the overall record one month after the invasion, Europe's contribution, though important, was rather meager: an economic embargo, humanitarian support for refugees in Jordan, and several strong political declarations.[28] Each country in Europe is found to have reacted to the crisis consistent with traditional behaviour patterns in modern European history by placing national and parochial self-interest above those of the collective.[29]

The inability of the Twelve to adopt a truly unified approach left the vision of political union badly tattered. And the question was asked: had Saddam Hussein brought the European Community to a halt? The dynamics which only two months before was propelling the

Community to monetary union, political integration and enlargement had been dissipated.

EUROPEAN CONFLICT MANAGEMENT: PHASE TWO

The hostages

As each European country was officially committed not to negotiate with Iraq, the task of gaining release of nationals held by the Iraqis was entrusted to 'unofficial' negotiators, with the several governments behaving as though ignorant of these 'private' negotiations. The precedent was Willy Brandt's trip to Baghdad only three days after the European summit decision not to send official government representatives to appeal, or to bargain with Iraq over the hostages.[30] He was the first in a long line of political figures to visit Baghdad, including even a British ex-prime minister, Edward Heath. Both men also stepped up their personal campaign in favour of negotiations with Saddam Hussein, arguing for example that Iraq should be given some assurances of non-aggression in return for withdrawal from Kuwait.[31] These non-coordinated European efforts were accompanied by an appeal from the Community to the Arab world to help redeem the hapless Western hostages.[32] On 6 December Western hostages were allowed to leave Iraq.

France's solitary game

On 17 September President Mitterrand reacted strongly to the flagrant intrusion by Iraqi soldiers into the French embassy located in Kuwait City. This blunder on Saddam's part led to closer French and European alignment with the US–British position. Closing ranks against Iraq, the European Community proceeded to expel all Iraqi military attaches,[33] just as steps were also taken to limit the movement of Iraqi diplomats allowed to stay behind.

But French policy still vacillated between one step towards solidarity and then another reversing course. Only a week after the expulsion of Iraqi personnel, in addressing the UN General Assembly in New York, President Mitterrand displayed a curious show of openness towards the Iraqi ruler,[34] putting forward a four-point resolution plan whose central message was that if Iraq merely expressed an intention to remove its troops and free the hostages, 'everything would become possible'. Moreover, diverging from the American position, he omitted the Security Council's demand that the legitimate Kuwaiti authorities be restored to power, and referred instead to 'the democratic expression of the Kuwaiti people's choices'. Mitterrand concluded further that after the end of the Gulf crisis all Middle Eastern conflicts should be discussed, including Lebanon and the Palestinian problem. Mitterrand's address deepened the gap between the two factions within the Community: the uncompromising camp led by Britain, versus the conciliatory camp led by France, with the clear support of Germany. Not surprising, therefore, is that a few days after Mitterrand's provocative speech allegations appeared that secret negotiations were under way between Paris and Baghdad.[35]

During the last three weeks before the 15 January deadline when the UN ultimatum would expire, France further intensified its diplomatic activity, launching a last-ditch effort to prevent war[36] should the proposed Baker–Aziz dialogue between Iraq and America collapse by 3 January. According to President Mitterrand, Saddam Hussein could still forestall military action simply by providing a definite timetable for pulling out his forces. This initiative consisted of sending Michel Vauzelle, a leading figure of the Socialist Party and a close friend and adviser to Mitterrand, to Baghdad.[37]

After meeting Saddam, M. Vauzelle said that 'everything remained possible', that 'Iraq should accomplish certain acts' and that he was 'neither optimistic nor pessimistic, but realistic'. Although his 'special envoy' had failed to obtain even some symbolic concession from Saddam, President Mitterrand persisted, sending Vauzelle to Tunis for a meeting with Yasser Arafat, suggesting Paris was ready to propose an international conference on the Palestinian problem if that would please the Iraqi dictator.

A final seven-point peace plan was next presented by Foreign Minister Dumas on 4 January. Its provisions were that:

1 Iraq should declare before 15 January its intention to leave Kuwait;
2 Iraq was then to receive full guarantees that it would not be attacked;
3 After the evacuation of Kuwait, there should be a review of all Middle East conflicts, particularly the Israeli–Arab one;
4 The Twelve would try to meet foreign minister Aziz in order to explain their position;
5 The Twelve supported the American initiative to organize a last meeting between Baker and Aziz in Geneva;
6 The European 'troika' should enter into contact with all other governments that had tabled peace plans for the Gulf crisis;

7 Security in the Middle East should be organized according to the model of the European Conference on Security.

Plainly, France wanted to allow Saddam Hussein to save face, without forcing him to admit defeat.

Closer to the deadline, Mitterrand repeated four crucial elements of the French position: that there should be no destruction of Iraq; that there should be free elections in Kuwait; that there should be an international conference on Palestine immediately after the evacuation of Kuwait; and that the Arab world should submit its solutions to the crisis[38] – all to no avail.

Last common efforts

One last debate within the Community focused on the need to preserve a distinctively 'European' contact with the Iraqi authorities by sending a senior figure to Baghdad. In addition, the new president of the EC, Luxembourg's foreign minister Jacques Poos, anxious to give his small country a role in defusing the crisis, did his best to promote the idea of yet another European initiative,[39] personally still convinced that Saddam would withdraw at the last minute.

Refusing to forfeit hope or a central role, the Twelve resolved that their final offer would be to invite Tareq Aziz to Luxembourg on 10 January.[40] Their deep conviction that Saddam would certainly accept the invitation in order to avert a military confrontation with the Western armada gave place to shock when Iraq flatly declined to come to Luxembourg. This Iraqi refusal, a reprisal for European cancellation of the Aziz meeting in Rome, symbolized the complete failure of European diplomacy ever since the invasion. Conciliation with Iraq had failed, possibly because Saddam appreciated that a 'United Europe', united as yet in name only, still remained a minor factor in the world arena and that a last meeting of Aziz with the 'troika' would be of no help.[41] The concluding European action before the military confrontation took place when the twelve foreign ministers came together in Geneva to meet UN Secretary-General Perez de Cuellar on his way to Iraq, requesting him to convey the Community's concern.[42] On the way back to New York, the UN Secretary-General reported his failure to convince Saddam, at which point the European Community abandoned plans for direct talks with Iraq and accepted the UN Secretary-General's advice that all scope for diplomatic initiative had been exhausted.[43]

CONCLUSION

With the outbreak of hostilities, the Twelve affirmed their solidarity with the United States, even as they stressed understandable disappointment with the failure of diplomatic efforts to force Iraq out of Kuwait. During the military campaign, two Community members, Britain and France, participated fully in the military operations. Following some criticism of French participation, President Mitterrand enlarged the involvement of French units, stressing repeatedly that France was a fully-pledged member of the coalition. This growing French involvement in air operations put the President and his Defence Minister at odds, however – Mitterrand's readiness to attack Iraqi territory in order to liberate Kuwait provoked the resignation of Jean-Pierre Chevenement at the end of January.

Within the European Community several debates were held during the war at every level: Commission, European Council, Council of Ministers, Parliament. The Twelve insisted on Iraq's responsibilities in the conflict, supported American operations, and went on to prepare for the post-crisis phase. They tried to avert the need for a ground offensive by appealing repeatedly to Saddam Hussein to leave Kuwait of his own will. They supplied generous aid to the victims of the war, for example refugees in Jordan. They tried to strengthen relations with Arab members of the coalition, and insisted on the urgency of an international conference under UN supervision to solve the Palestinian problem. The EC repeated that it was committed to a global approach in the Middle East.

In European parliaments, these political forces opposing the war remained a minority. They mainly tried to force European governments to press for a ceasefire, and came closest after the bombing of a civilian shelter in Baghdad; but the military operations were too brief for them to mobilize support.

The Community's inability to speak unanimously or act collectively had a short but negative impact on inter-European relations. London mounted criticism against the so-called supporters of a supranational Europe who spoke of federalism but did not hesitate to violate decisions taken collectively. Germany came under special attack, earning criticism for its seeming lack of concern or commitment at various moments during the crisis and for its hesitancy to support Turkey, a member of NATO. The British Press printed fresh allegations about the involvement of German business in providing lethal technology to Iraq, and also condemned Bonn for its insufficient financial contribution to the Western war effort. Belgium, too, was everely criticized by the British, who revealed the timid attitude of the Martens government in refusing to transfer some munitions from its tocks to British units.

Many asked the crucial question: how was it possible to explain European Community weakness in the face of a major international crisis, or the fact that the twelve member-states had been unable to act and react collectively in a uniform manner? Two alternative answers were given. For staunch supporters of European unification, i.e. France, Germany, Italy, the Benelux countries, and EC Commission president Jacques Delors, the main reason for failure was the structural weakness of the system of European political cooperation. For them, the EC had not developed means for crafting a common foreign or security policy. Their hope was that following the Gulf experience, the shortcoming might be rectified through an intergovernmental conference on political union. Britain and Denmark, for their part, claimed the Community's failure to produce a credible collective response dampened expectations as to what may emerge from the intergovernmental conference. If anything, in their view, the crisis showed that the instincts and national interests of European countries were still widely apart, and rather than narrowing had grown with time.

On the whole, the Gulf crisis has been a relatively brief episode used by both European schools of thought in support of their rival claims to European unity: the federal approach, which underscores strengthened Community-wide institutions, or the non-federal format, which builds on national interests and sovereignty.

NOTES

1 For an analysis of the state of European integration on the eve of the invasion of Kuwait, see *Europolitique*, no. 1607, 28 July 1990.
2 On the reasons for which it would be easy to use the oil weapon, see *Financial Times*, 3 August 1990, and *Le Figaro*, 6 August 1990.
3 For an analysis of EC first sanctions, see 'EC hits Iraq with ban on oil and arms', *Observer*, 5 August 1990, and 'EC takes swift action in sweeping embargo aimed at halting Iraq', *Wall Street Journal*, 6 August 1990.
4 On the possible consequences of the oil embargo, see 'Europe, hausse générale du super', *Le Figaro*, 8 August 1990.
5 See 'The limits of an assets freeze', *Financial Times*, 6 August 1990, and *Le Soir*, 7 August 1990.
6 On the reactions of the Iraqi embassy in Paris, see *La Libre Belgique*, 6 August 1990.
7 See 'Tokyo and Beijing join EC in sanctions', *Herald Tribune*, 6 August 1990.

8 On EC's action after the decision of the UN, see 'UN trade embargo gains support of many nations', *Daily Telegraph*, 8 August 1990.

9 For an evaluation of the embargo's efficiency, see 'Iraq faces tough food problems if sanctions work', *Financial Times*, 8 August 1990.

10 On the problems of a blockade of Iraq, see *Guardian*, 8 August 1990.

11 On the firm attitude of Mitterrand, see 'France bolsters Gulf forces, promises weapons to Saudis', *Wall Street Journal*, 10 August 1990, and on the rightist opposition's support, see the interview of Jean-Francois Poncet in *Le Monde*, 13 August 1990.

12 *Financial Times*, 16 August 1990.

13 On European answer to Baker, see 'NATO's Members Join in Tough Response to Iraq', *Daily Telegraph*, 11 August 1990.

14 For an analysis of the German position, see 'Kohl says he's willing to send ships', *Wall Street Journal*, 16 August 1990.

15 For an analysis of the Italian position, see 'De Michelis plays "even-handed" card', *Times*, 17 August 1990.

16 For an analysis of the Spanish position, see 'L'Espagne suit à contre-coeur', 17 August 1990.

17 For criticism of the Belgian position, see 'Une mission prudente en deux temps', *La Libre Belgique*, 14 August 1990, and 'Pussillanimité belge face au chantage', *L'Echo de la bourse*, 14 August 1990.

18 For a first criticism of European Community's position, see 'Waverers in need of a firm message', *European*, 10 August 1990; 'No time for timidity', *Times*, 10 August 1990; 'La CEE unanime, mais pour faire quoi?', *Le Soir*, 12 August 1990; 'Divided nations revert to type in the face of crisis', *European*, 17 August 1990; 'Isolationism à la mode', *Sunday Telegraph*, 19 August 1990.

19 On the possible role of WEU, see 'Sheltering behind a political fig-leaf', *Guardian*, 31 August 1990; Union to justify European force', *Daily Telegraph*, 21 August 1990; 'European defence group to discuss stronger action', *Financial Times*, 21 August 1990; 'WEU members planning to present a more unified stance against Iraq', *Wall Street Journal*, 21 August 1990.

20 On Margaret Thatcher's attitude, see 'Thatcher does not see a negotiated end to conflict with Saddam', *Times*, 27 August 1990; 'Thatcher attacks allies' slow response to crisis', *Daily Telegraph*, 31 August 1990; 'Europe's Gulf effort under fire from Thatcher', *Times*, 31 August 1990.

21 See 'US presses for NATO countries to send troops', *Times*, 11 September 1990; 'Unwilling to follow . . .', *Wall Street Journal*, 12 September 1990.

22 The data on the hostages from various countries are in *Le Monde*, 20 August 1990.

23 See *Daily Telegraph*, 22 August 1990; and 'EC ministers warn they will respond if citizens are harmed', *Irish Times*, 22 August 1990.

24 In fact the EC response was tempered by concern that the hostage release might be jeopardized by further anti-Iraqi measures in Europe. Each government tried secretly to achieve a deal with Saddam. On the way the hostage question divided the Europeans, see 'EC trapped by hostage dilemma', *European*, 31 August 1990.

25 See, 'Mitterrand sonne l'alarme', *Liberation*, 22 January 1990; 'France sending ground forces as screw tightens', *Guardian*, 22 August 1990.

26 For example, on Le Pen's attitude, see *Le Figaro*, 13 September 1990.

27 On the European Parliament's attitude, see 'Euro-MPs diplomacy vote is snub for Bush', *European*, 14 September 1990; 'Le Parlement Européen se prononce pour un embargo strict', *Le Monde*, 14 September 1990.

28 *European*, 10 August 1990.

29 *Sunday Telegraph*, 19 August 1990.

30 See 'Brandt's trip to Baghdad splits EC alliance', *Guardian*, 2 November 1990; 'Chagrined, Bonn aids Brandt trip', *Herald Tribune*, 6 November 1990; 'Brandt mission to Baghdad sparks fears of disunity', *Guardian*, 6 November 1990.

31 See 'La multiplication des missions officieuses à Bagdad sucite une polémique au sein de la CEE', *Le Monde*, 6 November 1990.

32 See 'EC enlists outside support on hostages', *Independent*, 13 November 1990.

33 See 'Military attaches thrown out in EC response to raids in Kuwait embassies', *Independent*, 18 September 1990; 'EC ousts Iraqi military staff, may press for air embargo', *Wall Street Journal*, 18 September 1990; 'Iraqi diplomats expelled by united Europe', *Daily Telegraph*, 18 September 1990.

34 On Mitterrand's address to the UN General Assembly, see 'M. Mitterrand propose à Bagdad une solution diplomatique en quatre étapes', *Le Monde*, 28 September 1990.

35 See, 'France denies negotiating with Iraq on Gulf conflict', *Financial Times*, 2 October 1990.

36 On Europe's last efforts at the end of December, 'EC hopes to talk to Iraq if US fails', *Herald Tribune*, 20 December 1990; 'Les Européens prendront une initiative en janvier', *Le Derniere Heure*, 20 December 1990.

37 On Vauzelle's mission, see *Liberation*, 3 January 1991; 'Golfe, Paris avance un pion', *Le Quotidien de Paris*, 3 January 1991; 'EC Gulf unity threatened by French mission', *Times*, 3 January 1991; 'Vauzelle, un émissaire tres officieux', *Le Figaro*, 4 January 1991.

38 On Hussein's last visit, see *L'Echo de la Bourse*, 3 January 1991, and 'Compromise plan by King Hussein', *Daily Telegraph*, 3 January 1991.

39 On Poos's intentions, see *La Libre Belgique*, 3 January 1991, and 'Luxembourg expects Iraq to pull out at last minute', *Times*, 3 January 1991.

40 On the European initiative for Aziz to come to Luxembourg and Saddam's rebuff: 'Les Douze proposent a M. Tarek Aziz une recontre le 10 janvier', *Le Monde*, 7 January 1991; 'Un camouflet pour les Douze', *Liberation*, 7 January 1991; 'Baghdad ignore les Douze', *Le Quotidien de Paris*, 7 January 1991; 'Europe, after Iraqi rebuff, renews offer of talks', *Herald Tribune*, 7 January 1991.

41 On the proposal to meet in Algiers, see 'L'Irak rejette une nouvelle proposition des Douze', *La Libre Belgique*, 10 January 1991.

42 'Les Douze vont à Genève', *Le Figaro*, 1 January 1991.

43 'M. de Cuellar, après Bagdad, se tourne vers les Douze', *La Libre Belgique*, 14 January 1991.

Part IV
Ripples worldwide

13 Third World arms exports to Iraq before and after the Gulf War

Gil Shidlo

INTRODUCTION

The recent Gulf War once again focuses attention on the international arms industry and weapons transfer patterns. For Iraq succeeded in obtaining a vast arsenal of advanced weapon systems from diverse sources – in the developing as well as the developed world – without which Saddam Hussein could not possibly have entertained a military option against Kuwait. The war in the Gulf demonstrated rather clearly the consequences of extensive international trade in conventional weapons. Traditionally Iraq's main suppliers – the former Soviet Union, China, France and the USA – viewed arms sales and transfers primarily as instruments of foreign policy, and up to a certain degree as a means to enhance economic motivations. International trade, however, proliferates advanced weapons and often involves collaborative production arrangements with far reaching consequences as in the case of Iraq. This chapter explores the form and dynamics of the international arms industry, the intricacies of technology transfers and equipment sales by looking at four developing countries and their arms sales patterns to Iraq prior to the Gulf War. These four countries which were major arms suppliers to Iraq among Third World nations, present an interesting trend which will be harder to control and will obviously accelerate the proliferation of modern weapons and increasing over-capacity in worldwide weapons production.

Arms production in the Third World, neglible up to the 1960s, has risen dramatically since then. Post-World War II arms production in effect started in Argentina and North Korea, with large-scale arms production then extending to an increasing number of industrializing countries, such as India, Israel and South Africa in the early 1960s, Brazil in the late 1960s, South Korea and Taiwan in the early 1970s and Singapore and Indonesia in the late 1970s.

This chapter will centre however mainly on Argentina, Brazil, China and Egypt. These four countries have penetrated the international arms market and become significant exporters also. Not suprisingly, their arms exports performance shows marked expansion during the mid-1980s corresponding with burgeoning arms purchases by Iran and Iraq. In all instances this arms emphasis reflects an amalgam of strategies, economic and political motivations.

The development of local arms industries have often stemmed from strategic considerations – local arms race (e.g. Brazil versus Argentina); ensured security of supply (e.g. Egypt; Argentina after the Falklands conflict); self reliance and regional power aspirations (China, Brazil, Argentina, Egypt). In recent years, economic incentives play an important role in motivating developing countries to undertake extensive arms production, especially with the Third World's huge external debt (e.g. Brazil, Argentina and Egypt). Until the early 1980s, China was a prime example of a country whose motivation in supplying arms was political rather than economic. The end of the Cold War and the accompanying decline in defence spending have both weakened the political foundation for continuous arms transfers and enhanced the economic motivations for international arms sales. Governments in developing countries tend to help their military industries in search of export markets to compensate for insufficient domestic defence budgets as well as to spread development costs of new weapon systems (e.g. ballistic missiles).

THIRD WORLD ARMS INDUSTRIES AND EXPORTS TO IRAQ

Argentina

Like its neighbour, Brazil, Argentina has an extensive arms industry. In 1920, Argentina attempted for the first time to produce military equipment. In 1941 the Dirección General de Fabricaciones Militares (DGFM) strengthened state activity in this area by linking it to the general industrialization effort. All branches of the armed forces were involved in the production of arms. The independent development of the arms industry, was one of necessity and not of choice. As a result its decision to remain neutral during World War II, Argentina was excluded from all wartime liaisons. Thus, as early as 1938 the Argentinian navy designed and built boats in its shipyards. Later production included patrol launches and frigates. German technicians assisted both the airforce and the army in the designing and

Table 13.1 Third World arms exports to Iraq, 1982–90

Weapon systems	Quan-tity	Type
Main battle tanks	1,500	Chinese T-59/69
Armoured personnel carriers	650	Chinese YW-531
	380	Brazilian EE-11
Towed artillery	90	Egyptian D-130, 122 mm
	96	Egyptian D-30, 122 mm
	720	Chinese Type 59-1;
Multiple rocket launchers	66	Brazilian ASTROS II SS-30
	20	Brazilian ASTROS II SS-60;
	150	Egyptian BM-21
	100	Egyptian Sakr-30
Ground attack fighters	30	Chinese J-6.
Air superiority fighters	40	Chinese J-7.
Anti-ship missiles	128	Chinese C-601
	72	Chinese Hal-Ying 2;
Trainer aircraft	20	Argentinian IA 58A Pucará;
Radars	13	Brazilian ASTROS Guidance Fire Control Radar;
Armoured cars	200	Brazilian EE-9 Cascaval;
	300	Brazilian EE-3 Jacara Scout Cars;

Source: Compiled from SIPRI Yearbooks (1980–91), *World Armaments and Disarmaments*; *The Military Balance 1990–91*, published by the IISS, London 1990.

manufacturing of aircraft and heavy artillery, machine guns and munitions. The initial impetus from German cooperation helped to establish Argentinian Research and Defence. In order to strengthen further its Research and Development (R&D) capacities, Argentina, similarly to Brazil, joined the trend of co-production. The transfer of a certain degree of R&D was combined, in the case of Argentina and in the case of many other developing countries, with pre-existing productive capacity. The success of R&D in developed countries has stimulated the transfer of sophisticated weapon systems to developing countries contributing to an increase in demand for more advanced weapon systems by the recipient countries. Local industries get a considerable boost through sub-contracts and licences. Less-developed countries attain the same levels of profitability and expansion as the developed ones through sub-contracts, licences and co-production. The first military transfers from the developed nations to the less developed ones were always in the form of finished products while keeping the monopoly on the production technology.[1] In this way they created both a dependent market and a market that does not

Table 13.2 Arms exports to Iraq by other countries, 1982–90

Weapon systems	Quan- tity	Type
Battle tanks	1,500	Soviet T-54/55/M-77;
	1,500	Soviet T-62;
	850	Soviet T-72;
	30	British Chieftain
Light tanks	100	Soviet PT-76;
Infantry fighting vehicles	1,500	Soviet BMP
Armoured personnel carriers	Total	Soviet BTR- 50/60/80/152;
	4,770	Soviet MTLB;
		French Panhrad M-3;
		US M-113A1/A2;
Self-propelled artillery	150	Soviet 2S1; 152 Soviet 2S3;
	100	US M-109;
	85	French AUF-1 GCT;
Towed artillery	Total	Soviet D-74/30, M-1938,
	3,000	M46, M-1937, M-1943;
		US M-114;
Multiple rocket launchers	360	Soviet BM-211;
	200	Soviet BM-13/16.
Surface-to-air missile launchers	160	Soviet SA-2
	150	SA-3
	992	Soviet SA-6/7/8/9/14
	100	French–German Roland
Surface-to-surface missile launchers	50	Soviet Frog-7
	350	Soviet Scud-B (mobile and
		fixed).
Attack helicopters	40	Soviet Mi-24
	20	French SA 342
	30	SA 316
	13	SA 321
	4	French–German BK 117
Ground attack fighters	90	Soviet MiG 23
	64	French Mirage EQ5/200;
	30	Soviet Su-7
	70	Soviet Su-25
	16	Soviet Su-24
Air superiority fighters	25	Soviet MiG-25
	150	Soviet MiG-21
	24	Soviet MiG-29
	24	French Mirage F1-EQ
Radar	10	French Tigers

Source: Compiled from SIPRI Yearbook 1980–91, *World Armaments & Disarma-ments*; *The Military Balance 1990–91* (London: IISS, 1990).

truly need R&D of its own. With the growing competitiveness in the R&D industry in the developed countries, Third World countries were viewed as markets where advantages might be exploited to balance trade between the industrialized nations and the Third World. In short, the transformation of R&D into a more profitable industry demanded markets larger than mere exports of arms, leading to the transfer of military technology to Third World countries. While the period from the end of World War II to the mid-1960s saw a transfer of military technology through the sale of finished arms to the Third World, it was superseded by transfer through sub-contracting, licensing and co-production agreements.[2] Manufacturing under licence is one of the most significant ways of transferring military technology to the Third World. In the case of Argentina, links with Britain, France, Belgium, (West) Germany, Italy and the USA contributed to the development of its arms industry.

From the mid-1970s to the 1980s arms production activities in Argentina increased considerably following the military takeover of 1976.[3] The military government invested heavily in the state-run arms industry. Until 1983, the Argentine army had the leading role in domestic arms production through the Director General of Military Manufacturers (DGFM). During the early 1980s the DGFM was the largest firm in Argentina and one of the largest in Latin America, with an annual turnover of US$ 2.2 billion.[4] By 1983, the financial holdings of the DGFM extended to some thirteen industries which employed between 14,000 and 15,000 workers and held shares in at least twenty-two Argentinian companies.

In April 1985, the Ministry of Defence submitted a draft bill to the executive branch proposing the creation of the General Savio State Corporation to replace the DGFM, whose founding decree was to be repealed. All companies under the DGFM's control were to be administered by the new military-industrial complex. All military weapons and equipment purchases, as well as military exports, were to be centralized under the Ministry of Defence which would act in consultation with the Joint Chiefs of Staff. Although the Alfonsin administration cited budgetary reasons behind the reorganization efforts, most analysts believe that a less publicized aspect of the policy was the democratically elected government's desire to restrict the military's influence on the national economy.

Historically, Third World countries have acquired their ballistic missiles from the superpowers – either the United States or the Soviet Union. While the United States has supplied missiles to two countries only, South Korea and Israel, the Soviet Union provided ballistic missiles to at least nine countries. By the mid-1980s, the superpowers began losing control over the market in ballistic missiles. One of the reasons was that the USA no longer exported ballistic missiles to the Third World. Efforts by both Israel and Saudi Arabia to obtain US missiles in the 1980s were futile. The mid-1980s also saw the emergence of a trade in Soviet-supplied missiles. Several countries which had received ballistic missiles in the past from the Soviet Union re-exported them. For example, Iran was supplied with Scud B missiles from Libya and North Korea in 1984 and in 1985. In 1988, North Korea supplied Iran with 100 ballistic missiles.

In 1988, the People's Republic of China delivered intermediate-range ballistic missiles to Saudi Arabia – thus becoming a first-time exporter of ballistic missiles. Currently, a large number of Third World countries are designing and building missiles without having to buy completed systems from the developed world. One of the first Third World countries to develop ballistic missiles was Argentina.

In the 1960s and early 1970s Argentina was the most advanced Third World nation in the field of rocket research, developing with US support sub-orbital sound rockets able to reach altitudes of up to 500 kilometres.[5] After almost a decade in abeyance, the programme was revived in 1982, the year of the Falkland Islands war. The Argentine programme has adopted an approach of acquiring assistance from the industrialized world. Similarly to Brazil, Egypt, India, Iraq and Libya, Argentina was assisted by West Germany with its missile programmes. It is interesting to point out that while West Germany has never built a ballistic missile for its own use, its engineers are familiar with US state-of-the-art missile technology.

> During the 1980s, a leading West German defense contractor, Messerschmitt-Boelkow-Blohm (known as MBB) designed the Kolas missile, a conventionally armed ballistic missile designed for attacks on air bases and other critical targets. It appears that MBB worked closely with a US company, Martin Marietta, which was responsible for building the Pershing II intermediate-range ballistic missile. As a result, MBB seems to have been intimately familiar with the most advanced US missile technology.[6]

Argentina is known to have at least three ballistic missile designs although none is known to be operational. Technology for the programme was acquired from various sources, such as the USA, Germany, France and Italy. The Condor I, which was first displayed in 1985 is a solid-fuel, single-stage rocket with a range of 100–150 kilometres. In late 1987, it was revealed that the Argentinians were developing the Condor II which is believed to have a range of 800 kilometres. The Condor II programme is a collaborative venture with Egypt and financed in part by Iraq. MBB and MAN (Maschinenefabrik Augsburg-Nurnberg), West German defence companies, are believed to have provided assistance to Argentina and Egypt in the development of the missile. MAN was believed to have built the mobile launchers of the Condor. SAGEM, a French aerospace company, was reported to have provided the guidance package for the Condor II missile.[7] An Italian company, SNIA-BPD, provided propellant technology for the Condor as well. The latter company, has expertise in the area of solid fuel booster rockets as it manufactured them for the European Arianne space launch vehicles.[8] Argentina's ballistic missile programme is highly sophisticated unlike others such as North Korea, Iraq and Egypt which rely on Soviet Scud B technology, a fairly old one.[9]

Brazil

Arms production by Brazilian industry began in a limited manner in the early 1960s with the manufacturing of rifles, pistols, and machine guns under licences secured from Belgium, Italy, and the United States. From that small beginning a large thriving industry evolved. During the next three decades aggressive Brazilian arms salesmen, spearheaded by military attachés cornered a significant portion of the world's arms deals. The current status of the Brazilian arms industry, as the leading arms producer and exporter among the industrializing countries, and the sixth largest arms exporter in the world, can be traced back to the military government decisions made in the 1960s. Convinced that Brazil was on the way to becoming a first-line power in the world, knowing that modernization of the armed forces was prerequisite to that development, and lacking the necessary capital to buy expensive weapons abroad, the military leaders encouraged the development of the domestic arms industry. Brazil's armed forces, however, could not possibly absorb the production of a major arms industry, and exports became mandatory. In a very short time the arms manufacturers had earned reputations for producing weapons and equipments of high quality and moderate technological complexity at reasonable prices, quickly attracting the attention of many Third World countries. Furthermore, there were no political connotations to the Brazilian arms deals as was the case with the Soviet Union and the United States, the two leading exporters. Already by the 1980s about fifty countries were using Brazilian military equipment or weaponry.

The development of Brazil's arms industry can be divided into three distinct periods. The first phase, (1964–67), began with the presidency of General Castello Branco, during which there was no clear programme for the defence industry. As part of a general plan to revive the economy which was in recession, the military government decided to cut back in military imports from the USA while reverting to the local industry. Civilian industries which were idle were revived with injection of government orders for jeeps, trucks, tents, trailers and communication equipment. As part of the military government's Plan of Industrial Mobilization price subsidies to Brazilian products were provided in order to make them more competitive.

The second phase, (1967–78), was characterized by the development of new, larger and more sophisticated weapons, designed to compete in the international market. The defence industry began also to manufacture domestic aircraft and single engine planes. During this period of vast economic growth (referred to as the Brazilian 'economic miracle') the defence budget was greatly expanded. Various European governments, as well as the USA, placed restrictions on military exports to nations with bad human rights records. Various West German industries began to produce their tanks, optical equipment and precision goods in Brazil after the signing of a military agreement between the two countries in 1975. Italy and France concentrated their investments in aeronautics projects, space technology and the production of helicopters while the United Kingdom invested in the production of ships.

The third phase, (1978–88), can be characterized as one of increased arms production and an intensification of the drive for external markets. The end of formal US–Brazilian military ties in 1977 and Argentina's defeat in the Falklands enhanced the capability of the military industrial complex to lobby for larger resources and investments.

In November 1981, Ernane Galveas, the Finance Minister led a group of fifty-five businessmen on a tour to the Middle East, reportedly resulting in lucrative arms contracts in addition to contracts for many other products. Exports of transport and training aircraft, armoured vehicles as well as tanks grew fast. The main customers were Iraq and Libya who wanted rugged Brazilian weapons as an alternative to army equipment from industrialized countries. In addition to armoured vehicles and aircraft, production of missiles and artillery was started. In the early 1980s it can be assumed that total

Brazilian exports of arms surpassed US$1 billion and the employment in arms production was estimated at about 100,000 workers. The Iran–Iraq war, in particular, stimulated arms exports by Brazilian companies. Iraq has been Brazil's largest customer, purchasing armoured personnel carriers, missiles, and aircraft, often in exchange for oil.

The giants of the Brazilian armaments industry are Engesa (Engenheiros Especializados, meaning specialized engineers) – the leading manufacture of wheeled vehicles in Latin America – and Embraer (Empresa Brasileira Aeronáutica – Brazilian aeronautics enterprise) – the country's foremost manufacture of aircraft. Engesa manufactures and exports the Urutu, an amphibious armoured personnel carrier, as well as two other armoured vehicles which have become well known to military forces around the world – the Cascavel and the Jararaca. Iraq purchased large quantities of Brazilian equipment and, in effect, became a proving ground for Engesa-built armour, which was said to have performed admirably in combat during the Iran–Iraq war. More than 1,000 Cascavel armoured cars were exported to Iraq during the 1980s as well as a few hundred Jararaca scout cars and Urutu armoured personnel carriers. One of the star products of Engesa, although not exported to Iraq, is the Osorio tank. The advantages of the Osorio over its rivals – the West German Leopard-2 and the French AMX-30 – are its price (half of that of its rivals); its ability to withstand attacks of most anti-tank rockets; and its invulnerability to chemical bombs and nuclear radiation.[10] Engesa also produces and exports a wide range of trucks for the military. The arms manufacturer's financial problems began in 1987, when its biggest customer, Iraq, defaulted on a US$80 million payment to the company.[11]

Embraer, manufactures and exports both civilian and military aircraft. In the early 1980s it exported Xingu jet trainers and Xavante jet fighters. The latter is a ground attack jet built under licence from Aeronautica Macchi of Italy and is powered by a Rolls Royce turbojet engine. The Xingu is a twin-turboprop general purpose transporter and advanced trainer and has been exported to Colombia, Britain, Belgium and some Middle Eastern countries.

Brazil began its rocket research over three decades ago and has several ballistic missile and space launch programmes in progress. Brazil is one of the nine newly industrializing countries who possess or is developing indigenously surface-to-surface missiles with ranges of 600 to 2000 km. Brazilian missile production is undertaken by two firms, Avibrás and Orbita, coordinated by a Joint Command of the Armed Forces. Avibrás, a privately owned firm is one of the leading export companies – over US\$340 million in 1987. One of the company's first projects was to assist the Institute for Space Activity (Instituto de Atividade Espacial – IAE) and the national Space Research Institute in the Sonda I, II, III, and IV experimental sounding rocket and satellite launch vehicle research programs.[12] The Sondas series, which were developed with West German, French and Chinese assistance, gradually grew from small sounding rockets into seven-ton rockets with a range of nearly 1,000 km. The first prototype of the Sonda IV, an 11-metre rocket weighing 7.3 US tons was launched in November 1987. The rocket has some 3,000 component parts, of which 70 per cent were purchased locally. Technological assistance was provided by West Germany's MBB, also reportedly participating in Argentina's Condor II.[13]

Avibrás used the Sonda series as a basis for its ASTROS-2 family of artillery rockets which have been exported to many Third World countries. The main clients for the latter were Iraq, Libya and Saudi Arabia. The Avibrás Artillery Rocket Bombardment System ASTROS II multiple rocket launcher was deployed by the Saudi army during the Gulf War. One of the main constraints in developing ballistic missiles is the enormous expense. For this reason Avibrás which had difficulties in obtaining finance to develop a new generation of missiles, cooperated with the Iraqi and Libyan governments. Iraq funded part of the ASTROS II, while Libya financed part of the long range missile programme. There are also reports that the Saudis, using Brazilian technology, financed the manufacture and development of various types of arms in Brazil.[14] A Saudi military mission to Brazil visited Engesa and Avibrás in 1984 and was reported to be interested in combat tanks, missile launchers and training and patrol aircraft.

In an interview published on 2 September 1991 by daily newspaper *Fôlha de São Paulo*, João Verdi Carvalho, Avibrás Aerospacia executive, said the company intends to continue investing in weapon research and development, despite the cash flow crisis caused by the end of the Iran–Iraq war. Avibrás' main product continues to be the Astros system (a ground-to-ground missile launching system) used by Iraq during the Gulf War. In the 1980s, Iraq spent US\$1 billion on Astros System acquisitions. According to Verdi, major weapon research projects currently underway include new warheads for the Astros System (a highly-powered incendiary, and another designed to 'craterize' airport runways). He also referred to the FOG-MPM missile, equipped with a fibre-optic guidance system for targeting tanks, helicopters, bunkers and other fortifications.[15]

Egypt

The Egyptian arms industry, employing about 100,000 people, exported a large proportion of its total production to Iraq. Although Egypt is often classified as a re-exporter of weapons it also exports domestically produced and designed equipment as well as weapons built under licence. The defence – related industries are diversifying and building more sophisticated weaponry, including co-production of the American M1A1 battle tank. Arms exports, including massive sales to Iraq, have amounted to nearly US$1 billion per year. The majority of Egyptian weapons are exported to Middle Eastern countries as well as to Africa (e.g. Zaire, Somalia, Sudan). Brzoska and Ohlson[16] identified three main reasons for Egypt's emergence as a leading Third World arms supplier in the 1980s:

First, sales to Iraq serves the purpose of reintegrating Egypt in the Arab fraternity; second, sales to the neighboring countries in Africa are part of the US-Egyptian regional containment policy towards Libya; and, third, Egypt has unique know-how and experience in the reverse-engineering, manufacture and overhaul of Soviet weapons, which abound in many countries in the region.

Egypt's arms industry consists of two different types of production. The first type of production line was established in the 1960s with assistance from the Soviets and manufactured small weapons ammunition and components and missile types. Although there was a decline in Egyptian-Soviet relations from 1972 onwards this production line continued. It also seems that significant amounts of Soviet equipment remained in use by the Egyptians for the remainder of the 1980s. This enormous stock and expertise in Soviet armaments helped Egypt retain its position in the Third World industries. At this time the other line was started with an ambitious plan to set up an Arab arms industry. Egyptian planners for several years have been intrigued with the idea of combining Egypt's managerial ability and industrial labour force, Arab oil money, and foreign technological assistance to develop a joint arms industry.

In 1975, Egypt, Saudi Arabia, Qatar, and the United Arab Emirates announced the joint establishment of the Arab Military Industries Organization, with an initial capitalization of the equivalent of more than US$1 billion to be contributed equally by the four member states. The bulk of the arms manufacture would take place in Egypt. The name of the joint venture was Arab Organization for Industrialization (AOI), but before it was able to develop into a major producer of arms, AOI foundered on Arab discontent with Sadat's peace initiatives towards Israel. After the withdrawal of its partners Egypt continued to use the title and AOI negotiated with several Western companies to engage in joint weapons or equipment production in Egypt. After signing the Camp David Accords in 1978, Egypt was able to acquire the most advanced US military equipment, as well as co-produce it, with the notable exception of ballistic missiles. For example, arrangements were made with American Motors Corporation to produce jeeps and with British Aerospace to make Swingfire anti-tank guided weapons. Parts for the French Mirage aircraft were also manufactured in Egypt. During the 1980s, Egypt exported 70 F-7 fighter aircraft (Chinese version of MiG-21) to Iraq as well as 80 EMB-312 Tucano trainers built under Brazilian licence. The Tucano is licensed – produced by Egypt, though Embraer produces and ships all of the parts to Egypt for assembly.

The refusal of the USA to enable Egypt to purchase ballistic missiles, even after the signing of the Camp David Accords, resulted in the development of a domestic missile industry. 'The only Arab nation with large military industries, Egypt started by reverse-engineering Soviet BM-21 short range artillery rockets for mass-production, including large-scale exports to Iraq.'[17] In the early and mid-1980s, Egypt collaborated with France to manufacture a missile named the Sakr-80, to replace its FROG missiles. North Korea and Iraq were also partners in an Egyptian effort to upgrade its ageing Scud missile force.

Another joint project was revealed in late 1987 – the Badr-2000 or more commonly know as the 800-km range Condor-II. According to the *Washington Post*, Iraq was behind the Argentine–Egyptian project as this would avail it of a missile to carry nuclear warheads. While an Iraqi connection is not impossible this has not been conclusively established. The *Post* has previously published inaccurate information on the Condor, when it put the range of the missile at nearly 10,000 km. Nevertheless, Egyptian–Iraqi work on modifications to the Soviet-supplied missiles used against Iran, as well as Egypt's assembly of Brazilian Tucano's planes for Baghdad's benefit, lend support to the assumption that Iraq may be interested in the Condor/Badr.

In 1989, Egyptian Head of State, President Hosni Mubarak, confirmed that Egypt had dropped out of the project. Mubarak added that Argentina and Iraq were going ahead with it. Although Argentinian sources did not confirm or deny any reports concerning the Condor-II, the latter was believed to have run into technical difficulties and a huge cost over-run.[18]

On 28 May 1991, Argentina's Defence Minister announced that all components, parts and facilities used in building the Condor-II were to be deactivated, dismantled, converted or made unusable. The Americans, with Israel in mind, were upset by the project, which was conducted jointly by Egypt and Argentina and partly bankrolled by Iraq – at least until the UN embargo began to bite. The USA's discontent with the project and the inability of Iraq to continue to finance the costly Condor-II put an end to the triangle partnership. Another possible explanation for the latter is that most senior officers in Argentina's army and navy are probably glad to see the last of the Condor rocket as they foresaw that the money would be better spent on their own projects.[19]

China

One of the four developing countries who have exported arms to Iraq since the early 1980s has been China. China's entrance into the international arms market in the 1980s was closely related to reforms in the defence industry and the leadership's desire to acquire the foreign technology needed to modernize its army's weaponry. Until 1980 friendly developing countries were provided with arms at concessionary prices. Like all great powers, China has pursued policies that it saw most useful in assuring its own independence and security. While in the past this included active support for world revolution, policy-makers have more recently emphasized good relations with other states. Chinese leaders have often stressed their role as the leading Third World state in the South's struggle against both the Northeast and the Northwest. Around 1980, China decided to sell arms for profit to absorb excess capacity in the military industry, make military enterprises more economically viable and earn the foreign currency required to purchase foreign military technology.

> China's military budget has declined in relative terms because the country is putting most of its funds into economic development. Instructed to pay for much of its own modernization, the military has engaged some of the country's best brains and well-connected sons in its drive to earn foreign exchange by selling weapons abroad.[20]

Although China continued to sell military hardware at generous terms to some of its traditional friends and weapons customers, such as Pakistan, North Korea, Egypt, Sudan, and Somalia, the rapid increase in weapon sales in the 1980s was mostly due to the hard currency sales to Iran and Iraq. As the only country consistently supplying major weapons to both sides, it used the war to become a major supplier.

Studies carried out by the United States Arms Control and Disarmament Agency in the mid-1980s indicated that from 1979 to 1983 Chinese arms sales ranked eighth in the world, for a total of about US$3.5 billion, of which an estimated US$2.1 billion went to Middle Eastern countries. By 1987, China had jumped to fifth place ranking behind the United States, the Soviet Union, Britain and France. According to SIPRI statistics for 1982–6 – China ranked as the fifth largest exporter of major weapons to Third World countries, approximately on par with (West) Germany, Italy and the UK. The arms trade earned Beijing more than US$12 billion in the 1980s – almost half of it from supplying both sides in the Iran–Iraq war.

Looking at Table 13.1 – Third World arms exports to Iraq – one can see that a significant proportion of the Chinese arms exported to Iraq were Soviet weapons or clones of Soviet arms. For example, 1500 T-59/69 main battle tanks. This is not surprising as China's defence industry produced weapons and equipment based predominantly on Soviet designs.

It seems that China increasingly substituted the Soviet Union in a profitable niche of the arms trade: the capability quickly to supply simple, yet functional weapon systems at low prices. Furthermore, China is modernizing its arms industry as is evident from its hosting of two international arms shows in Peking in 1986. Six Chinese arms manufacturers displayed new arms and equipment which were aimed mainly at Third World markets.[21] Many of the Chinese weapons displayed incorporated Western technology. The Chinese version of the MiG-21 (F-7) incorporates British GEC avionics while the Chinese version of the MiG-19 incorporates Aeritalia avionics. The F-8II, China's newest fighter, will incorporate US avionic kits. Other weapons, such as tanks, armoured personnel carriers and artillery incorporate foreign sub-systems as well as foreign assistance in the designing and production from such countries as Austria, Germany, Israel, the UK and the USA.

While the export of conventional weapons which are mostly updates of decades-old Soviet technology is attractive only to Third World countries which cannot afford anything better, ballistic missile technology enabled China to develop an up-market niche. Since the late 1980s, China has been offering for sale at arms exhibitions and advertising the capabilities of a new short-range ballistic missile (SRBM) called the M-9. The latter uses solid fuel, has a maximum range of 600 km and is mounted on a truck for transport and launching.

New evidence indicates that the Chinese are peddling missiles and nuclear technology to Third World customers in defiance of multilateral efforts to ban such sales. The performance of US high-tech hardware in the Gulf War, has strengthened even more the pressure on Chinese commanders to modernize the arsenal by raising money through arms sales. With China's defence budget so low the People's Liberation Army has to increase the sale of expensive weapons to customers overseas. According to US intelligence reports, China has secretly built a nuclear reactor in Algeria, sent Pakistan parts for its M-11 missile system and negotiated the sale to Syria of its M-9 missiles.[22] The meeting between President Bush and Premier Li Peng in the UN on 31 January 1992 emphasized the worry that China is not honouring the international accord against missile related technology.[23]

THE FUTURE OF THIRD WORLD ARMS TRADE WITH IRAQ

Iraq was the leading importer of major weapons in the Middle East during the 1970s and 1980s. In the early 1970s the USSR was, basically, the sole supplier of weapons to Iraq. From the mid-1970s relations between the USSR and Iraq deteriorated. One reason being that the USSR chose Syria as its main ally after Egypt had turned away from her in search of Western support. The leaderships of the Ba'th party in Iraq and in Syria were bitterly opposed to each other. The alleged Soviet support for Iraq's Communist Party was another reason. Thus, the Iraqi military began to diversify the sources of supply ordering mainly from France and Italy. During the Iran–Iraq war, the Iraqi military had difficulties with spare parts for its Soviet weapon systems. Countries such as China, Egypt and certain East European states with large stocks of Soviet-made weapons or with arms manufactured under licence from the USSR, became important suppliers. Other beneficiaries were the arms industries of Brazil, Argentina, Italy and France.

For the last two decades Iraq has become one of Brazil's most important trading partners. But the pattern of trade between the two has greatly favoured the oil-rich Iraqis. The Brazilians determined to redress this imbalance chose to transform Iraq into a focal point of their arms sales drive to the Third World.

The foundation of the special relationship between the two

countries is formed by oil. Nearly 50 per cent of Brazil's oil imports came from Iraq (in the late 1970s at a rate of more than 400,000 barrels per day). After the Iranian revolution, Brazil's dependence on Iraqi crude increased even further as Iraq became the world's second leading oil exporter. In 1981, Brazil stepped up its oil purchases to 500,000 bpd. This increase in oil imports enabled Brazil to buy crude at preferential prices. In 1980, the two countries signed a special wide-ranging trade and cooperation agreement. Brazil received important supply agreements and also allowed its State Owned Oil Company – Petrobras – to become heavily involved in technical operations in Iraq. Other state owned companies, mainly those involved in the steel industry were awarded export contracts. The Iraq–Iran war heightened Iraq's need for military supplies. Since the mid 1970s, Iraq sought ways to reduce its near absolute dependence on the Soviet Union as a military supplier. In 1978 the first major arms deal between Iraq and Brazil, involving the sale of 200 armoured vehicles was reported.[24]

Argentina's smaller oil imports from the Arab world – from Libya during the Peronist government, and from Saudi Arabia during military rule – as well as its voluminous exports to that region, greatly benefited its economy. For a number of years Argentina's main Arab trading partner was Egypt. It is also important to emphasise that among twenty-five other Latin American countries, Argentina is one of the very few to have a trade surplus with the Arab world. Taken as a whole, Latin American trade with the Arab world has been most advantageous to the latter, resulting in accumulated surpluses of over US$59 billion in the period between 1974–84. Brazil is responsible for three-quarters of this.

Diplomatic relations with Middle Eastern countries were among China's first Third World ties. Since the Cultural Revolution, official relations have been established with all Middle Eastern states except Israel, Bahrain, Qatar, and Saudi Arabia. China's strong interest in the region reflects fear of the destabilizing effects of both Islamic fundamentalism and political extremism. While at first China had ties with the more politically conservative Arab states such as Egypt, Morocco and Jordan, it has improved ties, since 1981, with Iraq, Iran, and South Yemen, in order to compete with the Soviet Union. It is important to stress that while in the past arms and technology services to Third World countries were considered by Beijing as aid it is now used as a source of foreign exchange.

The danger of proliferation of advanced arms technologies in the Third World is not a new issue. Missiles and their component technologies were placed under stricter monitoring than other convenional weapon systems mainly because of a possible linkage between nuclear proliferation and missile delivery capabilities. One way of restricting missile related exports can be seen in the agreement on Missile Technology Control Regime (MTCR). The MTCR notwithstanding, missile-related exports continue to be perceived as important to many industrialized countries' diplomatic and commercial objectives. The provision of military technology production to Third World countries is partly the unintended consequences of US policies. The rebuilding of Europe with the assistance of the USA following the Second World War resulted in the development of highly competitive arms industries seeking markets in the Third World.

The Gulf War did not diminish Middle Eastern countries' appetite for more sophisticated weapon systems. The lack of cohesiveness between the different players involved in the US calls for restricting arms sales to the Middle East (and other conflict-prone regions) will undoubtedly result in an increased arms export to the Middle East in the short term. The collapse of the Soviet Union and its increased interests in domestic policies will certainly reduce its role in policing the region. Eastern Europe is another potential weak link. Former Warsaw Pact states have a large supply of weapons. Possession of many Soviet-made weapons, coupled with their need for hard currency will probably result in the 'dumping' of weapons to Third World buyers. Third World countries such as Brazil, China, Argentina, North Korea and Egypt, also have the capacity and the need to export advanced weapons, finding willing buyers in the oil-rich Gulf states.

The transformation of the structure of the international system resulting from the end of the cold war, is applying an immediate downward pressure on defence expenditures in the developed countries. The decrease in East–West tensions facilitates the implementation of budget cuts and considerable force reductions, leading to a search for alternative markets – namely the Middle East. The proliferation of the arms industry around the world coupled with the proliferation of the ability to produce modern arms has led to the arming of allies as well as adversaries without making a distinction. In the post-Gulf War era this trend is likely to increase, benefiting mainly Third World countries on the lookout for a 'new' and better merchandise.

International military business is building up a dangerously armed world with grim prospects to politically unstable regions. Arms imported to the Middle East have raised considerably the stakes associated with political instability. Two good examples are the Islamic revolution in Iran, where modern weapons outlasted the government they were meant to keep in power, and the war in the Gulf

where sophisticated weapons systems were turned against their suppliers. There is no doubt that without the stimulus of an East–West
military confrontation leading to polarization it will be considerably
more difficult to justify the continuation of arms proliferation to Third
World countries either in political or military terms. The UN might be
assigned an active role, being a more appropriate vehicle to pursue
multilateral restraint of arms exports both conventional and
unconventional.

Success in limiting proliferation to Third World countries might be
considerable as the developing nations depend heavily on transferred
defence technology. Licensed production and other forms of collaboration in arms technology is central in building and strengthening those
industries in the Third World. As developing countries are weak in
R&D and advanced technology this might be an effective way to
control and limit to an extent further proliferation of arms. While the
USA and any other Western countries cannot stop Third World
countries from building their defence industries, a coherent policy on
transferring arms to them will, undoubtedly, make a very large
difference, and in a coherent and defined policy lies the future of the
arms industry and proliferation in Third World nations.

NOTES

1 Bernard Lietaer, *L'Amerique Latin et L'Europe Demain*, Paris:
  Universidaire de France, 1980.
2 Augusto Varas, *Militarization and the International Arms Race in Latin
  America*, Boulder, Colorado and London: Westview Press, 1985.
3 Jacquelyn Porth, 'Argentina' in James Katz (ed.) *Arms Production in
  Developing Countries*, Lexington, Mass.: D.C. Heath, 1984.
4 V. Millan, 'Argentina' in Michael Brzoska and Thomas Ohlson (eds) *Arms
  Production in the Third World*, Philadelphia: Taylor and Francis, 1986.
5 Sipri Yearbooks, *World Armaments and Disarmaments*, 1970–90,
  Stockholm: International Peace Research Institute.
6 Seth Carus, *Ballistic Missiles in the Third World: Threat and Response*,
  New York: Praeger – published with the Center for Strategic and
  International Studies, 1990, p. 22.
7 Seth Carus, as Note 6, pp 22–3.
8 *Sipri*, 1989.
9 *Latin American Weekly Report*, 6 October 1988.
10 *Latin American Weekly Report*, 14 December 1984.
11 *Journal do Brasil*, 10 August 1991.
12 Congress of the United States Office of Technology Assessment (1991)
   *Global Arms Trade: Commerce in Advanced Military Technology and
   Weapons*, Washington DC: US Government Printing Office.
13 *Latin American Weekly Report*, 13 October 1988.

14 *Latin American Weekly Report*, 12 October 1984.
15 *Fôlha de São Paulo*, 2 September 1991.
16 Michael Brzoska and Thomas Ohlson *Arms Transfers to the Third World, 1971–85*, Sipri, Oxford and New York: Oxford University Press, 1987, p. 118.
17 *Sipri Yearbook*, 1989, p. 294, see Note 5.
18 *Latin American Weekly Report*, 5 October 1988.
19 *The Economist*, 8 June 1991.
20 'China boosts arms sales in Mideast', *Washington Post*, 4 April 1988, p. A20, col. 1.
21 *Sipri Yearbook*, 1987, p. 196–7, see Note 5.
22 'China: for sale tools of destruction', *Time*, 22 April 1991, p. 44.
23 'The US seeks curbs on China's sprawling arms-sale business', *Wall Street Journal*, 31 January 1992, p. A1.
24 *Latin American Weekly Report*, January 1981.

14 Petroleum prices, politics and war[1]

Gil Feiler

Iraq's brief takeover of Kuwait introduced a new dimension into Middle East oil politics. Iran and Iraq had been careful not to permit differences over oil to become involved in their war with each other. By contrast, in the 1990–91 Gulf crisis, petroleum issues became highly politicized once Saddam Hussein practised coercive diplomacy, resorting to overt military force in a brazen attempt at achieving his oil-related objectives. The purpose of this chapter is to explore the interactions between petroleum prices, politics and war in contemporary Middle East affairs, and particularly as a crucial dimension in Iraq policy.

The period, 1985–89, saw a substantial revival in crude oil production and exports by member countries of the Organization of Petroleum Exporting Countries, OPEC, that was due both to increases in world oil consumption and to a limited growth in supplies deriving from non-OPEC sources. Total crude oil production by OPEC member countries increased from a low of 15.5 million barrels per day (bpd) in 1985 to about 21.5 million bpd in 1989.[2] By virtue of a severe downturn in oil prices, however, net incomes declined sharply, especially from 1986 onwards. Whereas, in 1985, OPEC oil exports amounted to $134 billion, the following year's slump in prices resulted in a sharp decline in exports, to $80 billion (1987 dollars). The sharp drop in prices in 1986 stemmed directly from a failure by the oil-producing countries to coordinate a response to changed market conditions. Revenues have recovered since then, yet are still far lower than previously.[3]

Some Arab members of OPEC – primarily Kuwait and the United Arab Emirates (UAE) – have been known to favour lowering prices and breaking quotas to gain larger shares of the market. Others, such as Iraq and Iran, have preferred to see the price of OPEC's oil rise as steeply as possible. Where Iraq is concerned, this is because it has come to depend almost entirely on oil revenues for its foreign currency earnings. Kuwait, by contrast, has had no interest in seeing oil prices pushed too high, largely because, having come to rely as heavily on its various investments in the West as it does on revenues from oil, it fears the slowdown in world economic growth likely to ensue from excessively high oil prices.

According to estimates made by *Arab Oil and Gas*, over-production, coupled with the fall in prices since 1986, resulted in a $263.1 billion decline, between 1986 and 1989, in oil revenues jointly earned by all OPEC countries, including a drop of $29.1 billion for Iraq.[4] The countries most seriously affected by this massive reversal have been those, such as Iraq, Iran and Algeria, with the largest populations and for which higher oil prices were vital if their respective foreign debts were to be repaid. Iraq required particularly substantial amounts of oil revenue, partially for the purpose of financing the reconstruction of an economy badly damaged during its war with Iran (1980–88), and partially to fund its ambitious armaments programme. But its programmes for economic reconstruction and military re-equipment were hampered by decreased oil revenues, which dropped still further in 1990.

Iraqi President Saddam Hussein, emerging from eight years of war with Iran as probably the strongest of the Arab world's dictators, focused his criticism on two of the region's weakest political and military actors, Kuwait and the United Arab Emirates, and whose oil pricing policies directly contradicted his own. Iraq's ruling Ba'th party newspaper, *al-Thawra*, in a key May 1990 article asserted some states 'had violated their OPEC quota and had flooded the market, ignoring the interests of other states in the region, including Iraq'. The article insisted that 'at a time when Zionist and imperialist circles are clearly waging campaigns against Iraq, certain states are pursuing identical goals by increasing the amounts of oil they are pumping to the markets . . .'. At a press conference held at about the same time in Baghdad, Foreign Minister Tareq Aziz cautioned 'those who are irresponsibly playing with the price of oil to achieve very limited gains, must know that they are committing a grave mistake . . . and it is our duty to warn them not to continue'.[5] Oil Minister Issam Abdul-Rahim al-Chalabi added that 'countries violating their production quotas ought to appreciate the grave economic and political developments which may ensue from such behavior'.

Following an OPEC emergency session held in Geneva, the thirteen OPEC oil ministers, in attempting to arrest further declines in world oil prices, which had amounted to 25 per cent since the beginning of 1990, pledged on 3 May 1990 that overall OPEC output would

Table 14.1 Gulf countries' excess oil production in April 1990

Country	(million barrels per day) Production	Quota	Excess
Saudi Arabia	5.7	5.38	0.32
UAE	2.1	1.095	1.005
Kuwait	1.8	1.5	0.3
Qatar	0.4	0.37	0.03
Iraq	2.9	3.14	(0.24)

Source: *Petroleum Economist*, June 1990, p. 193.

thereafter be substantially less – 1.445 million bpd (see Table 14.1) lower than the 23.5 million bpd produced in April.[7] The output reductions agreed on were primarily (71 per cent) offered by the Gulf states. Saudi Arabia promised a reduction of 430,000 bpd, while Kuwait and the UAE indicated that they would cut their output by 400,000 and 200,000 bpd respectively.[8] A few days later, in an official government statement, Saudi oil minister Hisham Nazer reaffirmed Saudi Arabia's commitment to the May agreement.[9] Whether Kuwait would make good on its promise, though, appeared to remain an open question.

Iraq, accordingly, began applying pressure on the leaders of the major Arab oil producing countries. In a closed forum, Saddam went so far as to threaten the Gulf states, categorically demanding they adhere to the oil policies he was advocating. In consequence, the oil ministers of Saudi Arabia, Iraq and the UAE, during the Arab summit in Baghdad in the last week of May 1990, agreed to advise respective heads of state to discuss the matter with Kuwait's Emir Sheikh Jaber al-Ahmad al-Sabah.[10]

Several weeks after, Kuwait's Oil Minister Sheikh Ali Khalifa al-Sabah indicated that his country would revert to its export quota of 1.5 million bpd and announced that Kuwait had stopped all spot sales to an already saturated market.[11] This gesture aside, it appeared that of all the OPEC producers the only one which honoured the May 3 agreement to cut production was Saudi Arabia, the world's biggest oil exporter, which did in fact reduce output by about 400,000 bpd.[12]

The Saudis also issued a sharply worded call to other OPEC producers to join in cutting excess output, demonstrating undisguised irritation at the tardiness exhibited by fellow members in executing output cuts needed to erase the world oil glut (for world consumption, see Table 14.2) and to which they had committed themselves.[13] Oil prices initially stabilized after the Saudi cut, but subsequently fell

Table 14.2 World petroleum consumption, by region, 1987

Region	Amount (million barrels per day)	Percentage of total
United States	16.7	26.6
Other North America	3.0	4.8
Central/South America	3.6	5.7
Western Europe	12.6	20.1
Eastern Europe/USSR	10.8	17.2
Middle East	2.8	4.4
Africa	1.8	2.9
Far East/Oceania	11.4	18.2
World total	62.7	100.0*

Source: US Department of Energy, *International Energy Annual 1988* (November 1989), as quoted by Michael A. Toman, 'What do we know about energy security?', *Resources*, no. 101, Fall 1990, p. 4.

again when oil industry executives estimated that, overall, the OPEC members had collectively cut output by no more than 900,000 bpd – far less than the 1.45 million-barrel reduction pledged in early May.[14]

An oil surplus occurred in June 1990 which sharply pushed prices still lower. The Kuwaiti Oil Minister may have declared on 5 June that his country's adherence to the accord reached in Geneva was 'not open to doubt',[15] yet Kuwait quietly continued to produce more oil than its allocation.[16] In mid-June, OPEC therefore suddenly found itself in its gravest crisis since the oil price crash of 1986 when spot prices averaged around $14 per barrel, down from the $20.50 per barrel posted in early January (see Table 14.3). In the words of the OPEC secretary-general: 'oil prices hit rock bottom'.[17]

In attempting to cope with the impact of a war debt estimated as high as $80 billion,[18] Saddam became increasingly outraged by the policies of his neighbours, principally Kuwait and the UAE. Flexing his military muscles, he sent envoys to the Gulf states' capitals with the message that he disbelieved their protestations of having truly cut individual country oil exports.[19] Iraq tried to explain its stance by claiming that the fall in oil prices tended to harm those countries, like itself, which had large populations and which were saddled by huge overseas debts, much more than it harmed 'OPEC members with small populations and with per capita incomes among the highest in the world'.[20] Iraqi deputy prime minister, Saadoun Hammadi, blaming Kuwait and the UAE for the drop in oil prices, declared that, for every decline of one dollar in the price of a barrel of oil, Iraq would lose one billion dollars per year.[21] At a late-June press conference in Kuwait, he

Table 14.3 World crude oil prices (dollars per barrel)*

| | Price | |
Date	OPEC	Non-OPEC
Before the crisis		
1990		
1 January	19.69	20.44
2 February	18.47	19.00
9 March	17.36	18.16
6 April	16.02	16.80
4 May	14.50	14.97
1 June	13.84	14.62
6 July	13.38	14.06
After the crisis		
1990		
20 July	15.39	15.80
27 July	16.43	16.94
3 August	17.67	19.00
27 August	28.51	28.58
7 September	27.11	28.36
28 September	35.79	36.76
5 October	33.56	35.06
26 October	28.09	29.55
2 November	30.76	32.30
7 December	25.76	27.74
1991		
4 January	23.86	24.98
25 January	16.82	20.30
8 February	16.48	19.24
1 March	14.63	16.80
5 April	15.08	16.57
3 May	16.42	17.86
14 June	15.81	16.52

Source: Eli Arom, 'Oil price data files', Tel-Aviv: Israel Institute of Petroleum and Energy.
Note: *Average price (FOB) of internationally traded oil only.

stated that 'anything below $25 a barrel is definitely not a fair price', accused Kuwait of violating its 1.5 million bpd quota by producing 2.0 million bpd in May (compared with 1.8 to 1.9 million in previous months), and concluded that 'the blade has reached now the bone, after cutting through the flesh'.[22]

Notwithstanding this barrage of Iraqi charges, Kuwait's new oil minister Rashid Salem al-Ameeri indicated that for its part his country badly needed an increase in its OPEC output quota in order to offset a substantial budget deficit'.[23] A few days later, though, Kuwait appeared willing to defer its demand for a higher output quota until such time as prices were restored to the $18 per barrel target to which OPEC was striving.[24]

Following an 11 July meeting in Jeddah, at which the oil ministers of Iraq, Kuwait, Qatar, Saudi Arabia and the UAE discussed the glut of crude on world markets, the impression was that the main OPEC producers, including Kuwait, in the end would abide by their respective oil production quotas and refrain from seeking any increase in those limits until prices reached $18 a barrel.[25]

Thus, oil prices slowly inched upwards on the expectation of cuts in supply. But Kuwait immediately made it clear that, nevertheless, a larger percentage of the market was still due it, if only because its reserves justified being permitted to produce up to 12 per cent of total OPEC volume, compared with around 7 per cent in July.[26] On 16 July, the Kuwaiti oil minister went so far as to declare that the decisions just reached at Jeddah supported Kuwait's demand 'to raise its oil production quota in the fourth quarter of this year [1990] after prices are brought under control'.[27]

As the 25 July date for the Geneva meeting drew near, Iraq warned fellow OPEC members that any violation of the cartel's production quotas would be tantamount to a declaration of war.[28] Most of the speech delivered by Saddam Hussein on 17 July, as part of celebrations marking the anniversary of Iraq's 1968 revolution, was devoted to an impassioned denunciation of what he described as a politically motivated conspiracy between the USA and some Gulf states to drive oil prices down. The Iraqi president openly threatened to resort to military force if the Arab Gulf nations, continued driving oil prices down by exceeding their production quotas. He said that 'raising our voice against the evil is not the final resort if the evil continues . . . cutting necks is better than cutting [our] means of living'.[29] On another occasion, he said: 'if words fail to protect Iraqis, something effective must be done to return things to their natural course and return usurped rights to their owners'.[30] No OPEC member state had ever been so strongly intimidated by another OPEC member and threatened by military force.

Simultaneously, Iraq chose to revive its longstanding border dispute with Kuwait, demanding the return of $2.4 billion in oil allegedly 'stolen' from Iraq's al-Rumaila field by the Kuwaitis. Iraq also began to insist that the $35 billion or thereabouts, which it had received by way of loans from Kuwait, Saudi Arabia and other Gulf states during the Iran–Iraq war, simply be erased. In portraying itself as the one country which had defended Arabs against the Iranian revolutionary menace during the Iran–Iraq war, Iraq was now demanding its reward.[31]

In the face of this Iraqi stridency, Kuwaiti newspapers began to adopt a more conciliatory tone, and its Prime Minister, Crown Prince Sheikh Saad al-Abdullah al-Sabah, even went so far as to summon Kuwait's 'parliament' for an emergency session behind closed doors to discuss the Iraqi accusations.[32] But neither Kuwait nor the UAE did much more than assert their plans to curtail production remained unchanged. 'Kuwait has already started to cut its output in line with the Jeddah agreement,' said a Kuwaiti official, 'and it will continue to do so.'

Iraq's hard line against Kuwait, however, continued. *Al-Thawra*, organ of the ruling Ba'th Party in Iraq, commented (19 July 1990) that 'the ink of the oil agreement [in Jeddah] . . . was not even dry when the Kuwaiti oil minister announced that Kuwait would increase its oil production in October'.[33] A few days before the scheduled Geneva meeting, Iraq escalated its coercive strategy of intimidation one step forward when its troops advanced to the Kuwaiti border in conjunction with demands that measures be adopted promptly for an increase of about 50 per cent in the price of crude oil. Most diplomats and analysts reckoned that the Iraqi military deployment amounted to little more than a show of force, mounted in anticipation of the crucial talks to be conducted in Geneva.[34]

Meanwhile, in part by virtue of a certain degree of pre-conference arrogance which some OPEC countries chose to exhibit, and partly as the outcome of the aggravated controversy between Iraq and Kuwait, world oil prices actually rose as the date for OPEC's Geneva conference approached. Everyone was aware that the 25–27 July meeting promised to test whether Iraq was capable of achieving its aims by threatening its smaller neighbours with military action. In the event, the agreement reached at the conference represented the most credible attempt ever made by OPEC to force crude oil prices upwards via stringent control of output volume. The production ceiling of 22.491 million bpd, it was decided, would remain unchanged until the end of 1990. Iraq called on OPEC to push prices up to $25 per barrel, but was eventually compelled to compromise with the stand of most OPEC ministers, who favoured a target price no higher than $21 per barrel. The agreement reached represented a coalition of interests among the most powerful Gulf countries – Saudi Arabia, Iran and Iraq.[35]

Iraq certainly appeared to have scored a major political victory, forcing Kuwait and the UAE to reduce their oil production and intimidating OPEC into consenting to raise oil prices. Once the conference was over, and after the basket price had recovered by nearly $4 from the low point of around $14 per barrel registered in June,[36] market watchers issued predictions that by the end of 1990 the price of $21 per barrel agreed on would more than likely be exceeded.

Much earlier, in mid-June 1990, Egyptian oil minister Abdel-Hadi Kandeel had predicted the oil price crisis would end in no more than two months 'within the framework of a fruitful dialogue between oil producers in and outside OPEC'.[37] And, indeed, the crisis did climax after two months, but in an entirely unexpected manner. For on 2 August 1990 Saddam Hussein, unappeased, invaded Kuwait.

One immediate side-effect of the invasion was to produce renewed turbulence in the world oil market. On 6 August, the international community imposed a trade embargo on Iraq, sanctioned by UN Security Council Resolution No. 661, in attempting to force Iraq to withdraw from Kuwait. The embargo proved entirely successful in preventing the sale or export of oil either from Iraqi or Iraqi-occupied Kuwait. In an editorial published on 21 August 1990, the Baghdad daily *al-Iraq* predicted the UN embargo and the US-led naval blockade of Iraq would result in far scarcer oil supplies and a consequent rise in oil prices. This, *al-Iraq* incorrectly assumed, would bring the American economy to 'total collapse'.

A principal economic consequence of the Iraqi invasion, was, indeed, a further rise in oil prices, and to a level higher than they had been for many years. Application of the international embargo cut world supply by about 4 million barrels daily (17 per cent of OPEC supply), to barely more than 20 million bpd in August 1990, pushing prices some four dollars above OPEC's $21 a barrel minimum reference price. Overnight, the world oil market outlook changed dramatically.[38] There was considerable anxiety, in particular, lest the Saudi Arabian oil fields clustered around Ras Tanura, less than 200 miles south of Kuwait, should suffer grievous damage in battle, for a disaster of that magnitude might easily result in the world's losing up to 7 million barrels of oil a day, equivalent to 11 per cent of daily consumption.

Saudi Arabia and Venezuela immediately began calling for an emergency OPEC conference aimed at increasing oil output to compensate for Iraqi and Kuwaiti crude oil being withheld from world markets. Saudi authorities announced on 7 August plans to step up production by 2 million bpd, while Venezuela indicated its preparedness to expand output by 500,000 barrels a day. Most OPEC members, however, preferred not to meet under the threat of military hostilities in the Gulf.[39] The Iraqis, for their part, made it clear they considered any attempt at quota busting by OPEC members to constitute acts of aggression against their country.[40]

This failure to convene an OPEC meeting, in and of itself, worked to force oil prices upward. Only in the last week of August, by which time world oil prices topped $31 a barrel (their highest since December 1982), did the majority of OPEC ministers express willingness to meet for informal consultations (Vienna, 26–28 August),[41] followed by a formal meeting in Vienna (29 August) to discuss how to respond in concert to the Gulf crisis.[42] The agreement reached there represents their delayed response to Iraq's invasion of Kuwait, and proved to be a political victory for Saudi Arabia.[43] The Saudis, having the advantage of considerable spare production capacity together with US military support, refused to permit crude oil prices to soar freely, irrespective of whether OPEC agreed or not. Still they sought official OPEC approval for their increase in production.[44]

The decision taken by a majority of the OPEC states was to suspend temporarily those output quotas established by their July production agreement and to raise overall crude-oil output from 20 million bpd to a ceiling of 22.5 million bpd so as to help hold down petroleum prices during the Middle East crisis.[45] The bulk of additional crude oil was to come from Saudi Arabia, Venezuela and the UAE. Not surprisingly, and to little avail, Iraq, Iran and Libya voiced their opposition to the very notion of any kind of production increase.[46] Iran, with no spare production capacity, claimed that 'raising output was a big mistake by OPEC because this was the best opportunity to demand that industrial countries use their stockpiles'.[47] Saudi Arabia had apparently been informed, by an Iraqi official, that the earnings from any increased oil production ought to be channelled to Iraq.[48]

Following the Vienna Agreement, September OPEC production reached more than 22 million bpd, compared with an August low of around 20 million bpd.[49] Nevertheless, because of the apparent lack of progress towards peace in the Gulf and the gathering anxieties over oil supplies, which reached their climax in mid-September, oil prices soared to their highest levels since the early 1980s (see Table 14.3). By October, oil prices were twice the level at which they had stood at the time of the Iraqi invasion of Kuwait (August 2), and oil spot prices had soared to over $40 per barrel. The main reason, though, that the price of oil doubled within less than two months was not the halt in Iraqi and Kuwaiti oil exports, but rather the fact that market analysts suspected interruptions in the flow of Saudi Arabian oil in the near future and advised stockpiling of petroleum strategic reserves.

By mid-December, though, expectations once again rose that peace might yet somehow be preserved in the Gulf. This unduly optimistic assessment was momentarily influenced by Iraq's consent to conduct high-level talks with the USA and by rumours that it might agree to release all of the foreigners it was holding hostage. This wave of optimism, allied with a timely softening in market fundamentals, combined to send oil prices down, to the lowest level recorded in over three months (see Table 14.3). Simultaneously, at their meeting in Vienna, the OPEC ministers decided that they would maintain high oil output while the Gulf crisis lasted, but once it was over would restore production controls and defend their $21 per barrel reference price for oil so as to avoid any chance of a glut in world oil supplies and a consequent collapse in prices.[50]

An indication of the volatile nature of petroleum pricing in times of international crisis came, when on 4 January, Iraq's presidential envoy to India made remarks in New Delhi to the effect that, were the USA to initiate a war in the Gulf, Iraq would promptly blow up all oil installations in the Saudi peninsula. Coming hard on the heels of Saddam Hussein's own announcement that his country would never quit Kuwaiti territory and that his people ought to prepare for war,[51] this declaration sent oil prices surging upwards again in the first week of January 1991. But immediately thereafter, in response to reports of success for the massive US-led allied air strikes against Iraqi military installations in Iraq and Kuwait, which commenced on 16 January, oil prices plummeted, registering the largest price fall ever recorded for a single day (the biggest decline, amounting to $10 per barrel, was posted on 16 January 1991, the day that war was declared).

Three contemporary developments in effect contributed to the sudden downward trend. The first was a sense of relief that Saudi Arabia's vital oil installations were now unlikely to sustain significant damage. Secondly, the International Energy Agency and the US government adopted immediate emergency measures, with President Bush ordering the sale of 33.75 million barrels from his country's 585 million barrel strategic reserve.[52] Finally, prices fell, too, in reaction to an announcement by the Soviet Union of a diplomatic initiative to achieve an immediate ceasefire in the Gulf. For these reasons the previously dominant prediction that crude oil prices might soar to $65 per barrel if war broke out[53] did not come true.

Once the war did end, but only in March, OPEC realized it would have to act resolutely to stem any further collapse in prices. Its ministers therefore agreed to convene in Geneva on 11–12 March 1991 for the purpose of negotiating oil output cuts. On the eve of the talks, however, Saudi Arabia signalled it would dig in its heels against any OPEC demand for a quick return to oil production controls. After all, it was presented with a bill of some $50 billion to pay for the Gulf War. Furthermore, Riyadh acknowledged the world expected to be compensated for more than 4 million bpd of lost Kuwaiti and Iraqi production. Accordingly, Saudi Arabia proceeded to open wide its oil taps. Consequently, therefore, in attempting to balance the now diminished level of world demand, OPEC ministers were obliged to declare a new output limit for OPEC members of 22.3 million bpd, which actually represented a reduction of no more than 1 million bpd (representing 5 per cent of the total) from February's independently estimated 23.3 million bpd.[54]

CONCLUSIONS

One major source of Iraq's animosity to Kuwait appears to have been primarily economic: the product of outrage and frustration at its own dire financial plight, which the decline in oil prices had exacerbated. According to Saddam Hussein's interpretation, it was persistent overproduction by Kuwait and the UAE which had caused world oil prices to collapse. In addition, Iraq also saw itself as justified in pressing creditors in the Gulf to waive Iraqi repayment of debts amounting to billions of dollars, and borrowed to finance its protracted war with Iran. Last, but not least, Baghdad sought $2.4 billion as compensation for the crude oil it accused Kuwait of having stolen from Iraq's South Rumaila field on the disputed Iraq–Kuwait border.

Iraq, indeed, can be said to have had a fairly powerful case in the matter of world oil prices. Its economy was completely dominated by oil. In 1989, more than 61 per cent of its GDP came from oil-related activities and about 99 per cent of its exports in that year ($14.5 billion, out of total exports amounting to $14.6 billion) derived from crude oil.[55] Saddam Hussein knew his country was faced with an enormous financial problem and that he had no alternative but to solve it by radical means. His chief motivation in invading Kuwait, therefore, was to lay his hands on its oil reserves and substantial financial assets. Over and beyond that, he entertained a number of additional major ambitions. As Robert Mabro phrased it in his study, 'The First Oil War', Iraq, to be sure, had broad political and regional objectives, but its primary and most acute desire was to alleviate its economic disaster.[56]

Whatever his other motives, though, Saddam cannot be said to have exaggerated the importance of oil revenues to Iraq. Thus, the immediate issues providing Iraq the pretext needed for its invasion of Kuwait were certainly those associated with oil pricing policies and oil revenues. Oil issues, indeed, were central to the war. The Iraqi invasion, in sum, was launched on the strength of Saddam Hussein's accusation that Kuwait and the UAE were undermining Iraq by producing too much oil, thereby depressing prices.

Daniel Yergin has noted that oil crises tend to begin with the spectre of shortage, and to end with actual surplus.[57] Indeed, anxieties over what disaster might occur to world oil prices in the wake of the Gulf crisis – with some commentators at the time predicting an allied attack on Iraq would lead to a lengthy war and double oil prices to $65 a barrel[58] – were unfulfilled. After an initial surge, oil prices steadied at about $25 per barrel and, once the war was over, reverted to around $16 per barrel. This pattern of relative stability tends to reinforce a growing conviction that the 1990–91 Gulf oil crisis does not resemble the two principal crises of the 1970s (the 1973–74 Arab oil embargo and the 1979 Iranian revolution). Rather, the world is now far better equipped to take disruptions in oil supplies in its stride.[59]

Nonetheless, the Gulf crisis and its aftermath do highlight the intrinsic instability featured by the world's largest oil basin, the Middle East's strategic Gulf.

NOTES

1 I wish to express my gratitude to Mr Eli Arom for his kindness in supplying me with much material and for making several useful suggestions on an earlier version.
2 International Monetary Fund (IMF), 'World oil situation: recent development and prospects', *World Economy Outlook*, May 1990, p. 97.
3 *Petroleum Review*, May 1990, p. 266.
4 *Arab Oil and Gas*, 1 August 1990.
5 Reuter (Baghdad), 3 May 1990.
6 Reuter (Baghdad), 4 May 1990.
7 On this meeting, see: *Middle East Economic Survey* (*MEES*), vol. 33, no. 31, 7 May 1990; *Petroleum Intelligence Weekly*, 7 May 1990; *Wall Street Journal*, 29 May, 1990. It should be noted that the new level has not been determined in a formal, signed accord.
8 *Energy Economist*, no. 103, May 1990, p. 18.
9 *Wall Street Journal*, 6 May 1990.
10 Rawhi Abeidoh, Reuter (Baghdad), 29 May 1990.
11 *Oil & Gas Journal*, 21 May 1990, p. 20.
12 OPEC Keeps cool in face of market downturn', *Middle East Economic Survey*, vol. 33, no. 34, 28 May 1990, p. A1; Nicholas Moore, Reuter (London), 24 May 1990.
13 Nicholas Moore, Reuter (London), 31 May 1990.

14 According to Subroto, OPEC's secretary-general. See: *International Herald Tribune*, 16 May 1990.
15 *Middle East Economic Survey* 11 June 1990.
16 *Arab Oil and Gas*, 16 June 1990.
17 Jennie Kantyka, Reuter (Singapore), 12 June 1990. For crude oil prices in June, see *Oil Market Trends*, June 1990, p. 9.
18 *The Economist*, 28 July 1990, p. 48.
19 Subhy Haddad, Reuter (Baghdad), 19 June 1990.
20 Reuter (Abu-Dhabi), 27 June 1990.
21 Rawhi Abeidoh, Reuter (Nicosia), 26 June 1990.
22 Hamza Hendawi, Reuter (Kuwait), 26 June 1990; Rawhi Abeidoh, Reuter (Nicosia), 28 June 1990.
23 Reuter (Nicosia), 2 July 1990.
24 Nicholas Moore, Reuter (Algiers), 5 July 1990.
25 For communique issued at the end of the Jeddah meeting, see *Arab Oil and Gas*, 1 August 1990, p. 4. See also: *International Herald Tribune*, 12 and 13 July 1990; *Wall Street Journal*, 13 July 1991.
26 See the words of the Kuwaiti oil Minister quoted by Reuter (Algiers), 14 July 1990.
27 *Al-Qabas* (Kuwait), 16 July 1990.
28 *International Herald Tribune*, 19 July 1990.
29 *Wall Street Journal* and *Financial Times*, 18 July 1990.
30 Eric Hall, Reuter (Dubai) and Ian Mackenzie, Reuter (Nicosia), 17 July 1990.
31 Quoted by Steven Butler and Victor Mallet, *Financial Times*, 25 July 1990. See also: *International Herald Tribune*, 19 July 1990; *Jerusalem Post*, 19 July 1990.
32 Reuter (Nicosia), 18 July 1990.
33 *International Herald Tribune*, 20 July 1990.
34 *Middle East Economics Survey*, 23 July 1990, p. A1. For text of the speech and the memorandum, see section C and D, *International Herald Tribune*, 21 July 1990.
35 See the report by Ian Seymour in *Middle East Economic Survey*, vol. 33, no. 43, 30 July 1990, pp. A1–A5. The text of the OPEC press release can be found on pp. A4–A5. See also: *Financial Times*, 28–29 and 30 July 1990; *International Herald Tribune*, 28 July 1990.
36 For the price trends, see 'Oil futures climb higher on uneasiness in Middle East', *Wall Street Journal*, 2 August 1990.
37 Reuter (Cairo), 12 June 1990.
38 *Oil and Gas Journal Newsletter*, 6 August 1990; *Petroleum Intelligence Weekly*, 3 September 1990.
39 *Middle East Economic Survey*, 29 August 1990; *Arab Oil and Gas*, 16 August 1990; *International Herald Tribune* and *Wall Street Journal*, 16 August 1990.
40 *Arab Oil and Gas*, 27 August 1990, p. 26.
41 Iraq and Libya did not attend the informal discussions in Vienna.
42 *International Herald Tribune*, 25 August 1990.
43 For the full text of the agreement, see Reuter (London), 29 August 1990.
44 For this and for Saudi Arabia's own reasons for wanting to put more oil on the market, see *Energy Economist*, no. 107, 1990, pp. 18–19.

45 For the text of OPEC's Vienna Agreement and analysis, see *Middle East Economic Survey*, 3 September 1990, pp. A1–A4; *Wall Street Journal*, 29 and 30 August 1990; *Financial Times*, 29 August 1990.
46 *Middle East Economic Survey*, 27 August 1990, pp. A1–A2.
47 *International Herald Tribune*, 31 August 1990.
48 *Energy Economist*, no. 107, p. 18.
49 *Petroleum Intelligence Weekly*, 1 October 1990, p. 3.
50 *Middle East Economic Survey*, 17 December 1990, pp. A1–A2; *Arab Oil and Gas*, 16 December 1990, pp. 5–6; *International Herald Tribune*, 13, 14 and 17 December 1990; *Wall Street Journal*, 14 December 1990; *Financial Times*, 14 December 1990.
51 Sarah Cunningham, Reuter (London), 7 January 1991.
52 *Oil and Gas Journal*, 21 January 1991, p. 20.
53 See for example Reuter (London), 8 January 1991.
54 *Middle East Economic Survey*, 18 March 1991, pp. A1–A4; *Arab Oil and Gas*, 18 March 1991; *Wall Street Journal*, 13 March 1991, p. 11. See the full text of the statement issued by OPEC at the end of the meeting in Reuter (Geneva), 12 March 1991.
55 Economist Intelligence Unit, *Iraq: Country Report*, no. 1, 1991, p. 3.
56 Quoted in *Petroleum Intelligence Weekly*, 27 August 1990, pp. 7–8.
57 See Daniel Yergin *The Prize: The Epic Quest for Oil, Money and Power*, New York Simon and Schuster, 1991.
58 See for example the words of Egypt's oil minister, quoted by Reuter (Cairo), 27 October 1990.
59 Israeli economic analysis Eliahu Kanovsky, thus, accurately predicted that the price rise would be of short duration. Quoted by *International Herald Tribune*, 4 August 1990.

15 The Gulf War and the media

Dina Goren

The international mass media played an extraordinary role throughout the extended Gulf crisis and short war, starting with the invasion
of Kuwait on 2 August 1990 and continuing even after the last tank
had ground to a halt on Iraqi soil in early March of the following year.
Literally every public move, military or political, received saturation
television coverage, mostly in real time, or was featured extensively on
the front pages of newspapers throughout the world. What follows is
an attempt to analyse efforts made by the media to furnish their
audiences or readership with both visual and verbal data about the
war, and to find out whether, as a result, the public was truly kept
well-informed, or, alternatively, manipulated.

Like the war itself, the media's coverage of the Gulf War divides into
three phases: the military build-up, a period of softening up the Iraqi
opponent, and the actual ground fighting.

THE ALLIED TROOP BUILD-UP AND DEPLOYMENT

In the course of this preliminary phase, lasting five months, the United
Nations Security Council endorsed the policy the demonstration of
force proposed by President Bush, half-a-million US troops were
transferred to Saudi Arabia and a multinational military coalition was
put together.

While the number of US troops being deployed steadily increased
from a projected ceiling of 50,000 to nine times that number, very little
public debate took place in the US Congress, the major papers, or TV.
Although the media did devote space to background stories on
logistical complexities and international perspectives, there was little
discussion about the overall policy adopted by the President. In his
analysis of how the *Los Angeles Times*, the *New York Times*, the
Washington Post and 'Nightline' (a very popular American TV

programme which usually deals with analysis of current public events) covered the crucial first six weeks of the build-up, James Bennet, editor of the *Washington Monthly* concludes that these 'influential, supposedly adversarial sources of news' never asked such questions as: 'Are any troops needed? If so, how many are enough? How many casualties would be too many?'[1] Criticism of the policy of deployment was mostly relegated to the op-ed pages. An outstanding example is a letter to the President, entitled 'If my Marine Son is Killed . . .', which was published on the op-ed page of the *New York Times*, on 23 August 1990, later to be widely quoted.[2]

By contrast, the military build-up itself received extensive coverage, particularly on television, bringing an endless number of colourful human interest stories about 'our hometown boys stationed in the desert'.[3] Coverage of this kind is found to enhance patriotism and foster national consensus, at least in the early days of any military engagement.

Saddam Hussein's cynical treatment of Westerners held hostage had the same effect. On 23 August 1990, television networks broadcast Saddam 'visiting' a roomful of captive British women and children, and then turning to caress the head of one little boy. Rather then gaining him sympathy or support, such stage-managed media events only incensed foreign viewers. 'If anyone wondered whether the analogy of Saddam Hussein to a predecessor agressor and mass murderer, Adolf Hitler, might be an exaggeration', reacted columnist William Safire – 'all doubt was removed yesterday, when the Iraqi dictator forced the world to triage'.[4] Negative perceptions in the West was strengthened by pictures of tens of thousands of foreign labourers fleeing from Kuwait and Iraq through the desert.

In contrast, media in the Arab and Muslim world bought the Iraqi campaign of misinformation, coming out with claims that 40 per cent of American servicemen in Saudia Arabia were infected with AIDS; American troops were massacring Saudi demonstrators; and the Pentagon had shipped 5,000 Egyptian prostitutes to the American troops in the desert kingdom.[5] Under the misperception that public opinion mattered in Iraq as much as it did in the USA, President Bush seized on Saddam Hussein's offer to appear on Iraqi television. Hussein himself was accorded extensive exposure in western media.[6] According to Elihu Katz the media on both sides: 'were enlisted in psychological warfare, delivering messages back and forth between the spokesmen of both nations, and cooperating in the attempts of each leader to "speak over the head" of the other'.[7]

THE SOFTENING-UP PHASE

A second distinctive phase began on 16 January with the air offensive against Iraq, to which the latter retaliated by sporadically firing Scud missiles against Israeli and Saudi targets, causing considerable damage to property and a few fatalities. Much of the criticism concerning the media's role in the conflict is based on its performance throughout this phase. The media in general and CNN in particular succeeded in creating an illusion of ubiquity: making audiences worldwide believe that whatever happened, or was reputed to have happened, was being relayed to them in real-time coverage. In fact, much of what went on never reached the media, while much of what was said, particularly during the first days, was simply not true. What really was happening, namely the systematic softening-up operation conducted from the air, was presented, on the American side, as a bloodless operation of surgical precision.

'The military's most striking success . . .' as one writer observed after the war 'came from its well-planned and inspired decision to flood the world's television screens with fascinating video tapes of smart bomb strikes that never missed and with detailed official briefings'.[8] Such filtering and flooding of military data presented war in a new light. Viewers were no longer confronted with the horrors of mangled flesh, blood and sweat of combat, as seen during the Vietnam War. Instead articulate men in immaculate uniforms explaining troop movements with the aid of multicoloured maps were shown. So, too, distant impersonal military objectives being hit, recorded by TV cameras mounted on the bombing aircraft. As one observer put it, 'Technology loves other technology, and so the Gulf war, in the absence of real footage, has become a war of hardware and description of hardware; not since WWII have we with such avidity learned the type and shape and capabilities of the engines we have invented to prosecute the war'.[9]

High-tech warfare thus combined with advanced media-technology to create a new, aesthetisized view of combat.[10] Audiences exposed to such presentations thus had little reason to be antagonistic. Public support for the war was further enhanced by extensive coverage accorded the ecological havoc created by Saddam's orders to flood the Gulf with crude oil and set Kuwaiti oilwells on fire. The sight of oil-drenched dying cormorants featured on magazine covers and TV screens, like those of burning oil fields, conveyed the subliminal message that Saddam was not just an enemy on the battlefield but demonic and a threat to life as such.

Viewed from the Iraqi side, the war was presented differently. Throughout the period in question Saddam chose to present himself as entirely in control of the situation. He used frequent appearances on TV, relayed round the world on CNN, to threaten his adversaries and describe the horrible defeat in store for them at the hands of his own invincible army, in what he promised would be 'The Mother of All Battles'. Only when it suited his policy, as in the case of the bombed air raid shelter, did he permit foreign camera crews to film and show scenes of damages inflicted on his country and subjects. The bombed ruins of what was said to be a baby formula factory, were helpfully identified with a sign in English: 'BABY FOOD FACTORY'. CNN's Peter Arnett was careful to call the attention of his viewers to the fact, thereby hinting that the sign was affixed there solely as propaganda, and outsmarting the Iraqi military censor.

Representatives of American and world media assigned to covering the war from Saudi Arabia in their own way encountered limitations circumscribing their ability to report the war freely and accurately. After extensive debate with US media executives, in the middle of January the Defense Department issued its definitive rules for combat coverage in the Gulf, with permission to be at the front restricted to Pentagon-organized pools of reporters under constant military escort only. This pool system itself had its antecedents following the Grenada operation in 1983, where the media had been denied access altogether.[11] Which means it was used for the first time only during the US operation in Panama.[12] These rules in effect ensured full control by the military of all news coverage. Similar press control applied to British reporters covering the UK's 30,000 troops in the Gulf, while French reporters were obliged individually to sign a statement accepting restrictions on their freedom of movement.[13]

One of the results according to veteran war correspondent Malcolm Browne is that 'For most news people most of the time, the Gulf war has been played out in the Dahran International Hotel'. In his description, during the first month of the war 'Americans in camouflage uniforms sprawl indolently over sofas facing an array of television monitors, where it seems the war never ends: cruise missiles whiz down Baghdad streets, howitzer and tank guns boom, military briefers sum up from Riyadh . . . and commentators explain what it all means . . .'.[14] In one notable exception, when CBS correspondent Bob Simon and his TV crew tried to get near the action relying on their own resources, they were apprehended by the Iraqis and jailed for the duration of the war. Most daily reports from Saudi Arabia consequently were filmed against the backdrop of hotel swimming pools, with correspondents covering the action from Baghdad (and occasionally from Tel-Aviv), doing 'stand-ups' from their hotel windows, against darkened skies lit up by incoming Scud missiles.

GROUND-FIGHTING

The third phase of the Gulf confrontation, the land war, began on 23 February and ended after only five days. During this time Kuwait was 'liberated' and Iraqi ground forces surrounded, hit hard or allowed to retreat. In preceding weeks, while the Iraqi ruler and his propaganda machine were threatening to defeat the 'infidel' coalition forces in the name of Islam, President Bush had been comparing Iraq's armed forces to those of the Third Reich. In the United States, the news media gave a good deal of attention to dire predictions about the outcome of an imminent ground war. Edward Luttwak, an often quoted 'defence expert', for example, warned 'the widely circulated estimates of 30,000 US casualties, including 10,000 killed, are becoming credible' and that 'at more than 5,000, Iraq's tank force is greater than what any coalition could possibly transport and deploy against it'.[15] Contrary to these predictions, the ground war was over almost before it had started. So swift that there was no time for the ugliness of war to emerge. Moreover, the number of US casualties proved minimal.

One can only speculate as to the possible impact of media coverage had the war dragged on. As it happened, media representatives could hardly catch up with events, and, for the most part, were not even allowed near them. Less than one in seven out of approximately the thousand journalists covering the war were ever allowed even near the scene of action.[16]

THE VIETNAM SYNDROME: BLAMING THE MEDIA

Ever since the end of the war in Vietnam, blaming the media, and television in particular, for whatever went wrong in its conduct has become a part of American political discourse. Television, according to this argument, bears direct responsibility for the American public's disenchantment with the war, as well as for its continued loss of confidence in the prowess of American armed forces. Subsequent administrations have even come to exploit this notion in their dealings with a more hostile Press, notwithstanding a great deal of evidence to the contrary.

In fact, the majority of media representatives covering the Vietnam war rarely diverged from the official version.[17] Most reports originated in the 'Five o'clock Follies', as daily briefings by US military spokesmen in Saigon were derisively termed.[18] Briefing the Press at a safe distance from where the actual fighting was going on, therefore long precedes the Gulf War. Moreover, in the case of Vietnam, journalists began diverging from the official line at a relatively late stage, only when they began to go after information on their own and realize that stories originating from official sources, in Saigon as well as in Washington, did not necessarily reflect the truth. As a result, the administration lost credibility.

On the other hand, it should be pointed out that, even though military censorship did not exist officially in Vietnam, there is no record of any operation compromised as a result of Press coverage. Out of more than two thousand sets of press credentials issued during the war in Vietnam, only six were revoked for damage to military security.[19] When asked to recall the name of even one journalist breaching security in Vietnam, Henry Kissinger replied: 'I can think of some reporting that jeopardized national security, but none in the field'.[20] What Kissinger had in mind were leaks out of Washington.

Criticism of the administration's policy in Vietnam also did not originate within the media, merely reflecting a change in the public mood and national consensus, which gradually turned against the war.[21] It was while covering Vietnam that the Press began to adopt an adversary position towards the government, refusing to accept its versions at face value and ready to 'rock the boat' on matters of foreign and military policy. It was from this position that the Press proceeded to publish the Pentagon Papers and to uncover the Watergate affair, encouraged by the 1967 Freedom of Information Act, subsequently reinforced by the US Supreme Court ruling as legal, the publication of the Pentagon Papers by the *New York Times*.[22]

This trend towards greater openness and transparency in national security policymaking continued throughout the 1970s, only to be reversed during the Reagan Administration. The decision to keep the Press out of Grenada is but one example. According to Hedrick Smith, a former Washington bureau chief of the *New York Times*, the Reagan White House engaged in 'the most sweeping efforts of any modern administration to restrict the flow of information in peacetime'.[23] It also limited the scope of the Freedom of Information Act and increased the quantity of classified information; it even sanctioned the reclassifying of information already in the public domain.[24] As a result, the Reagan Administration was successful in keeping secret its activities in Central America, and almost succeeded in the Iran–Contra affair, which did not reach the American Press until divulged by a small Lebanese publication.[25] By the same token, British success in the Falklands and US success in Grenada were ascribed to the Press having been kept at arms length.[26]

The Bush Administration's handling of the media during the Gulf War can only be understood against this background. The question remains, however, why the media allowed themselves to be manipulated to such an extent? To answer this question one has to look at changes that have occurred in the nature of news and the manner in which it has come to be gathered and presented, as amply manifested in the course of the Gulf War.

CNN: TECHNOLOGY AND THE END OF FREE JOURNALISM

Foremost among these changes is the advent of CNN, with the illusion of omnipresence and live reporting it has created. While the war lasted, praise of the network was almost unqualified. On January 28, *US News & World Report* Atlanta correspondent Matthew Cooper wrote that

> The gulf war has established CNN as an entirely new kind of global information system – an intelligence network that serves not only 70 million households but also world leaders. Both Defense Secretary Dick Cheney and Joint Chiefs of Staff Chairman Colin Powell dubbed CNN the best source for discovering the extent of the Baghdad bombing . . . Saddam Hussein reportedly has all his bunker TVs tuned to the network. Iraqi officials often delay press conferences until CNN reporters arrive. Jordan's King Hussein has ordered his royal staff to monitor CNN around the clock. . . .[27]

Writing in *Time*, on the same day, Susan Tifft pointed out that CNN was supplier of news in 103 countries, and was seen in offices and hotels throughout the Middle East.[28]

Yet even before the war was over, observers began to express doubts. Thus, in an article published on the op-ed page of the *New York Times* on 22 February, David Halberstam admitted his addiction to watch 'the dazzling technology of this war, covered live and in color by satellite', but noted that immediacy did not necessarily mean better, more thoughtful, reporting

> For if the technology has improved, then the editing function, the cumulative sense of judgment – the capacity of network news

executives to decide what to use and how to use it, and how to blend the nonvisual and visual – has declined in precise ratio to the improvement in technology.[29]

With the end of the war Elihu Katz, writing with the advantage of hindsight, believes that 'there was non-stop information without interpretation, and non-stop interpretation without information'. Unlike the other networks, Katz points out, CNN uses satellite connections not only to collect news but to distribute it as well.

> At first glance this sounds like the ideal deployment of new media technology. The only trouble is that it eliminates the editor . . . the CNN ideal is to do simultaneous, almost live editing, or better yet, no editing at all. CNN journalism almost wants to be wrong.[30]

What both Halberstam and Katz fail to point out is that CNN's *modus operandi* afforded the powers-that-be a perfect setting to control and manipulate its output. This has been true not only in the case of Iraq, where Peter Arnett's every movement was strictly controlled, the electronic equipment he used permanently monitored and his output fully censored. It was no less true on the other side: CNN reporters, in Saudi Arabia as well as in Israel, could only broadcast from where they were permitted to venture. Briefings by generals were relayed again and again, as was information provided by the Pentagon to CNN's defence reporter in Washington, much of which turned out to be patently false. It is true that some experts called upon to interpret events did not endorse the administration's policy; but enough was said by other experts and by government spokesmen so that the official line prevailed.

Although it is usually believed that the development of new technologies has improved television's ability to cover events round the world, this is not entirely the case. Minicams and satellite broadcasting actually compromise to the quality of coverage. 'Because it is now possible to fly a crew to the scene of a crisis and instantaneously send back information, television is even more addicted to "parachute journalism" than before'.[31] Another reason are the prohibitive costs of maintaining permanent foreign correspondents and news bureaus around the world. Reporters having no time to develop contacts and a variety of sources, and those whose knowledge of any given country is doubtful, will depend almost entirely on information handed them by official sources.

Of the legions of correspondents present in Saudi Arabia during the war, only a handful had any knowledge about the country and its complexities. Nor were they able to speak Arabic. As there had been little demand for military correspondents since Vietnam, few of them were available to cover the Gulf War.[32] Not many among the news personnel crowding the daily briefings held by the generals therefore possessed the necessary expertise to ask them questions which might have spoiled their show.[33] The military, on the other hand, had been preparing for just such a contingency. Soon after Vietnam the US army had begun to train its personnel in techniques of 'marketing the military viewpoint, primarily by seeing to it that only "upbeat" reports went to the public'.[34]

Furthermore, as mentioned earlier, the pool system afforded the military complete logistic control over the news media. Out of nearly a thousand reporters and camera crew members, accredited by the military in Saudi Arabia, of which some 80 per cent were American or working for American news-organizations, only about 125 were allowed into the pools; the rest were officially banned from the front lines. Even then, pool reports had to be cleared with the military before being filed.

THE POLITICAL AGENDA IS SET BY THE GOVERNMENT

All of the elements and restrictions discussed here contributed towards shaping the quality of reporting during the Gulf War. Ultimately, however, the nature of coverage was determined by the basic fact, so often obscured by government and media alike, that in matters concerning foreign policy, particularly in wartime, governments have the last say. At its best, the media can succeed in exposing flaws in the execution of policy, or in the arguments proposed to justify it. For the most part, however, media exposures have little effect on policy itself. To quote Philip Geyelin, who edited the *Washington Post*'s editorial page throughout the 1970s:

> The presumption of authority as well as credibility, ordinarily gives the government the high ground. Yet another built-in advantage to the government is its monopoly on secret intelligence and classified information – its ability to say, as government officials have so often said to those in the media, something to the general effect of "If-you-only-knew-what-we-know".[35]

Needless to say, this monopoly is especially crucial in wartime, when it is reinforced by the public's acquiescence to prior restraint on the media so as not to encourage demoralization or otherwise hamper the war effort.

As a general rule, even in democratic regimes, governments tend to use what *they* define as a threat to the security of the nation to engender support and achieve consensus. For most of the century, and in most countries including the United States, the media went along, voluntarily refraining from 'rocking the boat' on issues of foreign and military policy in times of crisis. Examples to the contrary, where the media assumed an adversary position to government policy, are the exception: in the USA and Vietnam, in France during the Indo-China and Algerian wars, and in Israel over the Lebanon war.[36] Common to each is that (a) the military action was prolonged, and (b) the war ended badly for the outside intervening power.

The pattern, therefore, does not repeat itself in the Gulf, where the fighting was short and the coalition did triumph. Besides, President Bush had the upper hand in contending with the media by deliberately exercising another prerogative borrowed from the Second World War experience: government's ability to define the meaning of information and to determine the symbolic setting in which it is to be placed. This helped avoid evoking the Vietnam trauma of dissonance and dissent; it also overcame the wish of doves, and some of the media, to avoid armed combat by condemning their appeasement of a new Hitler.[37] By using World War II as a model and by presenting Iraq as a military power almost equal to the USA, the President could tell the public that 'this was no longer just a confrontation of ideologies; it was a moral crusade of good against evil'.[38] Accordingly, defeat of Baghdad became a prerequisite for the survival of Western civilization. Saddam Hussein, flattered by this designation as a leading world military power, unwittingly played into Bush's hands.

Casting Saddam Hussein in the role of a latter-day Hitler enabled the President to divert media attention from the plight of the Iraqi civilian population, even though correspondents stationed in Baghdad were reporting it. Somewhat ironically, the World War II frame was also evoked by CNN reporters Bernard Shaw and, at a later stage, Peter Arnett, whose broadcasts from Baghdad reminded more than one observer of Edward R. Murrow's famous broadcasts during the London blitz.[39]

When it later became clear that Saddam's army was nothing like the army of the Third Reich, it was Bush himself who discarded the World War II frame. He could thus go back on his previous pledge to fight to the finish and eliminate the Iraqi despot.

One can only speculate on what would have happened had the war taken a different turn, or dragged on. Nonetheless, an indication of how the media might have performed in such an event might be found in the role they played after the war ended, in connection with the Kurdish revolt in northern Iraq. Unlike their colleagues during the war itself, journalists covering the plight of the Kurds fleeing Iraqi persecution were left alone to do their job without interference. Coverage of the massacre and exodus of the Kurds, dramatically and tellingly featured on television, generated public pressure resulting in the slowdown of America's withdrawal from Iraq and the actual dispatching of troops to help the victims.[40]

In this case, government, by intent or by default, relinquished its hold on the media, thereby enabling the latter, for its part, to demonstrate its potential for independently influencing both public opinion and policy. This worked, however, by creating an emotional rather than rational policy setting, illustrating that 'when it comes to pictures of human distress, the camera is not patriotic. It favours the victim who happens to be in focus'.[41]

NOTES

1 James Bennet, 'How the media missed the story' in Micah L. Sifry and Christopher Cerf (eds), *The Gulf War Reader*, New York: Times Books, 1991, pp. 355–67.

2 The letter was written by Alex Molnar, professor of education at the University of Wisconsin. It was publicized widely. Reprinted in *Gulf War Reader*, pp. 207–9.

3 Lawrence K. Grossman, 'A television plan for the next war', *Nieman Reports*, vol. XLV no. 2, Summer 1991 pp. 27–31.

4 William Safire, 'The Hitler analogy' *New York Times*, 24 August 1990, reprinted in *Gulf War Reader*, see Note 1, pp. 210–12. The term 'triage' is defined by Safire as 'the most excruciating choice faced by ethical people' for example, when someone, in an overcrowded field hospital has to decide which of the wounded is to be saved.

5 Elaine Sciolino, 'Iraq's propaganda may seem crude, but it's effective' *New York Times*, 9 September 1990.

6 On more than one occasion, in recent years, US television organizations, when faced with the dilemma of affording a platform to hostile spokesmen at the cost of losing an exclusive story, have chosen the first alternative.

7 Elihu Katz, 'The end of journalism: notes on watching the war' forthcoming.

8 Grossman, op. cit. (see Note 3).

9 Ken Burns, 'The painful, essential images of war', *New York Times*, (arts and leisure section) 27 January 1991.

10 David Ohana, 'The camera is the new frontier', *Ha'aretz*, 20 September 1991 (in Hebrew).

11 Winant Sidle, (Maj. Gen.) 'The public's right to know', *US Naval Institute Proceedings*, July 1985.

12 Peter Andrews, 'The media and the military', *American Heritage*, July/August 1991, pp. 75–8.

13 *Time*, 21 January 1991, p. 27.

14 Malcolm W. Browne, 'The military vs. the Press', *New York Times Magazine*, 3 March 1991, p. 28.

15 H. Joachim Maitre, 'Journalistic incompetence', *Nieman Reports*, Summer 1991, pp. 12–13.

16 Browne, op. cit. Note 14, p. 29–30.

17 Peter Braestrup, *Big Story*, New York: Anchor Books, 1978, ch. 1.

18 David Halberstam, *The Powers that Be*, New York: Dell Edition, 1979, pp. 699–711.

19. Andrews, op.cit., Note 12.

20 Quoted in Sydney H. Shanberg, 'A muzzle for the Press' in *Gulf War Reader*, see Note 1, p. 371.

21 Halberstam, op. cit., Note 18.

22 *New York Times Co.* vs. *United States*, 403 U.S. 713 (1971).

23 Hedrick Smith, *The Power Game*, New York, Ballentine Books, 1988, p. 432.

24 Floyd Abrams, 'The new effort to control information', *New York Times Magazine*, 25 September 1983.

25 An elaborate attempt by the Reagan Administration to topple Gaddafi through consistent manipulation of the media, is described at length by Gregory R. Nokes in his paper 'Libya: a government story' published in Simon Serfaty (ed.) *The Media and Foreign Policy*, New York: St Martin's Press, 1990, pp. 33–46.

26 Sidle, op. cit., Note 11.

27 Matthew Cooper, 'The very nervy win of CNN', *US News & World Report*, 28 January 1991, p. 44.

28 Susan Tifft, 'Far ahead of the pack', *Time*, 28 January 1991, p. 37.

29 David Halberstam, 'Television and the instant enemy', reprinted in *Gulf War Reader*, pp. 385–91.

30 Katz. op. cit., Note 7.

31 David R. Gergen, 'Diplomacy in a television age: the dangers of a teledemocracy', in Simon Serfaty (ed.), *The Media and Foreign Policy*, New York: St Martin's Press, 1990, pp. 47–64.

32 Maitre, op. cit., Note 15, pp. 13–16.

33 Peter Braestrup, quoted in *Columbia Journalism Review*, March/April 1991.

34 Reported by Tom Wicker in the *New York Times*, quoted by Grossman, op. cit., Note 3, p. 28.

35 Philip L. Geyelin, 'The Strategic Defense Initiative: the President's story', in Simon Serfaty (ed.) *The Media and Foreign Policy*, New York: St Martin's Press, 1990, pp. 19–32.

36 Dina Goren, 'Beyond censorship: informal methods of directing media coverage in security matters', in Shimon Shetreet (ed.) *Free Speech and National Security*, Dordrecht: Martinus Nijhoff, 1991, pp. 195–203.

37 As has been shown by Daniel Hallin, US media were, for decades, using the Cold War as a frame in order to package the wars in Korea, Vietnam and Central America as ideological wars fought in order to hold the Communist threat in check. See Daniel Hallin, 'Hegemony: the American

news media from Vietnam to El Salvador: a study of ideological change and its limits', in David Paletz (ed.), *Political Communication Research: Approaches, Studies, Assessments*, Norwood, New Jersey: Ablex, 1987, pp. 3–25. By the time of the Gulf War, the Cold War frame was no longer available.

38 Katz, op. cit., Note 7.
39 Tifft. op. cit., Note 28.
40 Daniel Schorr, 'Ten days that shook the White House', *Columbia Journalism Report*, July/August 1991, pp. 21–23.
41 Walter Goodman, 'TV flexes its muscles and takes some punches', *New York Times*, 24 February 1991.

Part V

Future prospects for calm after the storm

16 Conflict resolution under the veil of uncertainty: the Middle East

Gad Barzilai and Gideon Doron

INTRODUCTION

One of the most discussed issues in the course of the Gulf crisis was the Arab–Palestinian–Israeli conflict and its possible linkage to termination of the Gulf crisis. The results of that war are complex, and yet two developments stand out clearly: the first is American hegemony in the Middle East; and the second, the potential for an American-led regional alliance in the Middle East, composed of Israel and those Arab states – Egypt, Jordan, Saudi Arabia and Syria including Lebanon – which endorsed America's military and political-diplomatic efforts during the crisis. The purpose of this chapter is to deal with the possibilities for resolving the Arab–Palestinian–Israeli conflict in light of these two changes in the aftermath of the shared Gulf experience. Also to provide a theoretical framework through which regional instability can best be understood.

Termination of compound conflicts involving more than two political actors has not been adequately analysed in the literature of conflict resolution, in part because such situations, by their very complexity, discourage the integration of theoretical models with empirical fact.[1] When a compound conflict features additional intervening variables like territory, religion, nationalism, economic and cultural elements – as is the case of the conflict in the Middle East[2] – scholarship usually opts for detailed historical and situational narrative over theory and generalization. Hence, very little systematic research guided by theory has been conducted on Middle East conflict.

Interstate and intercommunal conflicts, including wars, are a familiar phenomenon in the Middle East dating back to biblical times. In the twentieth century and especially after World War II, a salient pattern of aggression sems to have emerged between principal as well as marginal regional political units. Israel, established in 1948, has been directly involved in many, but not all, those conflicts which contribute to regional instability. Arab and Palestinian enmity has been conducive to what may be defined as 'a cycle of aggression'; Israel is found to have been involved in at least one 'all-out war' with one or all of her Arab neighbours in each decade. Beyond the Israel–Arab conflict zone, Syria, Iraq and Egypt initiated or were involved in wars against Lebanon, Kuwait, and Yemen respectively. The Palestinians too, were responsible for a comparable 'cycle of aggression' in Jordan and Lebanon during the 1970s and 1980s.

Our analysis concentrates on structural relationships existing at two levels: between the local actors, and between them and the superpowers. We endorse Gilpin's assertion that power distributions determine international structure.[3] Yet, because his approach is too heavily based on formal cost-benefit analysis – a method which often relies on a set of empirically unrealistic assumptions and inaccurate data[4] – it falls short of providing an entirely satisfactory explanation, forcing us to take a somewhat different route.

Two concepts borrowed from game theory are found to aid in understanding the emergence and prevalence of Middle East conflicts: 'balance of power' and 'equilibrium' between the local antagonists. Our main thesis is that regional instability derives from the ultimate ineffectiveness of the bipolar international system which so affected this part of the world until the late 1980s. The US–USSR global rivalry spilled over to rivalry between the regional actors, each closely associated with one or the other superpower. While the latter were able to enforce stabilized relationships within their respective group of client states, they were far less effective in imposing stability between members of different groups, and between them and states not identified with one or other superpower.

These interrelated layers of relationships between the superpowers, between the regional political units, and between the superpowers and the regional units, have changed most significantly. Since 1988, when the United States, almost by forfeit, achieved regional hegemony, this uncontested new American status – only further underscored in the Gulf contest – is conducive to attaining stability, peace and even cooperation among traditional rival states.

CAUSES OF REGIONAL INSTABILITY: WHEN THE TAIL WAGS THE DOG

While the Ottoman empire ruled the Middle East, for four centuries ending in World War I, the region was considered relatively stable in comparison to Europe where such a central hegemonial power did not exist. Between the two World Wars Britain and France shared responsibility for the area. Under their supervision international borders were redefined and new states created. Lebanon, Jordan and Kuwait are three examples of states that emerged from larger political units (Syria, Palestine and Iraq respectively) as a result of arbitrary choices made in London and Paris, often insensitive to ethnic distributions. Nor did they necessarily take into account historical and territorial claims that were subsequently to become a constant source of regional tension. Thus, in the 1990s Damascus continues to treat Lebanon as an integral part of 'greater Syria';[5] some Israeli politicians regard East Bank Jordan as the true Palestinian homeland and ultimate solution to the Arab–Israeli conflict;[6] while Iraq of course, justified seizure of Kuwait on 2 August 1990, as simply reclaiming her rightful, historical 'nineteenth province'.

Britain and France then stepped aside to make room for the new emerging US and Soviet hegemonial contenders, whose Middle East involvement took place gradually, filling the vacuum created in the 1950s by withdrawal of the European powers. By then the two newcomers found themselves increasingly involved in supporting various political and client states.[7]

Cold War competition and containment turned the Middle East into a veritable strategic zone of confrontation, until the area became a mere reflection of the basic bipolar structure of the international system as a whole. Indeed, the rigid superpower relationship in the eastern Mediterranean came to resemble a zero-sum game, whereby a loss of influence in one country, Egypt for example, by the Soviets would be considered a direct gain by the Americans. Likewise, when a regional actor scored over another in a local dispute the superpower patron rightly perceived the victory as its own. Thus, for instance, Israel's achievements during the 'war of attrition' with Egypt were considered by the Nixon Administration as their own victory over the Russians.[8] Consequently, the administration rewarded Israel with a sizeable assistance package.[9]

Nonetheless, in time both superpowers learned to regard total victory in the region as merely one alternative to total defeat. Each increasingly came up against both domestic and contextual limitations imparing their manoeuvrability. The Soviets were aware of their economic disadvantage compared to the USA, just as American decision-makers confronted deep anti-colonial sentiments especially in the Arab and Muslim countries. Against these cultural, ideological and economic constraints, each superpower attempted to optimize gains by enlarging its sphere of influence, and by minimizing the influence of its rival, and frustrating the other side's ability to cause damage.

As it turned out, non-alignment and neutrality, Yugoslavian or Indian-style, proved a clear failure in the Middle East because the assertive superpowers left the smaller local countries no choice. Indeed, dependency by this region on the superpowers became its most distinctive trait. But, by way of compensation, or retribution, the pressures exerted by the developing countries on the superpowers were heavy, and their desire for ongoing economic and military assistance equally insatiable.

Interestingly, both superpowers deduced their respective regional strategies from similar core defensive objectives. Perceived safety represented the main common objective for Americans and Soviets alike. Russian traditional concern for the security of its southern border led them to consider the Middle East as crucial. And although direct territorial security cannot be offered as an American rationale, it too showed an eagerness to develop a strong military presence in the Mediterranean–Persian Gulf rim as a function of responsibility towards southern Europe, NATO allies and Middle East friendly regimes. Characteristic, however, of action–reaction spirals, America's naval presence infringed on the sense of safety desired by the Soviets, who, in countering this perceived threat, sought for, and then exploited any 'opening' in the region. They thus penetrated Egypt, the largest Arab state, by offering a major arms deal in 1955, and by sponsoring construction of the Aswan Dam. In the 1960s and 1970s other Arab countries like Syria and Iraq (as well as the PLO) became integral parts of the Soviet regional coalition.

That the regimes in these countries embraced an anti-colonial, anti-West brand of Arab socialist ideology made it easier for the Soviets to legitimize their involvement. However, they did not lose sight of their real interests, consistently avoiding potential ideological disputes and maintaining good relations with Arab regimes that repressed local supporters of communism.[10]

Safety or security are abstract objectives needing to be translated into operational terms. In this respect, American regional goals overall are found to have been different, more specific, and often diametrically opposed to those of the Russians. America is committed to the security of Israel; it wishes to guarantee a free flow of Arab oil to the West; and, it wished to check the expansion of Soviet influence in the region.[11] The priority assigned each of these varied from one administration to another. Thus, the Eisenhower Administration was less committed to Israel's security than say, the Johnson or Nixon

Administrations; nor was the Kennedy White House as preoccupied with the oil goal as later ones. Similarly, regional policies dominated by the anti-Soviet objective also varied in intensity and means of execution depending on the administration in office.

Stability, often cited as a primary American objective,[12] is more of a means than a goal in itself. When interest dictated, certain acts were designed to produce counter-stabilizing effects, with CIA activities in Iran in 1953 leading to the downfall of Premier Musaddeq indicative of actions intended to change a prevailing status quo.[13] The 1991 War in the Gulf fits this model.

During the Johnson Administration, Israel came to be valued as an American ally. But because of strong Arab opposition, the American coalition had to be built in the 1970s without Israel's formal participation, Iran and Saudi Arabia substituting for it as a major pillar. Nonetheless, when the United States wanted to support its coalition partners without being directly involved, Israel was called upon to provide her services.[14]

Thus, for example, when the PLO and Syria threatened the survival of the Jordanian regime in September 1970, President Nixon and Secretary Kissinger orchestrated with Israel the latter's deployment of troops on the Syrian border to assure King Hussein's regime – formally an enemy of Israel, a member of the Arab confrontation states and a country that only three years earlier had fought against the Jewish state.[15] Seymour Hersh[16] summarized this strange turn of events as follows:

> Kissinger and Nixon, exhilarated by their successful showdown with the Soviet Union, would continue – until forced otherwise, to view the basic problem in the Middle East as one of containing the Soviets and its client states . . . Israel was seen as a bulwark of that policy. A regional American partner willing to intervene without questions on behalf of the Nixon–Kissinger view of the world.

American and Soviet strategists shared one other important mutual interest in the region. Both resolved to act quickly to contain any local dispute from escalating to the international level,[17] which served as a major restraint on local quarrels. Hence, the parameters or 'rules of the game' guiding internal regional conflicts, even those considered 'total wars,' became well established; two in particular:

1 Established boundaries of a regional state are not to be changed through war;

2 No foreign or regional power can intervene uninvited in another regional state.

These conventions for regulating the scope and intensity of conflict between regional members are found to have been violated on two occasions: Israel captured Arab lands during the 1967 war, and Iraq unilaterally invaded Kuwait in 1990. Otherwise, foreign aggressors were either invited by the legitimate authority in the states they entered, or they returned occupied land after the dispute was over. Arab summits, UN rulings, or threatened direct involvement by one of the two superpowers served as sufficient inducement for the fighting parties to follow the above specified rules. Even Israel's intervention in Lebanon in 1982, as well as repeated Syrian entry into the country, came only after one side or another in the conflict asked the external regional power for help.[18]

The record shows that regional instability, is not solely a function of Israel, nor is it limited to state aggression activated by territorial ambitions. So too, have the interests of the regional states often precipitated local disputes without regard for the interest of one or both superpowers and often in direct opposition to them. Israel's decision to invade Lebanon in 1982 was not necessarily compatible with American interests, although it has been argued that Secretary of State Haig 'gave the green light to Minister Sharon'.[19] Again, Syria's decision to participate in the 1973 war is believed to have been taken against the advice of the Soviets.

The U.S.S.R. wanted to restrain Arab enthusiasm from bringing about an American reaction that might harm Soviet interests or develop into a confrontation, or an Israeli reaction (e.g. nuclear strike) that might develop into a dangerous complication for the Arabs and the Soviets.[20]

Such unilateral and unendorsed local initiatives eventually forced the superpowers to coordinate their efforts more closely in keeping a lid on ubiquitous disputes.

Regional instability in the Middle East was also a function of the structural relationship between each superpower and the members of its regional coalition. When members of one coalition were in dispute with members of another, the potential for conflict increased greatly, because communication between antagonists from different coalitions was mostly indirect; signals and messages on reducing local tensions passed through the superpowers, making the flow of information slow, indirect and beholden to third parties. And because the superpowers

		Soviet Coalition	
		A	NA
American	A	1 ; 1	4 ; 2
Coalition	NA	2 ; 4	3 ; 3

Figure 16.1 The 'chicken' game
Note: A and NA denote an aggressive and non-aggressive strategy respectively. The numbers denote values of outcomes obtained from strategy choices made by the players, where four is the best outcome and one is the worst.

often had their own separate agendas, local disputes tended not to be suppressed but rather encouraged, in accordance with the 'chicken' game, or paradigm.[21] This game is presented in Figure 16.1.

The game of chicken has no dominant strategy, one which would yield better outcomes than those possible by a choice of an alternative strategy. The game's outcome, known as Nash Equilibrium, is not unique and therefore is not stable.[22] In fact, chicken results in either (4 ; 2) or (2 ; 4) outcomes. The outcome 1 ; 1 which is the worst for the two players and may be the consequence of unlimited war (i.e. a mutual choice in aggressive strategies) is spared from the players by the structural rules imposed by the superpowers and the players themselves as described above. A (3 ; 3) outcome, too, is unreachable because players have incentives to break out of the equilibrium resulting from mutual non-aggressive choices and obtain a better result through aggression. Thus, the overall equilibrium was an aggregation of the following preferences:

S (Stability) > L (Limited War) > P (Peace) > A (All-out War)

The events preceding and following the 1973 October War serve as illustration. When Israel emerged triumphant in 1967, the equilibrium which resulted (4 ; 3) was unacceptable to Egypt and Syria. Relying on Soviet military assistance, they attempted to alter the outcome; the 'war of attrition' represented an unsuccessful attempt to obtain a (2 ; 4) result. They tried again in October 1973, but again, with US backing, Israel maintained its dominant position and territorial holdings. Indeed, so successful was the Israeli counter-offensive and deep thrust into Egypt that Moscow demanded Israel accept an immediate ceasefire and threatened direct military intervention. To which the United States reacted by declaring a nuclear alert.[23] A potential (1 ; 1) outcome could have resulted. The superpower lesson was patently clear – the inperative need to prevent similar situations in the future.

		Egypt	
		A	NA
Israel	A 2 ; 2		4 ; 1
	NA 1 ; 4		3 ; 3

Figure 16.2 The prisoners' dilemma game between Israel and Egypt
Note: Labels of strategies and value of outcomes are the same as in Figure 16.1.

DETERMINANTS OF REGIONAL STABILITY: WHEN THE DOG WAGS THE TAIL

It is possible for stability to be imposed when mutual superpower interests dictate local stability. In 1956 the Russians and Americans forced Britain, France and Israel to relinquish their achievements. However, in a bipolar context, when local gains are interpreted from a zero-sum perspective, symmetrical interests as a basis for cooperation are hard to come by. True, superpowers, even when acting alone, or in coordination with the UN, can move independently to prevent or to terminate a conflict not of their own making. Yet, if one of the superpowers is pleased at developments on the battlefield, it may be slow to intervene.

It is comparatively easier for the superpowers to restrain their own coalition partners, even those with a tendency to fight against each other, than those in the rival camp. In 1967, even though perceived of as a Western ally, Jordan went to war against Israel. Syria, a member of the Soviet coalition, fought the PLO another member, in Lebanon during the 1970s and 1980s.[24] Nonetheless, in-house conflicts can be more effectively stabilized simply because the superpowers need not regard preferences and potential reactions of the other global power. A superpower also can provide regional players with positive incentives, encouraging them to act in a non-aggressive manner.[25] Upon their refusal, the superpower has the capacity to impose its own preferences on the local players, thus inducing them to adopt stabilizing policies. The circumstances that led Egypt to move from the Soviet-led regional coalition in the early 1970s to the American side illustrate this point.

The decision by President Sadat in 1972 to expel the Soviets from Egypt may have led to the 1973 War, assuming Moscow had refused to sanction Sadat's choice of war;[26] but it also constituted the first step in a long journey ultimately resulting in a peace treaty between Israel and Egypt in 1979.[27] The peace agreement is an important milestone,[28] and an indirect derivative of these early developments,[29] that is best captured by the 'prisoners' dilemma' game[30] presented in Figure 16.2.

The game in Figure 16.2 has a unique and stable equilibrium because each player has a dominant strategy (aggressive). The outcome of the game when both players choose their best strategy is the equilibrium (2 ; 2). The equilibrium outcome (3 ; 3) is better for both, but because it results from the selection of a non-dominated strategy it cannot be the outcome of the game. Such an outcome may be obtained only when a third party intervenes and enforces his own preference on the players. In other words, a change in the rules of the game caused by the inclusion of outsiders enables movement from an aggressive to non-aggressive equilibrium. This happened in 1979 when the peace treaty was concluded.

The main problem to be solved in a prisoners' dilemma type game is the absence of trust between the players. The two parties to the conflict need not trust each other to affect a cooperative outcome (3 ; 3) when they can rely on the services of a third party. The third party should be willing to deliver them. President Sadat understood this point well. In fact he said that '99.9% of the cards in the Middle East game' are in the hands of the Americans.[31] Jimmy Carter was willing to play his hand. The assurances both regional countries received in the form of monitoring stations and actual American presence in the Sinai, as well as long-term commitments for foreign aid and military assistance contributed to stability and cooperation between the former antagonists. Consequently, they have much to lose and little to gain from violating the peace agreement.

The structural relationship described above need not result in a cooperative outcome of the (3 ; 3) type, nor need it lead to a formal peace agreement. Since 1967, both Israel and Jordan, members in the Western coalition, are locked in a stable (2 ; 2) equilibrium. Although there were many meetings between the leaders of these two states and even one explicit agreement (the so-called London Document signed in 1987) detailing their future relationship, stability could be obtained *de facto* but not *de jure*. This is because the leaders of the two states and of the United States are apparently still not convinced that formal peace is preferable to practical stability.

TOWARD COOPERATIVE REGIONAL EQUILIBRIUM

The analysis shows that certain conditions and structures to induce stable regional equilibrium are more compatible than others. Such conditions have prevailed in the Middle East since 1988, and were reinforced following the Gulf crisis.

Mikhail Gorbachev's decision to end the Cold War resulted, among other things, in a drastic reduction of military and financial support to the Kremlin's Middle East regional allies. Regional allies were led to understand they could no longer rely on the free, automatic support of the Soviets in their local disputes.[32] This paved the way for the United States to become the regional superpower. Since acts of state aggression are difficult to conduct – and conduct successfully – without superpower support, the likelihood of their occurrence has been reduced, as Saddam Hussein can confirm.

Thus, the new equilibrium has been the aggregation of the following preferences:

S (stability) $>$ P (peace) $>$ L (limited war) $>$ A (all-out war)

Such an inference stands, of course, in direct contradiction to the outbreak of the 1991 war in the Gulf involving Iraq and the American-led international coalition. In 1988, Iraq emerged from eight years of war with Iran – a war closely monitored by the Soviets fearing danger to their southern borders,[33] and decided to correct historical 'mistakes' and in August 1990 invaded Kuwait. This act violated, in effect, the two institutional rules specified above. By threatening to employ non-conventional means against countries that would try to prevent her from sustaining the new holdings, Iraq was also questioning the validity of the superpower's fear of transforming local conflict into a global one. The Iraqi challenge was taken up by the United States and in the course of forty-two days she and her allies destroyed much of the non-conventional capabilities of the Iraqis, forcing them to leave Kuwait. The Soviet Union did not materially participate in these events, thus strengthening American hegemony in the area.

The political and military capabilities of an American-led international coalition are demonstrated by the Gulf War. Only a direct presidential order from the White House prevented the occupation of Baghdad. Despite disagreements between members of this grand coalition in regard to specific aspects of the military operations, and notwithstanding the tendency of the Arab countries, Syria and Saudi Arabia in particular, to be more restrained than the Bush Administration in defeating Saddam's regime, the general tendency within the international multifarious alliance was that of cooperation and even coordination. Considering the natural obstacles to establishing efficient channels of communication with and between a religious state like Saudi Arabia, a radical state that supported anti-Western terror all over the world as Syria, and moderate Arab states with strong internal Muslim pressures such as Egypt and Morocco, it was a telling American achievement.

Global understanding held together in the primary desire of each participating state to avert what seemed to be Saddam's primary aim of acquiring regional and even international predominance. Facing this fragile coalition, the USA fostered inter-allied understanding by using its ability as superpower to punish an opponent or, alternatively, to reward supportive leaders.

This patience and sensitivity certainly paid off. Saddam's efforts to divide this alliance by, among other means, manipulating Arab and Muslim masses, failed. In this direct confrontation between a regional power and a foreign, Western power, the latter gained wider approval within the Arab world at the height of the crisis. The Bush Administration also demonstrated the right calculation in not striving to occupy Baghdad. By doing so it avoided a severe political crisis, especially as termination of the war neared.

This becomes one of those exceptional cases in history where the end of a war actually paved the way for greater cooperation in the international system and for a new equilibrium. By not humiliating the Arabs and by restraining Israel, the Administration signalled its qualifications as a global monitor over world oil resources, and potential for leading an emerging regional alliance rising above basic differences between Third World and Western industrialized countries. The Arab countries also acquired new hope for addressing their structural economic problems and in identifying a broker for promoting a negotiating process with Israel.

By contrast, little of real substance has changed in the internal political setting of the political players in the aftermath of the war. Traditional modes of relations between rulers and ruled in each of the Middle East countries remain similar to those existing before the war. What has happened though is the transition from Arab dependency on two rival great powers to dependency on a sole superpower with a demonstrated global reach. For the first time in recent history one global actor has power to oversee regional developments without intimidation by a rival external power, thus profoundly influencing economic, military and political patterns.

On the other hand, the cost to the Middle East countries was marginal. None of the Arab countries participating in the American-led alliance nor Israel have had to compromise their core political positions. The evolution of the negotiations between Syria (and Lebanon), Egypt, Jordan, the Palestinians (including the PLO) and Israel owes more to American persuasion than to self-initiated policy revisions.

Nonetheless, the larger, extra-regional structural changes have had their significant impact. The ability of the USA to be considered an honest broker has forced Israeli and Arab negotiators gradually to enter into channels of unprecedented communication ranging from mutual appearances before the international mass media to exchanging position papers and draft proposals, and even to direct conversations. This could not have happened in the earlier Cold War structure of polarization, when the Arab countries and Israel were subordinated to the status of proxies for the rival superpowers.

Since 1988, the reduction of Soviet regional influence led to two other developments in the region involving the PLO and Syria. In November 1988, the PLO declared that it rejected terror and was willing to recognize Israel's right to exist within secure borders. This declaration provided the legal grounds for America to begin talks in Tunis with the PLO, from which the Soviets were excluded.[34] Syria, too, benefited from her newly established relationship with America. The Pax-Syrian imposed in Lebanon was accepted by the Americans and was unopposed by the Israelis.

Hence, the new structure which left the United States practically as the sole regional superpower, enabled a more flexible reward/punishment policy towards the local players. Syria and the PLO were rewarded, while Iraq was punished. The intensity of the punishment, as the Gulf crisis shows, depends also on the extent to which local power foci endanger American interests connected to oil production and prices.[35] The extent of the reward, following this crisis, need no longer be significantly dependent on the American ambition to out-match the Soviets, as was the case during the bipolar system in earlier years. Thus, interstate stability in the Middle East following the Gulf crisis is to be dependent upon, and may be obtained through decisions in Washington more than in each of the regional capitals.

Enduring local disputes, whether intercommunal (in Iraq or in the Israeli-held territories, for example) or interstate (Turkey–Iraq, Israel–Lebanon) pose new challenges to the USA, and almost compel it to consolidate America's stand in the Middle East. For any withdrawal by the USA and abrogation of primary responsibility must lead to escalated conflict inimical to worldwide stability and to a more intensive process of nuclearization of the Middle East that is absolutely prejudicial to any world order, new or old.

One must constantly bear in mind when addressing the post-1991 Middle East that this is an area where the combination of religious fundamentalism, political radicalism and nuclear physics do have a real potential for breeding nuclear disaster. Efforts at imposing the ceasefire agreement on Iraq and to dismantle its non-conventional capabilities prove the central role the USA must play, with or without global partners. Revelations about the extent of Iraqi militarization prior to the war are a red alert. Whatever also, arms control – both conventional and nuclear – and demilitarization arrangements must be implemented in the area. Destruction of Iraqi military facilities confirms that a US-led international peace camp also has the practical enforcement means to accomplish such a goal.

The posture of the USA as dominant international broker in the Arab–Israeli conflict will enable it to suggest and enforce linkage between territorial aspects of the dispute and the needs of all the regional political players to reach an understanding regarding non-conventional weapons. Special relations with Israel also enables emphasizing to Jerusalem that only peace will ensure Israel's safety. Similarly, the USA alone can persuade the Arab states that peace with Israel will permit the latter to forgo any nuclear option in favour of diplomacy.

CONCLUSIONS

There are several levels of conflict in the Middle East. In so far as these conflicts exhibit international features the analysis presented identified the United States as a potentially major stabilizing power. The structural relationship between the antagonists and the United States enable such stability. In many ways it is up to the Americans to bring traditional enemies to the negotiating table.

Interstate conflicts are not, however, the only form of disputes in that region. The new hegemonic power can do very little in the short run to control counter-stabilizing effects generated by Islamic fundamentalist religious movement. It is very difficult to resolve conflicts which are defined on religious grounds. Policy positions based on religion usually reflect uncompromising 'objective truths'.[36] In almost every Arab Middle Eastern state these movements have gained in strength in the course of and following the Gulf crisis out of opposition to the American presence and their threat to the stability of the ruling regimes, which cooperated with the USA against Iraq, is quite real. A redistribution of state resources may, however, help modify the potency of these movements. This is because these movements mobilize support from the poor masses. Thus, an improvement in the economic well-being of these masses, an area where the West can certainly help, may perhaps contribute to future stabilization on this dimension.

The Palestinian condition is another unsolved problem which

affects regional stability.[37] Since 1988, this problem can no longer be perceived as a local problem to be taken care of by the Israelis and the Jordanians. Moreover, the Gulf crisis has proved the linkage between different conflicts in the area. On this matter, however, the United States can play a major and decisive role as the analysis in part two shows. It may be less effective but still true in taking an active role in the internal affairs of Lebanon. There, stability may be obtained through the Syrian proxy in coordination with the policies of another regional proxy – Israel. The combined efforts of these two states in Lebanon may result in a learning effect: the local leaders may learn that it is far better to live in peace with each other than in war.

The modern history of the Middle East has shown that superpower intervention and the regional reflections of overall structure of the international global system, are important factors in understanding the sources and dynamics of conflicts and their resolutions. Cultural and personal variables especially in domestic matters should not, however, be ignored. The new international structure constitutes the necessary condition for peace and stability, the right leader, of the Sadat type may add the sufficient dimension.

This is to say that no international structure can breed peace unless some basic micro-level conditions are met. Moderate processes of secularization, democratization trends, balance of deterrence, etc., are all important variables conducive to peace. In the Middle East in the aftermath of the Gulf crisis the new international structure enables these variables to take effect because the imposition of order and peaceful modes of interstate and intercommunal relations is gradually becoming a reality.

NOTES

1 Bruce B. De Mesquita, 'Theories of international conflict: an analysis and appraisal', in Ted Gurr, (ed.), *Handbook of Political Conflict*, New York: Free Press, 1980, pp. 361–98; Richard Mansbach and John Vasques, *In Search of Theory: A New Paradigm for Global Politics*, New York: Columbia University Press, 1981; James Morrow, 'Social choice and system structure in world politics', *World Politics*, vol. XLI, 1, October 1988, pp. 75–97; Bruce Russett, *The Prisoners of Insecurity*, New York: W.H. Freeman, 1983; Kenneth Waltz, *Theory of International Politics*, New York: Random House, 1979.

2 Fred Khouri, *The Arab-Israel Dilemma*, Syracuse, New York: Syracuse University Press, 1985; Yair Evron, *The Middle East*, London: Elek, 1973; David Vital, *Zionism: The Formative Years*, Oxford: Oxford University Press, 1982.

3 Robert Gilpin, *War and Change in World Politics*, New York: Cambridge University Press, 1981.
4 E.J. Mishan, *Cost-Benefit Analysis*, New York: Praeger, 1976.
5 Moshe Bylopolsky, *The Soviet Union in Syria's Strategy*, unpublished MA thesis, Tel-Aviv University, 1990; Yair Evron, *War and Intervention in Lebanon*, London: Croom Helm, 1987.
6 Gideon Doron, 'The principle of "no envy": a rational solution to the Israeli–Palestinian Conflict', *State, Government and International Relations*, 31, Summer 1989, pp. 8–10; Aaron Klieman, *Israel, Jordan, Palestine*, Beverly Hills: Sage Publications, 1981.
7 Elie Kedourie, 'Britain, France, and the Last Phase of the Eastern Question', in J.C. Hurewitz, (ed.), *Soviet-American Rivalry in the Middle East*, New York: Praeger, 1969.
8 Gideon Doron, 'Oil and/or the olive branch: the Nixon Administration choices in its Middle East policies', paper delivered at the Sixth Annual Presidential Conference, New York: Hofstra University, November 1987.
9 Nimrod Novik, *The United States and Israel*, Boulder, Colorado: Westview Press, 1986.
10 John Badeau, 'Internal contest in the Middle East', in J.C. Hurewitz, (ed.) *Soviet-American Rivalry in the Middle East*, New York: Praeger, 1969, pp. 170–86.
11 Gideon Doron, 1987, op. cit., Note 8.
12 American Enterprise Institute, *Conversations with Harold Saunders: U.S. Policy for the Middle East*, Washington DC: AEI, 1982.
13 Kermit Roosevelt, *Countercoup: The Struggle for the Control of Iran*, New York: McGraw-Hill, 1979.
14 Shlomo Aronson, *Conflict and Bargaining in the Middle East*, Baltimore: Johns Hopkins University Press, 1978, p. 126.
15 William Quandt, *Decade of Decisions: American Policy Toward the Arab-Israeli Conflict 1967–1977*, Berkeley: University of California Press, 1977.
16 Seymour Hersh, *The Price of Power: Kissinger in the Nixon White House*, New York: Summit, 1983, p. 249.
17 Zeev Maoz, *Paths to Conflict*, Boulder, Colorado: Westview Press, 1982, pp. 206–7; Abraham Ben-Zvi, *The American Approach to Superpower Collaboration in the Middle East, 1973–1986*, Boulder, Colorado: Westview Press, 1986.
18 John Devlin, 'Syrian policy in the aftermath of the Israeli invasion of Lebanon', in Robert Freedman, (ed.), *The Middle East After the Israeli Invasion of Lebanon*, Syracuse, New York: Syracuse University Press, 1986, pp. 299–322.
19 R.K. Ramazani, 'The impact of Khomeini's Iran', in Robert Freedman, (ed.), *The Middle East after the Israeli Invasion of Lebanon*, Syracuse, New York: Syracuse University Press, 1986, p. 155.
20 Shlomo Aronson, 1978, op. cit., Note 14, p. 182.
21 Steven Brams, *Superpowers Games*, New Haven, Connecticut: Yale University Press, 1985.
22 John Nash, 'The bargaining problem', *Econometrica*, 18, April 1950, pp. 155–62.
23 Howard Sachard, *A History of Israel*, New York: Knoff, 1982, pp. 783–4.

24 Moshe Bylopolsky, op. cit., Note 5.
25 Whitley Bruner, 'Soviet new thinking and the Middle East: Gorbachev's Arab–Israeli options', *Comparative Strategy*, 9 (4) October–November, 1990, pp. 385–401.
26 R. Hrair Dekmejian and Gideon Doron, 'Changing patterns of equilibria in the Arab–Israel conflict', *Conflict Management and Peace Science*, 5 (1) Fall, 1980, pp. 41–54.
27 Matti Golan, *The Secret Conversations of Henry Kissinger: Step by Step Diplomacy in the Middle East*, New York: Quadrangle, 1976; Abraham Ben-Zvi, *Between Lausanne and Geneva: International Conferences and the Arab–Israeli Conflict*, Boulder, Colorado: Westview Press, 1990.
28 Itzhak Rabin, *A Service Notebook*, Tel-Aviv: Maariv, 1979.
29 William Quandt, *Camp David: Peacemaking and Politics*, Washington DC: Brookings Institution, 1986.
30 Gideon Doron, *Rational Politics in Israel*, Tel-Aviv: Ramot, 1988.
31 *New York Times*, 6 April 1978.
32 Whitley Bruner, op. cit., Note 25; Huntington Samuel, 'America's changing strategic interests', *Survival*, 33 (1) January–February 1991, pp. 3–17.
33 Efraim Karsh and Rausti Inari, 'Why Saddam Hussein Invaded Kuwait?' *Survival*, 33 (1) January–February 1991, pp. 18–30.
34 Whitley Bruner, op. cit., Note 25, p. 393.
35 *Adelphi Papers*, 'America's Role in a Changing World', 256, part 1, Winter 1990–91.
36 Joseph Agassi, *Religion and Nationality*, Tel-Aviv: Papyrus, 1984.
37 Alan Taylor, *The Arab Balance of Power*, Syracuse, New York: Syracuse University Press, 1982.

Name Index

Abd al-Karim, Qassem 64
Abd al Hadi Mahadi (Dr) 87, 101
Abd al-Nasser, Gamal 36, 44, 61
Abdallah, Bishara 45, 68, 70
Addleton, J. 126
Agassi, Joseph 294
Ajama, Fouad 27
Allison, Graham T. 27
Ameeri, Rashid Salem al- 254
Andreotti, Giulio 197
Andrews, Peter 275
Arafat, Yasser 43, 74, 80, 81, 88, 89, 94, 95, 100, 101, 131, 142, 156, 222
Arens, Moshe 159, 182, 183
Aronson, Shlomo 293
Arnett, Peter 66, 267, 271, 273
Asad, Hafiz al- 44, 48, 49, 73, 185, 197
Awn, General Michel 44
Ayalon, Ami 49
Aziz, Tariq 38, 49, 58, 199, 201, 202, 222, 223, 251, 227

Badeau, John 293
Badran, Mudar 158
Bakatin, Vadim 193
Baker, James 26, 46, 47, 80, 92, 94, 181, 184, 186, 188, 199, 214, 218, 222
Bakr al-Hakim, Muhammad 52, 66
Baldwin, David A. 189
Bandar (ambassador) 69, 73
Barton, A.H. 144
Barzilai, Gad 129, 144, 145, 159, 279
Ben-Zvi, Abraham 176, 190, 293, 294
Bennet, James 265, 274
Braestrup, Peter 275

Brams, Steven 293
Branco, Castello 238
Brandt, Willy 61, 125, 221, 227
Brecher, Michael 25, 26, 27
Browne, Malcolm 267, 275
Bruner, Whitley 294
Brzoska, Michael 249
Bull, Hedley 10, 26, 29
Bush, George 8, 44, 45, 46, 60, 63, 80, 93, 155, 164-7, 174, 175, 176, 177, 180, 181, 184, 186, 188, 196, 197, 202, 203, 206, 245, 259, 264, 265, 268, 273
Bylopolsky, Moshe 293, 294

Cantori, Louis J. 27
Caras, Seth 248
Carter, Jimmy 287
Ceausescu, Nicolae 52
Chaudhry, Kiren 61, 85
Cheney, Dick 50, 77, 78, 270
Chevenement, Jean-Pierre 215, 224
Chomsky, Noam 133
Cobban, Helena 190
Coser, Lewis 132
Craig, Gordan A. 28
Cuellar, Perez de 223

Delors, Jacques 208, 225
Demchak, Chris 158
DeKmejian, R. Hrair 294
DeMesquita, Bruce B. 292
Devlin, John 293
Dishon, Daniel 50
Doron, Gideon 279, 293, 294

Eagleburger, Lawrence 149
Eitan, Rafael 148

Evron, Yair 293

Feiler, Gil 250
Freedman, Lawrence 26, 27
Friedman, Thomas L. 50
Fukuyama, Francis 27

Garnham, David 27
Gates, Robert 197
Gensher, Hans Deitrich 215, 219
George, Alexander L. 28, 190
Geyelin, Philip 272, 275
Gilboa, Eytan 190
Gilpin, Robert 293
Glaspie, April 25, 59
Goldberg, Giora 144, 159
Goldberg, Jacob 29, 67, 84
Goldberg, Andrew C. 29
Golan, Matti 294
Gorbachev, Michael 74, 150, 191,
    193, 196, 197, 199, 201, 202, 203,
    204, 205, 287
Goren, Dina 264, 275
Greilsammer, Ilan 159, 208
Grossman, Lawrence 274

Habash, George (Dr) 92
Habermas, Jurgen 133, 145
Haig, Alexander 284
Halberstom, David 270, 271, 275
Halliday, Fred 9, 17, 26, 27, 28
Hallin, David 275
Hammadi, Saadoum 253
Hasan, Salah al- 85
Hassn, Haled al- 93, 94, 96, 101
Heath, Edward 61, 125, 221
Hermann, Charles F. 25
Hersh, Seymour 283, 293
Herz, John 28
Hoffmann, Stanley 21, 26, 28, 29
Holbraad, Carsten 28
Horelick, Arnold L. 190
Howatme, Naif 92, 93, 96
Huntington, Samuel 28, 294
Hussein, Saddam 8, 21, 24, 25, 33–
    50, 51–65, 72, 73, 74, 76, 78, 81,
    88, 89, 91, 94, 104, 109, 111–15,
    130, 131, 141, 142, 146, 147, 149,
    209, 210, 213, 214, 217, 220, 221,
    222, 223, 250–63, 265, 266, 270,
    273, 288

Inbar, Efraim 144, 145, 146, 158, 159

Jackson, Jesse 125
Jefferson, Thomas 167
Jervis, Robert 189
Joergenson, Ankar 123
Johnson, Lyndon 164, 165

Kaldor, Mary 29
Kandeel, Abdul-Hadi 257
Kanovsky, Eliahu 263
Karsh, Efraim 25, 26, 51, 65, 66,
    158, 294
Katz, Elihu 265, 271, 274, 276
Kedourie, Elie 293
Keohane, Robert O. 26, 28
Khalil, Samir al 66
Khomeini, Ayatollah 12, 48
Khouri, Fred 292
King Hussein 29, 38, 39, 42, 43, 45,
    47, 57, 73, 148, 151, 157, 185, 186,
    227, 270
King Fahd 37, 38, 68, 72, 73, 75, 76,
    78, 79, 80, 81, 82
King Hassan 33, 34, 41
Kissinger, Henry 269, 283
Klein, Menachem 87
Klein, Yitzhak 191
Klibi, Chedli 38, 49
Klieman, Aharon 7, 293
Kohl, Helmut 211, 215
Krasner, Stephen D. 28

Lange, David 125
Le Pen, Jean-Marie 125, 227
Legum, Colin 50
Levi, Shlomit 145
Levine, Herbert M. 29
Lietaer, Bernard 248
Lijphart, Arend 29
Lodge, Henry Cabot 168, 171
Lubbers, Ruud 216
Luttwak, Edward 28, 268

Mabro, Robert 260
Maddy-Weitzman, Bruce 33, 50
Mansbach, Richard 292
Maoz, Seymour 293
Marquez, Gabriel Garcia 10, 26
Mathews, Jessica Tuchman 28
May, Ernest R. 28
Mayall, James 27, 28

Mearsheimer, John J. 9, 26, 158
Millan, V. 248
Miller, Judith 49, 66
Mishan, E. J. 293
Mitterrand, François 197, 214, 215, 220, 221–2, 224, 226
Morrow, James 292
Moser, Sheila 25, 26
Mubarak, Husni 36–41, 45, 57, 73, 197, 242
Mueller, John 26
Mylroie, Laurie 49, 66

Nakasone, Yasuhiro 125
Nash, John 293
Neeman, Yuval 158
Novik, Nimrod 293
Nuseiba, Seri 126, 135
Nye, Joseph 26, 28

Offen, Elizabeth N. 103
Ohlson, Thomas 249

Paige, Glenn D. 25
Peng, Li 245
Peres, Shimon 136, 143
Pickering, Thomas 28, 36
Poos, Jacques 223, 227
Porth, Jacquelyn 248
Powell, Colin 270
Primakov, Yevgenii 125, 193, 194, 196–8, 201, 202, 206, 207
Prince Abdallah ibn Faisal 68
Prince Bandar ibn Sultan 50
Prince Khaled ibn Sultan 71, 72

Qadumi, Faruq al- 92
Quandt, William 178, 189, 293, 294

Rabbo, Yassir Abed 93, 96
Rabin, Yitzhak 131, 153, 158, 294
Rafsanjani 74
Ramazani, R. K. 293
Rautsi, Inari 25, 65, 158, 294
Reagan, Ronald 179, 190
Reich, Bernard 189, 190
Renan, Ernest 29
Rizopoulos, Nicholas 27
Roberts, Adam 27
Rochlin, Gene I. 158
Roosevelt, Franklin D. 165, 170, 172
Roosevelt, Kermit 293

Roosevelt, Theodore 168
Root, Eliahu 168
Rosenau, James N. 9, 16, 25, 28
Ross, David 25
Rossiter, Clinton 133, 145
Rothstein, Robert L. 27
Rubinstein, Alvin 158
Rusk, Dean 165
Russett, Bruce 28, 292

Sachard, Howard 293
Sadat, Anwar al- 286, 287
Safire, William 265, 274
Samir, Hulaileh 102
Sandler, Shmuel 158
Sarid, Yossi 144
Schorr, Daniel 276
Segal, Zeev 145
Semerdzhiyev, Atanas 126
Seymour, Ian 262
Shahak, Amnon 145
Shaked, Haim 50
Shamir, Yitzhak 131, 135, 136, 137, 139, 147, 148, 156, 157, 185, 186, 188
Shath, Nabil 93
Shaw, George Bernard 273
Shaw, Martin 133
Sheikh Ali Khalifa al-Sabah 252
Sheikh Jaber al-Ahmad al-Sabah 252
Sheikh Saad al-Abdullah al-Sabah 256
Shevardnadze, Eduard 192, 193, 195, 196, 198, 199, 200, 204, 205, 206
Shidlo, Gil 231
Shultz, Joseph 179
Simmel, George 132, 145
Simon, Bob 267
Singer, David J. 28
Small, Melvin 28
Smith, Hendrick 275
Smith, H.A. 175
Solarz, Steven 50
Spiegel Steven L. 27
Sprout, Harold 28
Sprout, Margaret 28
Stohl, M. 134, 145
Sununu, John 197

Sutterlin, James, S. 28

Taylor, Alan 294
Thatcher, Margaret 213, 218, 226
Thompson, Kenneth 26
Tifft, Susan 270, 275, 276
Tripp, Charles 66
Tucker, Robert W. 163

Vandenberg, Arthur 172
Varas, Augusto 248
Vasques, John 292
Vauzelle, Michel 222
Vital, David 292

Volodin, Eduard 205

Waldheim, Kurt 125
Walt, Stephen M. 26, 29
Waltz, Kenneth 292
Wilkenfeld, Jonathan 25, 26
Wilson, Woodrow 165, 171, 172, 175
Wolfowitz, Paul 69, 149
Woodward, Bob 50

Yaniv, Avner 158
Yel'tsin, Boris 205
Yergin, Daniel 261, 263

Subject Index

AIPAC 183, 188
Al-Rumaila 38, 58, 59, 202, 255, 260
Algeria 39, 40, 41, 49, 227, 245, 251
America see United States
American–Israeli dyad 176–90;
  special relationship paradigm 177,
  178, 179, 181, 187, 188, 189
American–Kuwaiti Defense Treaty
  79
Amnesti International 53, 66
anti-Iraq bloc 14, 180, 181, 198
Arabs (including Israeli Arabs) 96,
  134, 135; boycott 156; identity 89
  inter-Arab relations 33–50, 71, 72,
  73, 77–81, 88, 89, 92, 93, 134, 150,
  180; new regional order 93–5, 157,
  158
Arab and Muslim media 76, 88, 265,
  267, 268; misinformation 265
Arab Cooperation Council (ACC)
  35, 36, 43, 48, 57
Arab–Israeli conflict 34, 36, 42, 48,
  88, 89, 130, 132, 143, 146, 150,
  152, 157, 176, 180, 181, 193, 194,
  195, 196, 279 281; Arab–Israeli
  peace process 23, 37, 39, 45, 46,
  47, 80, 90, 92–5, 98, 99, 150, 155,
  157, 183, 184–9, 289–91
Arab League 33, 35, 38, 39, 40, 41,
  43, 48, 58, 59, 219; Arab League
  Resolution 195 40
Arab Maghreb Union (AMU) 35
Arab Organization for
  Industrialization (AOI) 241, 242
arms race (arms control) 9, 16, 22,
  79, 151, 153, 154, 247–8, 291; arms
  embargo (against Iraq) 205, 210,

211, 212; regional arms race 144,
  151, 155, 291
arms sales: Argentina 231, 232–7,
  238, 240, 242, 243, 245–8; Brazil
  154, 231, 232, 233, 236, 237–43,
  245, 246, 247; China 154, 231, 232,
  233, 236, 237, 240, 242, 243–5,
  246, 247, 249; Egypt 232, 236, 237,
  241–3, 245, 246, 247; France 211–
  12, 231, 235, 236, 237, 238, 242,
  244, 245; India 231, 236;
  Indonesia 231; Italy 235, 236, 237,
  238, 239, 244, 245; Iran 232, 236,
  244, 246; Iraq 231–49; Israel 231,
  236, 242, 243, 244, 246; Libya 236,
  238, 240, 241; North Korea 154,
  231, 236, 237, 242, 243, 247;
  Singapore 231; Saudi Arabia 236,
  240, 241; South Africa 231; South
  Korea 231, 236; Soviet Union 231,
  236, 237, 241, 242, 244, 245, 246,
  247; Taiwan 231; US 231, 235,
  236, 237, 238, 241, 242, 243, 244,
  247
anti-Iraq coalition 198
arms transference 153, 154, 231, 233,
  235
Asians 120; displacement
  (migration) 103, 104, 105, 109,
  111, 116, 117, 118, 125
Association for Civil Rights 141
Aswan Dam 282

Baghdad summit 37
balance of power 9, 19, 24, 28, 29,
  34, 37, 89, 150, 166, 168, 169, 173

Ba'th Party 35, 38, 52, 53, 54, 64, 65, 72, 81, 245, 251, 256
ballistic missiles 17, 130, 137, 143, 144, 232, 235, 236, 237, 239, 240, 242, 244, 248
bandwagoning 29
Bangladeshi displacement (migration) 105, 106, 113, 114, 116, 117, 119, 120, 123
Belgium: reaction to invasion 225, 226
Brazil: displacement (migration) 106; trade agreement with Iraq 246
Britain 281; military involvement 213, 214, 215, 224; press coverage 267; reaction to invasion 219, 221, 222, 225
Bubiyan and Warba Islands 59, 202

Cairo summit 42, 43
Camp David 92; Accords 242, 286–7
Casablanca Arab summit conference 34
Casus Belli 8, 153
censorship 75, 82, 136, 137, 269
chemical weapons 130, 142, 147, 152, 153
'Chicken' Game 285
China 122; displacement (migration) 106, 114, 116
CNN 83, 266, 267, 270–1, 275
Condor I, Condor II 236, 237, 240, 242, 243
constitutional dictatorship 133
Cold War 17, 26, 35, 166, 169, 173, 179, 185, 231, 287; policy of containment 173–4; US–USSR global rivalry 280
conflict management (crisis management) 7–8, 25, 83, 149; conflict resolution 23, 279–94; game theory: balance of power 280; equilibrium 280, 287–8; theoretical model 279, 280
consensus 15, 18, 23, 33, 39, 40, 45, 68, 74, 81, 92, 97, 130–3, 137, 138, 139, 140, 141, 156, 265, 273
Conventional Forces in Europe (CFE) 195

Damascus Declaration 45, 46, 77

Democratic Front for the Liberation of Palestine (DFLP) 92, 93, 95, 96, 97, 98
deterrence 16, 28, 91, 116, 148, 149, 153, 158
Djbouti 40
displacement (migration) 103–26, 130, 265; economic impact 119–22
'disaster studies' (war studies) 130

economic sanctions 23, 42, 43, 60, 113, 156, 167, 194, 198, 202, 203, 213
Egypt: arms sales *see* arms sales; and coalition against Iraq 23, 33, 34, 38, 39, 40, 41, 44, 46, 181, 219; displacement (migration) 103, 105, 109, 111, 112, 113, 116, 119, 120, 121, 123; and regional affairs 35, 37, 40, 45, 46, 67, 69, 70, 73, 76, 77, 79, 80, 81, 241; war with Yemen 280
Engesa 239, 240
environment 27, 28, 122, 266
Embraer 239, 242
equilibrium *see* regional instability
European Community (EC) 22; Arab–Israeli conflict 149; disintegration between EC nations 217–23, 224, 225; eastern Europe 52, 247; economic sanctions (including oil embargo) 209, 210, 211, 213, 219, 220, 225; foreign policy 208; impact of the invasion of Kuwait on inter-European relations 208–27; military involvement 214, 215, 217, 218; security 209; unification 35, 46, 208, 225
European monetary system (EMS) 208; ECU 208, 219
Falklands War 232, 236, 238; media and censorship 236, 270
Fatah 92, 93, 95, 96, 97, 98
Front de Liberation Nationale (FLN) 41
France 114, 119, 214–15, 218, 219, 225, 281; media 267, 273; military involvement 213, 214, 217, 220, 224; solitary initiative 221–3

Freedom of Information Act (1967) 269
fundamentalism (also Islamic fundamentalist movements) 9, 35, 41, 47, 49, 65, 75, 77, 83, 92, 148, 246, 290, 291

gas masks 134, 135, 137, 152
GCC (Gulf Cooperation Council) 35, 37–41, 44–7, 68, 69, 74, 77, 78, 79, 80
Germany 114; reaction to Gulf challenge 215, 218, 219, 222, 225, 226; military involvement 216, 218; weapons industry 236, 238, 240
Glasnost 74
Gulf security 46, 67, 68–70, 77–9
Gulf Crisis Financial Coordination Group 183
Grenada Operation: media and censorship 267, 269, 270

Hajj 74, 82
Hamas 92
Helsinki Summit 194, 196
High Court of Justice
hostages 13, 60, 61, 104, 113, 114, 213, 219–20, 221, 226, 227, 259, 265
human rights 238; *see also* Amnesti International
humanitarian aid 114, 122–3, 212, 220, 224

India displacement (migration) 103, 105, 106, 109, 113, 114, 115, 117, 119, 120; *see also* arms sales
Indonesia 116
international arms industry 231–49 *see also* arms sales
Intifada 47, 87–93, 97, 98, 100, 101, 102, 130, 135, 140, 141, 142, 151, 153, 179
Iran: American policy toward Iran 12, background to the Gulf crisis 34, 35, 44; displacement (migration) 104, 114, 117, 118; extinguishing oil fires 122; inter-Arab relations 46, 48, 71, 74, 77, 81; foreign policy 24, 74;

fundamental muslims 12, 34, 64; normalized realtions with EC 219; oil 250, 251, 256, 258
Iran–Contra Affair 270
Iran–Iraq War 1, 17, 34, 35, 43, 51, 52, 55, 56, 57, 60, 64, 111, 150, 239, 240, 244, 245, 250, 251, 255, 288
Iraq: army/arms capability 8, 71, 78, 130, 142, 146, 147, 231, 245; dismantling nuclear capabilities 290–1; displacement (migration) 103–27; interaction between oil, politics, war 250–63; inter-Arab relations 35, 40, 67, 68, 71; internal affairs 28, 78; internal affairs leading to invasion of Kuwait 51–9, 260–1, 284; invasion of Kuwait 18, 33, 37, 38, 39, 41, 47, 51, 59, 67–74; game theory *see* conflict management; Palestinian cause 147; penal code 53; the Popular Army 55; Republican Guard 54, 61, 63; the war 47, 157, 180, Saddam's strategy 60–3, 91, 147, 259, defeat and aftermath 47, 63, 64, 65, 79, 80, 81, 83, 92, 101, 122, 289, 290; Western media coverage 264–268, 270, 271, 274; manipulation of the media in Iraq 266, 267, 268, 273
Islamic Jihad 92
Israel army/ military capabilities 138, 139, 149, 180; civilians 130, 132, 133, 153; displacement 125; foreign policy 27, 177; government 146; Israel Defense Forces (IDF) 149, 152, 153, 154; pressure from US 177; as provider of services to US 283; regional instability 280; regional peace negotiations 47, 176, 184–9; security 142, 143, 153, 154, 156, 134, 135, 136, 146; settlements 94, 155, 182, 184, 188, 189; strategic considerations 146–59; (see American–Israeli dyad); *see also* Arab–Israeli conflict; *see also* occupied territories
Italy 218, 219, 225, 226

Japan 14, 23, 68, 114, 119, 123, 169
Jeddah meeting 38, 58, 255–6
Joint Defense Pact 33, 40
Jordan 281; displacement
    (migration) 103, 104, 109, 111,
    112, 113, 114, 116, 119, 120, 125;
    inter-Arab relations 34, 35, 36, 39,
    40; Jordanian–Palestinian
    delegation 94, 186; links with
    Europe 218–19; and peace process
    98, 143; political realignment 23,
    41–3, 67, 71, 73, 80, 81; strategic
    consequences during Gulf crisis
    148, 149, 151–2

Knesset 133, 135, 136
Kurds 9, 14, 15, 18, 19, 131, 274;
    displacement (migration) 103, 104,
    117–18, 119
Kuwait: American objectives in
    liberation 200; armed forces 41;
    burning oil fields 62, 266;
    displacement 103–26, 143; and
    Gulf security 77–9; leading up to
    the invasion 8, 33, 37, 38; oil 57,
    58, 148, 250–61; reactionary
    leadership 89; reconstruction 46,
    48, 122; regional instability 280,
    281; right for sovereign existence
    51, 213, 281; Saddam's reasons for
    invasion 51–2, 56–61, 147;
    vulnerability 14, 68; women's
    rights 77
Labour Party 136, 143
Lasswellian Model 132, 140
League of Nations 167, 168, 169,
    170, 172
Lebanon 14, 20, 22, 37, 39, 40, 42,
    43, 44, 48, 50, 104, 280
Lebanon War 135, 138–79
Libya 23, 34, 39, 40, 240, 246
Likud 132, 135, 136, 143, 144, 147,
    148, 151, 157
linkage (linkage theory) 10, 16, 26,
    28, 47, 89, 91, 93, 111, 141, 146,
    147, 176, 182, 183, 185, 188, 189,
    222, 193, 195, 197, 279, 292
loan guarantees 182, 183, 184, 188,
    189
1987 London Accords 186

Madrid Conference 157
Mauritania 39, 40
media 9, 36, 37, 117, 118, 119, 132,
    136, 137, 148, 157, 264–76; as
    adversary 265, 269, 273;
    enhancing patriotism 265, 272;
    illusion of live coverage 270–1;
    issues of policy 273; manipulation
    272, 266–8, by government 269,
    272–4, 275
messianism 100–1
migrant labour 115, 120, 123, 124,
    125
Moledet Party 135, 136
Morocco 33, 34, 40, 41, 69, 72
Napoleonic Wars 170
nation-state 14, 27
NATO 23, 172, 173, 180, 209, 214,
    215, 217, 218, 226
North Africa 35, 44
North Korea/ Korea 25
North Yemen/Yemen 35, 39, 40, 43,
    44, 50, 67, 70, 71, 73, 80, 81, 280

Occupied Territories (West Bank
    and Gaza Strip, Judea and
    Samaria) 42, 43, 47, 80, 87, 91–9,
    102, 111, 112, 131, 132, 134, 135,
    140, 141, 144, 151, 156, 182, 188,
    189
October War (1973) 285, 286
OPEC 37, 57, 58, 210, 250–60
oil 58, 148, 156, 209, 250–63, 266,
    290; oil embargo 210; oil
    production, import and export:
    Britain 211; China 212; Denmark
    211; Germany 211; Gulf countries
    252, 255, 256; Japan 212; US 255;
    oil revenues, oil prices 57, 150,
    250–61
Ottoman Empire 280–1

Panama: Military operation and the
    media 267
Pakistan 109, 113, 115, 116, 117,
    119, 120, 123, 245
Palestinian National Council (PNC)
    87, 96, 99, 100, 101
Palestinians: displacement
    (migration during Gulf crisis) 103,

111, 112, 119, 121, 123, 151, 152;
inter-Arab relations 42, 43, 44, 46,
47, 61, 81, 92; multilateral peace
design 186; Palestinian identity 89,
90, 134; Palestinian issue 93–4,
151, 157, 141, 142, 147, 183, 193,
195, 198, 224, 291–2; Palestinian
state 131, 143, 144, 151, 157; the
PLO and Intifada 87–102;
political realignment 23;
polarization between factions 95–
101; as targets of retribution 111
Patriot Missiles (patriot batteries)
138, 139, 149, 152, 183
Peace Now movement 140
peace process (see Arab–Israeli
conflict)
Pentagon papers 269
permissive consensus 138, 141, 142
PLO 39, 40, 43, 47, 67, 73, 74, 80,
81, 87–102, 121, 130, 131, 132,
144, 150, 151, 185, 290
Popular Front for the Liberation of
Palestine 92, 95, 96, 97
power (resources) 15, 26, 177; power
assets 177; power capabilities 177;
great power supremacy 166–75
Prisoners' Dilemma 286–7
process analysis 19–25; domestic
process 21–2; interstate processes
22–3; systemic processes 23–5
public opinion 42, 62, 166, 167, 177,
180, 181, 183, 187, 188, 189, 220,
274; public opinion polls 178, 182,
215

Qatar 105, 121
Qur'an 75, 82

Ratz Party 131, 137
Reagan Doctrine 163, 165
Reagan administration 269, 275
refugees *see* displacement

regional instability 279–97;
American goals and limitations
281–3; causes 280–6; regional
equilibrium following Gulf crisis
287–92; Soviet goals and
limitations 281–3; superpower
regional strategies 282, 283–7

remittances 120, 122
Research and Development (R&D)
233, 235, 248
Russia (see USSR) 81

Saudi Arabia 33, 34, 39, 40, 41, 42,
43, 45, 93, 181, 214, 217, 219;
armed forces 70, 71, 79, 153;
Desert Storm 67–86; displacement
103, 104, 105, 112, 115, 116, 121,
122, 123; foreign policy 67, 72–4,
81; oil 210, 246; political and
social reforms 74–5, 76, 81–2;
royal family 70, 72, 74, 75, 77, 82,
83; women's rights 76, 83
Scud Missiles 14, 62, 91, 130, 132,
139, 146, 147, 148, 149, 152, 158,
180, 234, 236, 242, 266, 268; Scud
B 237
SDI (strategic defense initiative) 180
self determination 141, 144, 165,
167, 175
Shi'ite 62, 64, 65, 81, 104
Six Day War 93, 141, 284, 285
Somalia 40
Soviet press 192, 194, 195, 200, 206
Soviet Union (see USSR)
'Soyuz' (Union) 200
Sri Lanka 119
Sudan 39, 40
Sunna 82
Sunnis 65
Supreme Soviet 198, 200
Syria: armed forces 41, 46, 69, 71,
153; boycott of Baghdad summit
37; inter-Arab relations after the
war 45, 46, 67, 77, 79, 80, 81, 92,
93; Kurdish minority 118; Pax-
Syriana 44, 290; peace process 47,
95, 98, 183, 185, 186, 187; political
realignment 23, 35, 39, 40, 41, 42,
44, 73; regional instability 280,
283, 284, 285; supporting
terrorists 219, 288
Ta'if Accord 44, 50
Tehiya Party 135
Third World 16, 63, 91, 114, 124;
arms exports to Iraq 231–49
Tikriti clique 65
Truman Doctrine 163, 165

Tunisia 39, 40, 41, 43, 111
Turkey 15, 23, 44, 103, 104, 109,
113, 116, 117, 118, 120, 217, 218,
219
Tzomet party 148

unemployment 103, 112
United Arab Emirates (UAE) 38, 41,
57, 58; oil 210, 250, 252, 253, 255,
256, 258, 260, 261
United Nations (UN Security
Council) 14, 18, 23, 28, 40, 44, 74,
81, 91, 147, 154, 164, 167, 169,
170, 172, 174, 175, 192, 194, 195,
209, 221, 284; UN Charter 169–72,
196, 198; UN economic santions
24, 42, 43, 45, 113, 193, 194, 212,
219, 226, 257; UN Security
Council Resolution 678 18, 198–
200, 203, 207, 264; UN Security
Council Resolution 660 202; UN
Secuity Council Resolution 661
40, 257; UN Security Council
Resolution 338 93; UN Security
Council Resolution 242 93, 182
United States (USA): American
'imperialism' 91; attainment of
stability 280, 288–9; Congress 93,
178; foreign policy 47, 150, 172,
173, 183; Eisenhower
administration 282; great power
realignment 163–75, 179, 204;
hegemony in the Middle East 155,
279, 280, 288; Johnson
administration 282, 283; Kennedy
administration 283; military
involvement 39, 46, 61, 63, 72, 76,
77, 78, 81, 88, 149, 150, 154, 213,
257, 259, 264, 268; Nixon
administration 281, 282; policies
toward Israel 92–3, 155, 176–90,
282, 283; policy toward Iraq 12,
64, 92; policy toward Arab states,

Palestinians, PLO 93–5, 155;
political intentions 90, 91, 92, 146,
156, 201; political order 172;
superpower rivalry 17; Senate 69,
171, 172; US-led coalition 279,
288; US Senate Foreign Relations
Committee 28
USSR 12, 14, 17, 23, 27, 29, 74, 92,
95, 101, 114, 115, 122, 123, 150,
154, 155, 169, 172, 174, 179, 180,
245; Jewish emigration 36, 94,
155, 157, 182, 184; policy during
Gulf crisis 191–207, 209; political
influence in Europe 52, 191;
reduction of Soviet regional
influence 287–91; Soviet regional
coalition 282

Venezuela 210, 257, 258
Vietnam 164–5, 173, 174, 273
Vietnam syndrome 60, 268–9, 273
Vienna agreement 258, 259, 263

war coverage: CNN 266, 267, 270–1,
275; *Los Angeles Times* 264; the
New York Times 264, 265, 269,
270, 274, 275; 'Nightline' 264;
Washington Post 264, 272;
Warsaw Pact 12, 23, 195, 247
Western Alliance 172, 173, 174
Western hostages in Iraq *see*
hostages
(Westphalia, Treaty of 10, 13, 14, 27
Western European Union (WEU)
217, 226
world order (new wold order) 10, 13,
16, 18, 23, 26–8, 45, 144, 163–75,
290

Zionism 36, 38, 58, 92, 131, 135,
151; Zionist left/Israeli left 131